ALSO BY WILLIAM SAFIRE

LANGUAGE

Quoth the Maven
Coming to Terms
Fumblerules
Language Maven Strikes Again
You Could Look It Up
Take My Word for It
I Stand Corrected
What's the Good Word?
On Language
Safire's New Political Dictionary

POLITICS

The First Dissident
Safire's Washington
Before the Fall
Plunging into Politics
The Relations Explosion

FICTION

Freedom
Full Disclosure

ANTHOLOGIES

Lend Me Your Ears: Great Speeches in History

(WITH LEONARD SAFIR)

Good Advice for Writers
Leadership
Words of Wisdom
Good Advice

IN LOVE WITH NORMA LOQUENDI

IN LOVE
WITH
NORMA
LOQUENDI

William Safire

Illustrations by Keith Bendis

Random House
New York

Grateful acknowledgment is made to *The New York Times* for permission
to reprint 75 "On Language" columns by William Safire from
October 15, 1989, through April 28, 1991. Copyright © 1989, 1990,
1991 by The New York Times Company. Reprinted by permission.

Illustrations by Keith Bendis

Library of Congress Cataloging-in-Publication Data

Safire, William.
In love with Norma Loquendi / William Safire.
p.   cm.
Includes index.
ISBN 0-679-42386-9
1. English language—Usage. 2. English language—Style.
I. Title.
PE1421.S223   1994
428—dc20   93-36847

Manufactured in the United States of America

23456789

FIRST EDITION

To Rufus and Henry,
James and Heidi

Oh, somewhere on Elysian plains
   Where the light breath of Zephyr stirs
The bosky groves and silvan lanes
   Reserved for Lexicographers;
Where with your kind in that long spell
   Of peace which no intruder varies
You couch on beds of asphodel
   Gently discussing Dictionaries . . .

—Sir Owen Seaman's tribute to Sir James A. H. Murray,
   first editor of the *Oxford English Dictionary*

INTRODUCTION

The subject is copulation.

That is known in the trade as a grabber of a lead, attracting on false pretenses those browsing through a family newspaper and looking vainly for sexual arousal.

Whatever *copulation* means to you, to those of us in the language dodge it means "linking," or as Henry Kissinger used to say, *linkage.* A *copulative verb* is a hooker (there's a mnemonic that will work)—a linking verb, or as a title-writer would say, the grammar connection. As verbs go, it's a wimp; no get-up-and-go that we expect from that most exciting of the parts of speech. ("I am a verb," said Ulysses S. Grant, in the best self-description of a man of action.)

The copulative verb has no such daring destiny; its function is merely to connect the subject to the word that describes or identifies it. This linking verb is "into relationships," denoting a state of being or sensing. In "You smell good," "They look sad" and "I feel pretty," *smell, look* and *feel* are linkers. In the sentence "I am Flotus," so useful in establishing the acronymic identity of the First Lady of the United States, *I* is the subject, *am* is the linking verb and *Flotus* is the predicate nominative.

The what? The *predicate nominative.* The predicate, which includes the verb, is the part of the sentence that says what is happening to the subject. The *predicate nominative* is the noun or pronoun part of the predicate that follows a linking verb and stands equal to the subject, referring to it or identifying it; in "This is your President speaking," *is your President speaking* is the complete predicate, and *President* the predicate nominative that stands for the subject, *this.*

If you respond to this heavy pedagogy with "I am bored," *I* is the subject, *am* the linking verb and *bored* the predicate adjective. If you choose to tell me, "You are a bore," *you* is the subject, *are* is the linker and *bore* is the predicate nominative. *Nominative,* rooted in "named," means "noun" or "pronoun." Got it?

Now we come to why you need to have gotten it. The other day, in the elevator, I ran into Jim Schlesinger, the former Cabinet everything. He glared at me and said one word: *"Him?"* Others in the elevator assumed the pronoun referred to the President, an assumption automatically made in the nation's capital. (*"Her?"* would, of course, be taken to refer to Flotus.)

I understood the coded reference. Jim is a purist, an old-line stickler, a man of moorings and standards. He was calling me to account for this reference to Stanley and Livingstone in a previous column: "Here's this white man who could be him (yes, *him,* not *he*)."

My first alert to this apostasy came from Michael Molyneux, who presumes to edit this piece in New York. He pointed out that purists would demand *he* as predicate nominative, not *him,* which is in the objective case. That is why I added the parenthetical defiance.

As expected, the Gotcha! Gang struck. My "Uofallpeople" file bulges with missives like these: "I'm still in shock over your writing 'who could be *him* (yes, *him,* not *he*),' " gasps Edythe Mintz of Bloomfield, New Jersey. Over in Monmouth Beach, Harry Kaplan writes: "You have destroyed my faith in the infallibility of Safire. I'm afraid I must ask you for substantiation of your stand." From the District of Columbia: "Dazzled as I am by your confidence, I cannot think why it should not be *he,*" Edward Weismiller writes. "You must believe that the 'could' makes the difference. But 'could be' is still a conjugational form of the verb 'to be,' and a noun or pronoun following that verb must be a predicate nominative."

Safire's Rule for Predicate Nominatives: *The grammatically pristine form of "Woe is me" is "Woe is I" (or even "Woe am I"), but go tell that to Ophelia and Isaiah.* In *Hamlet,* Ophelia sighs, "O, woe is me, / T'have seen what I have seen, see what I see!" Desperate nominativeniks would say Shakespeare changed *I* to *me* to set up a rhyme with *see,* but at about that time, translators for King James were rendering Isaiah 6:5 as "Then said I, Woe is me! for I am undone; because I am a man of unclean lips." If that does not loosen the "must" of those insisting on the nominative case of pronouns following a linking verb, then there is nobody here but we chickens. (*"Us* chickens" is the way the idiom goes, and when the idiom raises good grammar's pot, the wise grammarian folds.)

Captain Oliver Perry's best-remembered line in 1813 was "We have met the enemy, and they are ours." The cartoonist Walt Kelly, playing on that line in "Pogo," used conversational idiom when he wrote in 1970, "We have met the enemy, and he is us." Today that use of *us* is more common than the hypercorrect "he is we" would be. And nobody plays around with the pronoun in Toys "R" Us.

Why does *it is me* sound better? English word order usually places a direct object, not a subject, after a verb. In his eminently sensible *Grammar of the English Language* in 1931, George O. Curme favored the nominative *I* to the objective or accusative *me,* but he acknowledged, "The plain drift of our language is to use the accusative of personal pronouns as the common case form."

Language is not mechanical. When an officious adviser of President William Howard Taft spoke of "the machinery of government," Taft said in wonderment to a friend, "You know—he really thinks it *is* machinery." The structure of language is at least as artistic as politics. The rules laid down by its elites are to be respected, and in writing usually followed, but in the end democracy, which goes by the name of common usage, will work its will. The teacher's duty, like the leader's duty in politics, is to resist cheap change and keep good order, but when the population challenges the order over a period of time, Norma Loquendi—the everyday voice of the native speaker—is the heroine who changes the order and raises a new Standard.

She has drawn a bead on the predicate nominative. If you linger too long on the ramparts, gallantly defending the correct form past its moment, she will let you have it between the it-is-I's. When a word sounds as if it is the object, use the objective form. When Norma knocks, say, "It's her," not "It's she." (If you object to this new order, stick with the old "Not I"; you cannot consistently say, "Not me.")

Go to a police lineup some day; if the witness leaps to his feet, points to the suspect and shouts, "That's *he*!" the prosecution will surely lose the case.

Woe Is Not Me

Weary news clerks humming "Ol' Man River" have been hauling into my office great bales of mail containing reader protests about the piece on predicative nominatives.

Most people manage to get through life without bothering their heads about the predicate nominative, which is the noun or pronoun embedded in a sentence's action section after a linking verb, like *mail-puller* in "You are a mail-puller." But there is a breed of language lover that clasps this grammatical category to its bosom, and insists with purist fervor on the nominative "I am he" rather than the sloppily objective "I am him," which is the choice of easygoing Norma Loquendi and me.

The offending sentence was my rule: "The grammatically pristine form of 'Woe is me' is 'Woe is I' (or even 'Woe am I'), but go tell that to Ophelia and Isaiah." My interpretation of Shakespeare and the Bible held that, in this use, *woe* and *me* were one and the same, and my point was to show a long history of the use of the objective *me,* when formal usage would dictate the nominative *I.* After all, if both Shakespeare's heroine and the biblical prophet said,

"Woe is me," who are the predicate nominatarians to insist on "Woe is I"?

One sack of mail set me straight on the original Hebrew. "I think the etymology of *Woe is me* is not a simple copulative phrase, a King James version of *I am woe*," writes Steve Pickering, a *New York Times* copy editor who has saved me from innumerable embarrassments and libel suits and otherwise drains my copy of impermissible zing. "It is rather a shortended version of *Woe is UNTO me.* To my mind, *Woe unto me,* in which *me* is grammatically correct as the object of the preposition *unto,* makes more grammatical and syntactical sense anyhow than *I am woe.*"

Rabbi George Barnard of Cincinnati agrees: "You should leave the prophet Isaiah out of the fight. He said, *'Oy li,'* which would be more literally translated as 'Woe to me.' He therefore took no position on predicate nominatives." Anne Mendelson of North Bergen, N.J., notes that "Martin Luther's German translation of the Bible renders Isaiah 6:5 as *Weh mir,*" and Robert Frankum of Huntington, L.I., translates this passage as "Woe unto me," adding: "The *me* is an old dative form, and historically never was or could have been a nominative form. Semantically, then, *woe* and *me* were never one and the same, linked by the verb *be,* but rather *me* was the recipient of *woe.*"

O.K.; I concede that the King James Version threw me off, and that the Hebrew biblical phrase should be translated as "Woe unto me," with *me* the object of the preposition *unto.* Chalk one up for the Gotcha! Gang.

Does that make me, as Prof. Caldwell Titcomb of Brandeis University writes, "incredibly ignorant"? (Some people get really worked up about this.) My less-than-irenic academic correspondent holds that in both the biblical and Shakespearean examples, "the pronoun here is not a nominative at all: it is a dative. . . . In 'Woe is me,' the noun is not being equated with the pronoun. The meaning is 'Woe is to me' or 'Woe is unto me.'" He cites Isabella in *Measure for Measure,* on being told her brother is in prison, as responding, "Woe me!" without even a verb, and holds that the *me* here, too, is dative.

The reader who thinks this argument is getting out of hand may be asking, "What's this *dative* jazz?" *Dative* comes from the Latin *data,* "given," as in the phrase *data Romae,* "given at Rome"; it usually describes a grammatical case in which the action is given *to* an indirect object. When you say, "I gave him the business," the direct object receiving the verb's action is *the business,* and the indirect object is *him.* If you want to straighten the sentence out for examination, it goes, "I gave the business (to) him." *Him* is dative, object of the understood *to.*

So if you are determined to think of the *me* in "Woe is (to) me" as dative, object of the preposition *to,* you escape my "Woe is I" trap. To the loosey-goosey grammarians who want to justify "It's me," abandoning the rampart of "It is I," you reply: No fair! The *me* in "Woe is me" is really dative! Incredible ignorance!

I think Shakespeare knew what he was writing. If he had wanted to say, "Woe is to me," he would have said it (or if the poetic meter required three syllables, "Woe is mine"). Contrary to the opinion of all my activist-dativist correspondents, I think he did intend to equate *woe* and *me*. Sometimes the truth lies flat on the surface, and you only confuse yourself looking for "understood" hidden words. By *Woe is me,* he was saying "I am woe; the person of me and the emotion of woe are one and the same." It's an old and frequently used poetic device: Oscar Hammerstein 2d did it in the lyric "You Are Love."

Therefore, positeth the maven, we have an example of a pretty fair writer of almost four centuries ago using the objective case for a predicate nominative. No latter-day "understood" insertions of a preposition allowed.

I do not kid myself: at this point, relatively few of us are left in the room. It's down to the die-hard nominativeniks and their dativist allies, ready to dispute this all night. Most of my normal readers have gone on to less arcane articles, shrugging at the inside-baseball struggles of the pinheaded angels of grammar, hoping this paroxysm will pass and next week we will get back to the latest Presidential gaffe.

But if you are not a Latin scholar or dative caseworker and have resolutely come this far, consider this: Just as Lieutenant Greenwald in Herman Wouk's *Caine Mutiny* defended in the end the nation's need for sailors like Captain Queeg, we can all thank our cultural stars for the legions who are absolutely certain they are keeping the language's one true faith.

They have learned their lessons from revered teachers; they have lashed themselves to the moorings of linguistic standards; they have an honorable equity in the preservation of the complicated guidelines so hard come by. Having paid their dues in lifelong respect for the rules, they can properly demand to know: Who are these permissivists—the descriptive lexicographers, the anything-goes dialectologists, the finger-painting purveyors of common usage—to arrogate to themselves the keeping of the temple of our tongue?

That is why it is worth wading out occasionally into the syntactical swamp. Whom do we find out (oops! Recast)—Who is found there, guardians not always grim mingled with classicists moved to mock fury at contradictions to cherished certitudes? Who forms a chorus to challenge the solecisms of solipsistic soliloquarians? It's *them.* (Or, as they would say, clinging to their beloved predicate nominatives, *it is they.*)

IN LOVE WITH NORMA LOQUENDI

Account of No Account

Accused by Moscow, and by some American political figures, of failing to respond adequately to Soviet arms-reduction overtures, President Bush protested with a revealing figure of speech: "I think our handling of the Soviet account is pretty good."

Mr. Bush never served as an account executive in an advertising agency. He did, however, serve as director of Central Intelligence, and from that experience drew his *Soviet account* trope.

People who work for our Central Intelligence Agency refer to the organization as *the Agency,* or *Langley,* the Virginia town in which its headquarters are said to be situated, or *the Company.* From this last appellation (used as a title of a 1976 novel by John Ehrlichman) comes the extension of the business metaphor.

Daniel Schorr, when staking out the home of James Jesus Angleton for CBS in 1974, was invited inside by the counterintelligence chief. The orchid-growing counterspymaster, known within the Company as "Mother," picked up a phone during his interview and said, "Shalom," the Hebrew greeting meaning "peace." When the correspondent asked him why he had used that word, Mr. Angleton replied, "I have for a long time handled the Israeli account."

Did this use of *account* stem from *the Company*? I checked with Richard Helms, a former director of Central Intelligence, who was present at the creation of much spookspeak; he admits that connection may exist, but thinks that the sense of *account* to mean "assignment" came from advertising and may have been brought to intelligence by a former adman. "I used to be an ad salesman myself," he added, "for Scripps Howard."

The term *account,* meaning "area of responsibility," has evidently stuck in the President's mind. We tend to forget he was once a spook, and that the old lingo lingers to pop up later in life.

Acronym Watch

All you dinks know what *bogsat* is—"Bunch of Guys Sitting Around a Table"—but are you familiar with *Wysiwyg* and *Nimby*? That's "What You See Is What You Get" and "Not in My Back Yard." (When an acronym contains more than three letters, the word is not usually written in all capitals.)

Some acronyms lead to the creation of usable words. In Britain, a *sluppy* is a combination of Sloane Ranger, a well-dressed denizen of Sloane Square, and *yuppie,* based on "young urban professional."

The aforementioned *dink,* from "Double Income, No Kids," has been in use for a couple of years now, its coinage attributed to Ellen Farley of Donnelley Marketing, who says that dinks make up 7.4 million United States households. (Much of the aging part of the segment is called *woop*—"Well-Off Older People.") In spookspeak, *snies,* pronounced "sneeze," from Special National Intelligence Estimates, seems to be more than a nonce term. Acronymic conversation at the Central Intelligence Agency:

"Does the President want *snies* on these?"

"Nimby."

Wimp is not an acronym; the slang term, which has aggressively shoved aside the Yiddishism *nebbish,* is based on the verb *whimper.* However, it lends itself to double-playing, and to this year's best use of a slang term for acronymic coinage by the scientific community:

You physicists all know that the standard theory for the creation of large structures in the universe is Cold Dark Matter (C.D.M. for short; because the initials do not form a pronounceable word, it's not an acronym).

The theory assumes that a certain fundamental particle in nature has no other force or energy except gravity. "These theoretical particles," writes John Noble Wilford in *The New York Times,* "are called WIMP's, for weakly interactive massive particles."

You assign the lineage of wimp *to the verb* whimper, *and trace* wimp*'s recent mutation in the jargon of particle physics.*

*Enclosed is new evidence of the possible first occurrence of the word in its earlier avatar—*wymp. *"Wymps," a story by Evelyn Sharp in the September 22, 1896, issue of* Harper's Round Table, *defines the* Wymps *as a mischievous sub-species of fairies which inhabit a land of yellow fog at the back of the sun.*

I leave to others the task of defining the links between the solar Wymps *and their subsequent evolution into the realms of cosmic particle physics and more mundane matter.*

> *Harvey F. Bellin*
> *Weston, Connecticut*

This is to suggest that you reconsider your rather pat attribution of "wimp" to "whimper." During the 1930s and 40s, a regular feature of the highly popular radio program Fibber McGee and Molly *was the appearance of one Willis Wimple, a meek little fellow, browbeaten by his "big fat wife," and referred to consistently (by McGee) as "Wimp." I believe it is the consciousness of this image in the minds of a generation that has made the term a part of our language. (I always visualized him as being played by that most aptly named character actor, Donald Meek).*

> *Owen Goldsmith*
> *Mountain Ranch, California*

The counterpart to nimby *is* noomp, *which stands for "Not Out Of My Pocket." It's what right-to-lifers say about state-funded abortions. I think I first saw it in* The Economist *a couple of years ago.*

Wysiwyg *software has the counterpart* wygiwyg, *which stands for "What You Get Is What You Get," or "What You've Got Is What You're Getting." It's used in the software business to describe software that has bugs which its manufacturer can't or won't fix. I first heard it used last year by Mr. David Covert, then with International Treasury Systems, to describe the malfunctions of that company's products, as in "Why is the customer complaining? Don't they know they bought* wygiwyg *software?"*

The final acronym I have for you, also from software, is pnambic *(NAM-bic), which is the not-quite-accurate acronym for "Pay No Attention to the Man Behind the Curtain." It refers to pre-existing foundation software that a programmer has to use to build a new application, but can't tinker with, usually because he can't get the source code. An example of* pnambic *software is a computer's operating system, as in "The program that I'm writing dies where it shouldn't, but I think the problem is down in the* pnambic *code where I can't get at it."*

> *David S. Platt*
> *Woburn, Massachusetts*

I was surprised you did not mention quango, *an English acronym for quasi-nongovernmental organization.*

> *Paul H. Silverstone*
> *New York, New York*

Balloon Goes Up on War Words

Secretary of State James A. Baker 3d called Prince Bandar bin Sultan, the Saudi Ambassador, into his office and informed him: "The balloon is going up. This is your notification." And so a piece of military slang from World War I was used to carry out a formal agreement of notification before an attack was launched on Iraq from United States bases in Saudi Arabia.

The balloon in question was set aloft by British artillerymen in 1915 to notify gunners along the line to commence firing; the easily seen visual signal was more reliable than rudimentary methods of courier or telephone (although the sound of one gun might have been a sufficient signal to the other artillery teams). The phrase was adopted by the military in the United States and was extended to any signal of the beginning of any enterprise, action or excitement: Advertising executives liked to refer to a planned start of a campaign with a crisp *"The balloon goes up* next Monday."

Artillery in the war on Iraq also appears in an abbreviation used by airmen: viewers heard debriefing pilots say *triple A,* or A.A.A., which means "antiaircraft artillery," in reference to cannons and machine guns but not surface-to-air missiles, or SAM's. Missiles are frequently acronymed; the TOW stands for "tube-launched, optically traced, wire-guided," the SLAM stands for "standoff land attack missile," and the Iraqi FROG stands for "free rocket over ground." The missile that resisted the trend toward acronyms is the *Tomahawk,* from the Algonquian for "tool used for cutting or chopping." (Scud is not an acronym, but a NATO code word for the Russian missile.)

The war itself has not been named; that may have to wait until its end. (World War I, known at the time as *the Great War,* was not numbered until the onset of World War II; the comedian Sid Caesar, playing on the anachronism, did a skit of a doughboy in a tin helmet who shouted, "World War I is over!") It cannot be "the Kuwaiti war," though some called the day the balloon went up, January 16, 1991, *K-Day,* on the stretched analogy of *D-Day.* The usual method of naming a regional war by using the names of its participants does not apply: This is not the *Iraqi-Multinational Force War* because that is too mouth-filling, and because the allied side has not settled on *the coalition* (as used by the White House) or *the allies* (as used by most newscasters).

The hot word at the start of the allied bombing was *decimate:* Our side's aircraft was hailed far and wide on the air and in print for "decimating the enemy air force." Walter Cronkite on CBS corrected a colleague's use of the verb, which means "reduce by one-tenth," originally Latin for "kill every tenth man as punishment for mutiny"; sloppy writers use it as a confused intensifier after using *devastate,* which hardly needs emphasis. In time, unless purists persist, *decimate* will come to mean "destroy a large part of."

Briefingese soon became the language of military-civilian communication. *Mission,* in its old sense of "a single attack by a single plane," was replaced by the French-derived *sortie,* from *sortir,* "to go out," first used in this sense in a 1918 book, *En l'Air;* pilots could claim twenty sorties, leaving *mission* to a more strategic sense of "military or diplomatic goal."

French also triumphed in the briefing by Air Force Lieutenant General Chuck (Charles) Horner. He said, "In many cases, though, when there are ground forces deployed, you have them in deep *revetments* and bunkers." A *revetment* is "a protecting embankment or wall made of sandbags"; it comes from *revêtir,* "to reclothe," the sense extended to the protection of sand-clothed positions. The general paired this noun with the more familiar *bunker,* an 1839 noun from the Scottish *bonker,* "chest, box."

Even after being hit by Iraqi missiles, Israel was asked to maintain a *low profile;* this was synonymous with *lie low,* and though no dictionary I can find cites a military origin, I speculate that it originated in the description of tanks; a tank with a *low profile* is set low to the ground and more difficult to hit. (Lexicographical fame awaits the finder of an early military citation for this phrase.)

Euphemism is almost as central to briefingese as acronymism. *Avoidance of collateral damage* means "trying not to kill civilians"; *collateral* means "side by side; parallel." *Targeting* is used as a kind of euphemism for "aiming at," which is not such a terrible phrase, yet President Bush, when asked if we were trying to bomb the person of Saddam Hussein, fell back on the boiler-plate "We are not *targeting* any individual." This is because of the policy against assassination.

The euphemism for *bomb* is *ordnance,* a newer spelling of *ordinance,* a word meaning "command; directive; law." Without the *i, ordnance* is a general term for weaponry, but is used when *bomb, rocket* or *napalm* would seem indelicate. Thus, General Colin L. Powell in a briefing: "The aircraft got to its target, delivered its *ordnance,* and returned."

Reporters like the term *carpet bombing,* a dysphemism for "bombing in a close pattern to destroy a large area rather than specific targets." (A *dysphemism,* obviously, is the opposite of a euphemism.)

"I don't know if the *bogie* was chasing him," said Captain Steve Tate, an American pilot, "but I *locked him up,* confirmed he was hostile and fired a missile." This *bogie* means "an enemy aircraft," but *bogie* can also be "an unidentified aircraft or a suspicious blip on a radar screen"; to *lock on* is to fix a weapon on a target through electronic means. This can happen in a *fur ball,* meaning "dogfight," or more generally, the hectic tangle of aerial combat.

War also churns up old phrases. Marlin Fitzwater, the President's press secretary, said just before the January 15, 1991, deadline that any period Saddam Hussein's forces remained in Kuwait after that was *on borrowed time.* This was first spotted in an 1854 variant in *Notes and Queries,* quoting an eighty-one-year-old Yorkshireman: "I'se livin' on borrowed days"; the *English Dialect Dictionary* reported this 1898 use in Lincolnshire: "A man who lives *on borrowed time* lives on trespass-ground." It was popularized in American by Raymond Chandler, the mystery writer, in the 1939 novel *The Big Sleep* and by the movie *On Borrowed Time* that same year. It means "an unexpected extension of one's life."

Finally, *Zulu.* This name of a South African tribe is used by military men to stand for the letter *Z,* and—for no known reason—the letters *BZ* are used to transmit a message meaning "job well done." This is then extended to the phrase "Bravo Zulu." To the military, *Zulu* has a second meaning: Greenwich mean time, or G.M.T. When it is seven P.M. on the East Coast of the United States, and three the next morning in Kuwait, in Great Britain, where time begins, it is *0000 Zulu.*

My colleague Wolf Blitzer (CNN's Pentagon correspondent) has taken a lot of flak lately for reporting that Saddam Hussein's Republican Guard had been decimated. Everyone assumes Wolf meant the Guard had been destroyed. But decimated also means "one-tenth destroyed" and I think people should remember that. We don't know whether the Guard has been destroyed or just decimated but it seems to me just possible one-tenth of the Guard has been hit.

Frances Hardin
Correspondent
CNN
Washington, D.C.

You say, in reference to the Middle East war, "The war itself has not been named; that may have to wait until its end." Catalogers at the Library of Congress don't have the luxury of waiting until then to name it. We're expecting to have to catalog our first book about it any day now, and will have to create a subject heading to be used now and in the future both here at the Library of Congress and in libraries across the nation. Since in matters like this we base our decision on the form that is most commonly used in books, newspapers, magazines, and other media, as well as on patterns evident in other headings in our system, we'll probably call it the "Persian Gulf War, 1991." Of course we'll also make "see" references from other forms that we find, such as "Gulf War, 1991."

Unfortunately, we didn't do so well in the case of other wars. For the Vietnam War, for example, we selected the form "Vietnamese Conflict, 1961–" (and later, after the war was over, changed it to "Vietnamese Conflict, 1961–1975"). In hindsight we wish we had chosen "Vietnam War, 1961–1975." We could of course change the heading once again, but we've now used it 2,836 times, and our computerized system doesn't allow us to "globally" update a heading—each bibliographic record would have to be changed individually. We're well aware of what a job that would be—it was precisely for that reason that we didn't get around to changing our heading "European War, 1914–1918" to "World War, 1914–1918" until 1980!

Paul G. Weiss
Subject Cataloging Policy
Specialist
The Library of Congress
Washington, D.C.

Maybe Scud is a "NATO code word," but as far as Webster is concerned it is first and foremost a peaceful verb meaning, "to move or run swiftly." Not a bad name for a missile, and if you ask me, a little too good to be a coincidence.

Dan R. Friedman
New York, New York

I'm sure it was 1938 when I saw Paul Osborn's play, On Borrowed Time, *on Broadway. It had to be that year, because Leonard Maltin sets 1939 as the year of the film version.*

Jim Russell
Oakland, California

You mention the use of "Zulu" to indicate Greenwich time without an explanation of its derivation.

Each of the 24 time zones has been given a letter designation for easy identification by navigators, radio operators and the military. Starting with the letter "Z" (phonetics Zulu) and moving eastward, the zones are labeled A to M (skipping J), as far as the international date line (the 180th meridian). Similarly, moving west from the Greenwich meridian to the date line, the zones are labeled N to X. Thus, 24 letters are used to designate the 24 time zones, with J and Y not used.

> Herman Gross
> Great Neck, New York

I think I can explain the derivation of "Bravo Zulu."

The phrase is taken from the Allied signal book currently used by the U.S., NATO and other friendly navies. When I was in the Navy (1976–80), it was called the "ATP-1(B)," which stood for, as I recall, "Allied Tactical Procedures." Anyway, the code book provides tactical and administrative signals in a standard, condensed format, consisting of two letters followed by a number. Originally intended for use in flag hoists, the signals are now transmitted primarily by radio. A sample signal in the admin section would be "AD 28." Pronounced "Alfa Delta Two Eight," it means "Splice the Main Brace"— nautical jargon for "Let's have a beer."

"Bravo Zulu" comes from a special table in the ATP of supplementary signals, all beginning with the letter B, or "Bravo." When combined with other signals, they add a slight variation in meaning to the basic signal, such as "Prepare to . . ." "Commence . . ." or "I am ready to . . ." Thus, the example above could be altered to: "BA-AD28" (pronounced "Bravo Alfa Tack Alfa Delta Two Eight")—meaning "Prepare to Splice the Main Brace." Signal "BZ" (Bravo Zulu) is the last entry on the list, meaning "Well done." It's a standard "Attaboy" heard inevitably at the conclusion of training exercises (during my peacetime days). As your column points out, it's apparently being heard just as frequently following military engagements in the Gulf.

For a future column, you should also consider the origin of "Sierra Hotel." In naval aviation, it's the rough equivalent of "Yahoo!" and stands for "S——— Hot!" It can be heard clearly in at least one scene from the movie Top Gun. *No doubt that's also being heard over radio circuits after many a* fur ball *in the Gulf these days.*

> Andrew J. Schilling
> Tokyo, Japan

You are hopelessly out of date about Zulu Time and Greenwich Mean Time. The latter no longer exists, except that it is still used by the BBC and VOA. GMT was replaced years ago by Coordinated Universal Time, or UT. The coordination is done by the Bureau International de l'Heure (BIH) in Paris. The BIH was established in 1911 "to give time to the world." What the BIH coordinates is a world-wide network of 150 atomic clocks, and it keeps atomic time and earth time precise by adding a leap second now and again.

So what happened to GMT? For starters, the Royal Observatory is no longer at Greenwich; it moved to Herstmonceaux Castle in Sussex years ago. A museum and a brass strip locating the Prime Meridian are all that remain at Greenwich. You can still see the time ball. When the RGO was relocated, it took along its transit circle telescope, located exactly at the Prime Meridian. That was not so bad, because by then, the RGO had its own atomic clocks, and was a contributor to UT. Unfortunately, the Government ran out of money to maintain the clocks and the RGO had to let them run down. The New York Times had a wonderful headline then: "For Greenwich, England Has the Time, but Not the Money." That was the very end of GMT. The UK was reduced to being a user of UT, as disseminated by the BIH.

Greenwich once was really the place where the day began, but that, too, has passed. The International Meridian Conference in Washington in 1844 agreed that the Prime Meridian would indeed pass through Greenwich, and that world standard time would be kept by the RGO. This was not very satisfactory, since the establishment of a "time zone" based on Greenwich meant that it was one day in London and another day in parts of Western Europe. (The French declined to accept this and continued to use the "Paris Meridian" until 1911.) Another Conference, in 1925, moved the International Date Line to 180° running thru the Pacific Ocean. That's where the day begins, and has since 1925.

Dean Koch
Lowry Bay, New Zealand

There is no more Greenwich Mean Time or GMT. Because of international political pressures it is now called Coordinated Universal Time.

Now imagine you're attending your first classes at the Naval Academy on navigation. You create your own acronym. Just don't shout it out.

Frank B. Muller
New York, New York

Belladonna

How do we refer to the President-elect of Nicaragua?

Her name is Violeta (one *t*, and you can win bets on that) Barrios de Chamorro. Because she is the widow of Pedro Joaquín Chamorro Cardenal, and because she has not asked to be referred to as *Ms.*, she is in second reference *Mrs.* Chamorro.

Why do we see *Doña Violeta*? Because *Doña*, pronounced "DOH-nya," is a term of respect before a first name, somewhat like *Dame* in Britain. Russians also have a way of using a first name without showing disrespect or informality: *Mikhail Sergeyevich* is a respectful but warmer form of *Mr. Gorbachev*. Americans do not have a subtle middle way; it's either the honorific or the first name. We should do something about that.

Spanish names usually include the mother's family name after, not before, the father's family name; thus, it is Daniel Ortega Saavedra, which we second-reference as *Mr. Ortega*. A married woman or widow usually uses her maiden name in the middle position, as we often do, making *Mrs. Chamorro* seem natural.

Soon to be correct, if all goes well: *President* Chamorro.

"Russians also have a way of using a first name without showing disrespect or informality. Mikhail Sergeyevich" etc.

Mikhail Sergeyevich is not disrespectful because it uses the patronymic with the first name. Vich in Russian means "son of," as Mc *and* Mac *and, in Hebrew,* ben. *Mikhail's father was Sergei. The first name alone would be rather informal, if not disrespectful.*

Dan [Daniel L. Schorr]
Washington, D.C.

We do indeed have a subtle middle way. Too bad our Friends' usage is so little known. Quakers (The Society of Friends), insistently democratic, have long eschewed titles. Like royalty and bishops of the patriarchal world, they use first names when speaking to each other as peers. When speaking to elders, respected persons, or strangers for whom they deem the first name alone to be too familiar, they simply add the family name to the first. So William Safire, though you are a bit too establishment oriented for my taste, you are nevertheless my elder, respected person, and stranger. So there.

James Harrison
New York, New York

Among members of the Religious Society of Friends, otherwise known as Quakers, who do not lack respect for other human beings but who decided long ago to drop the honorifics that usually elevate some and demean others, it is customary to show respect by using both first and last names together. Thus referring to you or addressing you as "William Safire" shows respect without assigning you to any particular level of society, while "William" or "Bill" by itself would indicate familiarity. I have found it an effective way in the office, too, of fitting in with the first-name custom without sounding disrespectful (at least to my own ear).

Marilyn Sutton Loos
Radnor, Pennsylvania

How do you reckon that doña *is "somewhat like* Dame *in Britain"? Because they are both applied to women? Because they are used with first names? Because they start with "d"? Because they're foreign? That's about it for similarities, since* doña *is a term of respect that one can properly use with any grown woman, whereas only the Queen proclaims who can be called* Dame.

Mia Certic
San Francisco, California

Bespokesman

"He's reaching way upscale," wrote Jay Cocks in *Time* magazine recently about today's fashionable male, "to Armani and Ralph Lauren and the heady heights of *bespoke* tailoring."

"You have to show up in Bond-age style," Paul Hirshson of the *Boston Globe* wrote about a promotional party for a James Bond film, "meaning *bespoke* tailoring for men and something slick and sexy for women."

"Times are tougher, flamboyance is out," *Newsweek* wrote, following the trend toward Duke of Windsor styling. "The suits are available 'off the peg,' but there is even a growing interest in made-to-order, *'bespoke'* tailoring."

My interest is growing in whatever happened to *custom,* a word fading from our fashion vocabulary in a blizzard of British usage. Don't give me any of those non-U *made-to-order* suits; get away from me with that bottom-of-the-line *custom* blazer; to be suitably trendy, bespeak to me of *bespoke* tailoring.

No, I may not say "bespeak to me." One old sense of *bespeak* is "to foreshadow, foretell," as in "The President's move bespeaks action in the gulf." Another sense means "show, indicate." In a *New York Times* book review, John Maxwell Hamilton notes the paradox of the frequent theft of the Bible, the most stolen book of all: "The Good Book apparently *bespeaks* a merciful God."

Yet another sense of this offbeat word is "to ask for in advance" ("to bespeak the reader's patience") or the similar "to reserve, or book, seats before a performance." The seats that are taken, like the person betrothed to be wed, are said to be *spoken for.*

Now we are zeroing in on the meaning of *bespoke,* an adjective that means "ordered in advance" (I'll hear from the Squad Squad about that).

"The shoemaking trade," *Chambers's Encyclopedia* wrote in 1866, ". . . is divided into two departments—the *bespoke* and the ready-made." A half-century later in London, the *bespoke tailor* was born (probably on Savile Row, famed home of tailoring establishments; the present Japanese term for a Western-style suit is *sebiro*).

Why are there so few linguistic customers for *custom*? That word, from the Latin *consuescere,* "to accustom," is akin to *suus,* "one's own," as in *suicide,* a form of which a political candidate wearing a bespoke suit in a working-class district commits.

The Custom Tailors and Designers Association of America claims to be the oldest trade association in the United States, and its executive director, Irma Lipkin, insists that *custom* is here to stay: "*Bespoke* is British for what Americans call *custom*."

But usage by usage, stitch by stitch, the Britishism is patching over our word. We may be left with *customized*—"altered to fit"—or with *made to measure*—"tailored to specific measurements but not made on the premises for a specified customer." This bespeaks a victory for the Brits. (Is "Brits" an ethnic slur? I'd like to hear from Britons about that.)

The old sense of bespeak *means "to foreshadow, foretell." In this sense the word, as applied to British tailoring, refers to a tailor who has been appointed to make clothing for a member of the Royal family, so that his letterhead or store-front sign announces "By appointment to the king (or queen)." The tailor is thus bespoke by the crown, and carries the highest possible recommendation.*

> Victor A. Barbata
> San Francisco, California

Brits, Tommies, Poms, Limeys and Kippers

Once again, in the crunch, the *Yanks* find themselves side by side with the *Brits.*

Does this mean that *G.I. Joe* is slogging through the desert sands with *Tommy Atkins*? No; use of the American term *G.I.*, popularized in World War II after the initials for "Government Issue," has fallen off. Perhaps this decline occurred because the derivative term *G.I. Joe* must be accompanied by *G.I. Josie,* acknowledging the presence of women as members of the armed forces. No sobriquet has emerged as yet to characterize the American forces in the Persian Gulf; Vietnam-era *grunts,* however, is passé. (*Grunt,* a verb from before the twelfth century and a noun since the 1500's, is onomatopoeic. According to *The Times* of London in 1970, "Luckless victims of the American military machine are known as 'grunts,' a name said to be derived from their way of complaining as they trudge along the jungle trails.")

We do know what to call the forces from Her Majesty's government. *Tommy* is still used, taken from the name "Tommy Atkins" used on government forms, much as we use "John Doe" and "Jane Doe" (did the other fella, Richard Roe, ever get married?); however, the term preferred is *Brits.*

That's what we call them, but is that what they call themselves? In the interests of allied solidarity, the question was put to Lexicographic Irregulars a month ago: Do people from Britain, which seems to have triumphed over Great Britain and the United Kingdom as the name for that country, consider *Brit* an ethnic slur?

The scientific sample was selected on the basis of the famed *Literary Digest* poll of 1936 (which predicted Alf Landon would defeat Franklin Roosevelt) and is subject to a polling error of plus or minus 100 percent. The result: 64 percent of the British respondents say they are happy with the appellation *Brit,* 19 percent think it is an undignified clip of the term *British,* and the remainder prefer not to be addressed at all until proper introductions have been made.

A significant percentage objected to the term in which the question was couched: Both letters pointed out *British* has to do with citizenship, not cultural heritage. *English, Scottish* and *Welsh* are ethnic categories, they argue, for people from England, Scotland and Wales, all of whom can be called *Britons* because they are subjects of Great Britain, which unites those three cultures. Add *Northern Irish* to the above, as many do, and you get into a political argument.

A Canadian of British descent, Al Tassie, writes from Victoria, British Columbia, using the noun as an adjective: "I polled several Brit friends and not one objected to the word. A more popular word is *kipper,* and even the *kippers* call themselves *kippers,* at least in this neck of the woods. The derivation is obvious." Obvious to him, maybe. It could be from "English kipper," a herring or sea trout cured by smoking and served with elegance by Mr. Clark, morning headwaiter at Claridge's in London, or from *brit,* uncapitalized, used since the early 1600's to mean "the young of the herring." Maybe the young of the English were equated then with the little herrings; Eric Partridge pointed to slang usage of *kipper* to mean "serviceman" in World War II.

The use of *Brit,* capitalized, dates back to Old English; it is related to *Briton,* first used before the end of the thirteenth century. In Scotland, the shorter form was applied to the Strathclyde Britons at least until 1300, when King Edward I of England abolished "Laws between the Scots and the Bretts." After that, the short form was used only historically but popped up again in 1901 in a British sports page: "The Brit is at his old game." The clip wavered between adjective and noun use: "Are you trying to fool the Brit public?" asked Percy Wyndham Lewis in 1948; "Your working-class Brit is a glutton for celebrities," Stanley Price wrote in a 1961 book. In the United States the noun form prevailed.

That killed *Britisher,* and good riddance to that "odious vulgarism," which was what an incensed lexicographer called the American term. That irritation persists: Sheila Somner writes from St. David, Arizona, that she finds no objection to being called a *Brit,* though she prefers being known as *English,* and "I do take great exception to being called a *Britisher.* I don't call you an *Americaner.*" The *New York Times* stylebook is firm: "Do not use *Britisher(s).*"

(Tangentially, Ms. Somner offers an emendation of my recent discussion of *drop a dime on,* meaning "to inform on," from using a coin telephone to call the police. I veered off to define *the dime dropped,* meaning "sudden realization or comprehension"; she recalls *spending a penny* as a euphemism for going to the public toilet, where a coin was required to enter the stall. This was substantiated independently by Janise Bogard, a Brit living in New York who is a leading photographer of cats; she called to say, "*Now the penny's dropped* comes from going to the loo, luv.")

"I, as a Scot," writes Anthony Eaton of London, "may say that *Brit* is not an ethnic slur, as would be the use of *English.* . . . The word is usually used as a method of demonstrating affection and seems more commonly used by Australians and Americans than *pom* or *limey.*"

Limey (from the lime juice used by English sailors to prevent scurvy) is low-class and insulting unless used with jocular affection. *Pom,* from "pomegranate" in a rough rhyme with "immigrant," is an Australian derogation of immigrants from England.

"Let us turn the question around," Stephen Grover writes from All Souls College in Oxford, one of the minority who think (construe this *who* as plural) that *Brit* is a slur. "Is *Yank* an ethnic slur?"

Yank is sometimes intended as a slur, but it is not received as such, which is disconcerting to the insulter. Americans do not use it for themselves unless in referring to a New Englander, and then it is always *Yankee*, not the clipped *Yank*, which is a Britishism. (That's preferred to *Briticism*, though we prefer *Scotticism* to *Scottishism*. Go figure.)

Nobody can say with certainty where *Yankee* comes from; one popular theory points to the Dutch name *Jan Kees*, "John Cheese," a slur at a Hollander, applied by colonial Dutch in New Amsterdam to the English settlers (much as Australians now hoot at them as *poms;* little changes in etymological patterns).

What, then, should the Brits in the gulf call their comrades in arms from the United States? Whatever they like; as for us, we call each other *Murkens*.

The name of the country is not Britain or Great Britain, but the United Kingdom of Great Britain and Northern Ireland. Britain or Great Britain may be in popular use among permissive types like you, but then so is England, which is equally incorrect (but when did you ever hear of anyone refer to the Queen of Britain?). The term Great Britain refers to the island lying slightly east of Ireland, and was invented for the purpose of making Scots and English feel part of one nation (the Welsh were already stuck in England) when the Kingdoms of England and Scotland were unified. It is an artificial construct, derived from the name applied to the Celtic population that was defeated by the Angles and Saxons. On the other side of the Manche, the people who speak a language akin to Cornish and Welsh are called Bretons.

Bruno Stein
Professor of Economics
New York University
New York, New York

According to Professor T.G.E. Powell in his book The Celts *(Thames & Hudson Inc., N.Y., Library of Congress Catalog Card No. 79-63879) p. 21 et seqq., the Greeks sailing from their colony at Massilia (Marseilles) in the 7th century B.C. established the existence, through intermediaries, of Ierné and Albion, which were direct derivatives from the Old Irish Ériu (later Éire) and Albu, which was used by the Irish for Albion/Britain down to the 10th century A.D. After the voyage of Pytheas of Massilia c. 324 B.C. the islands were referred to as the Pretanic Islands and the name of the inhabitants would thus have been Pritani or Priteni. These are Celtic names. In modern Welsh Prydain means Britain, Prydeinig is British and Prydeiniwr is a Briton, Britisher or Brit.*

The Latin mispronunciation gave rise to Britannia and Britanni. Otherwise we would now be Prits.

Great Britain is derived from its comparison to Brittany (Little Britain) so named after British emigration from Britain to the mainland peninsula in the 5th century A.D. *In French: La Grande Bretagne and La Bretagne. The inhabitants of the latter are Bretons. My surname (pronounced as with an* r *in button) is derived from* Breton *and is simply an anglicized spelling of the French pronunciation.*

*The final word in your piece—*Murken—*you may know appears in Dr. Johnson's* Dictionary, *sometimes* Merkin *or* Mirken, *and was an adjunct used by women in the 18th century.*

> Philip Brutton
> Paris, France

G.I. does not mean "Government Issue" but rather "General Issue" as used in the "Big War"—W.W. II.

Government Issue is generally accepted but is incorrect.

> John Kalafus
> Washington, Connecticut

You make the parenthetical comment, "did the other fella, Richard Roe, ever get married?"

I do not know the answer to that question, but probably the most famous (or infamous) "Roe" of all is Roe v. Wade, *where the Roe in question is decidedly female.*

> Craig Werner
> New York, New York

"Pom" is a shortened or slangy version of "pommie" derived from the acronym POME—Prisoner Of Mother England.

> Clinton W. Alphen
> Glen Rock, New Jersey

An Australian once gave me a different original for the word "pom." He claimed that English prisoners in Australia had "POME," an acronym for "Prisoners Of Mother England," stenciled onto their shirts. He went on to say that Australians apply the term to British immigrants who are, metaphorically at least, still prisoners of their home country. Those who are particularly homesick are called "pining poms." Finally, "Pacific poms" are New Zealanders, though he did not say whether they pine for Mother England.

He gave me this explanation after we had quaffed beer in a French Riviera street cafe for several hours, a circumstance that could taint the authenticity of the etymology. Given, however, that pomegranates have no obvious connection with either England or Australia, and that the rhyme is rough, I find the Australian's explanation more believable.

Nicholas E. Flanders
Hanover, New Hampshire

Why "Nobody can say with certainty where Yankee *comes from"? James Fenimore Cooper said with great certainty that it derives from* Yengeese, *the Indian mispronunciation of "English." See* Deerslayer, *chapter 13 and throughout the* Leatherstocking Tales.

Thomas J. Snow
New York, New York

Perhaps there is a squad which watches for, and advises you about, translation errors in the column and, if so, you probably have learned already that the Dutch name "kees" should not be translated as "cheese." Your source has confused the word "Kaas" (which does translate as "cheese") with the name "kees" (which is derived from "Cornelis" and is equivalent to "Cornelius").

Charles B. Abbott
Hingham, Massachusetts

P.S. The Dutch word for a Briton (male) is "Brit."

"John Cheese" is not an accurate translation of Yankees. *While John in Dutch is most easily rendered as* Jan *(with the "j" pronounced as a "y"), the latter is a diminutive of* Johannes—*a Latin given name common especially among Dutch Catholics. Kees is actually a diminutive of Cornelis, another equally common given name. The actual Dutch word for cheese which you were seeking is* kaas.

As I understand it, the etymology of the word Yankees *goes as follows: The Dutch, pioneering settlers of* Nieuw Amsterdam *(now Manhattan) constituted the mercantile elite among the settlers in the Northern states. The landed gentry in the Southern states (certainly not the Dutch, but probably Irish, Scots and English) began to notice that many of those of Dutch extraction in the North all (curiously) bore the given names of* Jan *and* Kees. *It should, of course, be obvious that considerable antagonism existed between the mercantile and agricultural sectors of the North and South, so that at some point, those of primarily British extraction soon began referring to the Dutch as "those* Jan-Kees," *ergo* Yankees.

> *Johannes Cornelis Thomas*
> *Kozyn*
> *Arlington, Virginia*

There is a folk etymology for grunt. *Supposedly, it came from fresh troop replacements in Viet Nam, called Ground Replacement, UNTrained. Because troops were replaced on an individual basis, instead of by unit, new troops had to prove themselves to the old, surviving troops. Since an unskilled man could be dangerous in his ignorance of real combat, they were derogatorily referred to as NFGs (New F——king Guys).*

I must quarrel with your pronunciation of American. *LBJ always said, "My fellow 'murrikins." Students of* Dr. Strangelove *will recall President Merkin Muffley, a wonderful double pun.*

> *John F. Collins*
> *San Francisco, California*

You reminded me of Bob Hope's recent quip about his native land: "My parents were English; we were too poor to be British."

> *Ernest T. Cimorelli*
> *Cranston, Rhode Island*

The Bloopie Awards

"I can understand a liquor company not using the word *drunk* in an ad," writes Ernest M. Lorimer of Stamford, Connecticut, "but this sentence clanks and should have been rewritten."

The advertisement in question—and it was questioned by nine Lexico-graphic Irregulars—was for Gilbey's gin, and read in part: "Coincidentally, the martini has made a return as well. And it's still drank the same way it was sixty years ago."

Howard L. Lemberg of Bernardsville, New Jersey, snorts: "Really? I'll wager that the last time those folks at Gilbey's drank a martini, *drunk* was still the past participle of *drink*."

Drink (present tense), *drank* (past tense), *drunk* (past participle, sometimes used as an adjective, as in *he is drunk;* the past participle is also used in the present perfect tense, as in *I have drunk,* and the passive voice, as in *it is still drunk the same way it was sixty years ago when men were men*).

Here we are boozing it up at the annual awards ceremony so avidly awaited by readers and writers of America's advertisements: the 1990 Bloopies. The envelope, please:

For the most significant solecism written by a piece of software, runner-up is AT&T Word Processor, for "The built-in spelling dictionary instantly alerts you of any spelling errors." Pity it doesn't alert you *to,* not *of,* idioms.

Winner: Epson's new Equity laptop computer, for "You decide between a 20 megabyte or 40 megabyte removable hard drive." For two objects being decided *between,* use *and,* not *or.*

For the timeliest reminder of the difference between hens and people, a Bloopie to Tourneau watches, for "If you are fortunate enough to have an old watch or two laying around, now is the time . . ." The present participle should be the intransitive *lying,* not the transitive *laying,* which requires an object like a Fabergé egg.

For the fell clutch of circumstance in spelling old Americana, to Ralph Lauren's Home Collection, for "From very fine cotton to double-needle stitching and double-feld seams for added durability . . ." Edward Lavitt of New York points out: "As the son of a tailor, I learned early that when one wanted the raw edges of a seam to be covered, the cloth was sewn once, folded over and sewn again. After the second sewing, the seam became a *felled seam; to fell* is to make that seam." Thus, Ralph Lauren's "double-feld seams" is incorrect, unless it is an eponymous reference to a tailor named Doublefeld.

For the most distinct misuse of a homophone, a solid-gold Bloopie to Bergdorf Goodman, for the phrase "Discrete extravagance. . . ." The word meaning "cautious, prudent, wary, tight-lipped" is *discreet,* which forms a nice oxymoron with *extravagance,* but the homophone *discrete* means "separate, distinct, unattached, removed from," and cannot be what the copywriter for Bergdorf's had in mind. The confusion may be rooted in *distinct* and *distinctive*—the first meaning "set apart" and the second having a sense of "a cut above."

For the most creative display of pronoun-antecedent disagreement, Yonex tennis racquets: "Anyone who thinks a Yonex racquet has improved their game, please raise your hand." This mixes up the indefinite singular *anyone* with the third-person plural *their* and second-person singular *your;* double fault.

For going so far without the ability to count, the Infiniti car by Nissan: "In our minds, the balance of three things is essential to making a luxury car, luxurious. Performance. Comfort. Styling. No one idea is more important than the other." First, no need for a comma before "luxurious"; next, one-noun sentence fragments make little sense, but the technique is used so often in advertising it's become idiomatic; third, when you have three ideas, one is no more important than the *others,* plural—otherwise, you've lost an idea. (No award for the misspelling of *infinity*—the deliberate substitution of a letter makes it possible to copyright the name.)

Incidentally, the term *Bloopie Awards* has made it into a dictionary: In *Webster's New World Dictionary of Media and Communications,* lexicographer Richard Weiner defines the term as "tongue-in-cheek 'awards' for notable errors in grammar and other misuse of language. . . ." It's nice to be institutionalized.

The envelope, please, for two more awards:
"For the most recent example of a Gotcha Club member's omitting (and a famous language expert's overlooking of it) the *'s* before the noun form of

a verb—even in its negative form—*twin bloopies to Messrs. Lorimer and Safire for:*

'I can understand a liquor company not using the word drunk *in an ad, etc.' "*

Dolores Ginsky
Flushing, New York

Perhaps you will be interested in the reply I received from Gilbey's when I wrote to them about the odd wording of their ad.

Wendy Dellett
Alexandria, Virginia

Dear Ms. Dellet:

Thank you for your recent letter clearly stating your position on the question of "drank" vs. "drunk" in one of our recent Gilbey's magazine ads. As a matter of fact, you and several others with an unrelenting passion for the English language have sent us re-checking our facts. Fortunately for our copywriter, Webster's Ninth Edition of the New Collegiate Dictionary *(page 381) gives "drank" as both the past and the past participle form of "drink."*

Now we know attribution doesn't always ensure accuracy. So, although Samuel Johnson did say, "In all pointed sentences, some degree of accuracy must be sacrificed to conciseness," we have decided the passion of our consumers wins the day. We will be rewriting the line for upcoming ads.

But don't get us wrong, we were thrilled to get your letter!

Nancy T. Albert
Director of Communications
Gilbey's
Deerfield, Illinois

Edward Lavitt is wrong. What he describes is a French seam. *He obviously did not enter his father's trade. A* French fell *(or felled seam) is when the seam is stitched,* one *(edge, side) is trimmed close to the stitching, and the other edge is turned under and stitched flat to the underside of the garment.*

Ann Rosenhaft
New York, New York

You say that Nissan's use of the letter "i" at the end of the name of its Infiniti model "makes it possible to copyright the name." The notion of "copyrighting" the commercial label that a manufacturer applies to its product cannot be what you had in mind; surely you were referring to registration of the name as a trademark. The difference between ® and © is vast.

> *J. William Doolittle*
> *Washington, D.C.*

Gotcha! You get the Bloopie Award for Most Egregious Confusion of Intellectual Property Rights by One Who Should Know Better. Your comment on an advertisement for the Infiniti automobile is that, "the deliberate substitution of a letter makes it possible to copyright the name." But, notwithstanding the assumptions of the advertisement's copywriters, names may not be copyrighted, for they lack the requisite originality of authorship under the law. Thus, the Copyright Office's regulations provide:

> *The following are examples of works not subject to copyright and applications for registration of such works cannot be entertained:*
>
> *(a) Words and short phrases such as names, titles and slogans . . .*

37 C.F.R. §202.1 (Note the show-biz nature of this Federal agency: other agencies might not accept applications for registration, but the Copyright Office will not entertain them.)

Names may, however, serve as trademarks, when they identify the source of origin of some particular product or service. The further removed the name from a descriptive term the easier the acquisition of trademark protection; hence the fanciful spelling "Infiniti."

All this should have been patently obvious to a noted author and copyright owner.

> *I. Fred Koenigsberg*
> *New York, New York*

What? No mention of the biggest billboarded bloopie—Honey, I Shrunk the Kids!?? Or are you giving this horror a stoopie award?

> *Bee Hargrove*
> *New York, New York*

Ad Infinitum

This is not the place to come for legal advice. Ignore all advice other than grammatical in this space.

In handing out this year's Bloopie Awards to advertising copywriters, I decided not to knock the car that Nissan Motors has named "Infiniti," because it was not a misspelling of *infinity:* "the deliberate substitution of a letter makes it possible to copyright the name."

"Your statement bristles with error," thunders Professor Phillip Edward Page of the South Texas College of Law in Houston. "First, copyright law has nothing to do with the case. The protection available, if any, is the legally recognized value of the trademark. Second, misspelling is a merchant's gimmick to catch the eye . . . but is not in any way required to make the trademark protectable."

From Grand Rapids, Michigan, John E. McGarry points out that "one cannot 'copyright' a name. Copyright is given to the writing of an author under the Copyright Act of 1976. A name does not qualify as a 'writing' under the Copyright Act."

O.K., the verb I should have used was *trademark.* What about my notion that a properly spelled word was unlikely to qualify as a trademark?

"Equally erroneous," Mr. McGarry says. "Ordinary words can function as trademarks so long as they are not merely descriptive of the goods. The classic example of this is the mark 'Camel' for cigarettes. The term *infinity* does not appear to be descriptive of the Nissan automobile or of a quality of the automobile and thus could have been used as the trademark."

George P. Kramer of Hunton & Williams in New York informs me crisply (all letters from lawyers number the paragraphs; occasionally, an attorney will begin with a more informal "First . . .") that Nissan owns trademark No. 1,478,618 for "Infiniti." Other companies have trademarks registered "Infiniti" for golf clubs and hair-styling mousse.

"Under ordinary circumstances (and there are occasional legal exceptions)," writes the careful Mr. Kramer, "you cannot pre-empt an otherwise descriptive or generic word by simply substituting a letter. . . . *Strawberry* cannot be monopolized if you misspell it as 'strawberri.' "

Last-Minute Bloopie Entry

Pictures of seven ABC anchors—from Sam Donaldson to Diane Sawyer—are shown in an ABC ad, with this caption: "At ABC News, we have a singular mission—to report to you what is happening in the world."

Singular most often means "peculiar, eccentric, strange, quaint, exceptional," with the slang synonyms "offbeat, oddball, flaky"; some round-heeled lexicographers add "unique," and most point out that the word's early meaning was the same as *single,* but few suggest the word can now be used outside of *first-person singular* as a substitute for *single.*

ABC cannot mean its journalists have a nutty mission, nor can the network be suggesting that it is the only news organization with the mission of reporting what is happening in the world. It must mean "only one mission" or "a primary mission"; therefore, the word should be *single.*

In "One," the final number of *A Chorus Line* (which just ended its run on Broadway), a line describes a dancer this way: "One singular sensation, every little step he takes. . . ." *One singular* might be redundant, but the meaning—"peculiar, strange, exceptional"—is correct.

Bogie, Anyone?

The devil, long lingering in the details of language, now stalks the corridors of the Pentagon.

His aliases have included Satan, Belial, Moloch, Mephistopheles, Beelzebub and Lucifer, as well as the more informal Scratch, Old Nick and Old Bogey. In that last incarnation, the *bogie*—I prefer that spelling—may be related to *bugbear,* "an imaginary hobgoblin," known to generations of teeth-chattering children as "the bogeyman."

The apparent triumph of the Prince of Darkness (the Foul Fiend himself, not Robert Novak, the Washington columnist who has adopted his sobriquet) in the Department of Defense is what concerns linguistic souls today. Susan F. Rasky of *The New York Times* has alerted me to the sudden emergence of a hot word in Washington, a favorite of Pentagonians:

"Certainly we did enough to meet the *bogie* that the President asked us to meet," Secretary of Defense Dick Cheney told a congressional committee. On another occasion, he told the committee, "I'm trying to make some *bogies* that I've been given out there in the outyears that are very stringent." He also criticized former colleagues in the Congress who urged him to take cuts now "so that they can meet a budget *bogie* . . . to avoid sequester."

Not since *reclama*—"a request to superior authority to reconsider a decision"—raced through the speech of defenseniks has an unfamiliar noun so thoroughly possessed a SecDef.

Tens of millions of golfers, listening to the voice of the Pentagon, wonder why the nation's military is so entranced with being one stroke over par on a given hole. Speculative etymologists have held for nearly a century that a golfer's *bogie*—golfers more often spell it *bogey*—refers to the scratch value, or par, set up for the course, as if a player competes against a phantom golfer; this *bogeyman* with the unfailingly good score may be the same gentleman of the "Colonel Bogey March," a theme made familiar to Americans in the 1957 movie *The Bridge on the River Kwai.*

Thousands of air controllers are confused, too: To them, a *bogie* is "an unidentified aircraft; a suspicious blip on a radar screen, possibly a *bandit*"; in the armored ranks of the armed services, the term means "a supporting roller on the endless steel belt of a tank." Mothers of sniveling children use the noun *boogie* to refer to a lump of mucus in the nostril of offspring too well-trained to pick their noses.

Musicians also pronounce it *boogie,* a verb from the dance "the boogie-woogie," and are careful not to let it slip as a racial slur; gays and homophobes often confuse *bogie* with *pogey,* a term for a young homosexual that some old salts insist has roots in the Chinese language.

To movie buffs, *Bogie* is short for Humphrey Bogart, and the title of this piece—"Bogie, Anyone?"—is an almost subliminal allusion to the line—"Tennis, anyone?"—in the actor's first appearance on stage, in *The Petrified Forest.*

Bogie probably comes from *bogle,* a sixteenth-century Scottish word for "goblin." The *bogle* lives on in the phrase *to boggle the mind;* one who has been frightened into stupefaction by a *bogle* has had his mind *boggled.* The Standard English word *bogus,* "sham, spurious, counterfeit," probably also stems from that evil trickster, Old Bogey (also spelled *bogie* and *bogy*).

In one of his most devilish prestidigitations, this phantom of the links, scarifier of children and embodiment of evil has transmogrified himself into "a proposed budget goal," as defined by Major General Perry M. Smith, in his 1989 *Assignment: Pentagon,* subtitled *The Insider's Guide to the Potomac Puzzle Palace.*

Quick tangent: General Smith includes a useful glossary of the lingo of Fort Fumble, which includes *analysis paralysis,* "what happens when you study excessively"; *bells and whistles,* "hyperbole to sell a system"; *horseholder,* unhyphenated, "executive assistant," apparently a smidgen closer to the center of action than a *spear carrier;* and *tap dance,* "a slick briefing, usually lacking substance." My favorite is *face time,* which General Smith defines as "time spent near big bosses in attempts to impress them with your diligence and loyalty." Ask yourself, reader ascending the corporate ladder: Have you put in enough *face time* lately? End of tangent.

Could it be that Pentagon officials, using *bogie* to mean "proposed budget goal," are subtly hinting that it is all a chimera, a phantom figure conjured up to scare us all?

Perish forbid. (I believe that portmanteau of "Perish the thought" and "God forbid" originated on the radio show *Duffy's Tavern,* unless it was a Gertrude Berg television creation.) Extracted from a budget meeting to take my call, Secretary Cheney says: "It just means 'mark' or 'target.' It's standard lingo around here; I hear it all the time. You're right, I'm using it too much—Lynne, my wife, warned me about that a week ago." He stifled a sigh, and added, "After a year or so around here, you become one of them."

And Old Nick, the ancient Tempter and scratch golfer, takes out his wallet and—chuckling evilly—inserts another linguistic soul.

The word "bogey" or "bogie" has long been used by aircraft designers and engineers in other fields to identify weight, power consumption and other design goals. As a design evolves, it is continually monitored to make sure that the bogey is not violated.

Another usage: A bogie comprises the drive motors, gearing and wheels of subway and other self-propelled railway cars.

I do not know why the term is used by engineers but it certainly has no hidden or threatening meaning as you imply for the Pentagon usage.

> *Sylvan Gollin*
> *Claremont, California*

I have always assumed that this usage came straight out of railroading. The swiveling, unpowered set of wheels at the front of a steam locomotive was a "bogie"; among other things, it facilitated the negotiation of curves by the long, heavy engine. As I understand it, in budgeting for multi-year programs, a "bogie" is a hypothetical or target budget level for a future period (or "outyear"); its use in budget analysis permits consideration of various options, such as alternative current and near-term spending levels, program stretch-outs and the like. The rail-fiscal analogy, while not perfect, seems to me quite apt: It recognizes that, in both contexts, the bogie, while a relatively flexible (forward/future) projection of the (locomotive/budgetary) mechanism, is directly connected to and driven by the force (powered wheels/prior spending levels) behind it.

> *J. William Doolittle*
> *Washington, D.C.*

In the investment world a bogey is a standard or benchmark to which a money manager's performance is compared. (Secretary Cheney seems to come close with his definition of "mark" or "target.") Thus, the investment results of "growth managers" are compared to one "bogey," those of "value managers" to another and so forth. Consequently, each asset manager has an index which is his or her "bogey."

> *Harrison J. Goldin*
> *New York, New York*

Most salespersons who receive incentive income have a quota established. They must reach that quota before they begin to receive incentive pay. That quota is almost universally called "the bogie." Frequently heard complaint in bars is "They cut up my territory and raised my bogie—I'll starve!"

> *David McKean*
> *Frenchtown, New Jersey*

Your column on bogies recently appeared in The Times of India. *Recent events here have brought another meaning of the term* bogie *to mind. In British and, I believe, American English,* bogie *also means a set of railway wheels of the kind found at each end of a railway carriage or wagon (or waggon, if you prefer.)*

In Indian English, bogie *has been adapted to mean an entire railway carriage (whether passenger or freight), as in the description of a rail accident in which ". . . two bodies were found in the gallery of the first class bogies which had perched atop the general bogie. . . . Using (a) crane . . . a ten foot hole was made in the roof of the bogie." (*Times of India, *June 7, 1990, p. 1.)*

> *Steven A. Heinrich*
> *Mysore, India*

Those things in your nose aren't boogies, they're boogers. Any 9-year-old could tell you that.

> Beth Botts
> Chicago, Illinois

Drop the Gun, Louie

In the Washington bureau of *The New York Times* hangs a framed poster titled *Boulevard of Broken Dreams.* It is a painting by Gottfried Helnwein—inspired by the nostalgia and realism in Edward Hopper's painting *Nighthawks*—of four legendary people in a dreary diner at night.

Working behind the counter is Elvis Presley; sitting on one stool by himself, coat collar turned up, with a white mug of coffee at hand, is an unshaven James Dean; Marilyn Monroe, blond head tossed back in provocative laughter, is seated close to Humphrey Bogart, wearing a bow tie as Rick in *Casablanca,* staring glumly at a glass in front of him. All dead too soon, but their images shimmer in the shared, broken dreams of our national memory.

Make a mistake about the details of the careers of any of them, and a legion of rememberers comes at you with an admixture of dismay and delight, mock hurt feelings and a fierce possessiveness of trivia. We must not get the details wrong; it is a kind of sacrilege, as if any deviation from the recorded history disturbs their ghosts and muddles the misty orderliness of our sentimental past.

"You must be buried under the mail from all the faithful," writes Harvey Glassman of Fort Lee, New Jersey, "who wrote after falling off their chairs from hysterical laughter at your boo-boo. Playing tennis was not one of Duke Mantee's diversions, since the machine gun would have slowed him down."

This, along with so many other letters, is the voice of the Bogart fan—shocked, shocked at the following paragraph in a recent piece in this space about the derivation of the word *bogey:*

"To movie buffs, *Bogie* is short for Humphrey Bogart, and the title of this piece—'Bogie, Anyone?'—is an almost subliminal allusion to the line—*'Tennis, anyone?'*—in the actor's first appearance on stage, in *The Petrified Forest.*"

"Oh dear, as Edward Everett Horton would have said," writes Roy D. Pierce of Portland, Oregon. "Oh dear, oh dear, oh dear. Bogart's initial stage appearance was made not in Robert E. Sherwood's *The Petrified Forest,* but in John Colton's *Drifting* in 1922, 13 years before he played the wanted criminal Duke Mantee."

"The phrase *'Tennis, anyone?'* was spoken by Bogart in *The Circle,"* writes the actress Dorothy Cheney Quinan of Newtonville, Massachusetts. "Actually, 'I say, what about this tennis?' is the way my playbook read when I appeared in the play at the Keene Summer Theatre, regrettably not with Bogie."

There seems to be some dispute here on a phrase that has a hallowed, tension-breaking place in the American language. Lloyd T. Grosse of Eatontown, New Jersey, sends in this passage from Nathaniel Benchley's biography of Bogart: "Richard Watts Jr. [the drama critic] . . . swears that he heard Humphrey, wearing a blue blazer and carrying a tennis racket, come onstage and speak the immortal line *'Tennis, anyone?'* as the playwright's device for getting unwanted characters off the stage, but he cannot now remember the name of the play. Others tend to doubt that the words were ever spoken . . . and Humphrey gave a different version every time the subject came up." (Mr. Grosse adds, "Shouldn't that be tennis *racquet?"* but I refuse to be sidetracked.)

"The gangster Mantee may have been involved in many rackets," writes Don Koll of New York, "but tennis was not one of them." (O.K., it's tennis *racquet.)* "Mr. Bogart had the line (and it may have been 'Anyone for tennis?') in another play in the 20's, probably *Cradle Snatchers."*

Mr. Koll points out that other famous stage and movie lines are misremembrances: "Mae West did not say, 'Come up and see me sometime' in *Diamond Lil.* What she actually said was 'Come up sometime and [pause] see me." (Nor did Bogie say, "Drop the gun, Louie"—that was a parody. I have felt the lash of the broken-dreams legion on this type of error before: Write *play it again, Sam* in any context, and the sticklers will send you transcripts showing the line in *Casablanca* to read only *Play it!*—no "again, Sam." Their slogan seems to be "You *must* remember this. . . .")

Jay Shulman of Scarsdale, New York, reminds us that "Bogart referred to the romantic juveniles he most often played on Broadway as *'Tennis, anyone?'* parts. This anecdote is recounted in Joe Hyams's *Bogie.* The line itself may have never actually been said."

Was it said? *Bartlett's Quotations* in its fourteenth edition lists the phrase as a Bogart quote, his sole line in his first play; in *They Never Said It,* Paul F. Boller Jr. and John George wrote that the "actor denied he ever uttered it in play, movie or in person."

Is there no former interviewer who can come forward with a contemporaneous citation, directly from Bogart, on this important two-word expression of la-di-da superciliousness now used as a jocular subject-changer?

Here's a surprise: I am that person. In 1951, as a reporter for the "Close-

Up" column in the New York *Herald Tribune,* I was sent out by my bosses, Tex McCrary and Jinx Falkenburg, to interview Mr. Bogart and his wife, Lauren Bacall.

Even then, almost four decades ago, I had phrases on the brain. Here in hand is the yellowed clipping from the file I saved when the old *Herald Tribune* morgue closed down. I asked Bogie about his first line on stage:

"People forget how I used to look on Broadway," the actor reminisced. "There would be a crowd of charming and witty young blue bloods gathered in the drawing-room set, having tea, while the hero and the heroine get into a petty squabble. The writer couldn't think of any other way of getting excess characters off the stage, so the leads could be alone—and that's where I would appear in the doorway, in my flannels, hair slicked back, sweater knotted jauntily about my neck, four tennis racquets under my arm, breathing hard as I said my line: 'It's 40-love out there. Anyone care to come out and watch?' "

I had just turned twenty-one years old, but my bosses had taught me enough about reporting to cause me to put the question to the source directly: Did he, Humphrey Bogart, ever use the words *Tennis, anyone?* on stage? His unequivocal reply: "The lines I had were corny enough, but I swear to you, never once did I have to say *Tennis, anyone?*"

There it is, straight from the horse's mouth, settling the argument forever. This is no recollection of mine; it was transcribed in shorthand and written for the newspaper that day. It was as if Fate had put an incipient phrasedick in the right place with the right question to the right source at the right time.

You may be wondering: If the answer to the origin of *Tennis, anyone?* had been vouchsafed to me, personally, thirty-nine years ago, why did I not cite it in my piece a few weeks ago?

I forgot, that's why; it went right out of my head. When my recollection was refreshed, it all came back to me, counselor.

Of course, looking back over more than thirty years himself, Mr. Bogart may have forgotten—or perhaps he got bored with the frequent question and tried a different answer. As the Hyams biography indicates, the line in his first show was somewhat longer than two words, and in his recollection to early interviewers, he compressed it into a compound adjective: "*tennis-anyone* roles." That adjectival usage was then treated as the exact quotation, which it probably was not.

Bartlett's in its fifteenth edition has made a change—not from the confirmed Americanism *Tennis, anyone?* but a change in the sourcing—to a more accurate "attributed" to Humphrey Bogart.

I just read all this aloud to the broken-dreams poster. Elvis gave an appreciative wriggle, and James Dean's eyes flickered. As Marilyn smiled and squeezed his arm, Bogie said to read it again, Sam. (Here's lookin' at you, kid.)

Yes, Bogart never said, "Drop the gun, Louie," but in the film Across the Pacific, *he pulled a gun on Claude Rains and said, "Not so fast, Louie!"*

Marshall Anker
New York, New York

Who Jests at "Scarify"

In a recent piece about *bogies,* I referred to "Old Scratch," a term for the devil, as a *"scarifier* of children."

This almost intimidated Richard Walsh of Bedford, Massachusetts: "I feel sure that in referring to the bogeyman as a 'scarifier of children,' you were deliberately trying to entrap know-it-alls, but here I go falling for it." He went on bravely to write that the verbs *to scare* and *to scarify* were unconnected.

This was no entrapment or subtle mail pull; it is a mistake I must have been making all my life. Using the false analogy of *horror* to *horrify,* I assumed that another verb for the noun and verb *scare* was *scarify.* Wrong.

"To scarify," writes Carl Mezoff of Stamford, Connecticut, "means 'to make a series of scratches or cuts in the surface of something,' and not, as I assume you had intended, 'to frighten.' " (Some dictionaries do list *scarify* as a 1794 slang synonym for *scare,* but the standard sense of *scarify* offered by Mr. Mezoff dates back to the sixteenth century. Pronounce the slang term "SCARE-if-y" and the standard word "SCAR-if-y.") He adds that the highway department will use a machine to scarify, or rough up, the surface of a road that is being blacktopped. Sheldon Flory of New Lebanon, New York, points out another sense of "to scar ritually," as is done among some African and other tribal peoples.

Heaven the Thought

"Perish forbid," a portmanteau of "Perish the thought" and "Heaven forbid," was a nice malapropism of the 1940's. I speculated that it might have originated with the radio show *Duffy's Tavern* or with *The Goldbergs.*

"My mother, Gertrude Berg," writes Harriet Berg Schwartz of West

Nyack, New York, "did not use a thick accent in her portrayal of Molly Goldberg, but made the audience laugh at and with her by using inverted word order, upward inflection and hilarious mispronunciations. 'Perish forbid' sounds like her, but I am not sure if she originated the expression. Of course, 'button your neck' is forever to her credit."

The answer lies elsewhere. "Goodman Ace was no plagiarist," writes Allan Davis of Levittown, Long Island, and Helen R. Chapman of Key West, Florida, agrees: "Perish forbid you should have forgotten the Easy Aces— Goodman and Jane. It was Jane who used to say, 'Perish forbid!' " Ms. Chapman was so surprised at my oversight that "As Jane also was noted for saying, 'You could have knocked me over with a fender!' "

Boldly Prudent

"Democrats on Capitol Hill have been calling me *timid,*" said George Bush recently. "I have other, better words like *cautious, diplomatic, prudent.*"

Nothing more delights this department than a battle of the adjectives. When jousting politicians pick up the lance of synonymy, they sharpen the differences in words, giving hard edges to meanings we otherwise treat fuzzily.

"*Timidity* in the critique," observes Meg Greenfield in *Newsweek,* "is inferred from caution, hesitation and a reluctance to engage in any but fairly modest actions. . . . The term, as loosely used, conveys at least a tiny whiff of cowardice. . . ."

That's because *timid* is rooted in the Latin *timere,* "to fear"; in more than four centuries of English use, it has meant "easily frightened, apprehensive, lacking courage." Another sense is the more becoming *shy, bashful, diffident, modest* and *coy;* another is *introverted, withdrawn, reserved,* by which the psychologically kindly often describe the timid, but the sense most often meant is *fearful.*

Cautious, however, is rooted in the Latin *cavere,* also the source of *caveat,* an English noun for "warning" that Alexander M. Haig Jr. used as a verb in "Let me caveat that." The root word meant "to be on one's guard, to take heed," which has a connotation more of good sense than of fear. The synonyms of *cautious* are *wary, circumspect, careful,* which are not ordinarily pejorative, as *timid* is. A fox is *cautious;* a rabbit is *timid.*

An owl, symbol of wisdom, is *prudent.* This adjective comes from the Latin *prudentia,* an alteration of *providentia,* "foresight." Originally "the wisdom to see what is virtuous," the word is synonymous with *wise, sage, judicious, discerning* and, if you prefer the unfamiliar, *sapient.* All of these signify sound judgment, but *prudent* uniquely carries the connotation of "exercising self-restraint before taking action or making a decision."

Ms. Greenfield, in her column, pointed out that the charge of timidity "is enough to drive all but the most self-restrained politician to dangerous, nutty acts. . . . Self-restraint, incidentally, is also not to be confused with timidity."

On a brief trip to the United States to consult with President Bush before the Malta summit, British Prime Minister Margaret Thatcher eschewed the current crop of characterizations and came up with her own, praising Mr. Bush's "*measured* approach."

Yankee fiduciaries like the word *prudent,* and bankers cling to the legal principle of "the prudent man." When Sherman Adams came under fire during the Eisenhower Administration, and had to admit some breach of ethics, the word he chose that admitted least wrongdoing was submitted by his friend Tex McCrary: *imprudent.*

The adjective *prudent* and its noun *prudence* are without a form to apply to an individual because a *prude* already exists with another meaning from another root. This locution is from the Old French for "proud, valiant," as in *prud'homme* and *prudefemme,* which Sir Richard Steele had appropriated by 1709, defining the French term in his *Tatler* as "a Courtly Word for Female Hypocrites." *Prude* now means "an excessively prim person; a prig," and is by no means what the President has in mind in calling his policies *prudent.*

We have been placing *timid* on one side of a coin and *cautious, prudent* on the other, but not everyone accepts caution and prudence as automatically admirable.

"In politics as in love," James Reston said as he retired from *The New York Times* on his eightieth birthday, "there's a time when you have to kiss the girl. I think that this is one of those times in history, and we're holding back. I feel in my guts," he told the reporter R. W. Apple Jr., "that it's wrong—that this is a moment when we should do more than be prudent and cautious."

Ah, we are now into the synonymy of daring, the realm of the plunger. My favorite word in this lexicon is the Americanism *bodacious,* probably from the English dialect *boldacious,* an amalgam of *bold* and *audacious.* In the cartoon strip "Barney Google," by Billy De Beck, later spun off to "Barney Google and Snuffy Smith," Snuffy's wife, Loweezy, popularized the word by applying it to her nervy and often outrageous husband. The usage is current: In Rockville, Maryland, a computer store calls itself Bodacious Bytes.

In the new fluidity that follows the cold war, what is obviously needed is a bodacious President following a prudent policy.

The Bonding Market

"Mrs. Gorbachev and Millie *bonded.*" That good news was the word from Barbara Bush and must have caused much head-scratching at Tass. They knew that Millie was the name of the Bushes' (which should be pronounced "bush-iz-zizz") English springer spaniel, sometimes referred to irreverently as the First Dog, but what means *bonded*?

It has nothing to do, in this sense, with promissory notes, with aging whisky in a warehouse that has been insured, or with Ian Fleming's hero, 007. Nor does it refer to the coating of teeth with adhesive resins, to a sadomasochistic game, or to the *bonds of matrimony,* though that notion of "ties"—from *band,* "something that constricts"—offers a clue to the new meaning.

Bonding (the gerund form is the most common) is a word being lifted from psychology. (When I am ambivalent, I claim to be *torn,* because I am of two minds about *ambivalent,* and have a block about slipping into psychological jargon with *conflicted.*)

"*Bonding* was first emphasized in the late 1950's," we are informed by L. Michael Honaker, an executive of the American Psychological Association who apparently has a hang-up about his first name, "primarily in the work of John Bowlby. The term is taken from ethology, the study of animal behavior."

Early studies of the attachment process spoke of *imprinting*—as adult birds imprint their behavior patterns on chicks—and this needful knowledge grows as the newborn attaches to its own species.

Students of human attachment, who took into account Freud's discussion of the libidinal feelings of baby to mother (which laymen like to call "love"), seized upon the word *bonding,* and that term soon shook *attachment* loose.

"*Bonding* is a relationship," Mr. Honaker says, "in which a person maintains or restores proximity to another individual. Often it involves a tendency to defend that other person, and the attachment is sometimes exclusive or preferential."

The *Longman Dictionary of Psychology and Psychiatry* defines the term as "a close attachment, or affiliation . . . present in normal behavior but absent in . . . the sociopathic personality."

What about *male bonding*? This is what used to be called "camaraderie" or good fellowship, a hearty form of friendship now viewed with amused contempt by some feminists. In a 1979 reference to a Babylonian legend, Elizabeth Fisher wrote that "Buried within . . . the Gilgamesh epic is an adolescent-male myth of the wonderful world without women, which still surfaces in male writings. It is the earliest extant tale of male bonding and the diabolic influence of women."

These sinister excesses are no part of what most of us mean by *bonding.* Nonpsychologist fathers like to take a few days off from work to bond with newborn infants, and owners of just-purchased puppies need bonding time to wean the young dogs away from the alarm clocks placed in their beds, or pallets, to resemble the beat of their mother's heart. (I put an electric clock in the kennel, and the lonely pup howled all night; where do you find a clock that ticks anymore?)

"Getting to know and love" is the current meaning of *bonding,* a word that fills the need for a term to describe a stage beyond *befriending.* It now runs between people as well as between people and animals. The First Lady's spokeswoman, Anna Perez, reported that Millie followed Raisa Gorbachev around the White House residential quarters and "quivered with pleasure whenever Mrs. Gorbachev spoke to her," a sure sign of *bonding.*

Barbara Bush's use of the word bonding *to describe the relationship between Mrs. Gorbachev and the American presidential dog Millie did not occasion any "head-scratching" here at Tass, nor did it send us to the dictionary.*

Besides being reasonably proficient at the English tongue (even as spoken by Americans), Tass correspondents are getting to know more and more running dogs of capitalism, including Millie.

We ourselves have bonded *with quite a number of Americans, and, thus, had little difficulty understanding Mrs. Bush.*

> Igor Makurin
> Bureau chief
> Tass
> New York, New York

Modesty aside, I feel bound to note that the first use of male bonding both as a phrase and a concept was in my book Men in Groups, *Random House, 1969, as part of an argument about biologically linked sex differences, and since then it has passed into the language as a kind of omnibus reference to an array of male behaviors.*

> Lionel Tiger
> New York, New York

Why do you continue to impose impractical pronunciations on us? Don't conversational and written language have implicit practical discrepancies? If our President's name was George Bushes, how would you have me pronounce, "Bushes' " then? Bush-iz-iz-izz? Perhaps the rule regarding pronunciation of a plural's possessive should, in this case, be rewritten . . . for sibilant suppression's sake!

> Philip Sivilli
> Commack, New York

Bring Back Upper Volta

The people of Chad had good reason to change the name of *Fort-Archambault* to *Sarh,* and *Fort-Lamy* to *Ndjamena:* The new names are less warlike, contain no memories of a colonial past and are easier for local residents to pronounce. I will go along with this change in about a year, when I become sure the Chadians mean it and everybody knows where the two cities are.

But ixnay on *Burkina Faso.* That's the new name chosen by the government of Upper Volta, which apparently tired of being asked, "Whatever happened to Lower Volta?" (There never was one.) A spokesperson for that country's Mission to the United Nations said, "We changed the name because *Upper Volta* was a colonial name not from us but from the French government, and because we are more than just a location on the river Volta. *Burkina Faso* means 'country of incorruptible people.' " That's fine for them, and the United Nations can change all the metal place cards at the table, but it's still *Upper Volta* to me.

Safire's Law of Nation-Naming: You get only one crack at a new name in each century. Upper Volta's organizers had their chance when the country proclaimed its independence in 1960. When British Honduras, British Guiana and Dutch Guiana became independent after that, they called themselves *Belize, Guyana* and *Surinam.* Fine; but if they want to change the names again, they should be required to wait.

What about *Cambodia?* A bunch of genocidal Khmer Rouge came along and renamed the country being terrorized; why do we have to go along with their preference, *Democratic Kampuchea?* We know it's no democracy; besides, the key part of the new name is approximately the same as it was, with the spelling jerked around to please the local dictators; why should you and I kowtow?

Accommodationists, doves, assorted linguistic roundheels and spelling reformers will say, "A place is named whatever the local people name it," so if *Cambodia* sounds like *Kampuchea* in Khmer, that's the way we all must transliterate the sounds. *The New York Times,* to its credit, has never adopted *Kampuchea,* although it has recently started using *Myanmar* for the country most of us know as *Burma.* (If the copy editors want to lather themselves up with Myanmar-Shave, that's their business, but I'm still traveling down that old Burma Road.)

If local preferences are to dictate, and Rangoon is now meekly accepted as *Yangon,* why don't we call Rome *Roma,* as the Romans do? Or if we are transliterating sounds, write Paris as *Paree,* to match the French pronunciation? To be consistent, Vienna should be *Veen,* as citizens of what is spelled *Wien* pronounce it.

"People can call their countries and their cities anything they like," writes Byron Farwell, in a column for the *Blue Ridge* (Virginia) *Leader,* "but why must we English-speakers follow suit?" Only Latin American, Asian and African countries get this favored treatment; European countries and cities are not the objects of our deference. "For us, Norway is not *Norge,* Germany is not *Deutschland,* Spain is not *España* and certainly we do not call Finland *Suomen Tasavalta.*" (Maybe Denmark is Lower Tasavalta.)

Our refusal to adopt European names and spellings, contrasted with our acquiescence in non-European nomenclature, suggests that we are permitting a political bias to affect our linguistic judgment. That's a bad reason for inconsistency; it is surely patronizing and may even be considered reverse racism. (We treated the Union of Soviet Socialist Republics as we do the Europeans. The U.S.S.R. was not the S.S.S.R. "No one ever calls the country

Soyuz Sovetskikh Sotsialisticheskikh Respublik," Mr. Farwell observed. Nor was it the C.C.C.P., as no one wanted to get into the Cyrillic.)

When somebody wins a war, among the spoils is the name; I am prepared to accept the name Vietnam for what was *North Vietnam* and *South Vietnam,* and though it galls me, I call Saigon *Ho Chi Minh City.* And when nations merge, we have no reason for resisting a medling of names; Tanganyika and Zanzibar came up with the sensible *Tanzania,* which has a nicer ring than something like *Zantanganbar.*

Although the Sultan of *Brunei* was good for a $10 million loan when Ollie North said we needed the money, I am reluctant to go along with the addition of a second name to the Sultan's country. An ancient name for Brunei, *Borni,* was probably used centuries ago to refer to the whole island of *Borneo;* the Sultan now wants to call his nation *Brunei Darussalam,* presumably because of the confusion with the rest of Borneo. Let's wait a generation or so; if the nation has not been reshuffled or merged, or it has not purchased all Malaysia in a friendly junk-bond takeover, we can see if we want to cram in the second name on our maps.

You think this resistance to cavalier place-renaming is xenophobic? Then bring it close to home: The highest point in North America is Mount McKinley in Alaska (named after William McKinley when he was campaigning for the presidency), which some groups in that area are now lobbying to call *Denali.* That means "great one" and is the name by which the mountain is known locally.

I'm standing pat with Mount McKinley. From atop its 20,320-foot peak, you can almost see from Yangon to Mandalay.

Dear Bill,
See Winston Churchill's minute to the Foreign Office dated April 23, 1945 (on page 752 of Triumph and Tragedy*): "I do not consider that names that have been familiar for generations in England should be altered to study the whims of foreigners living in those parts." Sir Winston thinks "if we do not make a stand we shall in a few weeks be asked to call Leghorn Livorno, and the B.B.C. will be pronouncing Paris 'Paree.' Foreign names were made for Englishmen, not Englishmen for foreign names. I date this minute from St. George's Day."*
   O Winston, thou shouldst be with us in this hour!

Frank [Mankiewicz]
Washington, D.C.

I was in West Africa for the Times *when that name change took place. FYI,* Burkina Faso *can be translated not only as "Country of Incorruptible People"* but also as "Land of the Erect Men," and indeed, many preferred that rendering.

By the way, I always meant to do a story on the train that runs from the Ivory Coast to Upper Volta/Burkina Faso, mainly because I wanted to see the headline: "Pardon Me, Boys, Is That the Ouagadougou Choo-choo?"

Another item: The Ivory Coast in recent years has been insisting that it be referred to only in French, e.g., Cote D'Ivoire.

And one more thought for today: In your piece, you use the phrase "reverse racism," a locution that has been gaining popularity lately. To my mind, that retronym is politically loaded. It suggests that "racism" describes a biased attitude only on the part of whites toward blacks. It seems to me that racism is racism no matter the color of the practitioner.

Clifford D. May
The New York Times
Washington, D.C.

It is most unlikely that Denmark will ever come to be known as Lower Tasavalta, since Tasavalta is not a geographical name—it's the Finnish word for "republic"!

Louis Jay Herman
New York, New York

To celebrate the veritable Praha Spring of liberation on this subject which you have opened up, I'm going to douse myself with köln and take my Beijingese for a walk, then put the Warszawa Concerto and the Carnival of Venezia on the phonograph, mix myself a Moskva Mule or maybe pour myself a glass of oporto or bourgogne, set out my best Royal København, light up a La Habana while one of my prize White Livorno hens roasts in the oven and Bruxelles sprouts and Yerushalaim artichokes simmer in the pot, read about the Congress of Wien, and plan a journey on the Cape-to-al-Qahirah railway.

The Times long since went to München on this matter, and most people seem to feel that all roads lead to Roma; so set all sail (including the genova), and fight with the fury of the great Lisboa earthquake, for neither the Genève Convention nor the 's Gravenhage Convention applies, and no Firenze Nightingale will succor the fallen; you will yet make New York once again an intellectual Makkah, the Athenai of the West.

Thaddeus Holt
Carlisle, Pennsylvania

I am particularly exercised about the renaming of Chinese cities since I lived in China for my first 15 years. Chinese, as you probably know, is a tonal language. One word pronounced in four different tones has four different meanings—often totally unrelated. So, to properly call Peking by its Chinese name, one should pronounce it "Bei³ Tsing¹." No one over here does that so no one pronounces it correctly. It might as well be called Peking as far as the relationship to the actual name goes. T'ien An Men is another example. T'ien An Men means Gate of Heavenly Peace and is divided into three separate words. Over here it is pronounced as if it were one word with the accent varying depending on who's talking. The same holds true for all the Chinese cities that broadcasters try to pronounce with sometimes laughable results.

It is also interesting to me that with all the emphasis on Chinese names, no one calls China by its proper name, Chung Kuo, or Japan by its proper name. I can't remember it exactly, but it's closer to Nippon than Japan. The whole thing seems so artificial—the Chinese probably have Chinese names for our cities. Why can't we have English names for theirs? At least they would be pronounced correctly.

Barbara H. Ambler
Wayne, Pennsylvania

It is encouraging to know that someone at The New York Times *believes that a country (or city, and I assume anyone) has the right to call itself by any name it wishes and to spell it however it chooses. The epitome of arrogance on this subject, I believe, occurs in some dictionaries, e.g.,* Random House. *Their definition for "Rumania" is "a republic in SE Europe." For "Romania" they have "Rumanian name of Rumania." Similarly, for "Livorno," they have "Italian name of Leghorn." I didn't bother looking further.*

I wrote to The New York Times *a few weeks ago suggesting that the real name of the newspaper is "The Nu Yurk Tumes."* The New York Times *is merely what* The Nu Yurk Tumes *calls* The Nu Yurk Tumes.

Manny Hillman
Blue Point, New York

I'm with you all the way in regard to place names. I wish you had mentioned Livorno. I'm sure you know most of English-speakers call it Leghorn. My edition of the Encyclopaedia Britannica *handles it this way: If you look up "Livorno," it says: "see Leghorn." If you look up "Leghorn," there is a lovely, long and interesting piece about the ancient Italian port, never once mentioning that it is properly called, by the people who live there, Livorno. I know whose fault that is, don't you?*

The Brits—they just didn't want to take the trouble to learn how to say Livorno. Leghorn, indeed! Me, I call it Livorno and I flip the R, Italian-style.

Elaine Steinbeck
(Mrs. John Steinbeck)
New York, New York

Bubba, Can You Paradigm?

The televised feeding frenzy that calls itself "The McLaughlin Group" was dealing with redneck tendencies in one of our Southern states.

Eleanor Clift of *Newsweek* said, "This enhances Louisiana's '*booba*' image."

"*Bubba*," Pat Buchanan corrected.

"*Bubba*," agreed the host, John McLaughlin.

"*Booba, bubba,* it's not good whatever it is," shot back Ms. Clift.

One viewer, Roberta Shaffner of Bala-Cynwyd, Pennsylvania, writes: "What is this *bubba factor* anyway? I always thought of *bubba* as the Yiddish word for 'grandmother.' Am I missing something here?"

The Wall Street Journal agrees with you, Mrs. Shaffner. A 1982 article was headlined "Is the Stock Market Really Efficient? Go Ask a Bubba" and quoted a professor explaining that "bubba psychology is the study of what Jewish grandmothers know without benefit of graduate training."

Buba is a Hebrew word for "little doll" and may have been the source of an affectionate term for a small grandmother; however, the similar *baba* is also used for "grandma" in Russian and other Slavic languages, which makes the origin uncertain.

This much is indisputable: A grandmotherly *bubba* (with the *u* pronounced like the *oo* in *book* and not like the *oo* in *boob*) is not a brotherly *bubba* (with the *u* as in *bub,* which we still hear in the hostile "What's it to you, bub?").

The pronunciation is the distinguishing key. Set aside the *oo* of *boob,* from the German *Bübbi,* meaning "teat." Another sense of *boob*—"fool"—is from *booby,* possibly from the Spanish *bobo,* "silly, stupid" (used for a silly sea bird), ultimately from the Latin *balbus,* "inarticulate, stammering." H. L. Mencken combined *boob* with *bourgeoisie* to come up with *booboisie,* his derogation of the middle class.

Bubba with the book-sounding vowel is the word to describe the dispenser of chicken soup; the *uh* sound, as in "hub, rub, stub," is the hypocoristic form of "brother" and is sometimes followed by the snap of a wet towel. (Is hypocorism the use of pet names, sweetie? You got it, buster.)

According to the *Dictionary of American Regional English* (where Fred Cassidy and his team at the University of Wisconsin are already up to the letter *H*), the fraternal form of *bubba* is "especially common among blacks" and is mainly Southern and Southern Midland usage. Because citations show the shorter form of *bub* in general use more than a century ago, this may be a rare example of current black borrowing from old white slang.

We now have a noun used in direct address—that is, speaking to the person being called by the term *bubba.* This noun is in competition with a clip of the word *brother* to *bro;* we will see which one triumphs in popular usage, at which point we will go with the flow, bro.

But *bubba* shows signs of breaking from its narrow confine as a term of direct address or as the nickname of Southern football players, usually black (the best known is Bubba Smith, who gained fame as a defensive end for the Baltimore Colts). It now has a political coloration in the phrase *bubba factor.*

"*Bubba* is political shorthand for 'Southern conservative,' " reports Mr. McLaughlin. "Think of *bubba* as a synonym for *redneck* or *good ol' boy*—someone who speaks a rural, crusty prose and is hard to present to city folk. The *bubba factor* refers to Southern conservatives whose vote must be considered in an election."

The word has not yet sorted out its meaning. If it is a paradigm of a poor rural Southerner, its synonyms are *cracker* (someone who cracks his own corn, too poor to buy cornmeal) or *redneck* (possibly from a sun-scorched neck from bending in the fields), and its *factor* is white; yet the word, when used in direct address, is at least as often associated with blacks as whites. Is it possible we have the birth of a nonracial, or biracial, term for "imposing Southerner"? Watch this space, bro.

While there may be those who address their Jewish bubbas with the u pronounced as in "book," most people pronounce the u as in "buf" or like a clipped rendering of the first syllable in "bauble."

What distinguishes a Jewish grandmother from a large football player is the pronunciation of Bubba's second syllable. In Yiddish it is "Bubbeh" (short e) and is often Anglicized to "Bubbie."

Using the book-sounding vowel in "Bubbie" or in the diminutive, "Bubbela," turns the word into an endearment, e.g., "Bubbela, I love your column."

> *Laura Chasin*
> *Flushing, New York*

P.S. In Russia, the book-sounding Bubba was the midwife!

When it comes to "bubs" and "boobs," I think you may be setting your etymological sights too low, deriving "boob" from a German word for teat. It is true that in vulgar parlance, a woman's breasts are termed "boobs." But that is a different article (or rather, those are different articles) from the person—an ignoramus—whom one terms a "boob." The root of the latter word is the German "bube," meaning "boy," which in American argot has taken on a depracatory value, as in the phrase, "Only a boob would confuse a Bubbi for a Bube."

> *Jurgen Schulz*
> *Providence, Rhode Island*

Budget Brightness

"Just toss them a metaphor and cynical journalists go weak-kneed," wrote Michael Kinsley in *The Washington Post.* He was complaining about the attention given to the ordinarily stupefying "Budget of the United States Government" because Director Richard G. Darman enlivened the hefty tome with a personal introduction comparing the general perception of the budget to the Cookie Monster on public television's *Sesame Street.*

I enjoy bright writing in unexpected places and salute Mr. Darman for slipping some wake-up prose into the torpid, tumid, turgid world of governmentese.

The last time this happened at O.M.B. was in budget director Cap Weinberger's day, when he suggested that Nixonian economic projections could become a "self-fulfilling prophecy." When he sent the draft out for comment to a score of departments and agencies, every single one returned the document with that line crossed out: The turn of phrase generated universal horror. Cap the Knife pretended to accept the deletion, sent out eight more redrafts with the original thought excised, and then slipped it back in just before the budget went to the printer. He knew bureaucratic infighting better than most.

However, Mr. Darman—having dared to be colorful—invites close inspection of prose as well as numbers. Here are a few potshots:

"As all monsters are, Cookie Monster is initially intimidating." This is so grammatically correct as to be hopelessly stilted. What's the matter with the natural *Like all monsters*? Mr. Darman knows how to do it; later in the document, he writes, "Like education, drug abuse is a problem." That's, like, the way, man—no graceful writer would try "As education is, drug abuse is. . . ."

"The true cost of the previously planned and Congressionally-approved defense program is . . ." In this explanation of the absence of a peace dividend, Mr. Darman tries to have it both ways on hyphenation. When an adverb ending in *ly* modifies an adjective before a noun, no hyphen is called for. *Previously planned* is correct; *Congressionally-approved* is a mistake.

"Federal investments in the future will only achieve their objectives if they are effectively managed." Because this comes in the context of improved returns on investment, I think he means "In the future, federal investments will." (He could be talking of "investments in the future," but that is usually placed in the section under Education.) Worse, the man charged with keeping track of $1.23 trillion has misplaced his modifier; he does not mean "will only achieve," because achievement is not to be sneezed at. He means "will achieve their objectives only if."

A metaphor (in the case of the Cookie Monster, an analogy) is attention-getting. But in the future, Federal Budget Messages will achieve their objectives only if they are effectively copy-edited.

Dear Bill:
I notice you didn't go into the origin of the Cookie Monster, also known to very small children as Alistair Cookie. The Recognition Gasp is one of the daily nuisances anyone who's much on TV has to learn to put up with. The only time it's actually pleasurable is when it comes from kids.

As recently, when I was waiting at La Guardia for my grandson to arrive
from Vermont. An arriving young mother being clutched by a five-year-old girl.
They stop, move on, stop again. Hectic hissings and whispers between the two.
The mother says: "Well, go on, ask him. Don't be afraid." The tot heel-scuffs
for a moment or two and then patters over. Wide-eyed, open-mouthed, says:
"Are you the Cookie Monster?" "I am!" I expected she'd scream and beat it.
But she grinned in relief and embraced my knee! Talk about the catch in the
throat, a flow of brine tears.

Don't ever pass this on to Bush: he'd swipe it—"Gee whillikins! I guess it was
one of the most touching moments of my life."

> *As ever,*
> *Alistair [Cooke]*
> *New York, New York*

Cache in the Wry

"You have to do something about this right away," said R. W. Apple Jr., my colleague at the Washington bureau of *The New York Times*. He brandished a clipping: "It's spreading."

The offending usage was in a *Wall Street Journal* story about Robert Iger, a bold television producer: "Even if *Twin Peaks* caves in, it has already won ABC new cache in Hollywood as the hands-off network, eager for ideas that are daring and different."

The daring and different usage was *cache*. That word, pronounced "cash," is rooted in the French *cachet*, "to conceal"; a *cache* is "a hiding place, a place where stores are kept or left; anything kept in such a hidden place."

The word probably meant by the writer is *cachet*, pronounced "ca-SHAY," from the same French root, but with a quite different modern meaning: "distinction, eminence, prestige." Henry Fowler disdained the French term as "mainly a literary critics' word (*bears the c. of genius etc.*) and should not be allowed to extrude native words; *stamp, seal, sign manual*, are usually good enough for English readers." Sixty-four years later, most usagists would disagree about the lifted-pinkie quality that bothered Fowler; the word that had its origin as a seal on an official document—*lettre de cachet*—has a nice panache that distinguishes it from *distinction*.

The other word, *cache*, is still useful in its proper hiding place. In 1970, criticism was directed against American military officials in Vietnam for not finding the much-heralded hidden stock of weapons called Cosvn during the Parrot's Beak incursion. The President's counsel, Len Garment, poked his head in my speech-writing office to ask, "Can you check a *cache*?"

I daresay the villain is the printer and not your good self, but that French infinitive should be cacher, *not* cachet *(". . . rooted in the French* cachet *[sic], 'to conceal' ").*

Louis Jay Herman
New York, New York

What you call a "daring and different usage" of cache *was of course nothing but a lousy illiteracy, no doubt abetted by the utterly damnable habit (alternatively sanctioned by the* Ninth*) of spelling* cafe *and* frappe *without the acute accent.*

Louis Marck
New York, New York

1. *I assume you mean* cacher *(to hide) or is it* cachette, *which means a hiding place. By the way, French children playing hide and seek call it:* jouer à cache cache.
2. Cachet, *yes, it has the same root but here the original meaning is to squeeze or press, as in* apposer son cachet *(affix one's seal) or seal a letter:* cacheter.
3. Lettre de cachet *only refers to one thing: the letter of imprisonment or banishment bearing the seal of the king.* Cachet *is also the legal name for the fee paid a performer and also refers to any medication taken in capsule form.*
4. *Since you mention the Parrot's Beak, did you know that the French called it* Bec de Canard *(one man's duck is . . .)*
5. *Last but not least, did Leonard Garment also invent the story about the midget from Czechoslovakia fleeing across the border and asking the first person he saw—you've guessed it—"Can you cache a small Czech?"*

Alec Toumayan
Washington, D.C.

Cache memory in a computer is used to describe a reserved part of RAM that is used to make file transfers between disks and working memory occur more rapidly. The sense of a protected location for a special use certainly fits what your friend Apple said about Twin Peaks.

Edward J. Haupt
Montclair, New Jersey

"Cosvn" or "COSVN" referred not to a cache *of weapons but to a central command headquarters for coordination of Viet Cong and North Vietnamese military and political efforts in the South. Truong Nhu Tang, one of the founders of the National Liberation Front—the political arm of the Viet Cong, wrote in* A Viet Cong Memoir *(Harcourt Brace Jovanovich, 1985), "COSVN was, and had always been, people rather than a place. It was a leadership group made up of delegates from the Central Committee of the Workers' Party (Lao Dong), several of whom became members of the NLF Central Committee as well. COSVN executed the directives of the North Vietnamese Politburo and coordinated the action of the Party and the National Liberation Front." (p. 128)*

COSVN was a nerve center for a powerful revolutionary movement, fueled primarily by ideas rather than weapons. Our own main error was vastly to exaggerate the capacity of our enormous military firepower—including obliterating B-52 raids—effectively to counter the gripping vision of the other side.

> *Arthur Cyr*
> *Vice President and Program*
> *Director*
> *The Chicago Council on*
> *Foreign Relations*
> *Chicago, Illinois*

Calling Colin Colon

Here is a plaintive communication from Colin W. Getz of Tequesta, Florida: "My first name has been made prominent by General Colin Powell, chairman of the Joint Chiefs of Staff. The media are pronouncing the name "KOH-lin." You may think there is not much difference as to whether the name is pronounced "KOH-lin" or "KAH-lin."

"The problem arises," Mr. Getz continues, "when you are a young boy and people mistakenly call you KOH-lin. Fun-loving kids then ask you if you were named after a bowel (*colon*) or other idiots ask you if you are going to name your son Semi-Colin."

A *colin*, in pastoral verse, denotes a shepherd, based on the poet Edmund Spenser's use of the word in the sixteenth century. According to Eric Partridge's *Name Into Word*, the French name *Colin* is a diminutive of *Col*, itself a shortening of *Nicolas* or *Nicholas*. (It is unrelated to *Colleen*, from the Irish word for "girl"; save your postage.)

The preferred English pronunciation, says *Random House II*, is "KAH-lin," with the preferred German pronunciation "KOH-lin." The British are firm about it: "Why are you chaps calling KAH-lin KOH-lin?" asks Sir Basil Feldman, the Conservative party stalwart, on the phone from London. Sir Colin Campbell was a nineteenth-century field marshal; one of his current namesakes, a political columnist for the *Atlanta Journal and Constitution,* says, "My name is pronounced KAH-lin; my colleague from Texas with the same name pronounces it KOH-lin."

In the Pentagon, the high-rent E-ring facing outside has at least two Colins working there. One is Major Colin F. Mayo, who is an aide to the chairman and pronounces his name "KAH-lin"; the other is his boss, Colin Powell, who pronounces it the other way but is putting no pressure on his aide to conform. (They don't call the Pentagon "the Puzzle Palace" for nothing.)

"My parents named me KAH-lin," the general told an interviewer. "My parents were British subjects and they knew how the name should be pronounced."

But that was not what the other kids called him: "When I was a young boy, there was a famous American war hero at the beginning of World War II by the name of KOH-lin Kelly—I think that is an Irish pronunciation, I am not entirely sure—but my friends in the street, hearing that he had pronounced his name KOH-lin, started calling me KOH-lin." He is comfortable with both pronunciations, but prefers "KOH-lin," "much to the regret of my British friends who consider us a bunch of ignorant Americans for mispronouncing the name."

Colin P. Kelly Jr. became a United States war hero when his plane was shot down after he bombed a Japanese battleship. In posthumously awarding him the Medal of Honor, President Franklin Roosevelt wrote a letter to a future President to ask that the hero's infant son, Colin P. Kelly 3d, receive an appointment to West Point when he came of age.

"The young man did grow up, did want to go to West Point," General Powell recounted, "went to West Point and into the Army. He served in Vietnam as an armor officer, came back from Vietnam and went into the chaplaincy and became an Episcopal priest. I met him about nine years ago when he was a lieutenant colonel and I was a brigadier general, and I said, 'What's your name?' He said, 'KOH-lin Kelly.' And I said, 'Thank God, you have been mispronouncing your name all your life just as I have.' "

Colon comes from two Greek roots with the same spelling. One has an accent mark over the first *o;* it means "part, limb," and has evolved into the punctuation mark (one dot over the other) that decisively separates two parts of a sentence. The root without the accent means "food, meat"; (no, that's a semicolon) it has come to mean this: (there we go) the large intestine or bowel, a hoselike muscular organ where food is digested.

Which brings us back to the letter of Colin Getz: "My reason for writing this is that many people, proud of the prominence of General Powell, may be moved to name their son Colin. My advice to them is: *Don't.*"

Years ago F.D.R. summoned George M. Cohan to the White House of a quiet evening and privately presented him with a Congressional Medal of Honor for the inspiration his music spanning two wars created among the citizenry ... only to have a startled Congress rise up and retract the bauble mistakenly given. The MOH, of course, is bestowed only for extraordinary valor against an armed foe. True, Colin Kelly's son did attend West Point on the strength of a presidential proclamation, but his Dad's Medal of Honor was rescinded because post-war revelations clearly indicated his plane to have been shot down nowhere near the Japanese warship he was supposed to have destroyed.

Pete McGovern
Westport, Connecticut

*You say that "*colon *comes from two Greek roots with the same spelling," one with and one without an accent mark over the first* o.

Not so. In the intestinal colon, the initial Greek kappa *is followed by an omicron with an acute accent; in the punctuational one, the second letter is an omega with a circumflex. The usual transliteration for omega or "long o" is an* o *with a macron.*

The ultimate origin of the intestinal colon is doubtful, but etymologically speaking, no "food" or "meat" is involved. Some etymologists even deny it a separate identity, perhaps abetted by the fact that in the Greek progenitor of our "colic," the omicron has become an omega.

The punctuational colon, however, goes back to the Indo-European root (s)kel-, *whose basic meaning is "crooked." It has "derivatives referring to a bent or curved part of the body, such as a leg, heel, knee, or hip"* (American Heritage Dictionary). *Among its other English progeny are* isosceles, scalene, scoliosis, *and (according to Merriam-Webster)* calk.

As for the name Colin, it is most likely a diminutive of Nicholas.

Louis Marck
New York, New York

"Colon" doesn't come from two Greek roots with the same spelling. They are spelled differently: ηῷλον and ηόλον. What you take for an accent mark over the first o *is only an English dictionary's way of telling you that an omega is used in the Greek instead of an omicron.*

Thomas B. Lemann
New Orleans, Louisiana

You were almost on it with Spenser's use denoting shepherd, but you went astray on calling Colin a shortening of Nicolas.

The word col *in French means hill, and Colin signifies a hill-dweller, which later means shepherd for the grazing of the hills by their sheep.*

William Miles
Beverly Hills, California

The "KOH-lin"/"KAH-lin" controversy can easily be resolved using a simple 4th-grade spelling rule: A vowel followed by a single consonant is long; followed by a double consonant—short. Hence General Colin Powell has been pronouncing his name correctly all along.

As to the preferred British pronunciation, "KAH-lin"—anyone who has traveled in England knows it is folly to depend on a relationship between spelling and pronunciation in British English. Consider Leicester ("LESS-ter"), Worcester ("WOOS-ter"), Beauchamp ("BEE-chum"), Cadogan ("ca-DUG-an"), Frome ("FREWME"), Gloucester ("GLOSS-ter"), or even the BBC's Kuwait ("QUE-wait") and Sinai ("SY-nyai").

Consequently, even though our son was born in London, we spelled his name Collin to try to avoid the old Colin/colon homonymic pitfall.

Mary-Sherman Willis
Greenwich, Connecticut

I am troubled a bit about your assertion that the British use the pronunciation "KAH-lin." I know British Colins, a number of Colins from Scotland, Canada, New Zealand and Australia, and not one of them pronounces the name with the intonation advised by the doctor putting the tongue-depresser in your mouth. The "o" is pronounced as in "otter," which is not so open as "ah" and not quite so closed as "law," although it can actually approach the latter.

Actually, what you have gotten into somewhat unwittingly is the matter of vowel sound-shifts that have been occurring in American English. In America, the "o" in such words as "collar," "dollar," "cottage" and "hot" has come more and more to sound like "ah."

C. Loring Brace
Ann Arbor, Michigan

Callous, My Foot

Dr. Scholl's uses gimpy English.

"Callous Removers" is what the company calls its product to remove the hardened, thick skin properly spelled *callus*.

"We're asked this question every six months or so," says Joanne Brown, the Scholl Inc. public relations director. "The noun spelling is *callus,* but we use the adjective in *Callous Removers,* and the adjective is spelled with an *o.*"

A lame excuse. First, the label sent to me by Charles Dahle of Greenwich, Connecticut, says to apply the "adhesive side onto the callous." That means the adjectival spelling is being used mistakenly for the noun.

Second, the too-confident flack is stubbing her toe on her parts of speech: In *callous removers,* the word *callous* is not an adjective describing the noun *removers;* only hardhearted bankers who repossess cars might be called *callous removers.* In the Dr. Scholl misusage, *callus*—with a *u,* no *o*—is an attributive noun modifying *removers.*

Callus, from the Latin *callum,* "hard skin," means just that—hard skin. *Callous,* same root, gives a figurative extension to the numbness: "insensitive, unfeeling" is the meaning.

After my yearly bout with manual labor, what I proudly show on my hand is a *callus;* pitilessly giving Dr. Scholl's a boot for its insolecism is being *callous.*

Can You Handle This?

Accustomed to a rapid advance, General Norman Schwarzkopf showed he could beat a hasty retreat when he found himself in a controversy with the President.

"A poor choice of words" was what he called his use of the verb *recommend* in connection with the decision to end the ground war in Iraq after one hundred hours, allowing some Iraqi forces to fight again against rebel troops. "I would change the word 'recommend' to say 'we initially planned,' " he explained in his apology.

President Bush forgave his Desert Storm commander with a Shakespearean phrase, "much ado about nothing," which may have been adapted from "great ado about many small matters" in Richard Hyrde's 1529 translation of a Spanish scholar's work on the instruction of Christian women. But a useful lesson—perhaps even a profound one—can be drawn from the brief Schwarzkopf-Bush contretemps, which has stirred particular interest among

language mavens. (The plural of *maven* is *mavens,* not the Yiddish *mavenim*—it is now an English word, taking an English plural, so cut it out with the postcards.) That lesson is about the effect of subtle inflections and pronunciations on meaning, especially concerning dialect terms.

Here is the account given by Marlin Fitzwater, the presidential press secretary, of the conversation in the Oval Office on February 27, 1991: "President Bush said to General [Colin] Powell: 'What about Schwarzkopf? Is he on board? Call him.' Powell walked over to the desk in the Oval Office and used the hot line to Riyadh [Saudi Arabia]. He told the President: 'Norm says he can handle it. It's fine with him.' "

He can handle it. That was Mr. Fitzwater's report of what General Powell characterized as General Schwarzkopf's reaction. Were the words "I can handle it" actually used by the general in Riyadh? Let us assume, for the sake of linguistic analysis, that the Fitzwater report of the Powell report of the Schwarzkopf comment was a direct and accurate quotation, changing only the first person to the third person, and will not be contradicted by any recording to be released in the heat of future presidential campaign.

What does *I can handle it* mean?

"Print hides the voice," says Frederic G. Cassidy, chief editor of the *Dictionary of American Regional English.* "If I could have heard the gentleman *speak* it, I'd be more certain of what he really meant." One meaning, says the man from DARE, is "I can control something that needs control"; a quite different meaning, indicated by inflection, is "This hurts (my pride, dignity, sense of what I deserve), but I can accept it and not let my feelings show."

Allan Metcalf, executive secretary of the American Dialect Society, agrees: "On the one hand, it means 'I am handy enough to accomplish whatever task is handed to me.' On the other hand, it means 'Hand me all the abuse you want; I promise I won't fly off the handle.' To decide which meaning was intended, you look for the context in which the statement was handed out. Of course, a speaker who doesn't want to tip his hand might say, 'I can handle it' and keep both possibilities in hand." (In one pedagogical burst, Professor Metcalf illustrates the *hand-handy-handle* connection as well as five dialect usages of *hand,* a handsome effort.)

"I would like to have heard him say it," says David K. Barnhart, general editor (as distinct from specific editor) of Lexik House, "particularly the word *it;* the intonation pattern can turn a phrase from friendly to begrudging. Remember that General Schwarzkopf is in a subordinate position; he has to accept the decisions made by his superiors. The expression in this military context might be construed as saying: 'I can obey orders,' which can mean 'Your order is my command' or 'I will obey orders, even though I think it's a mistake.' "

There may be another way of getting a handle on this. Let us go beyond general lexicography to a specific field in which the expression has gained particular meaning.

"Yes, the verb *handle* is used in the psychiatric profession," says Dr. Leah Dickstein, a psychiatrist in Louisville, Kentucky. "Psychiatrists often ask, 'Can you *handle* it?' about a specific problem, and patients say, 'I can *handle* it.' A synonymous expression used more often is *deal with.*"

Let's go deeper; this department does not flinch from horrific revelation. "I suspect that the term *handle* is used more often by men than women," opines Dr. James Nininger, a psychiatrist in New York. "That may be because *handle* suggests being in control of a situation; men more often than women speak of 'handling it,' as being able to do something alone or being able to handle responsibility.

"The word *handle,*" Dr. Nininger continues, "provides an image that involves hands or a concrete handle to take hold of. Frequently the expression is used in the negative, as in 'I'm not sure I can handle it'—that indicates a breakdown, at least temporarily, in ego functioning or control. Put positively, 'I can handle it' means being able to negotiate the variables or complexity of a situation and not losing control of oneself."

O.K., Norman, stretch out on this couch. Relax. Forget about what that anonymous White House aide meant when he said you were suffering from "camera fatigue." Do not be conflicted by the necessary avoidance of conflict.

Cast your mind back to the day the war was about to end, life was simple, the media feared you and the public loved you, and that nice General Powell came on the phone from the Oval Office to talk about stopping the shooting sometime before it had been initially planned.

When you said, "I can handle it," did your tone indicate a meaning of "Just leave it to me," as imputed by General Powell, who added either the characterization or report "It's fine with him"? If so, then your words meant that you raised no objection to the suspension of hostilities at the time, and your subsequent imputations to interviewer David Frost were self-serving, inaccurate and deserving of your abject apology to your commander in chief.

Or by "I can handle it," did you mean "I know what a chain of command is; I can take the stress, I can negotiate the complexities and not go through the roof, even though I know history will condemn us all for letting those Republican Guard units free to blow all the Kurds away"? If that was your meaning, then you did indicate you would follow orders but did not agree with them, and your subsequent apology was intended to conceal an embarrassing difference of opinion that did exist.

Intonation is all. A phrase's meaning is conveyed not by words alone, but by body language, inflection, emphasis and structures so deep as to be unfathomable to the shrinking deconstruction worker. The lexicographers all make clear that the recipient of meaning had to be there, on the line, hearing the subtle sound, to know what was meant. As early semiosemanticists liked to say, "It ain't what you say, it's the way that you say it."

Dear Bill,

Re: "I can handle it"

The New York Times, *reporting on the Schwarzkopf flap, quoted a White House spokesman saying that "Mr. Bush was comfortable with his decision to stop the fighting on Feb. 28." "Comfortable"—as if he was talking about an old pair of shoes, not a decision of momentous consequence! There was a time when a President would have defended such a decision by insisting that it was "right" or "just" or even "expedient."*

When did this usage of "comfortable" become so ubiquitous? I suspect it came in with the "touchie-feelie" psychobabble of the last decade, the group therapy sessions of self-confession and self-absolution, the pedagogy of "self-esteem" (the mantra chanted by some school-children, "I feel good, I am good"). And while you're about it, you can tell me when we started to say, "I can live with it"—another form of self-validation. (Can you imagine Churchill saying that he was "comfortable" with the decision to bomb Dresden, or that he could "live with" the policies made at Yalta?)

Gertrude Himmelfarb
Washington, D.C.

Chappy Chanukah

According to the *New York Times* stylebook, the eight-day Jewish Feast of Lights that celebrates the victory of the Maccabees is spelled *Hanukkah.* Two *k*'s.

Webster's New World Dictionary lists the name (from the Talmudic Hebrew word for "dedication") spelled first with a single *k,* then with a double *k* (with or without a final *h*); the *American Heritage Dictionary* says to take your pick but that both are variants of *Chanukah.*

This dispute went to the Supreme Court, in a way, in *County of Allegheny* v. *the American Civil Liberties Union,* a decision holding that the public display of a menorah, the candlestick symbol of the holiday, had both a secular as well as a religious meaning.

Never before had the Court written that Hebrew word in a decision; a spelling decision was required, especially since the disputants spelled the holiday differently. Down came the word, Supreme Court–style: *Chanukah.*

"Why did the Court pick the more phonetic 'C' spelling?" asked the reporter Tony Mauro in *Legal Times.* "The Court's reporter of decisions was at a loss to explain, except to suggest that it came from author Justice Harry Blackmun's chambers that way. . . . 'It's a spelling of first impression,' says public information officer Toni House." That hardly seems the way to spell out the decisions of the nation's unappealable court.

We are dealing here with transliteration, the spelling in one language of sounds made in another, using letters of different alphabets that often do not directly correspond. In this case, the *ch* letters are intended to convey a fricative sound, as happens when you create friction by narrowing the flow of air along the top of your palate; the trouble with that in *Chanuka* is that the *ch* letter combination is confused with the first sound in *China.*

Well, then, how about *Hanuka?* Doesn't quite do the fricative trick, but comes closer, without going to the less familiar *kh* combination, as in *Khomeini.* However, the single *n* in *Hanuka* leads some logical English speakers to pronounce the word "Han-OO-kah."

The English spelling in use today that comes closest to the sound of the Hebrew word, in my book, is *Hannuka,* which leads most to "HAN-uh-kuh," a reasonably close approximation for those who resist gargling.

That's settled, then; remanded to the Supreme Court for review. Next year at this season, we will discuss other logical questions: Why don't we pronounce the *i* in *Christmas* the same way as the *i* in *Christ?* And why do we drop the *t* in *Christmas?*

As a Judaica librarian, I read your column on the proper spelling of the holiday Hanukkah with great interest. Three principal questions appear to be at issue:

(1) systematic romanization, (2) common usage, and (3) standard American spelling.

As far as romanization is concerned, there are several incompatible systems now in use. Prof. Werner Weinberg, of Hebrew Union College, prefers "Chanukah," basing his preference on "The American National Standard Romanization of Hebrew" (ANSI Standard Z.39.25). The nation's libraries employ a different romanization scheme: ALA/LC romanization, which was developed at the Library of Congress. (I am surprised that, in preparing your column, you did not get in touch with the relevant authorities at LC.) According to ALA/LC romanization, the holiday is romanized "ḥanukah" (ḥ with a dot underneath, denoting the guttural consonant). Hebrew book titles containing that word are invariably romanized by catalogers, using that spelling.

Because LC subject headings are based on common and accepted usage, subject catalogers rely on dictionaries and encyclopedias in establishing many headings. Because of this, LC subject headings for Jewish holidays usually diverge from their systematic romanizations. In the 2nd edition of Webster's dictionary, for example (I do not have ready access to the 3rd edition), the Festival of Lights is spelled "Hanukkah" (preferably) or "Hanukka" (alternatively). These spellings reflect out-of-date romanization systems, true, but they do have the advantage of being widely accepted, and of bearing a passing relation to the Hebrew pronunciation of the holiday. In the interest of promoting a single, standard American orthography, I would urge that, in such cases, you follow your editors' lead in accepting "Hanukkah" as the proper spelling for the holiday. (In effect, I am recommending that common usage take into account accepted dictionary spellings for proper nouns borrowed from other languages and alphabets, for the purpose of establishing a uniform American spelling. Systematic romanization remains appropriate for bibliographical description.)

Zachary M. Baker
Head Librarian
Yivo Institute for Jewish
    Research
New York, New York

Dear Bill,

The reason the "t" of Christmas *isn't pronounced is the same as the reason why the "t" of* listen, glisten, chasten, mustn't, whistle, thistle, often, soften, *etc. isn't pronounced: English underwent a sound shift in which [t] was lost if preceded by a spirant and followed by a sonorant; according to Jespersen (*Modern English Grammar, *vol. 1, 224–5), this loss took place in the 17th century. The difference between the vowels of* Christ/Christian *is due to a much* *earlier set of changes in which vowels in various contexts became short (this dates from before the Great Vowel Shift, i.e., at the time of the shortening,* Christ *was pronounced with [i:], which had not yet shifted to [ay].*

Jim [James D. McCawley]
Department of Linguistics
University of Chicago
Chicago, Illinois

Both . . . As Well As

I have five separate files on corrections to mistakes made in these columns. One is starkly labeled "Shame!" because that's how the letters begin; other files are "Say It Isn't So," "Not You Too," "Gotcha!" and "You, of All People." When all five files have a letter on the same subject, I respond.

"Say it isn't so," salutes R. Henson of New York City. " 'The display . . . had *both* a secular *as well as* a religious meaning.'!!!"

Harry Kaplan of Monmouth Beach, New Jersey, is a twofer: "For Shame! And you, Mr. Safire, of all people!!"

"I now find that you have joined the swelling ranks of semi-literates," adds Paul Streeten of Boston University, "who use the correlative *both* not as parallel to *and* but to the redundant (or alternative) *as well as.*" (Because his letter begins with "You, the guru of the English language, have let me down," I have that under "You, of All People.")

The sentence at issue is "The public display of a menorah, the candlestick symbol of the holiday, had *both* a secular *as well as* a religious meaning."

A conjunction conjoins, or just joins, two words or phrases; correlative conjunctions (like *neither . . . nor*) are used as a pair with at least one intervening word. My shocked correctors say I should have written either *both . . . and* or just left off the *both.* And there's no denying that the weight of authority and tradition is on their side.

Both Ted Bernstein and Eric Partridge, usagists I respect, hold that *both* is redundant when used with *as well as.* Merriam-Webster's anything-goes *Dictionary of English Usage* says it doesn't matter, which I ordinarily take to mean it does matter.

Let's noodle this around. The preceding paragraph begins, "Both Ted Bernstein and Eric Partridge"; is *both* necessary? It could easily be done away with, because the *and* does the conjoining job; still, the *both* adds emphasis that not just one, but two, of these giants of grammar and lexicography are against me. At the risk of redundancy, *both* . . . *and* drives the point home.

Now let's see how *both* works with *as well as*. "Both Ted Bernstein as well as Eric Partridge"; nope, it sounds funny. Doesn't quite fit in Norma Loquendi's unerring ear. Drop the *both* and try "Ted Bernstein as well as Eric Partridge." That works because the *as well as* is more emphatic than *and,* and doesn't need the extra stress of an opening *both.*

Both *both* and *as well as* are emphasizers; the precise writer should go with one or the other, but not both. Not because they are redundant (which they are, but so is *both* . . . *and*), but primarily because they result in emphasis overkill.

Therefore, I admit the error. Shame! Me, of all people.

Why did you end your column in which you admit the error of using "both" and "as well as" together by stating, "Me, of all people"? Did you do this because it sounds better than "I, of all people"?

> Maryanne Bruck
> Edison, New Jersey

Just make sure it's "Ted Bernstein and Eric Partridge . . . hold . . .", but "Ted Bernstein as well as Eric Partridge holds . . ."

> Robert Goodman
> Bronx, New York

Characters and Plots

I could write a great story and make a bunch of money, many would-be novelists tell themselves, if only I could think of a good plot.

Ray Bradbury is a poet, short-story writer and novelist with a worldwide following: The Russian poet Yevgeny Yevtushenko once recited for me a long and shining passage from one of Bradbury's science-fiction stories.

Zen in the Art of Writing: Essays on Creativity is a paperback by Bradbury (Capra Press, $8.95), in which he departs from the usual how-to advice to writers and imparts some of the nontricks of his trade. For those who write for money, he advises:

"The surgeon must not think of his fee, but the life beating under his hands.

"The athlete must ignore the crowd and let his body run the race for him.

"The writer must let his fingers run out the story of his characters, who, being only human and full of strange dreams and obsessions, are only too glad to run."

Then Bradbury passes on the secret that novelists know but plotters never grasp:

"The time will come when your characters will write your stories for you, when your emotions, free of literary cant and commercial bias, will blast the page and tell the truth.

"Remember: *Plot* is no more than footprints left in the snow *after* your characters have run by on their way to incredible destinations. *Plot* is observed after the fact rather than before. It cannot precede action. It is the chart that remains when an action is through."

Chop on, Chop at, Chop-Chop

The United States Secretary of State, a man long familiar with bureaucratic slang, was explaining to reporters how Israel, the United States and Egypt would decide on which Palestinians would attend a meeting to arrange for elections in the disputed territories.

"The three nations could in some way determine the Palestinian representation with respect to the dialogue," said James A. Baker 3d. "That would, of course, give Israel a *chop* on the representation."

Of course. But what was a *chop*? "It's a murky phrase to me," said a reporter at a follow-up briefing by the State Department spokesman, Margaret D. Tutwiler. "What is it exactly that the United States says Israel's reservations or control of the delegation amounts to? Do they have a *veto*? Do they have a *say*? Do they have a *chop*, whatever that means?"

Ms. Tutwiler (who has decided to interpret the title "spokesman" as embracing the female, thereby forthrightly rejecting *spokeswoman* or *spokesperson*, but that is on background from an official source who insists on anonymity) had no answer: "I can't get into that" was her way of evading a definition of *chop*.

This department, however, is fairly licking its chops at the opportunity to get into that because the locution is rich in its etymology and subtle in its range of meanings.

The figurative meaning of *chop* as a verb is profoundly affected by the particle following it. To *chop off*, in Washington parlance, is "to freeze; to withdraw support from and communication with; to remove from the circulation list of memos." To *chop about* means "to flail; to act indecisively or aimlessly; to issue contradictory statements." To *chop down* does not usually mean to destroy, but "to reduce in influence," as when a Cabinet officer chops down an attempt by a White House staffer to articulate policy; the more severe *chop up* means "to damage the reputation of; to mangle bureaucratically."

As a noun, *chop* also is affected by the subsequent preposition, and that is what directly concerns us here. To give someone a chop *at* is far different from giving a chop *on* something.

Take a chop at may have started in logging, but is now firmly rooted in baseball lingo as a synonym for *take a swing at* or *take a cut at*. (A *Baltimore chop* is a topped ball that bounces high off home plate or near the plate.)

But the Secretary of State promised Israel a chop *on*, not *at*, his draft proposal; this places the metaphor in a different league.

The Baker chop comes from the Hindi *chhap*, meaning "stamp, print, impression"; when the *Los Angeles Times* ran the Baker usage, it interpolated "stamp of approval." European traders carried this term to China, where it has been used in senses that later became obsolete in India.

In English, where *chop* began as "a bargain" and led to *cheap*, its other meaning of "seal" or "official stamp" was first used in 1614—"The King sent us his Chop"—which led to the word's meaning of "license, passport." William Dampier reported in his 1699 travel book that "The Governor or his Deputy gives his Chop or Pass to all Vessels that go up or down." That led to *chophouse*, meaning "customhouse"; elsewhere in the Empire, the *chophouse* referred to another derivation, from the French *couper*, "to cut or chop," and was a place where mutton chops were cooked and sold.

Meanwhile, in Anglo-Indian and in Hong Kong Chinese-English, *chop* came to mean "rate" or "quality." *First chop* was top quality, and William

Makepeace Thackeray's 1848 *Book of Snobs* contained this comment: "We are the first-chop of the world."

A *chop mark* was placed on coins and documents to verify authenticity, and gave the word another sense of "trademark, signature stamp." A *bargain-chop* was an option on opium (and some think it may have been the basis for *bargaining chip*). In pidgin English used by traders in what was called the Far East (now Asia), coolies were sent in a hurry, or *chop-chop*.

In the United States, we have used the noun *chop* mainly to designate a cutlet or a swing, or as a description of rough water, or—since the jaws chop food—as a synonym for "cheek, jaw," as in *chapfallen* (a variant is *chopfallen*) and *to bust one's chops*.

Chop did not gain that "seal of approval or verification" sense here until recently; perhaps it traveled to the United States' corporate scene from Japan, as businessmen like Mitsuo Goto, president of Nomura Wasserstein Perella, told *Fortune* in 1988: "It used to be that 40 or 50 people had to know. . . . Everyone had to put his chop on the idea. Now corporate strategy people have a direct line to the top."

More likely, it was taken up by Pentagon bureaucrats a generation ago. "*Chop* has been in use here for some time," says Major David Super, a Defense Department spokesman. "When we circulate a paper for coordination, the cover sheet will have a series of boxes for comments or signatures. We'll say, 'Please put your chop on this,' or just 'Chop this.' "

Thus, for diplomats from Foggy Bottom to the golden hills of Jerusalem, this differentiation: *to have a chop at* means "to participate actively in the play"; *to have a chop on* means "to have the right of approval." Maybe this lexical guidance will help calm the choppy water.

In U.S. Navy parlance "CHOP" means "CHange of OPerational control." When a Navy ship headed for the Mediterranean crosses a certain longitude west of Gibraltar, it CHOPs or is CHOPped from 2d Fleet to 6th Fleet, for example.

> Brooke Nihart
> McLean, Virginia

Within the Military Sealift Command, "chop" is an acronym meaning change of operational control. It is used as a verb and is synonymous with delegating, passing the buck, or moving it upstairs.

> LCDR L. Hannigan
> South Kearny, New Jersey

*During the air war in North Africa in World War II, a pilot who was shot down
was referred to as "getting the chop." As,*
  "Whatever happened to Safire today?"
  "Bill got the chop over Algiers."

> Jerome F. Downs
> Ex S/Sgt., U.S. Army Air
> Corps, 1942–1945
> San Rafael, California

*About "chop," you may be interested to know that the word is much used in
West African English, derived from your mutton chop to mean "food" to start
off with and then by extension "a meal," "nourishment," "payment," "prosper-
ity" or any of the verbs derived from those meanings.*

*Thus if a clerk or porter says, "You want to chop me?," he means that a small
service charge would be appropriate. On a higher level, a businessman who says,
"You chop me, I chop you" is suggesting that a mutually advantageous, if
slightly crooked, deal is possible. Flight Lieutenant Jerry John Rawlings, in a
reverberant phrase used before he seized power in Ghana, said of the former
order of things, "They are chopping Ghana small."*

*But the usage I liked best was in one of those enigmatic philosophic phrases
that are written on the back of public transport vehicles in Ghana and Nigeria.*
SEA NEVER DRY *is the most famous; there is also* MAN PASSES, GOD SURPASSES *and*
ALL END SIX FEET UNDER. *But, to return to our mutton cutlets, the one I saw
said:* ONE MAN NO CHOP. *This means that if you are by yourself, you don't eat
well, and then by extension that mankind to survive must learn to cooperate and
work together. It is a commonplace thought, but pithily expressed.*

> Ken Mackenzie
> Paris, France

You state: "In English, where chop *began as a bargain and led to* cheap, *its
other meaning of "seal" or "official stamp" was first used in 1614."*

*Actually, it is not a question of another meaning but of another word, for the
two words* chop *are completely unrelated. The word meaning "seal" is, as you
say in the preceding paragraph, derived from Hindi. However,* chop, *"bargain"
and* cheap *both go back to Old English and are ultimately traceable (via a
common Germanic loan-word) to Latin* caupo, *"shopkeeper, innkeeper." They
are thus related to archaic English* chapman, *"merchant" (whence* chap, *"fellow") as well as to German* kaufen, *"to buy," and* Kaufmann, *"merchant,"
and Danish* København *(Copenhagen), "Merchants' Harbor."*

> Louis Jay Herman
> New York, New York

In the world of jazz, when one says that a musician has "chops," that musician is being complimented on his great technical proficiency.

I assume that this began as a reference to players of wind instruments, who use their jaws or "chops," but it now applies to deserving players of all instruments.

Larry Lubin
New York, New York

There is a "chop" at the start of every football play. This chopping motion by the referee (white hat) indicates the ball is "ready for play." This chop also starts the 25- or 30-second count (college or pro) in which the offense must put the ball in play or be charged with "delay of game."

John Liddle
San Diego, California

You omitted "chopsticks" whose roots in south Asia may (might?) serve to amaze you.

James Day Hodgson
Beverly Hills, California

Why use "decide on" and "arrange for" instead of just those verbs?

David Schatsky
New York, New York

Chutzpah at Camp Greentop

Malcolm Forbes wasn't around to enjoy it, but his newest publication made its debut last month: *!Forbes von Burda* (with the exclamation mark in front), described as a "*business/lifestyle* monthly" (with a virgule separating *business* from *lifestyle,* part of the trend in which slash triumphs over dash).

It is published in German in West Germany. I am indebted to Max Frankel, *Chefredakteur* of *The New York Times,* for Frankelfaxing to me a copy of one of the new magazine's regular features, which this month is about the success of a fashion designer's company.

The new *!Forbes* column is titled *"Chuzpe des Monats,"* which translates to "Chutzpah of the Month."

That's what I call a great and gutsy title for a column in a German publication. The word *chutzpah,* even when spelled *chuzpe,* is not German, but Yiddish; better still, it is probably not the part of Yiddish that is German-based, but from the Aramaic *huspa.* In the United States, the vivid term was first used, and promptly defined, in 1892 by Israel Zangwill (coiner of "the melting pot") in this sentence: "The national *Chutzbah,* which is variously translated enterprise, audacity, brazen impudence and cheek."

To the new publication: !Welcome/good for you.

Relatedly, this just in: (You like *this just in*? It beats the archaic *which reminds me;* the tense, terse *this just in* encapsulates "Hold everything, I have just been handed this hard-copy bulletin," or "Wait—something's been pasted on my TelePrompTer"; I use the trendy verbal bridge when I want to feel like a stare-'n'-speak anchorperson or a weighty network anchor. Do not confuse the excited *this just in* with the stern but friendly *now this,* which introduces a commercial announcement, or with a first name spoken with an interrogative inflection, which means "back to you, anchor, and if you want to ask me any questions on my report, remember this damned earpiece keeps falling out.")

Back to which reminds me: In a recent piece, I banged my spoon against the highchair about the huge difference between German *unification* (just East and West Germany) and *reunification* (throw in Silesia, East Prussia, the Sudetenland, and now that we think of it, sweet Alsace-Lorraine). In the course of this isolationist tirade (get out those old buttons, "Who wants to die for Danzig?"), I referred to my colleague David Binder as one "who speaks fluent East European."

"And also fluent *Central* European," comes the correction from Daniel Schorr, senior correspondent of National Public Radio. "In the U.S., we tend to lump everything in the Soviet bloc as East Europe. But Germans, Austrians, Hungarians and Czechoslovaks call themselves Central Europeans.

"You will find references to *Central* Europe in speeches of Chancellor Helmut Kohl and President Vaclav Havel," Mr. Schorr continues, citing two Kohl usages within a minute during his Camp David press appearance with Mr. Bush. ("Seeing the major changes in Central Europe, East Europe, Southeast Europe," said Mr. Kohl, adding in slightly shorter form, "It is our joint interest that the reform policy in Central, East and Southeast Europe. . . .")

Why the insertion of two new European regions between East and West? "This reflects, I believe," writes Dan, "a cultural snobbery—Central Europeans want it known they are more civilized than those Slavs."

We have a version of that regional differentiation in the United States. Texans, New Mexicans and Arizonans usually do not like to be called Southerners or Westerners; they come from the *Southwest,* a culture distinct from South and West. In the same way, Europeans will resist identification as East and West from now on; with no simplifying Iron Curtain, even the East-West relationship is getting muddied up.

And that's not all (a hard-sell phrase that has replaced the conversational *What's more*). Let's go formal: *Moreover,* the name of our presidential retreat is undergoing fractionalization. If you were watching that Bush-Kohl news conference, you may have been surprised by the dateline flashed under their picture: "Camp Greentop, Md."

What happened to Camp David? F.D.R. called that Navy camp in the Catoctin Mountains "Shangri-La," after the unfindable place in James Hilton's *Lost Horizon,* and President Eisenhower renamed it after his grandson, David. What's going on here—a new name for each Administration? Does George Bush have a grandchild with an odd mop of hair who is named Greentop?

No; according to the White House Press Office, formerly the Office of the Press Secretary: "Camp Greentop is a little below Camp David. It's a separate area for press access, so the news conference was held there."

Formerly West Europeans held press conferences at Camp David; now Central Europeans hold news conferences at Camp Greentop. Oh, it's going to be a cold, multipolar world.

Let me add a correction to your notation of Daniel Schorr's correction regarding Central and East Europe. Not that people wore buttons about Danzig—or much else—in 1939, but if they had, the question would have been not "Who wants to die for Danzig?" but "Why die for Danzig?" This was the title ("Mourir pour Dantzig?") of an article published on May 4, 1939, in the Parisian journal L'OEuvre by Marcel Déat, then an independent socialist, after July 1940 a collaborationist. The skepticism which Déat expressed about Poland's military chances against the Third Reich was to be confirmed by the rapidity of the German conquest in September 1939. The underlying premise of his argument—that Hitler's immediate objective was solely Danzig—was, of course, an illusion.

Dan S. White
Associate Professor of History
State University of New York
Albany, New York

Cocking a Snook

"Most of us join in cocking a snook at the law," wrote *The Times* of London, "when we feel that we are being deprived of choosing for ourselves what to do on Sunday."

Harold Evans, now the president and publisher of Random House, had written in *Good Times, Bad Times* that Rupert Murdoch had successfully "cocked his snook at the Establishment." I called Mr. Evans to get the meaning of the phrase *cock a snook.* "Thumb your nose," he said.

For verification, I tried it on David Frost, also bilingual in English and American, who replied: "Thumb your nose, express visible derision. And by the way, whatever happened to *room service* in your country? The hotels are calling it *private dining.*"

A *snook,* a variant of *snooks,* is a gesture of derision or disdain; one sense of the verb *cock,* as in "cock the ears, cock a hat, cock a pistol," means "to set at a vain or defiant angle." An uncommonly vivid definition was put forth in the 1860 edition of John C. Hotten's slang dictionary: "a vulgar action employed by street boys to denote incredulity, or contempt for authority, by placing the thumb against the nose and closing all the fingers except the little one, which is agitated in token of derision." Nowadays, we employ all the fingers for wiggling.

The two languages, English and American, have the identical sign with the same meaning, described in wholly different phrases. Perhaps *snook* comes from the earlier *snoot;* we use our thumbs to lift or cock our snoots. Go to London, hit the pound sign and ask for private dining; snooks up.

I noticed your reference to Harold Evans's statement that Rupert Murdoch had "cocked his *snook at the establishment." It seems to me that the replacement of the indefinite article in "cock a snook" with the possessive pronoun is wrong, unless Evans meant that Murdoch actually put thumb to nose in the presence of that establishment.*

Is this a case where the literally described actions of street children have been replaced completely by the figurative? In American-English, we have many phrases using the possessive pronoun, "Steal his thunder," "Rip him off," "Lift his spirits," but they all refer to actions which cannot literally be accomplished.

In those situations where the action is doable, it is usually wrong to replace the article with a possessive pronoun, either because the resultant return from the figurative to the descriptive is silly (as in "Take a leak"), or downright dangerous (as in "Pull a boner").

Misuse and abuse of the indefinite article is rampant among those for whom

English is a second language. It has even led to a few jokes, including the one about the dope dealer's picnic: "A loaf of bread, a jug of wine and a thou."

Anthony J. Hope
Washington, D.C.

Conflicting Advice

The television reporter Robert MacNeil asked Vernon A. Walters, Ambassador to West Germany, about a diplomatic anomaly, concluding with "Don't you feel *conflicted* about that?" The Ambassador—an accomplished linguist—replied promptly, "Yes, of course I do."

"One can be *afflicted*," writes Phil Chimento of Durham, North Carolina, "but one cannot be *conflicted* because *conflict* is intransitive. . . . Kindly scold Mr. MacNeil for his solecism."

Because it follows a linking verb ("feel"), *conflicted* in this case is a predicate adjective—a past participle used as an adjective after a linking verb—and is not a verb. For that reason alone, Mr. MacNeil is not in error; however, *conflicted* is an interesting bit of psychojargon.

"*Conflicted* as a verb is fairly recent," notes Dr. Ellen McGrath, a Brooklyn Heights psychotherapist. "It's an active verb to describe an ongoing emotional experience. Therapists have to work on resolving what *conflicts* the patient."

To be *conflicted*, then, is to be under the stress of influences that tug in opposite directions. The term is too much in vogue; a better old word is *troubled*, with its synonyms "worried, upset, concerned." If you prefer to wow your friends with highfalutin language, try "Doesn't that give you *cognitive dissonance?*"

A lawyer or firm that is unable to accept an assignment for a client because of a conflict of interest is said to be "conflicted" or "conflicted out."

This informal lawyer's use is certainly in accord with your definition of "to be under the stress of influences that tug in opposite directions." And having to forgo a lucrative assignment, as I recently did, is an emotional experience as well!

Richard Lyon
Dallas, Texas

Contrariwisdom

"Regrettably," said the President, using a sentence adverb that causes stock-market speculators to hit the sell button, "the noon deadline passed . . ." Mr. Bush then laid the rhetorical and legal foundation for the allies' ground attack on Iraqi forces: "To the contrary, what we have seen is a redoubling of Saddam Hussein's efforts to destroy completely Kuwait and its people."

Though most of the world applauded the President's decision, not everyone accepted his language.

"Instead of tying himself in knots to avoid a split infinitive," writes Louis Jay Herman, master sergeant of the Gotcha! Gang, "the President should have done a little more work on his *contrary* phrases."

Rarely does anyone object to a speaker's avoidance of the split infinitive. In this case, however, *to completely destroy* would have been more natural—and carried greater impact—than Mr. Bush's ultracorrect "to destroy completely," or the alternative *completely to destroy.*

But what of *to the contrary*? The Gotcha! Gangster is unrelenting: "The use of *to the contrary* to negate or mark a contrast with a previous idea is becoming fairly frequent, but it's plain wrong. The correct phrase for introducing a sentence in this manner has always been *on the contrary,* whereas *to the contrary* is used as a grammatical complement to a noun."

Not always. Among the prepositions that once led into *contrary,* the *Oxford English Dictionary* cites *by, to, for, of* and *in;* in the sixteenth century, you could start a sentence with "to the contrarye" and nobody would write in. But in the last few centuries, a clean difference has developed between *on the contrary* and *to the contrary.*

Contrary—from the Latin *contrarius,* "opposite, hostile"—has most recently been in the news as *contra,* the name for Nicaragua's rebels. *Contrary* is an absolute (an adjective used as a noun) not subject to nuances or shadings or sneaky qualifiers; it is as absolute as *free* and *brave* in "the land of the free and the home of the brave."

We're talking about the noun that means "a position or thing that is diametrically opposite; the reverse." Set aside, for this argument, the adjective *contrary,* meaning "disagreeable, perverse, ornery," as in the nursery rhyme "Mary, Mary, Quite Contrary." The adjective's emphasis is on the second syllable anyway, in contradistinction to the noun form's accent on the first syllable.

The phrase *to the contrary* usually modifies or objects to a specific noun just mentioned; *on the contrary* usually marks a contrast with a whole argument or position that precedes it. The *to* pinpoints only the objectionable word; the *on* signals a complete refutation of the earlier argument.

For example, "This Constitution . . . shall be the supreme law of the land," wrote our Founders, ". . . any thing in the Constitution or laws of any State to the contrary notwithstanding." *To the contrary* refers to the aforementioned *thing.* In a similar way, Ralph Waldo Emerson, writing about curious traits of the English, reported in 1856, "The favorite phrase of their law is 'a custom whereof the memory of man runneth not back to the contrary.' " The specific word being countered contrarily (the "noun being complemented," in Mr. Herman's phrase) is *custom.*

On the other hand (I have already used *in contradistinction,* and I am running low on synonymous phrases), Shakespeare popularized the *on* phrase as a pointer to a general refutation that followed. "The great Duke came to the bar," said a character in *Henry VIII,* with "many sharp reasons to defeat the law. The King's attorney, on the contrary, urg'd on the examinations, proofs, confessions of divers witnesses."

Let's follow the Bard on this: Use *to the contrary* about a noun, *on the contrary* about an assertion or argument. To put both in a single sentence, "On the contrary, evidence to the contrary proves all the foregoing to be balderdash."

Contrariwise (coined in 1340 and still my favorite), what about the French *au contraire?* Doesn't that mean, literally, "to the contrary," and don't the French start sentences with it all the time, objecting to entire démarches? There's no *sur le contraire* in French; doesn't that suggest we should start our sentences with *to the contrary,* as President Bush likes to do?

No. Our popular President happens to have a tin ear. The American idiom is noted in *Dictionnaire de l'Américain Parlé,* by the lexicographer Adrienne (imagine Dr. Johnson's dictionary signed only by "Sam"), published in the United States by Norton. *Au contraire* is given as the definition of "on the contrary," with a world-wearily Gallic illustration: "I thought they were happy together, but on the contrary, they're splitting."

Cosmetological Chartist

Be careful of parenthetical remarks; these asides can get you into unexpected trouble.

In a recent sociological harangue in support of segregated women's colleges, I went off on this tangent: "(Barbara Bush . . . needs no defense from feminists eager to get right with home-working women. Mrs. Reagan had turned a small room in the White House living quarters into a glitzy beauty parlor; when the unpretentious Mrs. Bush used it for a whelping box in which her dog, Millie, could deliver and care for a litter of pups, I fell in love with the current First Lady)."

At first, the objections to this parenthetical pop centered on the use of *glitzy* as a modifier for *beauty parlor;* was I suggesting that this was an especially glitzy specimen, or implying that glitziness was in the nature of beauty parlors? My construction was imprecise; my intended meaning was that glitziness was characteristic of beauty parlors—but that, on sober second thought, is an unfair derogation of those tasteful salons where a person can sit under a dryer and read a good book.

Glitzy, a late 1960's coinage meaning "showy, ostentatious," is derived from the Yiddish *glitz*, "glitter," related to the German *glitzerig*, "sparkling." In the mid-80's, we seemed to be under a glitzkrieg. (While in this etymological mode, I should add that *whelp* is from the Old Icelandic *hvelpr*, perhaps imitative of the cry of a seal puppy.)

Then Nancy Reagan weighed in. Her official spokesman called to say the "little hairdressing salon" in the White House living quarters had been in place long before the Reagans moved into the White House. I tried to wriggle out by asking whether the beauty parlor had been made especially glitzy during the years of Reagan use, and was informed that the "upgrading of the area" was undertaken at the initiative of the National Hairdressers and Cosmetologists Association, and that the renovation was not Nancy Reagan's idea at all.

After a common (not *mutual*) friend called to discuss the general subject of accuracy, fairness and late hits, I called the hairdressers' trade association to check out the Reagan defense.

Sure enough, a spokesman verified that the hairdressing facility had been in place for more than twenty years, and they had a letter dated September 28, 1981, from Nancy Reagan thanking them for their work renovating the little room. She said Robin Weir, the Washington beauty-parlor operator who had had several First Ladies as clients, had organized the project and had all the chairs, dryers and wallpaper donated by manufacturers.

I called Mr. Weir. "The old place was a dump," he recalled, "and I started the renovation idea before the Reagans came in. It was installed in her first year, though, and she took the bashing for it." I am happy to set the record straight today.

However, in the course of this display of journalistic fairness, I noticed that the word *hairdresser* has been dropped from the association name. "Yes," said Kate Godfrey, who puts a good face on things at what is now the National Cosmetology Association, "the preferred word for a licensed professional is *cosmetologist*."

Is that like a *cosmetician*? "A *cosmetician* can refer to a person with little training," she explained, "who works, say, in a department store to sell and apply makeup."

Whatever happened to *beautician*, coined in the early 1920's? "That term suggests a person who does your hair," said Ms. Godfrey, avoiding the word *hairdresser*, which was coined in the eighteenth century. Skin-care specialists call themselves *estheticians*, she informed me: "The *esthetician* is more than a *cosmetician*, who just applies cosmetics to the outside; an *esthetician* knows your body inside out, using everything from massage to vitamins in caring for your skin."

Aesthetes may get riled at that takeover of the Greek term for "sensitive to the perception of beauty," but the beauty business seems to be dropping the *a* from the start of the word to avoid conflict.

I called Mr. Weir back and put it to him: What happened to *hairdresser*?

"You hardly hear that anymore," he replied. "*Hairstylist* has taken over. We do more than the old hairdressers."

Like dyeing hair? "Used to say *dye*," said the forthright Mr. Weir. "Then it was *tint*. Now it's *color*. Never say *bleach* anymore; people say, with a sneer, 'Her hair's been bleached.' Now we call it *prelighten*. Same thing."

Does anybody ever ask for a simple *set*? "The shampoo-and-set shop is for a more mature crowd," Mr. Weir said, "or people who want their hair like a helmet, hurricane-proof. The younger, hipper crowd will ask for a *rinse and blow-dry*."

Next call was to Milton Pitts, the presidential barber, who has been cutting (not *doing*) my hair for twenty years. "Can't take you today," he began, but was available for a quick answer on what he called himself: "I'm a *barber-slash-hairstylist*, which is the term for men's hairdressers. You looked a tad shaggy on television the other day, by the way." His work is *tonsorial*, from the Latin *tondere*, "to shear."

What other source would know the replacement for *hairdresser*? To Lucien Sriqui of Lucien et Eivind, where columnists send their wives to find out what's really happening in Washington: "I'm a *hair designer*," said the coiffeur. (*Design* is a hot word; most interior decorators call themselves *interior designers*, to the irritation of some interior architects.) Does he employ a *manicurist*?

"You mean a *nail technician*," he corrected. Gee; has someone mistakenly assumed *manicure* is sexist? "The word *manicure* is still in use," said Lucien, limiting the usage to its noun form; the *manicurist*, however, now does more than clip, buff and paint nails. "Many more techniques are in use," Lucien said. "Women ask for *tips*—fake nails, disco nails—and the *nail technician* knows how to *silk-wrap*. It's all part of the new cosmetology."

Cosmetic is from the Greek feminine of *kosmetikos*, "skilled at ordering or adorning," which in turn is rooted in *kosmos*, "order," as in "the order of the universe." The *-logy* ending means "doctrine, theory, science"; it sounds scientific but may not be, as *astrology* illustrates.

Which brings us back not to Nancy Reagan, to whom I am grateful for setting me off on this quest, but to a linguistic problem: Confusion is inherent in *cosmetology*, from a nineteenth-century French term, now being used to mean "cosmetic science," and *cosmology*, "the study of the origins of the universe," which some would argue is a subject almost as important.

I think *cosmetologist* is pushing it. Even *esthetician* has its drawback—sounds too much like "Estéelauder." It's not for me to issue diktats (although I insist on *fine-toothed*, rather than the clipped *fine-tooth*, in describing a comb-out), but here's one vote for a return to *cosmeticians* for people who sell and apply rouges and powders, and *beauticians* for people who work in beauty parlors or skin-care-and-massage emporia.

If they want to call a *facial* a *single-layer exfoliation*, that's O.K. with me, but just back off with that hot towel.

My goodness, you certainly packed a lot of offensiveness into a very little text. In just thirteen words—"where columnists send their wives to find out what's really happening in Washington"—you managed to imply that:

1. *columnists are male (or might not some have husbands?)*
2. *their wives are sent to beauty shops of their husbands' choosing (most of my friends choose their own)*
3. *Oh, most trite: women go to the hairdresser to gossip (most women I know go to have their hair done and then get back to their offices as soon as possible)*

My sympathies to Mrs. Safire. I hope she is at least getting a decent haircut.

Maggie Buchwald
New York, New York

Counting Census Mistakes

I could tell I was going to have trouble with the census people from the very first sentence of their guide: "Please use a black lead pencil only."

In that sentence, *only* is a half-misplaced modifier—not incorrect, but not as good as "Please use only a black lead pencil." In the following sentence, the census taker promptly contradicts the *only:* "Black lead pencil is better to use than ballpoint or other pens." In other words, black lead pencil is preferable to other writing instruments, but is not the only one acceptable. Drop the *only;* say, "Please use a black lead pencil."

(Wait—what other colors do lead pencils come in? Blue pencils and red pencils are called *colored pencils,* not *lead pencils;* a lead pencil is made not of lead but of graphite, which makes a black or dark gray mark—one that really turns on electronic scanners. I was tempted to cut that census direction to "Please use a lead pencil," but that would be wrong: "black lead" is a synonym for *graphite,* and many colored pencils have some graphite in them. Therefore, *black lead* is not a redundancy, and the point is clear that the adjective *black* is needed to discourage the use of colored pencils.)

I am supposed to have returned the form by April 1: "By doing so, a census taker will not have to visit your home." A dangle: *by doing so* applies to the subject of the sentence, *a census taker,* and makes the sentence appear to suggest that the census taker, not the late answerer, is doing the nondoing. The correct form—one that would make sense—is "By doing so, you may avoid the need for a census taker to visit your home, thereby upsetting your dog, causing the resident language maven to howl, etc."

The Census Bureau, which has had ten long years to get its forms straight, has a misplacement problem: "You'll find detailed instructions for answering the census in the enclosed guide." No; the census is not in the enclosed guide. Make that "You'll [ain't we familiar?] find detailed instructions in the enclosed guide for answering the census." Same misplacing problem with "List everyone who lives at this address in question 1a"; nobody at this address lives in question 1a. Make that "In question 1a, list everyone who lives at this address."

We now enumerate the mistakes in parallel structure.

"You'll [this is the reader-friendly form of "you will"; I presume it is used throughout the census documents to avoid the authoritative connotation of *you will,* as in the implied *you will return this form or spend time in the slammer*] find directions for completing the census on the form itself and the enclosed guide." The preposition *in* is needed before "the enclosed guide." The preposition *on,* used to introduce "the form itself," does not carry over and do the trick for the enclosed guide because *on the guide* would refer to the cover of the guide, and not to the guide itself. For parallel structure, and for idiomatic purity, you'll use "on the form itself and *in* the enclosed guide."

Parallelism takes another beating in "Do NOT include . . . Persons who are away in an institution such as a prison, mental hospital, or a nursing home." If you are using the article *a* before the first and third items in a series, parallel structure requires it in the second as well: "*a* mental hospital."

The Squad Squad, having lost its reach for redundancy in *black lead pencil,* will find happy hunting ground in "This means the place where the person lives and sleeps most of the time." *Lives and sleeps* is redundant in this context, but perhaps the census was eager to get around someone who might say, "He lives here, but he doesn't sleep here, and let me tell you about that . . ." However, the *place where,* though in frequent use, is in error, as are the *time when* and the *reason why;* a simple *that* avoids the problem in all cases. ("Theirs not to reason why" was great poetry, lousy grammar; the census bureaucrat's "enter the name(s) and reason(s) why" is poor form-writing.)

"If you are not sure if you should list a person . . ." That's one *if* too far. For a yes-or-no option, use *whether:* "If you are not sure whether you should list a person . . ."

The Comma-kazi Pilots Association will be up in arms at the cavalier treatment given commas in the 1990 form.

"Complete your form and return it by April 1, 1990 in the postage-paid envelope provided." A comma or some other punctuation must always appear after the year in a full date; cutting commas this way is no way for the government to cut costs.

"No one except census workers may see your completed form and they can be fined and/or imprisoned for any disclosure of your answers." Although short independent clauses joined by a conjunction do not require a comma, long clauses do: In this case, we need a comma before the first *and,* especially since another *and* appears in the middle of the second clause. Thus: "No one except census workers may see your completed form, [comma!] and they can be fined and/or imprisoned . . ."

Let not the serial comma go uncounted: "funding for . . . services for the elderly, child care, employment and training programs and much more." If "employment and training programs" is one phrase, as it seems to be, it should be followed by the final comma in the series, before "and much more." Throughout the census form, the final comma is placed before the last *and* or *or:* "state, county, and local governments"; "It's important to you, your community, and the Nation." Be consistent; use that last serial comma or do not, but don't go both ways.

You might think that people headquartered in the capital working on capitation would be careful about their capitalization. "The first census was taken in 1790," explains the guide, "in accordance with the requirement in the first article of the constitution." In that sentence, "first article" might well be capitalized, since it refers to Article I, which is capitalized, but this is certain: Any old constitution is spelled with a small *c,* but the one referred to specifically as our own is *the Constitution.*

What about homeless words? These are words ending in *-self* that get lost in a thoughtless usage of a reflexive verb. In the census form, the Asian or Pacific Islander category "includes persons who identify as Burmese, Fijian, Hmong . . ." The use of *identify* in this sentence must be reflexive, requiring an object that matches its subject: "who identify *themselves* as . . ."

So they missed a few words; they'll miss a few people. But when they get my filled-out form, the circular spaces dutifully filled in, some scanner will note the bureau's admonition printed near the end: "Please make sure you have . . . 1. filled this form completely." I have put a little caret after "filled," and written in the necessary word, *out*—but not in black lead pencil. I don't want to be the one who blows the computers.

In "their's (apostrophe ?) not to reason why": In addition to poetic license, in this example the word "reason" is used as a verb. The usual form of the error is to say, "the reason why" when "reason" is a noun.

Leslie N. Hale
Severna Park, Maryland

The Crackdown Watch

Will Mikhail Gorbachev *crack down* on separatist movements in the disintegrating Soviet Union? Can we expect a *crackdown* to begin in the three Baltic nations, illegally occupied by Soviet forces since the von Ribbentrop-Molotov deal of 1939?

As an intransitive verb phrase, *to crack down,* with its transitive state *to crack down on* (something or someone), or as a noun no longer hyphenated or labeled "slang," *crackdown* is in the news. Although it can be used by the forces of good—as in "*cracking down* on drug kingpins"—the term is usually used as a threat by feared repressors. The question arises: When did the term (not the practice it describes) slam into the language?

To *cry crack,* meaning "to give up, quit," was English and Irish slang in the nineteenth century; James Joyce recorded it in *Ulysses* in 1922: "He never cried crack till he brought him home as drunk as a boiled owl." This may have been one source.

Another meaning of *crack down* was spotted by Cassidy's Lexies at the *Dictionary of American Regional English,* "to lower and shoot a gun," as cited in Marjorie Kinnan Rawlings's 1938 novel, *The Yearling:* "There was two shells in the gun, and there stood the buck, jest waitin'. I cracked down and he dropped." Eric Partridge reported this sense as R.A.F. usage in 1940, "to shoot down (an enemy plane)," adding an earlier sense of "to suppress or reprimand" as service slang in the mid-30's.

A third possibility is the most obvious: *To crack* has meant "to strike with a sharp noise" since 1470, and in 1850 Harriet Beecher Stowe wrote a character's line in dialect in *Uncle Tom's Cabin:* "She oughter cracked me over de head for bein' so sarcy." From that sense of striking over the head, it is a short hop to "repressing; treating severely."

The term made its appearance in the Depression, probably in Washington, in this 1933 *Newsweek* reference to the National Recovery Administration: "The *'cracking down'* phase of the Blue Eagle's career opened last week." Two years later, *The Washington Post* reported "a threat of a *'crack-down'* by the middle-class group against those who put forward the legislation for abolishing public utility holding companies." The location of the usage was emphasized in this 1941 *Economist* citation: "Prophecies of a *'crack-down'* are busily circulating in Washington."

Evidently some bureaucrat in the Roosevelt Administration came up with a major coinage but never took credit for it.

What do the Russians call it? For this I turned to Bill Keller and Jeanne Pinder of *The New York Times*, experts in both the politics played and the language used in the Soviet Union.

Eduard A. Shevardnadze, in his angry speech resigning as Foreign Minister, used the word *diktatura*, "dictatorship"; this broad term encompasses the actions of a dictator but does not narrow it down to the synonym for *crackdown*. For that we have *silnaya ruka*, "strong hand," and more strongly, *zheleznaya ruka*, "iron hand," with its evocation of Stalin, that name based on the Russian word for "steel," *stal*.

Mr. Gorbachev doesn't use those phrases, of course; he prefers *reshitelniye mery*, "decisive measures," and some of his aides use another euphemism, *zhostkiye mery*, "strong measures." Correspondent Keller recalls mistaking that last phrase for the similar *zhestokiye mery*, which means "evil, brutal measures," for which he received a lecture from a Gorbachevite about how strong measures are not necessarily cruel.

Relatedly, let us now anticipate the re-emergence of a word that will gain wide currency if Mr. Gorbachev is removed, or if he cracks down on his own followers. That dread word is *purge*.

In Russian, the direct translation, *chistka*, is rooted in "to clean"; that meaning is also at the base of the English *purge*, from the Latin *purgare*, "to cleanse, purify." Even before it was adopted by the medical profession in the 1390's, the word was being used to mean "to clear of a suspicion of guilt, to establish innocence." Religion soon moved in: *Purgatory* is the place where people who have died in God's grace expiate their sins by suffering.

Where and when did the word first crack down on errant politicians? Thomas Pride was a colonel supporting Oliver Cromwell in the English Civil War; his regiment took part in the military occupation of London in 1648 on the road to regicide. With his troops assembled in front of the House of Commons, Pride read out a list of members suspected of loyalty to the King and arrested or otherwise excluded them; only then was a vote taken to bring the King to trial. This early example of vigorous lobbying was called "Pride's Purge."

The word kicked around for centuries, mainly used by doctors prescribing laxatives, until the era of Stalin and his secret police. H. G. Wells, in his 1933

Shape of Things to Come, wrote of "the eternal espionage, censorship and *'purges'* of the G.P.U."; the "show trials" of officials who had fallen from Stalin's favor were also called the *purge* trials.

Will the crackdown (taken to mean "on those not in power") lead to a purge (usually meaning "of those in power, but not at the top")? That, to use the favorite cliché of today's Kremlinologists, remains to be seen. Meanwhile, the Center for Security Policy in Washington has instituted a fax-distributed "Crackdown Watch." I'm waiting for the "Purge Patrol."

My recollection tells me it wasn't just "some bureaucrat" who first came out with "crack down," but old Ironpants himself, General Hugh S. Johnson, the head of the NRA. I recall reading in the paper that General Johnson had vowed to "crack down" on some laggards who weren't toeing the NRA line.

John C. Thomas
Wilmington, Delaware

I would add that the word "crack" is very widely used in Ireland today to describe that a "good time" was had! For example, "That was a crack last night" or "Last night we had a great crack!"

John Carey
Toronto, Ontario, Canada

The Crucial Trucial

Xinhua (pronounced "shin-hwa"), the Chinese news agency, reported from Cairo in English that an eighty-four-year-old sheik, Rashid bin Said al-Maktum, had died. The agency noted that "he was a founder of the United Arab Emirates, which was born in 1971 grouping seven emirates in the Trucial Coast under a federal system."

Trucial? The only time I had seen that word was in a piece by Irving Kristol in *The Washington Post* titled "Born-Again Isolationists," in which the neo-conservative leader chided some colleagues on the right for a narrow view of the national interest.

The reason for the need for United States intervention in the Persian Gulf, he wrote, "is simple: it is a serious challenge to our national interest to have any single, hostile power control the Middle East's reserves and supply of oil." That was why "we are intervening to ensure the freedom of Saudi Arabia and the Trucial States from domination by a resurgent Iraq."

The adjective *trucial* means "bound by a truce." The word is used almost exclusively to refer to the Persian Gulf states on the Oman peninsula that agreed, in the truce of 1835, to cease their sea warfare. In 1971, these seven semi-independent sheikdoms, long under British protection, formed a nation called the United Arab Emirates, with its capital Abu Dhabi.

Irving Kristol must have been reading the British statesman George N. Curzon's 1891 *Persia and the Persian Question,* in which "Trucial States" was coined. In the pronunciation of Gulf terms, *sheik* sounds like the French *chic,* though "shake" is also accepted; *emir* is "ih-MEER," though you can also get away with "A-meer" in a permissive crowd, and *trucial,* which shows you to be steeped in the history of the area, rhymes with *crucial.*

Dancetalk

Over the obituary of Martha Graham was this *New York Times* headline: "Choreographer Hailed for Creating a Language."

Newsweek, in its subhead, agreed with the use of language as a metaphor for her communication of emotion: "Martha Graham gave dance a new vocabulary." Laura Shapiro wrote in that article: "Upward spirals that propelled a dancer from kneeling to exulting, the leaps that ripped themselves from the ground . . . Graham's astonishing vocabulary seared the landscape of dance like a branding iron."

We're getting unabashedly artsy in this space today to answer this question: Why were *language* and *vocabulary* so often used to describe her contributions to dance? In this case, we deal with a lexicon of wordlessness, which seems to be an oxymoron; however, it is apt to treat the art of dance as silent speech.

The Times and other newspapers were obviously ready for Miss Graham's death; a lengthy "prepared obit" is on file for most celebrated figures in art and politics, and a newspaper of record knows that its obituary will be consulted by future historians with their CD-ROM libraries.

We have words to bridge the spoken and unspoken languages. One is *expression.* When some bit of dialect we use is met with a blank look, we say, "That's an expression," meaning "That's a figure of speech to express a meaning"; another sense of *expression* is "a suggestion of emotion," as when a face adopts a pained "expression." The Latin root means "a pressing out," shown but not necessarily articulated.

The gap between the spoken and unspoken is also bridged by *statement,* which can be made wordlessly in "a fashion statement," and by *idiom,* as in "the idiom of pantomime." The point is that language, most often used in the sense of a system of words, also has a sense of "communication by means other than words"—by signs, movements, touches, sounds, tastes (and, as any bloodhound can attest, smells).

In her *Times* obit (that's an expression; I use the clipped word rather than *obituary* to show off a breezy insiderhood), Anna Kisselgoff writes of Miss Graham's "invention of a new and codified dance language. . . . Powerful, dynamic, jagged and filled with tension, this vocabulary . . . set her above other dance innovators."

Are there any spoken words that describe the expressions in dance's mute lingo? "She used to speak of *contraction and release,*" says Janet Eilber, now a film and television actress, and from 1972 to 1985 a principal soloist in the Graham company. "She showed how to draw yourself into the center, the pelvic area, then release by sending emotions outward with great theatrical effect."

Miss Eilber, whose own dancing was described by balletomanes with gestures and eye-rolling that could be verbalized as "fantastic," offers this linguistic leap: "She developed a vocabulary of movements to describe emotion in physical rather than verbal language, using the torque of the body to show the twist and pull of pain or desire.

"She really did use and codify movements rarely used on stage before," says her longtime student. "In the premiere of the ballet *Deaths and Entrances* in the early 40's, she was wearing a glittering period gown. She went prone, then back up suddenly. When a member of the audience said afterward, 'You fell on the floor in that beautiful dress,' Miss Graham answered, 'But haven't you ever felt you were falling on the inside?' "

Language is not a metaphor or analogue for speechless artistic expression; on the contrary, as the Graham obituaries (from the Latin *obire,* "to go to meet, to fall") show, expression has a variety of languages, and dance is one of them.

It is obvious you know nothing about dance. If you knew something about it, you would know that all forms of dance have a vocabulary. Ballet has a French vocabulary: pliés, tendu, jeté, assemblées, *etc. The ballet vocabulary is the foundation of its technique. Tap dancing has a vocabulary:* flap, stamp, buffalo, shuffle, *etc. The vocabulary is combined to form new steps, as in* shuffle buffalo. *Sometimes songs are written using tap vocabulary, keeping step and destination in mind.*

I am already anticipating your argument. I am speaking of steps and not expression. It's okay to have a vocabulary of steps is what I'm sure you will say. However, expressive or modern dance became a viable, living dance form, and since all forms of dance have a vocabulary, isn't it logical or natural for a vocabulary to develop for expressive dance? Isadora Duncan removed the shoes and costumes, Ruth St. Denis looked to the East for inspiration, and Martha Graham created modern dance technique by defining it through a vocabulary of expressive movement. Not only does this new dance have a vocabulary, but guess what? Doris Humphrey, a contemporary of Graham, went so far as to say there are "phrases" of movement. The linguist in you must be livid by now! And this quote is likely to make you run from anyone who mentions they ever set foot in a dance class. Doris Humphrey describes in her book, The Art of Making Dances, *how to create a dance. She uses a language analogy in order to convey one aspect of this process:*

> *These one-bar phrases are arranged in various directions . . . at the end of which the student has nine of these measures which might loosely be compared to single words, like nouns in language . . . If the student knows how to complete them with syntax, grammar, and phrasing, he will have quite enough movement to complete a whole dance. (p. 47.)*

Humphrey's book was written just before her death in 1958. It appears that language and vocabulary have been connected with modern dance for quite some time, especially with its innovators. I don't believe Ms. Eilber, Ms. Kisselgoff, and the other quotes from The Times *and* Newsweek *went too far in their use of vocabulary and language in Graham's obituary. Dance is expressive, as you point out, but the process of creating that expression involves technique, and technique requires a vocabulary which the dancer/choreographer needs in order for expression to occur.*

Regina Paglia
Edison, New Jersey

You win the Fingernail-Down-the-Blackboard Award for your sentence that began, "We're getting unabashedly artsy in this space today . . ." Your abashedness was all too evident in your apparent need to warn your readers of what was ahead and your choice of the word "artsy" to distance yourself from the subject of your piece.

I can only guess that your weekday persona, the Washington tough guy, gained the upper hand for a moment or so as you were writing an otherwise enjoyable little essay.

Jerome Evans
Zephyr Cove, Nevada

Dark Words of Disapproval

A week before his arrest, Marion S. Barry Jr., Mayor of Washington, took umbrage at an article written about him by Bella Stumbo of the *Los Angeles Times.* The reporter quoted the Mayor, who is black, as saying of the Reverend Jesse Jackson, a new resident of Washington, "He don't wanna be no mayor."

Mr. Barry objected to the imputation to him of the use of black dialect, which he denied having used, observing: "Most reporters realize that in casual conversation, grammar may occasionally slip; they account for this by making appropriate corrections in the written text. That is only fair." The Mayor went on to say, in a letter to the editor, "In no way did I denigrate him," referring to Mr. Jackson, adding that "all the denigration in the article" was the reporter's, toward him.

The etymology of the word *denigrate* was promptly called to my attention by a media colleague, who wondered whether the Mayor was unwittingly using a term that illustrates how racism is buried in the language.

Niger is Latin for "black"; *denigrationem* is Late Latin for "a blackening." The *de-* does not mean "the opposite or reverse of," as *de-* so often does; in this case, as in *denude* and *declaim,* it means "completely"; thus, *denigrate* is rooted in "to blacken completely." The term was picked up as a verb in Old French meaning "to blacken" and transferred to English in the sixteenth century in the sense of "darken a good name," or "defame."

Historically, *black* and *dark* have signified "bad" (Satan was called the Prince of Darkness long before the self-styled meanie, Robert Novak, was born), and *white* and *light* have meant "good" (none but the brave deserve the *fair,* meaning "light-colored").

The question is: Should we now take cognizance of the prejudice inherent in this and try to root it out? For example, should an aide to the embattled Mayor of Washington have whispered to him, "You should not use *denigrate* in reference to Jesse Jackson, because the root means 'to blacken,' and for years we have been saying that black is beautiful"?

I think that is taking antiracism too far. Language is like a great coral reef, built of the fossils of millions of organisms; to go back through the language's development and to "correct" what we now see as wrong or cruel unnecessarily hacks away at the reef.

Of course, some words are now taboo; the epithet *nigger*—from *Negro,* from the same Latin *niger*—has been expunged from the vocabulary because it betrays contempt and gives offense. However, *boy,* when used toward a black, or African-American, male also gives offense, because of its use toward adults in days of slavery; we do not use *boy* in that context any longer, but we do not drop *boy* from the language in its general sense as "young male." Indeed, *home boy* is black English for "close friend," which is roughly equivalent to the CB user's *good buddy.*

Denigrate, though undoubtedly rooted in dark-light symbolism, is not to be *derogated* (its value lessened) or *deprecated* (disapproved of earnestly). Etymology is a key to understanding the development of meaning, not a weapon for correct-thought police. Mayor Barry has made his share of mistakes, and does not hesitate to charge critics with racism, but in using *denigrate* he did not blunder into unconscious racism. (He would have been more accurate in using *disparage,* "to subtly belittle," because that is more often applied to people than *denigrate,* which is usually used to run down ideas or values.)

Umbrage, a word used in the lead of this item, is from the Latin *umbra,* "shadow"; such darkness falling across a person was considered offensive to the one so cast in the shade, and *to take umbrage* is "to take offense" or to become more than miffed but less than outraged. A favorite word of writers about subjects who blaze back is the infrequently used *umbrageous,* "easily offended."

I must take umbrage at your blanket signification of black as meaning bad. It may also mean profitable, as in "my company is in the black."

Several other variable meanings come to mind: sunny yellow, and yellow as cowardly; fresh and vivid green, and green as inexperienced, nauseated, and envious; pink as faintly communist, and pink as healthy, as in "in the."

Then there are blackbirds and blackberries and beautiful black people, and the stupendously positive black, as in "in the" as in solvent, universally accepted as good.

Annabel Stehli
Westport, Connecticut

"White" is not always honorific in its connotation. Remember Melville's chapter on the "Whiteness of the Whale" in Moby Dick.

James M. La Sala
Cheshire, Connecticut

I understand your view that the word "denigrate" is not racism buried in the language. But what about the use *of the word "niggardly"? The word is derived from "niggard," which historically has nothing to do with race; however, the use of the word (especially in conversation) always surprises. The use of the word may convey racial prejudice or give offense to some; or maybe, it is simply a case of taking anti-racism a bit too far.*

George W. Bramblett, Jr.
Dallas, Texas

Degrading Attrition

"Too bitter is thy jest," says the King of Navarre in Shakespeare's *Love's Labor's Lost.* "Are we betrayed thus to thy *over-view?*"

Overviews, no longer hyphenated, are sought avidly by *bookers.* A *booker* is a person with a persuasive voice and professionally desperate demeanor, calling from what seems to be a boiler room, whose job it is to arrange the appearance of guests on television programs; this new job title is rooted in the British verb *to book,* "to reserve a place."

A booker called the other day to say, "Come on and give us your *overview* on war words." That usage substantiates an observation in a letter in my hand: "*Overview* is a word beloved by television news readers," writes Ralph A. Brooks of New York, "as are *upcoming, ongoing* and *offloading.* What's the difference between a *view* and an *overview?*"

A *view,* which until recently had a sense of "a thought," now connotes more of a slanted squint; an *overview,* on the other hand, has a loftier, almost Olympian, feeling. That word, used overmuch by the overpaid overseers of voice-over footage, has a meaning more comprehensive than "summary" and more pretentious than "survey." (Yes, there is an *underviewer;* in mining, this is a supervisor who works under an overseer.) I have just given you my view of *overview;* for an overview of that word, we must put it in a context of global military strategese, which to lexicographers is a *target-rich environment.*

Journalists tend to snicker at the jargon of military briefers, but we peddle our own prepackaged parlance, often overly compressed: "Good evening. Dan Rather, updating the war." The 1941 verb for "to bring up to date" requires another word or two to make grammatical sense out of the thought, which now suggests adding new technology to, or otherwise modernizing, the war: A leisurely "updating you about the war" or "updating the war news" would do the trick but might lose crispness and urgency, not to mention precious milliseconds.

Although *briefing* is a military coinage that has crossed over into general use, official military language is drawn more to the bloodless and the bureaucratic than the brief; it often takes secondary senses of words and makes them its own. (The World War II verb *to brief,* probably from the lawyer's brief, or written argument, means "to impart information concisely"; *to debrief* means "to receive information.")

The most common verb used in military briefings from Riyadh, Saudi Arabia, has been *to degrade,* which means to most people "to humiliate, to cause to be held in contempt"; correspondents think that being forced to cover a war without being allowed to see the fighting is fairly degrading. But a second sense, primary only to military people, is "to reduce in grade; to lessen in rank," and that sense is extended to "to weaken." When a general says, "Our attacks have degraded enemy forces," he does not mean that the enemy has been held up to ridicule, or even that his majors have been busted to captains; he means that the attacks have weakened the enemy. For some reason, the brass hate to use the word *weaken.*

Pentagonians like to verb nouns. ("To verb a noun," of course, makes a verb out of the noun *verb.*) *Attrition,* for example, means "the wearing down by friction; rubbing away." The first use of *war of attrition* was in 1914; "General Kelly says that Iraqi military targets are being *'attrited,'* " Robert and Margaret Lloyd write from London, and wonder if they are out of touch with United States usage. No; this is the military speaking to a much wider public than before, but using a term pioneered by Laurence Sterne in his 1760 novel *Tristram Shandy:* "So glazed, so contrited and attrited was it with fingers and with thumbs in all its parts."

Attrit and *degrade* are used interchangeably, but a careful commander would use *attrit* when he wanted to stress the wearing-down quality of the degradation process.

To avoid being degraded, the enemy will *hunker down.* This is a lively piece of old Scottish dialect adopted by the modern military. Perhaps of Scandinavian origin, akin to the Old Norse *huka,* "to squat," this term was first used when a Scot was observed in 1720 "hunk'ring down upon the cald Grass." This term for crouching or kneeling often implied a craven or frightened attitude, but has developed into a sense of crouching defensively in a mood of defiance. (It is probably not related to the Flemish *hunke,* "a large lump or piece," leading to the English "hunk of meat"; the Scots then gave *hunk* the meaning of "slut," and Americans in 1845 gave *hunker* the meaning of "conservative"; we now think of a hunk as a sexually attractive male, not necessarily a right-winger.)

Another bright metaphor introduced by pilots into this war is *trolling:* "It involves a search for supply vehicles or convoys, called 'movers,' " R. W. Apple Jr. writes in *The New York Times,* "on main logistical routes." He quotes Marine Lieutenant Colonel William J. Home on the term's origin: "It's very similar to fishing with your line out, hoping to find something." This boating reference recalls the World War II bilingual trope, *strafing the strasse,* meaning "looking for girls."

"The reports of *'friendly fire,'* a serious danger on any battlefield," were reviewed by John H. Cushman Jr. of *The Times.* This phrase describes a moment in warfare that causes shudders in airmen and artillerymen: when your bombs or shells are dropped by tragic mistake on your own troops. This is sometimes treated with macabre humor—"hell with 'em if they can't take a joke"—to conceal a sense of guilt that can last a lifetime. *Friendly fire* is an extension of *friendlies,* the word for one's own troops or allies, perhaps from the apocryphal line sardonically attributed to General Custer at Little Big Horn, "Those look like friendly Indians."

Saddam Hussein's contribution to the current war lingo is his bloodthirsty prediction of *"the mother of all battles"* to be fought on the ground. Western writers have picked this up as a simple maternal personification, like Virginia's designation as "mother of Presidents" or John Bright's 1865 phrase "England, the mother of Parliaments."

There's much more to it. In Arabic literature, *the mother of all battles* refers specifically to the battle of Qadisiya in A.D. 636, where the Arabs united under Islam to win a decisive victory against the Sassanian Persian army. This seventh-century fight continued to the walls of Ctesiphon; the Arabs triumphed, gaining the land west of the Tigris River for the cause of Islam.

When Saddam Hussein uses the phrase *the mother of all battles,* as he often did during the recent Iran-Iraq war, he wants to evoke the memory of that first great Arab victory. The ruins of Ctesiphon, the ancient Sassanian capital where the first significant Islamic conquest took place, lie twenty miles southeast of Baghdad. It may again become a *target-rich environment.*

Bill,

Not so: the use of degrade *in the sense of weaken is not primary "only" to military people. You haven't been hanging around with enough computer nerds.*

If, while I'm writing this memo, my computer suddenly blacks out, you won't get the memo. And when I complain, I'll be told I did something that degraded the system.

If, by contrast, the scrolling slows down and the cursor flutters nervously, giving me warning to fall back to pencil and paper, the nerds will tell me to be thankful the machine "degraded gracefully." Graceful degradation, with its overtones of Scarlett O'Hara, is one of the few compensations of working around computer people.

> *Al [Allan M. Siegal]*
> The New York Times
> *New York, New York*

I note your reference to "prepackaged parlance." I wonder if this is redundant, since anything that is packaged is done so before the fact.

I think "packaged parlance" would do.

> Bob Laurie
> *New York, New York*

You wrote about the propensity of Pentagonians "to verb nouns." That reminded me of a military usage I heard somewhere in the last two years (and had meant to share with you). After some sort of incident, possibly a launch-preparation problem, I heard (on the radio) a military spokesman say "the vehicle has been safed." I would guess the event was one of those situations where the space vehicle has to be emptied of its fuel. I thought this usage was unusual, but I guess it makes sense: (a) we have a problem, perhaps with dangerous (unsafe) potential consequences; (b) we take remedial action to resolve our problem; and (c) what was "unsafe" now "has been safed."

Ralph W. Richardson
Wilmington, North Carolina

Denouncing Denouncement

The Senate Ethics Committee's special counsel, in charging Senator Dave Durenberger of Minnesota with, among other lapses, padding his expense account, called for a punishment of *denouncement.*

This word is the noun form of the verb *to denounce,* which has a niche between "to criticize" and "to censure," and is closest in synonymy to "publicly to condemn, usually in a loud tone of voice." *Denouncement* was first used in 1544, and nobody can deny the noun its place in the backwaters of our vocabulary.

However, I rise here, Mr. President (that's how you talk in the Senate), to *reprehend, proscribe, reprobate* and even *damn* its use by my distinguished colleagues when another word has triumphed over it in common English usage.

The more familiar noun form of *denounce* is *denunciation.* It beat *denouncement* in fair usage combat, just as *renunciation* has whipped *renouncement;* why does the Senate (rooted, like *senile,* in the Latin *senex,* "elder") insist on dredging up the archaic alternative?

One word, one meaning, is my motto; when you use an alternative form to mean the same thing, you have wasted valuable space on the hard disk of your memory, and you have blocked the development of a different meaning.

For example, *to pronounce* spawned the noun *pronunciation,* meaning the sound of words, as well as the noun *pronouncement,* which means "declaration, usually pompous." Another example: *to announce* has given us *Annunciation,* capitalized, meaning "the revelation of the Incarnation to the Virgin Mary," as well as the more prosaic *announcement.*

Therefore, let us asperse, bad-mouth, revile, vilify and disparage *denouncement;* if we are to denounce anybody, a clear *denunciation* is in order.

A small but important omission in the last of your pieces, about denouncement: *I agree with you in disallowing the hidjus word. But in defining it you left out the idea of naming, disclosing, giving away the culprit. The denouncer is first and foremost an informer; there is announcement in denunciation. Latin* nuntius, *messenger, comes ultimately from* novere, *related to novelty = news.*

> *Yours,*
> *Jacques [Barzun]*
> *New York, New York*

Heartened today by your sound denunciation of denouncement, *I make so bold as to suggest you next call for the abolition of* abolishment, *an equally unnecessary and annoying back-formation much in favor at least hereabouts among young reporters delivering accounts of demands uttered by "activists" (syn.,* freeloaders*).*

I surmise the prevalence of this habit of inventing portmanteau words demonstrates the extinction of the junior high teachers who severely and exasperatingly enforced the study of vocabulary and resort to dictionaries. If these scriveners knew the serviceable existing noun, or at least where to ascertain whether one exists, they would not labor to invent locutions less felicitous.

> *George V. Higgins*
> *Milton, Massachusetts*

Done Deal

"There were words," writes the former speechwriter Peggy Noonan, in her deliciously irreverent *What I Saw at the Revolution: A Political Life in the Reagan Era.*

Using a run-on device, she then surveys the clichés of only yesteryear: "You had a *notion* instead of a thought and a *dust-up* instead of a fight, you had a *can-do attitude* and you were *in touch with the Zeitgeist.* No one had intentions they had an *agenda* and no one was wrong they were *fundamentally wrong* and you didn't work on something you *broke your pick on it* and it wasn't an agreement it was a *done deal.*"

By the time *done deal* reached print in 1979, its place in the lingo of business and political bargaining was a *fait accompli.*

That's because we have had no expressive word or phrase for "an irreversible agreement," an accord or understanding that had the connotation of "sorry, it's too late now to make a change, you missed the boat, that train left the station."

Three centuries ago, in a Charles Cotton poem, the phrase was nearly found: "She thought 't would be a done Thing Soon." That locution percolated in the language, appearing in Charles Dickens's *Christmas Carol* in 1843: "It was a done thing between him and Scrooge's nephew."

Finally, somebody in the 1970's—nobody knows who—used alliteration to transform a tired *done thing* into a lively *done deal.*

Overnight, the partly alliterative but not as punchy *signed, sealed and delivered* was undone; same with *wrapped up, buttoned up, all set, fini, in the bag, nailed down* and *yesterday's news.*

Having dissolved all these clichés, *done deal* lasted more than a decade, placing it beyond nonce-word status. Soon to be in all the dictionaries, the Americanism that unraveled *fait accompli* stands as a triumph of alliterative phrasemaking; it's all over but the shouting.

I believe Peggy Noonan's Washington crowd had the broke your pick on it *usage wrong. I'm not talking research here, but personal knowledge.*

I was born in Tonopah, Nevada, a silver-mining town, in 1922. My father was a miner, and I worked underground summers while going to college. I knew a lot of hard-rock miners. I became a reporter and editor on newspapers, and tend to remember colorful locutions.

A shift boss firing a miner might say, "You've broken (or busted) your pick with me." (The miner would tell his friends, "She's deep enough. I'm going down the hill.") Or the phrase might be used in a social estrangement: "She's broken her pick with me."

The point is that an ending is indicated. It doesn't mean working hard on something. The original idea was that a miner can't work with a broken pick.

The "broken pick" usage still is common in the West, and in the sense I've indicated.

William Friel
San Francisco, California

Egad, an Adage!

Bill Irvine, author of *Senile Felines,* a desk calendar of palindromes for 1991, published by Harcourt Brace Jovanovich, has checked in from the land of coming and going.

He predicts an increase in the space budget (A SANTA'S AT NASA) and shortages in Baghdad fruit stands (NO LEMONS, NO MELON). His editorial comment on the Persian Gulf: DRAT SADDAM, A MAD DASTARD. If this gives you a headache, try LONELY TYLENOL.

Empowerment and Denouncement

The energizing word among "bleeding-heart conservatives" (an oxymoron that Jack F. Kemp, the Housing and Urban Development Secretary, uses to describe himself and his followers) is *empowerment.*

The voguish political noun, coined in 1849 to mean "the gaining of power," has particular resonance among blacks. In 1978, the conservative Heritage Foundation attributed popularization of the word to the Students for a Democratic Society in the 1960's, which, said a Heritage release, "condemned the 'Establishment' and sought *'empowerment'* for 'helpless minorities outside the system.' " The assumption is that the word grew out of the S.D.S. slogan "power to the people."

As political empowerment was largely achieved, the word was applied to the need for economic clout. In 1976, Vernon E. Jordan Jr., then head of the National Urban League, said, "That goes to economic security, income maintenance, economic *empowerment*—the real basic issues of equal opportunity."

Everybody got into the *empowerment* act. Voter-registration groups pushed *electoral empowerment;* pediatricians espoused *parent empowerment;* after the Reagan re-election in 1984, the political pollster Pat Caddell, who had been a Gary Hart adviser in the Democratic primaries, opined sadly: "The issue was the *empowerment* of a generation. . . ."

Feminists have also made it their own: In a piece about the campaign to maintain Mills College in California as a women's undergraduate school, Amy Pyle of the *Los Angeles Times* wrote, "*Empowerment*—buzzword of the recent protests—actually has been the theme at Mills for some time."

The word was used by some black conservatives eager to move beyond integration to equal opportunities. Many liberals saw this as a denial of their achievement, or as self-help rhetoric unhelpful to entitlements, and were slow to pick it up. "The issue was black *empowerment,* not integration," Robert L. Woodson, a black critic of social welfare bureaucracies, insisted in 1985; he helped popularize the word among conservatives.

In a 1990 Rose Garden awards ceremony, President Bush said, "Each of these seven Americans provides a definition of the word that I have learned to respect so much, learned from Jack Kemp—*empowerment.*"

Since Mr. Kemp has apparently become "Mr. Empowerment," at least in the Bush Administration's corridors of power, I called him to get his short definition of the term. Not a man given to brevity, he worked on it for a while, cutting his definition down to this: "Giving people the opportunity to gain greater control over their own destiny through access to assets of private property, jobs and education."

This is a word that has crept up on lexicographers; because *empower,* the verb, has deep roots in the language, its usage as a political noun in recent decades was not noted. "We didn't regard it as anything that needed watching," says Cynthia Barnhart, a dictionary editor at Barnhart Books. "Then all of a sudden it started coming in."

Now we're all keeping an eye on it; obviously, *empowerment* is potent.

Enclavery Zone

First of all, it's pronounced "EN-clave" in English, not "ON-clave"; if you insist on pronouncing the first syllable in the French way, you should go with a French final syllable, "CLAHV." I'd stick to "EN-clave," just as I lick an ENvelope; only when we use whole French words should we adopt *ennui*'s "on-WEE or *en route*'s "on ROUTE."

The word, most often applied in diplomacy in recent years to suggestions for Palestinian Arab areas within the disputed territories of the West Bank, was thrust upon the world by the need to protect Kurdish refugees from the vengeance of Saddam Hussein.

The British Prime Minister, John Major, was the first to call for *enclaves* within Iraq for the fearful Kurds. But the Bush spokesmen resisted the word: "The Administration backed away from the idea of setting up a Kurdish 'enclave,' " wrote Patrick E. Tyler in *The New York Times,* "that might later be used as a claim to statehood by Iraq's Kurdish minority." Promptly, European leaders started talking more fuzzily about *protection zone* and *safety zone.*

President Bush's press secretary, Marlin Fitzwater, said, "The problem was that nobody wants a demarcation that says this is a permanent area or new country. . . . We need an area, call it what you will, of safety."

With no official using a term to describe the place, reporters used "informal safe haven" in their stories; "safe haven" was part of the headline in *The Times.* Although *safe haven* is redundant, the words have been linked so long as to become an idiom. Subsequently, *sanctuary* was evoked, as well as *buffer zone.*

Nobody used *mandate,* applied by John Maynard Keynes in 1919 to territory assigned to the League of Nations, because that would be too "official." And nobody (except the Kurds, a distinct people with a thousand-year-old culture) would use *Kurdistan* because that would imply a separate state.

What, then, was this area—inside Iraq, on the Turkish and Iranian borders above the thirty-sixth parallel—to be called?

Not yet decided. For the time being, it's "the area" or the "safe-haven territory," the name kept fuzzy because the nations protecting the refugees do not want to clarify (or complicate) matters by giving an area an identity and national life of its own with a name.

The synonymy: *Enclave* is moving toward a meaning of "permanent, delimited area" from its origin in the French verb *enclaver,* "to enclose." *Sanctuary* implies inviolability due to sacredness; when applied to a place rather than an idea, it now often pertains to wildlife, not human beings. *Asylum* is a state of shelter from persecution, but not a particular area. *Haven,* from the Old English "harbor," with a connotation of "refuge" dating to 1200, has the advantage of meaning both a place and a status of protection, with a diplomatically useful overlay of impermanence. *Refuge* is a fourteenth-century noun from the Latin *refugere,* "to flee from," and the 1908 *buffer zone* comes from *buff,* "to sound like a soft body when struck." *Zone* is an area usually characterized as a band or a strip. Broadest of all: *area,* leading to "area, call it what you will, of safety."

Ennui is not pronounced "on-WEE," but rather "ON-WEE," and "en ROUTE" is closer to the English norm of pronunciation than to the French, which should be "EN ROUTE."

As musicians have long been aware, when two notes of equal length and weight close a musical phrase, the second of these will always seem stronger. This is because the last note heard will always assume more prominence on account of being the most recent stimulus perceived by the brain. Hence, in order to make the two notes appear to be of equal weight, it is necessary to ease off a bit on the last note. In French there is no easing off on the last syllable, and hence the misperception of last-syllable accent.

Carl Bowman
New York, New York

You discuss the etymology of enclave, sanctuary, haven, refuge *and* buffer, *but in the case of* zone, *quite possibly the most etymologically interesting word of the lot, you merely say that it denotes "an area usually characterized as a band or a strip."*

Zone *is from the Greek word for "(woman's) belt," and its use in English parallels the figurative meaning of* belt, *as in* Bible Belt *and* Farm Belt. *It was formerly sometimes used in a literal sense in poetry, e.g., "Wit calls the Graces the chaste zone to loose" (from "Night Thoughts," by the 18th-century English poet Edward Young).*

Louis Jay Herman
New York, New York

You refer to the "thousand-year-old culture" of the Kurds, and you have used the same phrase in your political columns. I don't know how you define "culture," and I'm not an expert on ancient Southwest Asian ethnology, but standard references tell me that the Kurds have been an identifiable ethnic group on their present territory for a lot longer than 1,000 years. They are identified with the hostile "Carduchi" encountered there by Xenophon in 400 B.C., and individual clan names are said to be recognized as far back as the 6th century B.C. The Kurds appear as Gortukh, Kardu, Gurda, Kurtie, Kuti, etc. in Armenian, Persian, Assyrian, Hittite and even Sumerian records, possibly as far back as 2000 B.C. They are, in fact, one of the oldest ethnic groups in the world continuously identifiable on its present territory.

Michael Yamin
Gillette, New Jersey

Endgame War Game

"It's the beginning of the endgame," said William Quandt, one of the phalanx of former diplomatic officials, now in think tanks, who come crashing through television screens at each development in the Middle East. He was reacting to an announcement on the Baghdad radio that Iraq would consider withdrawal from Kuwait if a series of conditions were met, and his characterizing words were seized upon by ABC's Peter Jennings, John McWethy and Sam Donaldson.

That's because the catch phrase was what the Phrasedick Squad of the

etymological police admires as a double historical allusion with an extended word backflip. The base was in the French statesman Charles Maurice de Talleyrand-Périgord's assessment of the battle of Borodino, in 1812, when Russian forces under General Mikhail Kutuzov stopped Napoleon's army near Moscow: "It is the beginning of the end." (*"Voilà le commencement de la fin."*)

That judgment was picked up and given a memorable twist by Winston Churchill in November 1942, after British forces under General Bernard Montgomery defeated the German Field Marshal Erwin Rommel's Afrika Korps at El Alamein in Egypt. "Now this is not the end," said Churchill, alluding to the Talleyrand judgment. "It is not even the beginning of the end. But it is, perhaps, the end of the beginning." (I assume Mr. Churchill was evoking Talleyrand, and not Quince in *A Midsummer Night's Dream:* "That is the true beginning of our end." Makes a better point.)

Mr. Quandt, who served on the National Security Council during the Carter Administration, combined those allusions and added his substitution of an extended term for the word *end:* the *endgame.* That's a chess term coined in 1884 by Bernard Horwitz: "The real end game consists of a position where the method can be analytically demonstrated by which the slightly superior force can win." (The writer was not a grandmaster in syntax, but showed daring in neologism.) An endgame is the final stage, often after queens have been exchanged and many other pieces have been knocked off the board; one player is trying for a checkmate, and the weaker opponent is trying for a stalemate.

The two words have fused as the chess metaphor has been extended; in 1964, the Russian-born American novelist Vladimir Nabokov wrote, "We'll simply take the *endgame* position at the point it was interrupted today."

Was the Baghdad statement a "cruel hoax," as President Bush promptly dubbed it (to differentiate it, presumably, from a kind hoax)—or was it a *gambit?* That chess term, derived from the Italian *gamba* for "leg," suggesting the tripping of the unsuspected, means "the calculated risk of a minor piece to gain early position"; it has been extended to mean "stratagem." However, *opening gambit* is almost as redundant as *final endgame.*

There are several ways to achieve a draw without stalemate: a mutually agreed-upon draw; threefold repetition of position; perpetual check (often combined with the latter), and 50 moves without a piece taken. Stalemate occurs only when the player whose turn it is, although not checkmated, legally cannot move any piece. While it seems like a cheap draw, a draw is a draw. So a stalemate is a draw, but a draw is not necessarily a stalemate. (Opening gambit *may be* redundant, *but* gambit opening *is not.*)

> Elliott Weinstein
> Baltimore, Maryland

Many people use stalemate *to be synonymous with* draw, *but in fact a stalemate is a particular* kind *of draw. It occurs only when the player on move has no legal move available but is not in check. This situation is important to chess theory, but very rare in practice. The vast majority of draws are "by agreement," that is, a handshake over a position that neither player feels likely to win.*

Your comment that "One player is trying for a checkmate" is true, but only in the sense that a player who doesn't feel desperate is always trying for a checkmate eventually. One characteristic of the endgame is that the superior player is usually not *trying for checkmate directly, but trying to promote a pawn. Pawn promotion creates new force on the board and eventually (the superior player hopes) forces checkmate.*

Stalemate has a very wide currency for a rather arcane technical term, and the usual metaphorical meaning of deadlock *is essentially correct. To chess players, though, it calls up a picture not of deadlock on less even terms, but a position in which one side has come very close to winning altogether but has been outmaneuvered into a draw. In this respect, a true chess stalemate was exactly what Saddam Hussein was trying for when he embraced the Soviet peace proposal.*

> Edward Lense
> Columbus, Ohio

Face Time

A White House aide thrust into the limelight by Persian Gulf war preparations was described to Maureen Dowd of *The New York Times* as one who was "getting a lot of *face time* on national television."

This is a locution gaining currency but groping for specific meaning.

The print coinage of *face time* belongs to *U.S. News & World Report*, which in 1978 wrote that President Carter "drops by the White House press room . . . guaranteeing himself a few precious seconds of 'face time' on the evening TV news." The use of quotation marks suggests earlier spoken usage.

Three years later, Lois Romano of *The Washington Post* wrote that presidential counselor Ed Meese came to a book party "for what is commonly referred to in Washington as 'face-time.' " The Style section writer defined the term as "a handshake, a walk around the room and one drink." (That political parlance is more commonly called a *drop-by*.)

The sense of showing one's face to a gathering in person, rather than to an audience on television, was remarked by Jeffrey Schmalz in a *Times* article about Cornell University's 1983 hockey season: " 'Going to the games is positive face time,' said Alan Baren, a senior. (Translation: Having your face seen at the right place, at the right time, with the right people.)"

This sense was narrowed to a form of apple-polishing in Pentagonese.

Major General Perry M. Smith compiled a glossary to the insider lingo at Fort Fumble in his 1989 book *Assignment: Pentagon* that includes *"Face time:* time spent near big bosses in attempts to impress them with your diligence and loyalty." *Night face,* or after-hours contact, counts double; *weekend face* counts quadruple.

In the midst of the development of these related but not identical meanings came my own entry in 1985 in a survey of college lingo: "Happily, a recent term for necking—*sucking face*—is on the decline, replaced by the more romantic *doing face time.*"

The second half of that statement was disputed by Kara B. Kerker, then a senior at Cornell, who defined *face time* on campus as "the art of seeing and being seen," not associated with noisy osculation; her examples of ways that undergraduates collected F.T.U.'s (face time units) included "occupying the window seat in a popular town bar and throwing dead fish at the Harvard players during their hockey team's annual visit to Ithaca."

All this is unrelated to *saving face,* based on the Asian concept of dignity. The Chinese expression *tiu lien* means "to lose face," which is the loss of dignity before others; *saving face,* as in maintaining one's dignity, is an English phrase of the late nineteenth century modeled on the Chinese.

To pick up a few definition units: In current use, *face time* means "being noticed by a significant audience." In a corporate or political hierarchy, the locution involves the physical impression of one's attentive visage on an employer or superior, and also has a more general meaning of "exposure," as in "face time on television."

Although the two-word phrase has been with us for more than a decade, it has not yet fused, on the analogy of *bedtime.* Give it usage time.

Re: "Face Time"

At Princeton University from 1967–71 when I was there—and presumably before and since and perhaps even still—a "face man" was a hale-fellow-well-met sort of person. Shallow; face-only—that sort of thing. Coeducation began gradually in '69, so maybe this slang has changed. It was a terrific term, I think, and widely used (by hip and square, left and right).

Robert P. Slocum
White Plains, New York

Fair Exchange?

In June 1989, President Bush announced he was cutting off all "high-level *exchanges* of government officials . . . in response to the wave of violence and reprisals by the Chinese authorities against those who have called for democracy."

Six months later, Frank Sesno of Cable News Network revealed that Brent Scowcroft, the national security adviser, and Lawrence S. Eagleburger, the Deputy Secretary of State, had secretly traveled to Beijing within a month after Mr. Bush's statement. When asked about this, the White House issued a statement contending that *resuming a dialogue* with the Chinese was "to personally underscore the United States' shock and concern."

When asked at a news conference about this apparent discrepancy in what had been said and done about high-level *contacts,* the President corrected the questioner: "I said, 'No high-level *exchanges.*' "

In the President's mind, evidently, a *contact* is synonymous with a *dialogue* but is not synonymous with an *exchange.*

What, in the language of diplomacy, is an *exchange*? Margaret D. Tutwiler, the State Department spokeswoman, acknowledged that "it's not playing a word game" and took a crack at defining it: "An *exchange* falls into the category of—for instance, when we were at the Treasury Department . . . we led a delegation" that continued a series of visits to China. But this year, "that was canceled. . . . Any number of *exchanges* have been ceased."

A reporter tried to help, referring to a recent meeting between James A. Baker 3d and the Chinese Foreign Minister: "When the Secretary met Qian Qichen in Paris, he told us that this was not an *exchange* because it took place in a third country and that he said *exchanges* were when officials went from one country to the other. . . . The second Scowcroft-Eagleburger mission, I gather, was considered an *exchange*?"

Miss Tutwiler, perhaps sensing she was being entrapped, went out of the synonymy business: "I don't know if it was characterized as an *exchange.* Was it characterized as a *contact*? It happened."

Let's try others. George Jones, vice president of the American Foreign Service Association, defined *diplomatic contact* as "a term applied to a person who's the source of information for a diplomat or to the initiation of relations between two countries." Bernard Kalb, veteran diplomatic correspondent and State spokesman who's now busy on a writing project, stated: "The difference between *diplomatic contact* and *diplomatic exchange* is diplomatic gibberish."

Contact, rooted in the Latin for "touching," has a diplomatic meaning of "communication" in its broadest sense; *exchange,* rooted in *cambire,* Latin for "barter," has the diplomatic meaning of "transaction," which includes discussions and reciprocal visits. *Dialogue,* rooted in "to talk between," is closer in diplomatic meaning to *exchange.*

Thus, the hairsplitting Mr. Bush can claim his promise of "no *exchanges*" was kept; he never said "no *contact.*" However, this recalls the old punch line "But I never said *positively*" and puts us all on guard: The President may be narrowly construing what he says, and may not always mean what he seems to mean.

Fine Line

"We righties," I wrote in a political harangue, "come to our side's line of scrimmage with different mental sets." That was a neat trope, I thought; a football player comes to a motionless "set" on a line of scrimmage.

Watch those sports metaphors. "Your side doesn't have its own line of scrimmage," writes Donald Kennedy, member of the Nitpickers' League and president of Stanford University. "Neither do the other guys. Rather, the line of scrimmage is a singular domain, a plane passing through the equator of the resting football, and destined to become the point of collision between the burly biggies of the Right and their smaller, quicker opponents on the Left."

Football fans could argue that each team has its own line of scrimmage, at either end of the football; on this theory, only the center snapping the ball is allowed to be in the "neutral zone" where the football rests between the lines of scrimmage. However, the term *line of scrimmage* is usually used in its singular sense, for the imaginary line that passes through the most forward point of the ball (not, as is believed at Stanford, the ball's equator).

The corrected version: "We righties come to our side of the line of scrimmage with different mental sets. . . ."

Floating Naming Game

O.K., everybody, let's get organized. What are we going to call the get-together of the heads of the two superpowers next weekend?

President Bush spoke of it as "a chance to put our feet up and talk." He added a linguistic caveat: "This one isn't a summit. . . . 'Summits' take on a

definition, an expectation of grand design and grand agreements, and that's not what this is."

A White House official privy to the decision making last summer said the President spoke of it then as "a nonsummit summit." The Soviet Foreign Minister, Eduard A. Shevardnadze, fearlessly adopted the no-no word, modifying it as an "intermediate summit." The *Atlanta Constitution* noted the President's queasiness about overselling the get-together in its editorial headline: "The, Uh, Almost, Well, Kind-of Summit."

"We never say the word *summit,*" another White House official, who had not been so privy, told me soon after the public announcement of the sea-borne meeting off the island of Malta in the Mediterranean. "The *summit* is what will take place next summer. If I were to say *summit* in regard to what will happen next week, the entire eighteen acres that make up the White House complex would open up and swallow me. We have to think about the management of anticipation. It's a *meeting,* an informal *meeting.*"

Mr. Gorbachev and Mr. Bush may have the power to sit down and divvy up the world (we'll take East Germany and a Nicaraguan cutoff for a suspension of Jackson-Vanik and one round of a Bush GATT pick), but they have no say in what we call their deliberations.

It's a *summit.* Not all my colleagues agree: The *New York Times* editorialist referred to *the Mediterranean rendezvous,* and a *Time* magazine reporter alliterated *the mid-Med meeting.* A dyspeptic pundit called it *the last cruise of the Love Boat.* Another wag put forward *the schmooze cruise.*

But when Winston Churchill applied the word to the get-togethers of the heads of government in 1950, he used "parley at the summit" to mean just the sort of meeting that Mr. Gorbachev and Mr. Bush say they have in mind. "This conference should not be overhung by a ponderous or rigid agenda," said Churchill, "or led into mazes of technical details, zealously contested by hordes of experts and officials drawn up in a vast cumbrous array."

But how shall we distinguish it from other summits? Some like a geographic designation, as in the *Glassboro summit* of 1967; to these namers, the *Mediterranean summit* comes naturally, shortened to *Med summit* or hooted at as the *Club Med summit;* the more specific designation of *Malta summit* also leaps to mind.

This recalls Churchill's exhortation to Franklin Delano Roosevelt before the Yalta Conference of 1945—they were called *conferences,* then, or *Big [number] meetings*—"No more let us falter. From Malta to Yalta. Let nobody alter." (They aren't rhyming like that at the highest level anymore; the trouble was, Roosevelt faltered and Stalin altered. We can expect many headlines of "From Yalta to Malta" over thumbsuckers about the difference in the meetings of 1945 and 1989.)

More popular among phrasecoiners in the first flush of namings was the bobbing nature of the site. David S. Broder of *The Washington Post* chose *seaborne summit,* while John Broder of the *Los Angeles Times* preferred a hyphenated *summit-at-sea* (*U.S. News & World Report* dropped the hyphens in choosing the same phrase). The columnist Mary McGrory liked *floating summit,* while others chose *saltwater summit, shipboard summit, seagoing summit.*

I'll go for the *Malta summit,* because that's where the press will be covering it from, not counting the plucky types aiming their cameras from rowboats; besides, the natural comparison to Yalta, with its broken Soviet promises, may come in handy.

Be alert to the background of briny clichés. PRESSURE OF EVENTS FORCED SEA CHANGE IN BUSH POLICY was a *Los Angeles Times* headline, and any shift in position will be called a *sea change;* a few years ago, Tom Brokaw of NBC sent me a note that read: "Meredith Brokaw raises the question, 'Was the phrase *sea change,* now so in vogue, always used, and I was unaware of it?' My guess is that it is suddenly fashionable and not clearly understood. Any thoughts?"

Think Shakespeare. In *The Tempest,* the sprite Ariel sings:

> Full fathom five thy father lies,
> Of his bones are coral made:
> Those are pearls that were his eyes:
> Nothing of him that doth fade,
> But doth suffer a sea-change
> Into something rich and strange.

(If you think the Bard should have written "Of his bones *is* coral made," write him, not me.) From that metaphoric use of "profound change made by the action of salt water over time," the phrase—no longer a hyphenated term—has come to mean "transformation," the most extreme form of alteration. (Let nobody alter.)

THE 2 SHIPS OF STATECRAFT WILL MEET OFF MALTA was a *New York Times* headline; this portmanteau metaphor was a nice extension of *statecraft,* a word defined in dictionaries as "statesmanship" or "the art of leading a country," but now also carrying a connotation of "the tricks of the foreign-policy trade," perhaps influenced by the intelligence community's *tradecraft* and the manipulative sense of *crafty.*

We can expect a big run on the *ship of state* trope, which originated in ancient Greek poetry and was popularized by the lines in Henry Wadsworth Longfellow's 1849 poem "The Building of the Ship," about strengthening our nation:

> Thou, too, sail on, O Ship of State!
> Sail on, O Union, strong and great!
> Humanity with all its fears,
> With all the hopes of future years,
> Is hanging breathless on thy fate!

This was the poem sent by F.D.R. to Churchill in 1941, carried by the defeated presidential candidate, Wendell Willkie, offering encouragement to Britain in its travail. (Churchill responded with Arthur Hugh Clough's poem that ends with the line "but westward, look, the land is bright.")

In fact, Longfellow is having one of his biggest months in years in the run-up to the Malta summit. President Bush, perhaps unconsciously, called up that poet's phrase in explaining why he was having the kind of summit he had previously derogated: "I don't want to have two gigantic ships pass in the night because of failed communication."

Let's be generous; in a Churchillian way, the President was referring to the 1873 "Tales of a Wayside Inn," in which the American poet wrote a memorable passage about forgotten passages that may be applicable to statecraft today:

> Ships that pass in the night, and speak each other in passing,
> Only a signal shown and a distant voice in the darkness;
> So on the ocean of life we pass and speak one another,
> Only a look and a voice; then darkness again and a silence.

Fluffya Slang

Philadelphians are proud of their regional dialect, which is based on a pronunciation of compression; a "Fluffya Inkwire," for example, is what outlanders call a *Philadelphia Inquirer.*

A competing publication, The Fluffyadailynooz, has come up with an interesting slang usage unrelated to pronunciation. "Ex-Prosecutor's Plea Stalemated," goes a July headline of an article that was read with dread at the Department of Justice in Washington, where droves of Pennsylvania prosecutors recused themselves in the case. Then followed this subhead: "Won't Dime Drug-Using Pals, Feds Say."

What is the meaning of *dime* as a verb? "Since pay phones required ten cents per call for many years," explains Francis J. Hanssens Jr. of that city, "the phrase *to drop a dime on* came to mean 'to inform on.' The *Daily News* apparently believes that, even standing alone, *dime* can be used in that sense."

I salute the headline writer; it's good to see a colorful bit of slang hang in there in the face of inflation. *To stop on a dime* is still with us, because the ten-cent coin is our smallest, and the phrase means "to stop short"; however, the *dime store,* or *five-and-dime,* is Old Slang. So is "Suddenly *the dime dropped,*" said by one who was illuminated by understanding, as if the inserted coin finally operated the pay phone and the dial tone came on. (If anybody calls about this, I'll hit him with Really Old Slang: "It's your nickel.")

You quote an individual as saying that the phrase to "drop a dime on" means "to inform on." At least one reader takes serious exception to that interpretation.

Perhaps from too much association with the wrong kind of people, I can certify that "drop a dime on" refers to a judge imposing a ten-year prison sentence on a felon. A derivative phrase, in almost universal use in certain circles, is "doin' a dime" (in Attica, Sing-Sing, Atlanta or other government-provided facilities). "Doin' a nickel" is also used when appropriate.

Walter Meyer
Federal Bureau of
Investigation
New York, New York

Please do not be too hard on the "Fluffyans" who read the "Fluffya Inkwire." After all, you write for the "Nyawktimz." "Fluffyans" can't hold a candle to "Nyawkus" when it comes to dialect, especially to those who live on "Lung Guylend." Chauvinist!

Richard E. Thomson
Kill Devil Hills,
North Carolina

A Foreign Affair

From R. E. (Ted) Turner, founder of the broadcasting system that bears his name (I like those archaic formulations), has come this memo to personnel at his Cable News Network: "It is the policy of TBS that any person, event, etc. which [sic] is not part of the United States be referred to as *international* rather than *foreign*."

Why? "The word *foreign* implies something unfamiliar and creates a perception of misunderstanding," writes Mr. Turner, backing his stricture to employees with the threat of a fine payable to Unicef. "In contrast, *international* means 'among nations' and promotes a sense of unity." Excepted from the diktat: "cases in which the word *foreign* is part of the proper title [sic] of a person or thing," as in Best Foreign Language Film.

This is not the first time *foreign* has been attacked. In 1975, the House of Representatives Committee on Foreign Affairs was troubled by its name. Nobody would say so publicly, but insiders felt that *foreign* seemed old-fashioned, or at least too similar to the title of the Senate committee in the same field, and the word *affairs* had a double meaning. After four exciting years styled as "the Committee on International Relations," with snickers and hooting directed its way by the Senate Committee on Foreign Relations, the House committee changed its name back to Foreign Affairs; if the voters thought it meant that each member was visiting a Mata Hari on every junket, so be it. Thus did congressional tradition triumph over trendiness.

Not at CNN, at least as far as *foreign* is concerned. At Mr. Turner's network, there ain't no such thing as *foreign news;* it's all *international,* except for the domestic variety.

A threshold question arises: Does Mr. Turner have the right to issue such a ukase, even with such a high-minded motivation? The answer is yes. Journalism has long recognized the first law of freedom of the press: You own the press, you set the style.

(*The New York Times,* for example, insists on an honorific followed by the last name of an individual upon second reference; thus, "Saddam Hussein" becomes "Mr. Hussein." Behind the scenes, I fought using the honorific for him on the grounds of confusion with King Hussein and the practice of President Bush in referring to the Iraqi dictator with contemptuous familiarity as "Sad'm," but *Times* stylists, who will be in business long after Sad'm fades from the scene, do not want standards of courtesy to erode on this exception. Supercelebrities of history may not need honorifics—Jefferson and Stalin do not require "Mr."—and some first names stand alone, as Cher demonstrates, but "Mr. Hussein" remains. Years ago, I protested at having to refer to "Slick Willie" Sutton, the bank robber, as "Mr. Sutton" the second time around, and the rule was eased; as Slick Willie used to explain, that's where the money is. The point of this extended digression is to show first that style in each media outlet is what the boss says it is, and second that parenthetical remarks should be limited to a single sentence.)

The more substantive question is: Can we do without *foreign* in an antinational, multipolar world?

Foreign, with seven centuries in ethnocentric English, is based on the Latin *foris,* "outside"—let's go outside to the *forum* and debate. It means "situated outside a place, especially outside one's own country."

International plays in the same extrinsic ballpark with *foreign,* but is not precisely synonymous. A coinage by Jeremy Bentham in 1780, *international* replaced "of nations" in "law of nations." It originally meant "having to do with two or more nations" and has gained a more recent sense of "known or reaching beyond national boundaries."

Mr. Turner would insist that the connotation of *foreign* is "strange, alien, exotic," while *international* connotes nothing other than neutral intercourse; he would be right. But *international* does not always mean "foreign": We may say proudly that our Secretary of State, James A. Baker 3d, has become an international dignitary, but to those of us who are his compatriots, he is not a *foreign* one. If that word were banished entirely, we would have a new problem: What if we wanted to say that a merger with an over-the-air network that submerged the identity of CNN would be foreign to Mr. Turner's independent and entrepreneurial nature? We could not say it would be *international* to it; we could only say it would be *extraneous* (weak word) or *alien* to it.

As those of Slick Willie's successors who use an *alias* know, *alien* is rooted in the Latin for "other"; that word, too, has been the target of determined political euphemists. *Illegal alien* was at first replaced by *undocumented person,* which was surely an improvement over the slur *wetback,* but the Immigration and Naturalization Service points out that a visitor whose visa runs out while in this country is not truly "undocumented," and "persons" who are not aliens do not need documents; therefore, that agency has reluctantly returned to *illegal alien.* However, in general speech, the out-of-it *alien* is now applied mainly to visitors from other planets; if other-world-weary writers want to adopt a cause, that noun and adjective *alien* will soon be replaced by *interplanetarian.*

Mr. Turner's diktat (we international-setters call him Ted, but one style crusade at a time) would also make every *foreign* language an *international* language, which is a label better suited to such translinguistic concoctions as Esperanto, Interlingua or Volapük than to Welsh, Lapp or Murken. Moreover, the Chinese could no longer refer to old Nixon hands as *foreign friends;* the substitution of *overseas* or *international* for *foreign* would lose their meaning of "those who are not Chinese."

Easy on the ukases and the fines, Ted (a first name is stylistically permissible in a direct hailing; Mr. Sutton was not the only slick Willie). Instead, tell your employees that your network stylebook prefers *international* to *foreign* when that usage is suitable. But you cannot banish offenders to an international land.

Thank you for bringing to light Ted Turner's good intentions and the linguistic contortions it creates.

When the original memo/diktat surfaced some months ago it produced the predictable incredulity among CNN employees.

Washington bureau chief Bill Headline was credited with "I have an international object in my eye."

Then we realized Ted was serious.

Rebel reporters contemplated euphonic loopholes: President Bush has searched far'n wide for'n alternative to Saddam Hussein.

To the network's journalists this is an alien and Orwellian approach to communications and unlikely to produce its intended result of international amity.

Fortunately, the threatened fines have not materialized. In any event, I figured I could meet the spirit of Ted's determination and pay in an international currency. Rubles ought to do.

I enjoy your column and hope it keeps us honest.

Charles J. Bierbauer
Senior White House
Correspondent
CNN
Washington, D.C.

You included the phrase "a visitor whose visa runs out while in this country." I would have been afraid that the phrase refers to the visa's presence in the U.S., and so would have written "while he is in this country." The trouble is that the complete phrase, with my addition of only two little syllables, scans ill; "a visitor whose visa runs out while he is in this country" seems to clunk in the middle, as though going over a speed bump. Alternatively, I suppose, one could exit to a different way of saying it: "runs out during his stay."

Alberto Guzman
Bronx, New York

Foreign Guests and Hostages

At the beginning of the Persian Gulf crisis, reporters noted that President Bush was careful not to use the word *hostages* to describe foreign nationals not permitted to leave Iraq. "Do you believe the Iraqis are using those Americans as a *shield*?" was the way the question was put to Mr. Bush at a news conference.

The President, eager not to show the vulnerability of official concern, was equally circumspect about their status: "The status is inconvenienced people who want to get out . . . [but] the more we speculate, the less helpful it is."

From Baghdad, Ted Koppel of ABC reported that the word being used there by a foreign-ministry official was *restrictees.* This was a newer locution, milder than *detainees,* with the sense of "held but not arrested." A few days later, in the United States, the newsman said: "All this nonsense about using euphemisms like *detainees* and *restrictees* is . . . something that belongs in the garbage can. These people are *hostages.*"

Others continued to use *pawn* or *bargaining chip,* but the Iraqi Foreign Office preferred a term that was a euphemism for a euphemism: They dropped *restrictees* for *foreign guests,* which was knowingly so far from the truth that it carried a connotation of contempt.

Finally, George Bush saw no further use in avoiding the hard word that had so plagued his two predecessors: "When Saddam Hussein specifically offers to trade the freedom of those citizens of many nations he holds against their will in return for concessions, there can be little doubt that whatever these innocent people are called, they are in fact *hostages.*" The *Washington Times* headline underscored the impact of using the word for the fact: BUSH CALLS A HOSTAGE A HOSTAGE.

Internee was coined in 1918 when *Parliament Papers* referred to "State prisoners and internees" in Bengal. Article 80 of the Geneva Convention of 1949 on the protection of civilians in time of war says, "Internees shall retain

their full civil capacity and shall exercise such attendant rights as may be compatible with their status," and Article 34 states, "The taking of hostages is prohibited." *Human shield* is a hostage used to inhibit attack, originating in the kidnapping of bystanders by armed robbers.

Freebie

The budget deficit, once of considerable concern in Washington, was the subject of a question to President Bush: Would the Persian Gulf involvement knock his projections off? "It may cause for a rearrangement in how money is spent," he replied, scrambling his syntax, "because this is not a *freebie . . .*"

This slang noun means "something that costs nothing; a gift." In current usage, it has replaced *cuffo, gratis* and *on the house;* in terms of free tickets, it has replaced *Annie Oakley.*

"That meal was a freebie," wrote Louis Armstrong in his 1954 autobiography, "and didn't cost me anything." He added the definition because the word was then only about a decade old. His spelling, with the *-ie* ending, indicates that this coinage was part of the midcentury trend toward popularizing *sweetie, cutie* and the 1871 *goodie-goodie. Freebie* and *cheapie* grew up together; a consonant was added to *free* to make it work as the first of two syllables.

A second theory exists: Random House speculates that the final syllable should be spelled *bee,* if taken from the phrase *put the bee on,* meaning "to borrow money with no intention of repaying it." That's a good stretch, but fanciful.

The *-ie* ending is current: A news release has come in for what is described as a "new 4 lb. book"—*Lesko's Info-Power,* by Matthew Lesko—which shows "how to tap into the thousands of freebies and cheapies" from the United States government's "30,000 government goodies."

Sweetie and *cutie,* coined in the eighteenth century, are now often taken as sexist put-downs; Reagan operatives in the 1980 campaign infuriated many women at the Democratic candidate by distributing buttons reading "Cuties for Carter."

Cheapie has a pejorative connotation, derived from the tawdry sense of *cheap;* there are no *inexpensivies.* But *freebie* has a happy feeling; everybody wants to get on a *freebie list.*

Why do we need the word? *It's free* means the same as *It's a freebie* and has the advantage of brevity. A yearning evidently has developed for a nominative form of the adjective; when turned into a noun, the word gains a piquant personality it lacks as an adjective. "She's *sweet*" often introduces a *but,* but "She's a *sweetie*" does not. Similarly, "It's *free*" is nice to know, but "It's a *freebie*" impels you toward an item you want to get your hands on. The President's usage extends its sense to the cost of a gigantic enterprise.

Nominative *does not mean "of or having to do with a noun," as you appear to believe. It is the term used in languages with a case system to designate the case of the subject. Thus,* homo *is the nominative case of the Latin word for "man,"* hominis *is the genitive,* homini *is the dative, etc.*

The word you were looking for is nominal. *However, since this word is widely used in another sense, I think it would have been best to say: "A yearning evidently has developed for a noun form of the adjective."*

Louis Jay Herman
New York, New York

Friendly Enemies

Note from Justin Kaplan, editor of *Bartlett's Familiar Quotations:* "I wonder if you have been tracking the by-now inescapable axiom about the Iraqi crisis: *The enemy of my enemy is my friend.*"

Have I ever. H. L. Mencken, in his 1942 *Dictionary of Quotations,* listed "The friends of my friends are my friends" as a Flemish proverb, and "The enemy of my enemy is my friend" as a French proverb; yet everybody I ask about this says, "It's an old Arab proverb." (That's redundant; all proverbs and adages are old. They mean it's an old Arab saying.)

Tom Friedman of *The New York Times* offers as a clue this saying he has heard as a correspondent in the Middle East: "Me and my brother against my cousin; me, my brother and my cousin against the outsider."

There we are in the gulf, in strange bedfellowship with the likes of Hafez al-Assad, dictator of Syria, destroyer of Hama and invader of Lebanon, without a citation for the origin of *the enemy of my enemy is my friend* to show the rationale for uneasy alliances. Help from Lexicographic Irregulars is urgently sought.

Relatedly, Mr. Kaplan has gone deeper than the April 1978 sportscast of Dan Cook for the expression that modern phrasedicks are most often asked about: "The opera ain't over till the fat lady sings." He will use this 1976 citation found by Fred R. Shapiro of Yale Law School from *Southern Words and Sayings* (edited by Fabia Rue Smith and Charles Rayford Smith): "Church ain't out till the fat lady sings."

I like Mr. Kaplan's stated intention to credit the screenwriters for such lines as "Go ahead, make my day" and "Win one for the Gipper" in future editions of *Bartlett's.* Does this mean that speechwriters will get credit for famous lines delivered by public figures? That prospect causes some of us nattering nabobs of negativism to salivate at coinage glory and others (like Douglass Cater, at the last meeting of the Judson Welliver Society of former White House Ghosts) to express shock at the loss of what F.D.R.'s Louis Brownlow called "a passion for anonymity."

"Any attempt at systematic crediting would probably lead to nothing but trouble and confusion," Kaplan says, "since in most instances there's no demonstrable line between the speechwriter and the speaker." In the case of George Bush's *kinder, gentler nation,* we have learned from Peggy Noonan's memoirs that Mr. Bush emended her draft to include the word *gentler;* that means the collaborative effort will be attributed to the speaker, not the cowriter, which strikes me as proper. In *a thousand points of light,* Mr. Kaplan says, "Ms. Noonan should be given credit, at least in a footnote, since she discusses the phrase and its antecedents in some detail and has obviously gone 100 percent public. But this is an exception."

The editor of *Bartlett's* is thinking about *read my lips*. Nobody wants full credit for that.

"The enemy of my enemy is my friend." The author is Kautilya, in his book on politics and administration of government called the Artha Sastra *written in Sanskrit around 400 B.C. He was the Brahmin Guru of King Chandragupta Maurya who ruled India around that time and who was a contemporary of the Buddha.*

> *Prema Ramaswami*
> *Washington, D.C.*

Although the actual wording is not found in the Kautilīya Arthaśāstra, *a pre-4th century CE textbook of statecraft, the idea underlies the doctrine of "circles" that is fundamental to ancient Indian political theory.*

> *John Newman*
> *Assistant Professor of Asian*
> *Studies*
> *University of South Florida*
> *Sarasota, Florida*

The U. S. Navy has a saying "Messmate before shipmate, shipmate before stranger, stranger before a dog."
We borrowed it from the British, as we did many of our naval traditions. Vice Admiral W. H. Smyth, RN, quotes it in his Sailor's Word Book: An Alphabetical Digest of Nautical Terms *(London: Blackie and Sons, 1867).*

> *Daniel W. Greene*
> *San Diego, California*

I had occasion some years ago to ask Ted Sorenson whether he wrote "Ask not what your country . . . etc." He obviously had been asked that question many times before and gave a quick, practiced reply: "Ask not."
Cute answer. He preserved the anonymity you presidential speech writers affect, and yet got across to me that he did, in fact, write it!

> *Herman Gross*
> *Great Neck, New York*

Garden Party Whatsit

One of the great word-pictures in the American language is *the skunk at the garden party.* Think about it: There is the garden party, an elegant institution peopled with perfumed ladies in large hats and gentlemen in blazers and green pants who are holding gin fizzes. An expensive tent called a "marquee" is in place in case of showers; a few of the fellows slip off for a slow game of croquet, and into this strawberry-and-cream world meanders a small black animal with a white streak down its back and a bushy tail, with the potential, if it is frightened, of causing such a stink as to render anyone in the neighborhood an object of general repugnance for days. After a moment of silent horror, with the terrified guests and the frightened skunk staring at each other—panic is followed by havoc.

It's a nice, antielitist trope. I use it often, always in the negative, usually when taking a contrarian view of a widely accepted position: "Look, I don't want to be *the skunk at the garden party,* but . . ."

When the Nicaraguan strongman Daniel Ortega Saavedra arrived in Costa Rica, where American chiefs of state were gathering to congratulate themselves on the furtherance of the "peace process," he stunned them all by announcing his intention to break the ceasefire in his country.

A United States television reporter went on the air describing the stupefied reaction by using the great old expression. President Bush, at a subsequent press meeting, agreed: "That's exactly what happened," he said. "Mr. Ortega looks like that unwanted animal at a garden party. . . . We're not going to let this one little man who is out of whack with the rest of the hemisphere ruin a very good meeting."

Apparently Mr. Bush was about to use the full expression, *skunk at a garden party,* but then pulled his punch: Would it be proper for the United States President to characterize another head of state as a "skunk"? Would he be accused of name-calling? Would it somehow be taken out of the context of the phrase to allow Mr. Ortega to take personal offense, and make President Bush appear ungentlemanly?

These thoughts must have come to mind, or must have been suggested beforehand by an aide, causing the President to use a modification of the phrase: "that unwanted animal at a garden party . . ."

London's *Sunday Telegraph* explained the significance to British readers: "In using that term, President Bush stopped only just short of the full American colloquial expression, which is 'a skunk at a garden party.' "

This recourse to euphemism reduced President Ortega's capacity for riposte; instead of objecting to the skunk reference, or immediately wearing a skunk cap in defiance, the Nicaraguan attacked the other end of the phrase in a piece written for *The New York Times* Op-Ed page: "President Bush reacted with a torrent of personal invective. He accused me of spoiling the 'garden party' in Costa Rica. Well, life in my country is no 'garden party.' "

Thus did Mr. Ortega's publicist, denied the *skunk* opening, make what he could of the *garden party* as an elite image. It was not as effective as "He called me a skunk, that rat," or "Even a skunk doesn't weasel out of . . ." or whatever alternative animal metaphor he could have chosen.

Garden party—a gathering or celebration held on a lawn, with connotations of affluence—is a phrase first used by Anthony Trollope in his 1869 novel, *Phineas Finn:* "The Duke's garden party was becoming a mere ball, with privilege for the dancers to stroll about the lawn between the dances."

Skunk is of Algonquian origin: The Indians of the Atlantic seaboard called "the mammal who sprays" *sekakwa* or *squnck;* by 1840, it was being used, along with *polecat,* to mean a contemptible person. In 1813, an anti-Federalist wrote, "We here choose to let Mr. Madison 'skin his own skunks,' " and in the twentieth century, another use of the word in a rhyming simile was *drunk as a skunk in a moonshine still.*

In the phrase we are studying today, however, cited references are few and found mainly in politics.

"In 1984, I was the skunk in the garden party," said Colorado Democrat Pat Schroeder in 1987, "who said we women have to run like men do." She added ruefully, "May your words be tender and juicy, for people often serve them back to you."

In the presidential primary of 1988, former Governor Bruce Babbitt of Arizona said as he withdrew from the race that Jesse Jackson, Gary Hart and he "were sort of the skunks at the garden party, always saying 'This debate is supposed to be about something' and raking our fingers down the chalkboard."

Who coined this invaluable Americanism, and when? It's a mystery; the *Dictionary of American Regional English* has no reference to this expression in its files, but a staff member there reports its use in Wisconsin two decades ago. If anyone has an early citation, it will be welcomed by the entire etymological community, as well as by the genus *Mephitis* everywhere. You'd think it would have left a scent.

Here is a line from William Howard Moore's The Kefauver Committee and the Politics of Crime 1950–1952 *(1974), which dates the "skunk" at a "lawn" party back to the early 1950s:*

> In Congress the polite smiles barely concealed a bitter opposition born in part of jealousy and in part of the fear that the Committee's exposures would critically damage the Democratic party; in Senate cloakrooms, Kefauver reportedly had the appeal of a "skunk at a lawn party."

Charles H. McCaghy
Bowling Green, Ohio

Not to be the skunk at the garden party, but your description of a "black animal with a white streak down its back" sent me to the reference books. I thought you might enjoy the richly authoritative description in Lloyd Glenn Ingles's Mammals of California:

> *STRIPED SKUNK* (Mephitis mephitis) *. . . all-over black coloration, with two white stripes extending from the neck to the tail . . . In the Eastern United States some . . . possess only one slender white stripe from the nose to the back of the neck. . . . Such "black skunks" are not found among the Western animals.*

Owing no doubt to the dearth of garden parties.

> William Strider
> New York, New York

The German Answer

The German Question—in German, *die deutsche Frage*—is again in the world news. The question itself is widely understood to be "What is to be done about Germany?" The underlying question, however, of far greater historical linguistic import, is: Who coined the phrase? Did it enter the geopolitical arena in the 1930's with the rise of Hitler?

"Etymological immortality awaits" the discoverer of the first person to pose *the German Question,* I wrote here recently. With this incentive, two Lexicographic Irregulars came through.

"It was much earlier than the 1930's," writes Gary D. Stark, associate professor of history at the University of Texas at Arlington, "and probably as early as the Congress of Vienna." He provides a once-removed source: On the page preceding the title page of Wilhelm Röpke's 1946 *The Solution of the German Problem* is this quotation: "*The German Question* is the most somber, the most complicated, the most comprehensive problem of all recent history." The person quoted was Constantin Frantz, the date 1866, but no specific source was given.

For that we turn to Jens P. Drews of Harrisburg, Pennsylvania, who sends along a paper in German written in 1987 by Michael Dreyer that cites Constantin Frantz's article "Theorie der deutschen Frage," which appeared in the journal *Deutsche Vierteljahrsschrift* in 1866.

Frantz, explains Mr. Drews, was "an ardent opponent of Bismarck's *klein-deutsch* answer to *the German Question.*" Rather than seeing a little Germany, Frantz envisioned a Central European confederation, with Germany at its core, stretching from Finland to the Black Sea. "However, Frantz was not only a philosopher and political thinker," adds Mr. Drews, "but also a noted polemicist whose rabid anti-Semitism was an integral part of his journalistic as well as of his academic work."

In 1944, Kurt Waldheim wrote a dissertation on Frantz's work without mentioning the anti-Semitic arguments. "Given Waldheim's selective historical memory," writes my informant, "I would not at all be surprised if the Austrian President were to introduce parts of Frantz's thinking as his contribution to the ongoing debate over the future of Europe."

Now we're getting into polemics, not my intent in this space, but illustrative of the sort of dander raised whenever *the German Question* is mentioned. The phrase has been used in a more specific sense: The eleventh (and to encyclopedia buffs, the best) edition of the *Encyclopedia Britannica,* published in 1910–11, has an entry on *the Schleswig-Holstein Question.* (Did Denmark or Prussia control these duchies on the North and Baltic Seas, and would Great Britain permit Germany to become a sea power?)

"In German," writes Louise E. Hoffman, a history professor at Pennsylvania State University at Harrisburg, "the word *Frage* is used much as English-speakers would use *issue.*" True, which leads us to an earlier use of that formulation, put forward in a testy letter from an American scholar, Paul Irving Anderson, living in Aalen, West Germany: "What is bothering you is something that sounds similar and yet is miles apart: '*die Judenfrage,*' *nicht wahr?*" (Those last two words mean "hunh?")

Apparently *the Jewish Question,* posed by a trouble-making German philosopher, born a Jew, whose views have recently come under fire in the Soviet

Union, antedated *the German Question.* "I wonder if the phrase *the German question* was coined as a takeoff on Karl Marx's 'On the Jewish Question,' " writes Asli Göçer, at the department of philosophy, University of Massachusetts at Amherst: "This essay was written in the autumn of 1843 and published in the *Deutsch-Französische Jahrbücher.*"

Let's look at Marx's use: "To formulate a question is to resolve it," wrote the father of Communism. "The critical study of the Jewish Question is the answer to the Jewish Question. Here it is in brief: We have to emancipate ourselves before we can emancipate others." He presumably had in mind here the "liberation" from religion, both Judaic and Christian, which he was sure would lead to the emancipation of mankind.

Unless earlier citations come in, that's the etymology of *the German Question,* meaning to some "the German issue," and to others "the German problem." It is for this generation to come up with the German *answer;* language can only take you so far.

In that regard, this urgent message just in from Christopher Smart at the hard-line Hudson Institute: "Please settle this one before it's too late: Two *Germanys*? Two *Germanies*? I support the former, but we need a grammatical ruling before there is only one."

We're talking about uniting the two *Germanys.* Although the plural of nouns ending in *y* after a consonant is *ies,* the plural of proper names overrides that rule to preserve the name itself: Mr. and Mrs. Murphy and their two daughters are the *Murphys;* if both girls are confusingly named Mary, they're the *Marys.*

I anticipate a letter from a resident of the Canary Islands asking, "And what about the *Canaries*?" Similar postcards will follow from people in the Rocky Mountains and the Allegheny Mountains; the ranges are spelled *Rockies* and *Alleghenies,* contrary to the overriding rule laid down so authoritatively in the preceding paragraph.

These proper noun plurals have no singular form; one cannot say "I'm on a Canary Island" or "I plan to climb one Rocky Mountain." Because the plural represents a group, we *Sprachpolizei* permit a plural spelling at the end as if the proper name were an ordinary word. Do not be misled by this special situation, however: It's two *Germanys,* never two *Germanies.*

(Somewhere deep in a pyramid, inside a sarcophagus, underneath the wrapping of a mummy, an ancient grammarian is asking, "But what about us Ptolemies?")

Marx's essay was a two-part response—not really a review—to essays by another young Hegelian, Bruno Bauer. One of Bauer's essays was titled "Die Judenfrage" and was published earlier that same year. This seems to be the reason for the title of Marx's essay. So Bauer's usage does pre-date Marx's.

Judith E. McBride
Associate Professor
Department of Philosophy
Central Connecticut State
University
New Britain, Connecticut

Here is a little item to supplement your file on the "German Question." As you can see from the article copied below, the expression was current in the U.S. before 1866.

THE GERMAN QUESTION. *We don't exactly understand the merits and demerits of this question in Europe, but the German Question about here is: "Vat you dinks von 'ter Gonsdidushun?"*

Gold Hill News, *23 December 1863, p. 2, c. 1.*

(The "Gonsdidushun" was the Nevada constitution that, at that time, was being discussed in the County Convention and among the people of the state.)

The political context is probably still Bismarck's klein deutsch oder groß deutsch, *but it is interesting to note that the joke appeared in a West Coast newspaper, the Gold Hill News, in 1863. As you may know, Gold Hill was a neighboring town of Virginia City, Nevada, and had, just like Virginia, a sizeable percentage of Germans among its inhabitants at the time. Back then, jokes based on the immigrants' trouble with the English language apparently amused a lot of readers. The use of this kind of German-American dialect was widespread from the 1850's until the 1880's and writers such as Charles Godfrey Leland ("Hans Breitmann") and Charles H. Harris ("Carl Pretzel") built their reputation entirely on stories composed in this German variant of pidgin English.*

Holger Kersten
Berkeley, California

In the last act of Shaw's "Caesar and Cleopatra" (written in 1898) the following exchange occurs:
The scene is the esplanade in front of the palace with the populace assembled to await the arrival of Caesar, who is about to embark for Rome and home.

BELZANOR (the Egyptian captain): *A marvelous man, this Caesar! Will he come soon, think you?*
APOLLODORUS (the Greek artist): *He was settling the Jewish question when I left.*

Shaw, the satirist, seems to be saying, "Some things never change."

William Barbour
Brewster, Massachusetts

I was very surprised to read that the proper plural for East and West Germany is "Germanys." This conclusion is both unnecessary on its face and contrary to at least two hundred years of practice.

The word "Germany" comes from the latin "Germania," the Roman description of part of what we now call Germany. For the Romans, Germany fell into (at least) three parts: savage Germany beyond the Rhine and Danube; and the two Roman provinces, Upper Germany and Lower Germany. The existence of the two provinces may provide the reason that in French until the eighteenth century the word for Germany was "Les Allemagnes." In English, a quick look at my book shelf reveals that Edward Gibbon referred to the two Roman provinces as "the Germanies" in The Decline and Fall of the Roman Empire, *although I am quite sure that prior references could be found. This formation of a plural in the normal way for a territorial name ending in "y" was also used in the English name for the state that existed in southern Italy until the Risigormento, "The Kingdom of the Two Sicilies" (Sicily proper being one, the mainland including Naples being the other). On this basis "Germanies" must be at least an acceptable alternative.*

I do not find your argument about Murphys very convincing. Germany is not a proper name in the same way that "Federal Republic of Germany" or even "German Democratic Republic" certainly is. (If a commentator insists on speculation regarding the emergence of "Federal Republic of Germanys" in other parts of the world, I will cringe but will not object.)

It occurs to me that there are policy reasons for leaving the "y" intact in the case of a given name. The original spelling may reflect a meaning that could be altered by an alteration in spelling. Furthermore, people and countries are entitled to determine their own spelling of their name, which should be respected insofar as possible in forming the plural. These reasons do not apply to the name of a region, particularly when the name is in any case an English word unrelated to the one used in the original language.

I do not see why we must refer to the ancient domains of the Dukes of Burgundy (the Duchy of Burgundy in France and the County of Burgundy in the Empire) as the Burgundys and refer to the products of the Côte d'or and Côte de Beaune as burgundies. Why not restrict the rule on preservation of proper names to given names of persons, countries, companies, etc.?

John Kallaugher
London, England

Thank you for your explanation of the pluralization of nouns ending with "y." It made perfect sense to me.

Now, perhaps you can get the editors of your business section to refer to U.S. Treasury-issued securities collectively as "Treasurys" instead of "Treasuries." This would be in full compliance with your "rule of singularity" (e.g., Germanys vs. Rockies). It's also done correctly by The Wall Street Journal, *certainly the nation's financial newspaper of record.*

It's evident that your editors do pay some attention to you on issues of lexicography. After all, they caved on "Romania."

David K. Hoffman
Washington, D.C.

Shouldn't it read . . . "language can take you only so far"?

Harold Wolfe
Hartsdale, New York

Gifts of Gab

Give a word addict the quickest fix for Christmas: a good specialized dictionary.

Presume your word lover already has a general dictionary propped up on its stand. (Last year, somebody gave me a dictionary stand, which I have not yet put together because my dictionary has no entry under "quick assembly.") Now go one step further, into the lexicons of slang or specialities.

The 1990 word book of the year is the *Third Barnhart Dictionary of New English* (H. W. Wilson, $49) by Robert K. Barnhart, Sol Steinmetz and Clarence L. Barnhart. (They don't call it the Steinmetz dictionary, because

Sol went to Random House as executive editor of Random House dictionaries. Joe Esposito of Random House was just named president of Merriam-Webster, where the *Ninth Collegiate* has been on the best-seller lists for some two hundred weeks running, thus bidding fair to challenge the run of Agatha Christie's thriller *The Mousetrap* on the London stage. Publishers are raiding one another for lexicographers, a nice thing for the language dodge; see *poaching*.)

The Barnhart crowd is not perfect: The *bomfog* citation is only 1976, while the shorthand acronym for Nelson Rockefeller's frequently used "brotherhood of man, fatherhood of God" has been tracked to the 1964 campaign. But the dictionary is a mother lode of recent coinages: look up *body* in the *Barnhart Third*.

You'll find *body art*, coined in 1971 to denote the decoration of the human body "for some esthetic effect"; *body bag*, Saddam Hussein's favorite new threat, coined in 1967; and among others, *body clock*, the jet-setter's internal mechanism; *body dancing*, also called *touch dancing*, which used to be known simply as *dancin'*; *body jewel*, worn on the skin rather than the clothing (you mean you wear nothing in your navel?); *body language*, "the unconscious gestures and postures of the body as a form of communication" (and what does it mean when I stand arms akimbo?); *body mike*, used by singers who cannot understand how Ethel Merman did it; *body shop,* first "an automobile body repair shop" and more recently "a place of prostitution," and *body stocking* and *bodysuit.*

(I looked for *bodily fluids* in vain; this voguish euphemism is applied to blood, spinal fluid, semen, urine, saliva, tears and sweat; if Churchill were alive, we would hear "nothing to offer but *bodily fluids.*")

Eric Partridge may have been the last of the one-man lexies; researchers used to find him at a back desk of the main reading room of the British Museum. His classic English slang dictionary has been updated and condensed by Paul Beale. Partridge's *Concise Dictionary of Slang and Unconventional English* (Macmillan, $35) includes Cockney rhyming slang: *Insects and ants* stands for "trousers," based on the rhyme for "pants"; I presume it had a connection with the American "ants in your pants."

More affordable and accessible is *Slang! The Topic-by-Topic Dictionary of Contemporary American Lingoes, With the Most Up-to-Date, Colorful Expressions From *Computerese *Hollywood *Sports *Pentagonese *Wall Street *Politics *And Much More!* (yes, that's the title) by Paul Dickson (Pocket Books, $9.95 for the 295-page trade paperback). Advertised as "the only contemporary language guide arranged by subject!" (I'll have to talk with Paul about exclamation marks!), it contains such nice differentiations as *Trekker* for older fans of *Star Trek, Trekkie* for younger fans.

A Dictionary of Modern Legal Usage by Bryan A. Garner was published three years ago but has just come out in paperback (Oxford, $15.95 printed right on the back next to the bar code, and a legal book has a right to a bar code). Because the *Oxford Law Dictionary* project has been derailed, this book becomes all the more necessary in the library of Null, Null & Void. Legal eagles need to know the variations of *recusal, recusation, recusement,* dating only to 1958 and noted here to mean "the act of removing oneself as a judge" (though I would add "or prosecutor") and their difference from *recusancy,* "obstinate refusal to comply."

Where shall wisdom be found (Job 28:12)? In *Mene, Mene, Tekel,* a book by Eugene Ehrlich and David H. Scott (Harper & Row, $18.95) about the famous phrases in the King James translation of the Bible. Whether you have *feet of clay* or are willing to *fight the good fight,* fear the *handwriting on the wall* or love *the apple of one's eye*—or even wonder, *"Can the leopard change his spots?"*—you can find etymological pleasure in biblical roots.

In *Is There a Cow in Moscow?* Charles Harrington Elster, author of *There Is No Zoo in Zoology,* does his pronunciation thing again (Collier, $8.95 paperback). Most television reporters say it without the cow, preferring "MAHS-koh," despite the *NBC Handbook of Pronunciation*'s call for MAHS-cow, which is also the choice of most Americans. (Hit the *chill* in *Chilean,* too, and don't get swept up in the elitist "chi-LAY-in," which isn't even Spanish.)

The PBS series on the Civil War was notable for its use of direct quotations from letters of average Americans of that era. The literary pattern was direct, colorful, unself-conscious. The best book of this year that shows the natural language at work is *Diary of a Confederate Soldier: John S. Jackman of the Orphan Brigade* (University of South Carolina Press, $24.95), a quietly moving work edited with an introduction by William C. Davis, the historian who sees the war in microcosm in the brigade of Confederate Kentuckians. It's a fine source for phrasedicks, too: "At last the news came of the surrender of Johnston," Jackman wrote. "We knew then, that we had 'gone up.' " To *go up* meant "to lose"; that sense persists today in the lingo of actors, who use it to mean "to forget lines."

The Word's Gotten Out is the prolific Willard R. Espy's annual entry. (How many more phrases can there be with the word *word* in them?) This cheerful gallimaufry (Potter, $24.95) taught me the eponymous source of *vaudeville:* satiric songs from the Vau (valley) de Vire in Normandy were known in France first as *vaux de Vire,* changed in Paris to *vaux de ville,* which then crossed the Atlantic and played the Palace.

For wordniks with an interest in language controversy, there is *Forked Tongue: The Politics of Bilingual Education* by Rosalie Pedalino Porter (Basic Books, $22.95). She says to teach the kids English because the bilingual programs have been a flop. Dennis Baron, in *The English-Only Question* (Yale University Press, $22.50), traces the history of the U.S. English movement and comes out on the other side, holding that legislation to make English our official language is restrictive and discriminatory. One of these days I ought to take a position on this.

Finally, from the people who bring us the *Chicago Manual of Style,* we have *Style: Toward Clarity and Grace* by Joseph M. Williams (University of Chicago Press, $17.95). "It's harder to begin a sentence well than to end it well," he notes, preferring an opening based on topic rather than transitional metadiscourse (like *And therefore*), evaluation (like *Fortunately*) or time and place (like *Meanwhile, back at the ranch*). He's right, though I would prefer "Beginning a sentence well is harder than ending it well."

Greenhouse Effect

Professor Glenn T. Trewartha of the University of Wisconsin wrote in 1937 about "the so-called greenhouse effect of the atmosphere." He was explaining why he thought the earth was growing warmer, and that is the first use of *greenhouse effect* cited in the *Oxford English Dictionary* supplement.

But note that "so-called," which means that the first use of the phrase came earlier; a scientist who wants to coin a phrase says "which I call," never "so-called." Where, then, did the phrase originate?

Responding to that query in this space, John B. Wells and Kristi Rasmussen of the Bruce Company in Washington, D.C., note that an earlier term for *greenhouse* is *hothouse.* In 1930, the meteorologist W. G. Kendrew wrote a monograph published by the Clarendon Press using this simile: "The atmosphere may be likened . . . to the glass roof and sides of a hothouse. The glass allows the light rays of the sun to enter, but it obstructs the outward passage of the dark heat, into which the light rays are converted, from the inside that has been warmed by the sunshine."

As I get it, shortwave solar radiation penetrates the atmosphere to the earth's surface, where it is transformed into longwaves readily absorbed by carbon dioxide and other gases; that supposedly traps the heat and causes the earth's climate to warm. The theory was first expounded by the physicist John Tyndall in 1861, but he did not clothe it in the catchy *greenhouse* or *hothouse* trope.

The state of the coinage search, then, is: theory by Tyndall, metaphor of the hothouse by Kendrew, change to the greenhouse synonym by Trewartha.

This brings us to another environmental mystery: Who coined *global warming*?

That phrase, which became popular in the 80's, has political legs. Senator Albert Gore Jr. of Tennessee may ride it to the White House, attracting the support of those who believe that unchecked industrialization could lead to climate disaster. But President Bush, in a speech to clean-air enthusiasts, deliberately avoided the controversial term.

When a reporter noted that the President did "not mention the words *global warming* in his speech today," Marlin Fitzwater, White House press secretary, jocularly responded: "I listened to the speech, and I thought I heard it several times. How did I miss it?" The reporter pressed that the President said " 'climate change,' everything but" global warming. Then came the marshmallow guidance: "He believes there is a buildup in CO_2 that contributes to a phenomenon we don't clearly understand . . . but we are working on it."

Global warming is a phrase summarizing an issue that is heating up. This is a want ad for the originator to come forward and stand in the solar radiation.

I would like to think that Professor Trewartha's use of "so-called" reflected his knowledge that greenhouses do not perform their function by means of the mechanism which W. G. Kendrew ascribed to them. Although the earth's relatively high temperature is due to its atmosphere's greater transparency to incoming solar radiation than to outgoing (longer-wavelength) terrestrial radi-

*ation, and although this is commonly referred to as "the greenhouse effect,"
greenhouses themselves (a.k.a. "hothouses") do not achieve their high temper-
atures through the "greenhouse effect."*

Thomas L. Bohan
Portland, Maine

*In fact, an actual greenhouse does not operate by means of the "so-called
greenhouse effect." A real greenhouse works by trapping hot air. Light penetrates the glass roof of the greenhouse, heating the earth that, in turn, heats the
air above it. This hot air expands and becomes less dense. Normally, this heated
air would rise, as in a hot air balloon, but here it is trapped by the walls and roof
of the greenhouse.*

*In the summer, the roof is ventilated so the hot air can escape. Cool air comes
in the open doors of the greenhouse to replace the hot air that escapes through
the ventilation holes in the roof. Ventilation keeps the greenhouse cool regardless of glass's lack of transparency to long wavelength radiation.*

*In summary, a greenhouse works by stopping convection cooling rather than
by stopping radiation loss. Professor Trewartha showed his awareness of this
in his use of the expression "so-called." Despite its unsuitability for greenhouses, he realized that a similar concept might still be appropriate for discussions of global warming.*

Jack Olsen
Hoboken, New Jersey

*You refer to "shortwave solar radiation" in describing the phenomenon whereby
certain of the solar radiation reaching the earth is converted into infrared
radiation (which we experience as heat). I believe that you are guilty [of]
misusing the term "shortwave" in this context.*

*The electromagnetic spectrum (of which all radiant energy emitted by the
Sun is part) extends from very long wavelength, low energy waves referred to
as "radio waves" to the extremely short wavelength, high energy waves called
"gamma rays." While the spectrum is continuous, with no inherent physical
differences along it aside from wavelength and energy (which stand in an inverse
one-to-one relationship with each other, knowing one means knowing the
other), for reasons of descriptive convenience terms such as "radio waves,"
"micro waves," "infrared," "light," "ultraviolet," "x-rays," "gamma rays,"
etc., have been coined to refer to various parts of it. One of the terms used to
refer to a portion of the spectrum is "shortwave," which can be thought of as
near, overlapping or part of the "radio wave" portion of the spectrum, depend-*

ing on how one wants to restrict or expand the latter term. It is this "shortwave" portion of the spectrum that is used for shortwave radio.

The phenomenon that you are alluding to involves the absorption of radiation in the "ultraviolet" and visible light bands of the spectrum by the atmosphere or by the earth's surface, and the subsequent emission of some of the energy absorbed as "infrared" radiation (heat). While it is true that ultraviolet and visible light are of shorter wavelengths than infrared, it seems imprecise to refer to them as "shortwave," as that term is used to refer to an entirely separate part of the spectrum. Solar radiation of the shortest wavelengths, "gamma rays," "x-rays," and some of the shorter wave "ultraviolet" light reach the Earth, but they play no part in the "greenhouse effect," although they do raise other concerns.

Michael S. Duggan
San Francisco, California

Happy Soft Landings

HOW SOFT A LANDING?, headlines the latest newsletter of economic commentary from the Federal Reserve Bank of Cleveland.

Last summer, the president of the Federal Reserve Bank of San Francisco, Robert T. Parry, told a luncheon group that balanced growth "enhances the prospect that we can achieve a *soft landing*," which he defined as "a needed slowdown without a recession. . . . The goal is to have the economy grow at a slow rate relative to its potential to cause the rate of inflation to come down."

Evidently Fed officials find this metaphor useful, and when the Fed offers a trope, economists and business writers haul in the line. "Most economists expect the Fed to ease rates late in the fourth quarter," wrote a Reuters reporter, "as the economy slows further from a *soft landing* scenario into more of a skid."

Gerund economics has long been with us, as in *jawboning* and *smooth sailing,* but the gentle touchdown has become the reigning cliché. What would it be like?

"We've never had one before," writes Caroline A. Baum, a Treasury market commentator for Telerate Systems of Jersey City. "No one knows exactly what it will feel like when we get there. And there is only the most tenuous definition of what it should be."

That is why, says Ms. Baum, "economists turned to a nonsocial science like aeronautics for a term that would adequately describe a maneuver designed to land the economy softly without inflicting damage on itself or its payload."

Her etymological guess is on the mark. *The Times* of London, in a piece about lunar exploration, reported on March 28, 1958, that "Next (in difficulty) would be a *'soft'* (controlled) *landing* by an unmanned vehicle." The same phrase appeared that year in the *Proceedings of the Lunar and Planetary Exploration Colloquium:* "With a *soft landing* on the moon, one might put down a payload of 225 to 800 pounds. . . ."

The first use I can find of the space term in economic lingo was from *Newsweek* on September 17, 1973: "Even if the President succeeds in pulling in the rampaging economy for a *soft landing,* of course, the arrival will be nonetheless bumpy for many."

Now the metaphor is extended into many fields. A commodities dealer in 1985 said he wanted "to organize a *soft landing* for tin." An Israeli scientist announced recently that "We have provided a *soft landing* for a certain number of immigrants." A wine critic for the *Financial Times* complained that some Italian wines "are sparkling and too gassy for my taste" and hoped "to arrange a *soft landing* back into real wine at some point."

Soft landing is from astronautics; its opposite, *crash landing,* along with the toast *happy landings,* is from aeronautics. If the economy does achieve a level of steady, slow growth that lowers inflation while maintaining employment, we can expect space-minded economists to ask: "When do we blast off again?"

Healing Wings

Writers lift metaphors from old speeches and don't always attribute them. This is not plagiarism, only light lifting, but when conscience nags, it's better to slip in an attribution.

I lifted a Woodrow Wilson phrase once in writing a speech for President Nixon: that peace would come "with healing in its wings." It conjures peace as a bird, specifically a dove, and does all a poetic figure of speech should do.

Dutifully, I put the phrase in quotation marks, to show it was not original, but not until twenty years later did I get around to attributing it to Wilson. I closed a political column about the air war in Iraq: "As it succeeds, peace will come, in Wilson's words, 'with healing in its wings.' "

In comes this letter from Simeon M. Berman of Brooklyn: "The phrase originally appeared in the biblical book of the prophet Malachi: 'Unto you that fear My name shall the sun of righteousness arise *with healing in its wings*' " (Malachi 4:2).

If President Wilson were alive, he would explain that no citation is needed for a biblical phrase; listeners are supposed to know it. Sure.

Peace and healing on a wing may be prophetic and presidential, but we often remember phrases because of a lyric and melody.

A synagogue Sabbath hymn commonly sung in the 1930s and '40s, "Come, O Sabbath Day," has in its first line the phrase "Peace and healing on thy wing . . ."

> Matthew H. Simon
> Rabbi
> B'nai Israel Congregation
> Rockville, Maryland

Of course Mr. Berman knows the source for the "healing wings" trope and of course Woodrow Wilson, a Presbyterian schoolmaster, expected his audience to know it too. But untold millions in Britain and America are probably more familiar with it from Charles Wesley's typologized version of Malachi in the third stanza of "Hark, the Herald Angels Sing":

> 3. Hail, the heav'n-born Prince of Peace!
> Hail, the Sun of Righteousness!
> Light and life to all He brings,
> Ris'n with healing in His wings;

> Tom Ferrell
> The New York Times
> Book Review
> New York, New York

You needn't feel bad about borrowing a phrase from Woodrow Wilson without attribution, and then—after waiting twenty years to acknowledge the debt—finding out that Wilson himself had borrowed the phrase (unmistakably biblical) from the prophet Malachi. After all, you were not foolish enough to carve the words in stone, as "Monument Maker" Maya Lin did when she created the Civil Rights Memorial in Montgomery, Alabama.

The photograph in the Times *article shows the words "until justice rolls down like waters and righteousness like a mighty stream" inscribed over the name of Martin Luther King, Jr., who was clearly quoting the prophet Amos—ironically enough, the first of the Hebrew prophets to have a book of the Bible named after him: "Let judgment run down as waters, and righteousness as a mighty stream" (5:24 KJV).*

King's full statement was, "We are not satisfied, we will not be satisfied until justice rolls down like waters and righteousness like a mighty stream." Only when one is aware of the phrase's biblical origin and the context in which King used it can one feel the power that King intended his statement to have.

If King were alive today, "he would explain that no citation is needed for a biblical phrase; listeners are supposed to know it"(Safire).

Frank Salvidio
English Department
Westfield State College
Westfield, Massachusetts

(HED) Folo My Lede (UNHED)

"In the old days," wrote Herb Caen, the San Francisco columnist, "we pounded out the copy with two fingers and hollered 'Boy!' to rush this hot stuff to the composing room. Today you yell 'Boy!' and a girl arrives along with a member of the union grievance committee."

Waxing nostalgic (S. J. Perelman used to wax a fellow named Roth), Mr. Caen reminisced: "Gone the 'Boy!' of yesterday . . . gone with the demon rewrite man with the phone cradled to ear and cigarette burning his lips as he pounds out a perfect, tight, non-editable 'new *lede*' (never *'lead'*) on a fast-breaking story."

Why the spelling *lede*, never *lead*? The flecked beige copy paper and thick pencils are no longer to be found in the newly quiet newspaper offices where typewriters have been banished, and "pounding" the sensually ergonomic keyboard is as frowned on as smoking. The last time I wrote *-30-* to mark the end of a story, a copy individual at the other end of the modem wanted to know, "You don't trust anybody under thirty, or what?"

To remind me of the era of slug-it-slay, I keep a "turtle" in my surge-protected office. (Wouldn't mind a little surge now and then, but the technicians roll their eyes and say that is not meant to be.) The turtle is a heavy table, I think made of lead, on wheels; the valuable industrial artifact came from the composing room when that place was converted from hot lead to cool electronics. Each turtle held a page of type; mine contains the prepared obituary of Fidel Castro, who outlived the preparations for the coverage of his demise.

Note the use twice in the previous paragraph of the word *lead*, which you internally pronounced as if spelled "led," to rhyme with "bread." Of course, if the context were not metallic, but having to do with vanguards as in "new *lead*," you would have pronounced it with a long *e*, to rhyme with "new breed." You are blindingly quick and remarkably accurate at noting context and then pronouncing the word one way or the other; your pronunciation synapse works at twenty-five megahertz (a measurement of computer speed or multitudinous car rentals).

But you wonder: Why do I have to tax my brain to make this fast *led-lead* decision? Wouldn't it be easier if the noun for the metal were spelled the way it sounded (*led*, to rhyme with *dead*) and the noun for the beginning of a newspaper story were spelled the way it is pronounced (*lede*, or *leed*, to rhyme with *deed*)?

Led by the old hands of print journalism, a change toward simplified spelling is taking place. "Enclosed are two clippings using the word *ledes* to mean the introductory part of a news item," writes Janet Kiersted of Houston. One is from a column by Molly Ivins in the *Houston Post:* "Austin is abuzz (I love *ledes* like this: 'Washington is agog,' 'Paris is delighted'). . . ." The other is by Dave Shiflett of the *Rocky Mountain News:* "Horace Greeley . . . launched articles with armor-piercing *ledes.*"

You will not find this spelling in dictionaries; it is still an insiders' variant, steadily growing in frequency of use. But unlike telegraphese (*downhold* expenses, *instick earward*), tightness of space is not the impetus: *Lede* is no shorter than *lead*. What's behind its use?

"I've always heard that *lede* was a deliberate misspelling," says Carl Stepp, associate professor of journalism at the University of Maryland. "The wire-service formula reduced chances that a label of a story would appear in print. *Nulede* was used for 'new lead' because such obvious errors would stand out to the eye; the label could then be removed before the copy hit print."

Lede, as we shall spell it henceforth, was defined as "a noun to refer to the initial summary of the story, or as a verb to instruct the printer what to put first" by Dorothy Colburn, a Nebraska English teacher, in the February 1927 issue of *American Speech,* though she held to the standard spelling. The use of the old verb as a noun was daring: Samuel Johnson stigmatized its use in this new way, in the sense of "first place," as "a low despicable word." (Can you imagine what he'd think of the modern harmless drudges who call his early dictionary "a good *read*"? Perhaps *rede* would improve that vogue word; on second thought, I reckon not.)

As a variant, the spelling *lede* for *lead* dates to the fourteenth century; same with *hed* for *head,* and in the identical pattern, (HED) is now used as a journalistic shortening of "headline," and (UNHED) for "end of headline."

Will *lede* break out of its insider status and find its way into general use? Halfway down an A.P. story, far from the *lede,* is this recent usage in Canada: "Scott Schneider scored a pair of goals to help *lede* the Moncton Hawks to a 5–3 win over the Fredericton Canadiens . . .." In a 1984 *New York Times* article about a Mafia figure: "he provided important new *ledes* and evidence."

To suggest this is becoming standard would be misledeing (that doesn't work; you would have to drop the *e* before the *ing,* and that would change the pronunciation of the *e* before the *d;* stick with *misleading*). But it has earned its place as a variant spelling, soon to overtake the original spelling for the beginning of a news article. That's lexicographic news, but I have learned never to put the story in the lede.

He-e-e-re's George!

Time was, only one introduction was proper for the President of the United States. Nine words, no more, no less: "Ladies and gentlemen, the President of the United States."

Then, during the House Speakership of Tip O'Neill, well-intended but unnecessary words were added: "It is my high honor and personal privilege to introduce the President of the United States."

That broke the tradition. Nobody protested; no President turned to say, "Thanks for the fervent sentiment, Mr. Speaker, but nine words was all it took to introduce Lincoln." Letting the change go by without protest was a mistake.

Listen to the way television anchors do it these days: "Now let's go to the White House and President George Bush." Or "and here from the Oval Office is the President."

We've lost something. Is it because "Ladies and gentlemen" is passé? Is that old phrase soon to be replaced by "Listen up, you men and women"? Perhaps politicians in their introducing mode feel they must inject a personal passion into their introductions, or maybe television announcers are driven to show their individuality or importance through irreverence or informality.

But those nine words had weight. More is less; maybe we should give the traditional introduction another try.

If this appeal is ignored, I have what arms negotiators call a fallback position. The reader may recall a recent piece in this space about the Obsequious Concluding Interrogatory, the rising inflection on a name that is de rigueur among electronic reporters (". . . and that's all from here. *Dan?*").

How about this: "Ladies and gentlemen, the President of the United States. *George?*"

This sometime congressional correspondent enjoyed your piece on introducing the President. I agree entirely that the classic nine words need no elaboration.

I'm not so sure, though, that it was Tip O'Neill who introduced, as it were, a longer form. On Edward R. Murrow's marvelous "I Can Hear It Now" recording that covers the years 1933–1945, Sam Rayburn introduces Harry Truman to his first joint session of Congress as President with these words: "I have the great pleasure and the high privilege of presenting to you the President of the United States." Not precisely O'Neill's language, but awfully close.

> Keith R. Johnson
> New York, New York

Hitting Today's Ceiling

The lexicon of fury needs constant updating. In describing a person in a state of extreme rage—your boss, for example, or a red-faced baby in a highchair—you show your age or tolerance for clichés with *hit the ceiling, go through the roof, split a gut, blow one's stack/cork/gasket,* or *fly off the handle.*

You could turn to Standard English for *exploded,* or call the burning subject *infuriated, enraged, incensed, steamed up;* these are stronger than *angered, aggravated, maddened, ticked off* and much stronger than *piqued,*

peeved, put out. But these words, while all respectable, do not have the vivid imagery of *hitting the ceiling* or the preimplantation *flipping one's wig.*

Today's psychobabble preference is *out of control,* which leaves me cold. A far more expressive expression was the 1980's term *went ballistic.* When that was defined in this space as "driven up the wall in frustration, but not quite *bananas,*" a host of Pentagon readers blew sky-high. (That's from the nineteenth century, when the sky was considered high.) They did not dispute my differentiation of the state of acute anger from a state of craziness (*bananas, bonkers*); *ballistic* is to *kooky* as *up the wall* is to *off the wall.* They faulted my etymology, which held that the word *ballistic* was drawn from "a missile blazing skyward."

The essence of *going ballistic,* says the Gotcha! Gang, is "losing control or guidance." A missile *goes ballistic* when its trajectory or course is independent of any guidance or influence other than the laws of physics. An intercontinental ballistic missile *goes ballistic,* or unguided, when it re-enters the atmosphere; similarly, when a missile fired from a plane does not smartly follow its assigned course to the target, but flies straight as a bullet, the pilot will mutter that it *"went ballistic"* and it's not his fault he's not an ace.

With the onset of strategic-arms reduction, *going ballistic* lost its zing; it's a nonce term, like *gnarly* of the 80's and *fast track* of the 60's. Let us turn to physics and computer technology to help us into the 90's.

"When [Energy Secretary James D.] Watkins was first informed of the added cost," writes *Physics Today,* "he went *'nonlinear.'*"

"The mere mention of multiple entry points," writes David M. Bulman in *Computer Language*, "would cause the typical structured programming advocate to go *nonlinear*."

In *Personal Computing*, Michael Antonoff inserted bracketed definitions in a comment by the Nobel-winning physicist Arno Penzias: "People say things like 'Sorry for giving you a core dump' [for giving you too much information at once] or 'I went *nonlinear*' or 'I blew my circuit' [for not making sense]."

In this new usage, two senses are emerging for *nonlinear:* The first is the classic hit-the-ceiling meaning, the second a deliberate rejection of reasonableness. John Leo, a writer for *U.S. News & World Report* finely tuned to language change, obituated Abbie Hoffman with "A fan of Marshall McLuhan's, he went '*nonlinear*,' turning to arresting images and sound bites, on grounds that rational argument was dead anyway." In post-modern criticism, *nonlinear* has been used to describe literary works, like those that lack a definite plot line.

Ira Flatow of Stamford, Connecticut, who called this term to my attention, explains: "*Linear* means traveling in a straight line; in science and math, it refers to a graph depicting behavior as smooth and predictable. A *nonlinear* graph shows a curving geometric progression as in a tremendous release of energy in a short time. An explosion is *nonlinear*." He adds, "What *impacting* did for the 70's and *cusp* for the 80's, *going nonlinear* may do for the 90's."

Linear thinking is generally a put-down, synonymous with "unimaginative" or "too logical," but *linear programming* tries to deal with the way all parts of a system interact with all the other parts over time. The adjective's opposite, *nonlinear*, can be used for *wild and crazy* or the angrier *explosive;* it beats the dated *hitting the ceiling*, but I wouldn't go ape over it. (Sorry for the *core dump*.)

You missed the "true" meaning of the word "nonlinear." In physics, for example, a linear spring is one which extends in proportion to the force exerted on it. If a one gram force extends the spring one centimeter, then two grams will extend it two cm, five grams five cm, etc. A nonlinear spring is one which does not extend in proportion to the force exerted on it. For example, when the spring stiffness increases with increasing extension, if a one gram force extends the spring one cm, then a four gram force might extend it only three cm. Similarly, when the spring stiffness decreases with increasing extension, if a one gram force extends the spring one cm, a four gram force might extend it six cm.

Therefore, something is "nonlinear" when the response is out of proportion to the stimulus.

John R. Vig
Colts Neck, New Jersey

The origin of "going nonlinear" lies in an important property of a linear system, that its output is proportional to its input. Think of an ordinary hi-fi amplifier. If the input is within design limits, the music sounds fine. If the input is too large, the amplifier operates outside its linear range and "saturates," producing audible distortion. ("Saturation" is another term often used figuratively by us hairy-armed engineers.)

That, and that alone, is the origin of the word "linear." The concept of linear systems and their saturation for large inputs goes back to the 1930s. "Linear" does not refer to smoothness or predictability, as you quoted another reader having said. The usage of the word in the sense of "overload" rings true to a technically educated ear. The extended use you cited, by post-modernist critics, does not.

Myron Kayton
Santa Monica, California

In science and math, linear means exactly a straight line, not smooth or predictable. A quadratic curve is also smooth and predictable. Though a geometric progression is nonlinear, it is also predictable. The sense of nonlinear that is used in the quotations you cited is related more to the new field of chaos theory than to single nonlinear curves. In systems which feature nonlinear feedback, small changes can have corresponding large effects on the behavior of the system, resulting in wildly fluctuating or turbulent systems. In contrast linear systems, including those studied in linear programming, have the characteristic that changes in the state produce (linearly) proportional changes in the behavior of the system.

The best synonym for nonlinear *in the context described by you is* chaotic. *For a very readable account of the beginnings and basics of chaos theory, check out the book* Chaos, Making a New Science, *by James Gleick.*

Andrew S. Dean
Columbus, Ohio

As you say, "the essence of going ballistic . . . is losing control or guidance," but it is nonsense to say that "a missile goes ballistic when its trajectory or course is independent of any guidance or influence other than the laws of physics." Guided or not, the laws of physics always determine what happens; to say "gone ballistic" implies that some special control means—presumably ordinarily present—has become inoperable.

Regarding your explanation that an intercontinental ballistic missile goes ballistic, or unguided, when it re-enters the atmosphere, this also appears incor-

rect, since certain control means then become operable rather than previously, and others not, etc.

Julian H. Bigelow
School of Natural Sciences
The Institute for Advanced
Study
Princeton, New Jersey

You cite "split a gut" as a cliché for rage. In Illinois and Pennsylvania (I have lived 20 years in each) I understand common usage of this phrase to mean "to be convulsed with laughter."

Ellen Chatterjee
Allentown, Pennsylvania

How's That Again?

Sally Quinn, the Washington novelist, keeps an ear tuned to localisms. (She was the first to spot *sneaker,* a Waspism for "secret yen.")

The latest locution she's heard on the Georgetown-to-the-Hamptons circuit is *vujà dé,* pronounced "voo-zhah day." It means "the eerie sense that you never want to be in this place again."

In 1983 a line began appearing in my concert act which was later (April 1984) recorded on an album and on a cable TV special for HBO. Both were titled "Carlin on Campus." Here is the line:

> *I just had . . . it's weird. I just had that little feeling. Do you ever get that funny little . . . that kind of feeling . . . that* vujà dé? *You know? Not* déjà vu. *This is* vujà dé. *This is the strange feeling that somehow, none of this has ever happened before. And then it's gone.*

I know this information will not change the history of locutions, but pride of authorship insisted I tell you.

George Carlin
Los Angeles, California

If You Will

The National—the first all-sports daily newspaper distributed nationwide—was kicked off last month by the ace sportswriter Frank Deford. It appears to be a literate publication; one headline in its first issue over a story about the New York Knicks basketball center Patrick Ewing was "The Center Is Holding," an allusion to William Butler Yeats's poem "The Second Coming."

William A. Henry 3d, a classy writer who runs the section proudly labeled "Press" in *Time* magazine (others lump the print and electronic media together under *media,* but who ever heard of a "full-court media"?), posed this question in his coverage of the kickoff: Will the public support an all-sports daily? *Time* concluded that *"The National* is hard to assess because it is unprecedented—one might say, a whole new ball game."

Now we're into a whole nother problem: *Parrhesia* (accent on the *reezh*), the Greek word for "speaking boldly of something obnoxious," which can be stretched into a second sense of "excuse the joke."

This pre-emptive apology, *one might say,* is a rhetorical balk. It says to the reader, "Look, I'm going to do something egregiously pun-related, or outrageously metaphor-extending or simile-provoking, and you mustn't hold it against me—but for God's sake, notice it."

Some speakers self-conscious about humor, or worried that their audience will miss their hard-earned easy wit, use the internal flag at the conclusion of the thigh-scratcher, like the Fred Allen Senator who would add, "That's a joke, son."

The most familiar I-was-being-funny phrase is *so to speak.* This Britishism, originally meaning "in the vernacular" or indigenous dialect, was an aristocrat's apology for stooping to colorful downstairs language. In the United States, it remains a staple of academics who are cooling their schooling, so to speak. Another form of this elitist elocution, sometimes used self-mockingly, is *as they say,* "they" being the less refined types.

Politicians are *parrhesiacs* (preferable to *parrhesians*), too: *Forgive me, but* was Ronald Reagan's favorite way of sugarcoating some seemingly outrageous pill. This is a variation of *if you will permit me,* or *if you will forgive the pun,* often shortened to *if you will* and put at the end. Some writers are shy not only about making a funny, but also about appearing to be too literate or la-di-da in their apology aforethought. These cringing comedians pretend to be speaking in their writing, and use a transcribed articulated schwa—*uh* or *er*—as in "Some football commentators use language that, er, really came to play." Show off or shut up. Make your joke, or dazzle us with your double meaning, or skip rope on a trope without shyness or deprecation. But enough forelock-tugging and dirt-toeing; spare us protestations of "I know this is awful" or rib-digging reminders of "Get it?"

Wordplay is not foreplay; it may cause a groan or two, but won't provoke a passionate response. Man the ramparts of repartee with stout heart, persevere in your persiflage without shame—it's all good badinage, as it were.

I just had to act out my impulse to add to your family of preemptive apologies "to coin a phrase," which I have always assumed to be another Britishism."

Ray Woolley
Burbank, California

I Like Icon

At an official Soviet diplomatic reception for summiteers in Moscow, guests came up to me on the way out to express their gratitude at having been invited. In Russian-accented English, I replied that it was good of them to come.

Of course, I was not the host. This curious byplay took place because Gennadi I. Gerasimov, the Soviet Foreign Ministry spokesman, and I are look-alikes. We have been pictured side by side in a book entitled *Separated at Birth?* and I am not certain which picture is the one of him. (That will explain why Mr. Gerasimov—balding, stooped, bulbous-nosed—is invariably described in this space as "handsome"; it's a private joke.) We are *icons* of each other.

That uses the word in its original but not its current sense: the Greek *eikenai*, "to be like, resemble, look alike," gave birth to a noun (spelled *eikon*, *ikon*, and most frequently *icon*) meaning "image, material representation." The word was applied to paintings or other artwork of angels or saints in the Eastern Orthodox Church.

The meaning of *icon* has evolved to "revered symbol"; many who hold to a literal interpretation of the Bible apply the Second Commandment—"Thou shalt not make unto thee any graven image," with *graven* meaning "sculptured, carved"—to forbid statues or idols of religious figures, preferring instead representations in paintings, mosaics or bas-reliefs.

Now, in this time of symbol-fascination, *icon* is being worked harder by people who have tired of using *metaphor* as a voguish substitute for *paradigm, model, archetype, standard* or *beau ideal*. My *Times* colleague Karl E. Meyer pointed this out to me in an elevator recently, adding as he stepped off, "Perhaps the stretching of *icon* is a metaphor for our times."

Here come the citations:

"Rep. [Bill] Richardson (D-N.M.) denounced insensitivity of Japanese," reported *Communications Daily* in November, "in buying 'American *icons*' such as Rockefeller Center . . ."

New York *Newsday* identified Michael Milken in December as "junk-bond ex-wizard" and "the leading *icon* of the Booming 80's." A *New York Times* art critic described Roger Shimomura a year ago as an artist who "lavishes affection on the *icons* of American pop." The *International Herald Tribune* reported in October: "Communist protesters, showing no respect for capitalist *icons*, hurled eggs, flour and tomato sauce at Walt Disney Co. chairman Michael D. Eisner . . ."

Flipping through the thousands of uses of this hot new word in the Nexis file, I get the unmistakable message that the word's meaning is now "cherished symbol" extended far beyond religion.

That happened generations ago to a derivative word, *iconoclast*, "destroyer of images." Breakers of icons in the Eastern Church of the eighth century were so identified in English; by the seventeenth century, the term was applied to Protestants in the Netherlands who destroyed church icons.

Iconoclast's meaning was extended because the language needed a synonym for *rebel* and *insurgent* that had a particularly ideological or philosophical quality. When James A. Froude in his 1858 history of England referred to religious reform in writing of "the *iconoclasm* of [Hugh] Latimer," he extended the meaning of *iconoclasm* to a figurative breaking, with *iconoclast* as "the attacker of cherished beliefs and venerated institutions."

One of my favorite characters in American history is William Cowper Brann, known by the title of his collected works: *Brann the Iconoclast.* (I am indebted to Jack Kroll of *Newsweek,* who set me on the character's trail with a cheery "Just remember what happened to Brann the Iconoclast.")

He started a radical, racist, reformist monthly journal in Austin, Texas, in 1891 called *The Iconoclast,* and was roundly—often rightly—denounced as a sensation-mongering scoundrel.

Brann sold his printing presses to William Sydney Porter (O. Henry), who used the name for a humorous weekly. But Brann felt stifled writing editorials for the *San Antonio Express;* he bought back the *Iconoclast* name from Porter (who renamed his own publication *Rolling Stone*). Brann vituperated along until 1898, when he was shot in the back on a Waco street by an incensed reader; the mortally wounded writer whirled, drew his own gun and fired back at the assailant; both died, their sacrifice a testament to the power of iconoclasm in journalism and the importance of printing letters to the editor.

We have been drawn off the subject. To refocus: Why has *icon* suddenly shoved aside *symbol* and *metaphor*? (To put that issue more succinctly: Brother, can you *paradigm*?)

One reason is its adoption by computer users: "Another popular extension to the Macintosh interface," writes a magazine that calls itself *MacUser* (as Zola never said, *M'acUse!*), "is the use of *icons* in programs, which usually takes the form of an *icon* bar or a small window palette of *icons*."

An *icon* in computerese is a picture or symbol that appears on a screen to help the confused and irritated user find the way to a program or a file. The picture is cunningly related to the subject; a command to delete a file may be symbolized by a little wastebasket.

The root of this can be found in semiotics, the theory of the relationships of signs in language. In this ever-flagging field of study, very hot now in Eastern colleges, an *icon* is a sign chosen to stand for its object because it looks like, or triggers an association with, the thing it represents.

For example, assume you cannot read as you drive past a couple of gas stations. One sign shows a star; unless you are a Texan familiar with "the Lone Star State," you would not quickly associate the symbol with the name Texaco. Another sign shows a shell; you know immediately that means Shell Oil Company; in fact, many stations use the symbol without the name. The shell, more than the star, is an *icon* in semiotics; it triggers an association with the name, which in turn stands for the company.

What do semioticists call this quality, so desirable in a sign? *Iconicity,* and here is how they use it in a sentence: "Spoken language contains some sounds," wrote Charles W. Morris in his 1946 semiotics text, "which are clearly iconic ('onomatopoetic'); the extent of its *iconicity* is a difficult matter to determine."

Difficult for him, but easy for me now: *Crunch,* for example, is a word coined to imitate the sound of an icebreaker doing its thing, and I would give it an iconicity factor of 90 percent. That trivialization of a big concept will infuriate semioticians, already turning blue at being mislabeled "semioticists," on the analogy of *ethicists,* in the previous paragraph.

Let 'em holler, or more to the point, gesticulate frenziedly; on the menu of my screen is a little figure of a man in a cowboy hat, gun in hand, twisting to return fire. That is an icon of a language maven.

My home was in Waco, Texas, and Brann was shot on the street there. Before he died, he shot his assailant. This all happened across the street from my father's place of business and he saw it all. Shortly thereafter my father got Brann's work published, and that's the book Brann the Iconoclast.

Lois Keane
Bon Air, Virginia

I am sending you a Xerox copy of Chapter 6, on "Iconicity," from the 2nd edition (1989) of my 1979 book, The Sign & Its Masters.

Most of my colleagues—I have never seen a blue one—call themselves "semioticians," but a minority prefer "semioticists."

Onward and upward in your pursuit of Paradigms Lost and Paradigms Regained,

> Thomas A. Sebeok, Chairman
> Distinguished Professor of
> Linguistics and Semiotics
> and Professor of
> Anthropology
> Indiana University
> Bloomington, Indiana

I don't think under any definition can you and Gennadi Gerasimov be considered icons of each other. Look-alikes, yes, maybe even doubles, but not icons.

The word you are looking for is Doppelganger. *That is a much better description of the idea.*

> George Rowell
> New York, New York

Should you sponsor a competition for maximum iconicity, I nominate "SPLAT," the approximate sound perceived upon stopping a wet snowball with one's ear.

> Raymond Brandes
> Newark, Delaware

In Harm's Way

Both President Bush, a former Navy pilot, and Secretary of State James A. Baker 3d, a former marine, often use the phrase *in harm's way* to describe the position of members of American armed services in and around Saudi Arabia. That's not surprising: It's a naval term.

The phrase is rooted in its opposite: *out of harm's way,* coined by the English divine Thomas Fuller before 1661: "Some great persons . . . have been made sheriffs, to keep them out of harm's way." Apparently the sheriff's job was a political plum, not then dangerous.

In November 1778, the American naval captain John Paul Jones wrote to Le Ray de Chaumont, the French official in charge of assigning ships: "I wish to have no Connection with any Ship that does not sail fast, for I intend to go in harm's way." He was assigned a not-so-fast merchantman that he rebuilt and named the *Bon Homme Richard,* honoring Benjamin Franklin (*Poor Richard's Almanack*). Jones sailed in the way of the British frigate *Serapis,* and lashed his smaller warship to the larger in naval warfare's most memorable hand-to-hand battle; after the British ship surrendered, the battered *Bon Homme Richard* sank.

James Bassett, a press aide to Fleet Admiral William F. Halsey and later to Richard M. Nixon, chose *Harm's Way* as the title of his 1962 novel about naval action in the Pacific during World War II; John Wayne starred in the 1965 movie, *In Harm's Way,* in which the make-my-day line was "Sir, I have not yet begun to fight."

The hoary phrase has more power than the bureaucratic "in the face of impending hostilities."

"Is Concerned" Is Concerned

"I know that I am shouting into the breeze here, as far as what we're doing now," said former Secretary of State George P. Shultz to Stanford alumni about drug legalization, "but I feel that . . ."

George Carlin, the comedian and language student, clipped that item and sent it in with this comment: "Leaving aside for the moment the rest of the Secretary's language, I call your attention to a sin of omission which [sic] I have encountered more and more frequently in recent months: the dropping of the words 'is concerned' from the phrase 'as far as—is concerned.' "

You're right, George (Carlin, not Shultz). I have been keeping a dossier on this. My *Times* colleague Maureen Dowd (who slipped the old dialect word *tetchy* into a recent story, which was wisely not changed to *touchy* by copy editors) wrote last year about candidate Bush: "The Vice President said there was a double standard in the way Republicans and Democrats were viewed as far as class."

A reader, Ian Graham of Harvard's Peabody Museum, called her to task for leaving out "is concerned."

Is the phrase *as far as* turning into a preposition meaning *as for*? Richard Nixon was quoted as saying about former Israeli President Golda Meir, "Now, as far as Mrs. Meir—here's the essence of what happened." Jimmy Carter did the same thing: "As far as any investigation of members of Congress, however, I am not familiar with that at all."

But it would be wrong. *As for* and *as to* are good, short substitutes for *as far as . . . is concerned,* but the use of half of the last expression is not the same. The fact that all three begin with *as* does not make the two prepositions the same as the subordinating conjunction; all the more reason to stay alert to the easy confusion.

I know not what course others may take (wrote St. George Tucker to the biographer William Wirt, attributing to Patrick Henry the construction that later became famous), but as for me—or as far as I am concerned—give me *is concerned* or stop giving me *as far as*.

As for a good, short substitute for as far as . . . is concerned, *look no further than the last two letters of your last name.*

David Bernklau
Brooklyn, New York

Isn't It Rich?

"Don't tax you, don't tax me," goes the doggerel that former Senator Russell Long used to enjoy quoting. "Tax that feller behind the tree."

After months of peering and pointing, "that feller" turns out to be *the rich*. Who are they?

Some statisticians arbitrarily choose a family income of $80,000 a year as the affluence line (which I have just coined on the analogy of the poverty line), but magazines like *Forbes* and *Fortune* prefer making judgments of wealth on the basis of what people have rather than what they earn: $260 million is *Forbes*'s cutoff this year for its "richest 400" list, though most people would apply the word *rich* to any old multimillionaire.

(There's a word that's fading fast in an era of *megabucks*. A nuance of its meaning is expressed in this joke: "My friend Sam is a *multimillionaire*." "No, Sam may be a millionaire, but he's no *multimillionaire*. How much does he have in cash?" "Ten thousand dollars." "You're right—he's a *multimillionaire*.")

In the Depression years of the early 30's, *the rich* was a term used by socialist and populist politicians as an epithet, especially in promoting progressive taxation. The first citation of the slogan *soak the rich* is from James P. Warburg's 1935 book, *Hell Bent for Election,* in which President Franklin D. Roosevelt was charged with "being 'clever' when he tried to steal Huey Long's thunder by suddenly coming out with his *'soak the rich'* tax message."

The use of quotes around the phrase suggests an earlier usage, perhaps by Huey Long, the Louisiana Governor, whose slogan was "Every Man a King"; Joe Klein of *New York* magazine informs me that the phrase was associated with Fiorello La Guardia's campaigning in the early 30's. If anyone can find a specific citation earlier than 1935, send it in; phrasedick immortality awaits.

When turned into a compound adjective, the slogan becomes an attack on the attack: A *soak-the-rich scheme* uses the phrase as a device to damn those who would unduly penalize the wealthy.

What's the difference between *rich* and *wealthy*? Webster's New World Dictionary holds that *rich* "is the general word for one who has more money or income-producing property than is necessary to satisfy his normal needs; *wealthy* adds to this connotations of grand living, influence in the community, a tradition of richness."

Perhaps that synonymy is true when the words are used as adjectives—a *rich* family has to wait until its money ages before it becomes a *wealthy* family—but when used by politicians as nouns, *the wealthy* is not nearly as rich a target as *the rich*. You never hear of "the filthy *wealthy*," or "get-*wealthy*-quick schemes." In any populist coupling of the *needy* and the *greedy*, it's the *rich*—not the *wealthy*—that gives a stump orator more polemical satisfaction. Today, *the wealthy* are spoken of with less of an envious sneer than *the rich*.

Affluent is a bookish term, given a high-domed academic air by John Kenneth Galbraith's *Affluent Society,* and its subsequent alliterative use in "the age of affluence." No sloganeer would offer "soak the affluent" (although "marinate the affluent" might go as a bumper sticker in some hypereducated, low-income areas along the Charles River).

How do rich people describe their own economic circumstances? Out of modesty, a repugnance for ostentation or a desire to hide from the revenooers, most would demur from any identification as being *rich* or *wealthy,* reserving those words for those nouveau-riche showoffs down the street with the *opulent* lifestyle. The preferred admission, rather than assertion, of high economic status is "I'm *well-to-do."* A *New York Times* editorialist, sensing the political heft in the harsh word *rich,* wrote of the budget agreement: "*Well-to-do* families will pay more for Medicare, setting a constructive precedent."

Curiously, *rich* has long had a slang sense of "paradoxical, rich in irony" (using *rich* there to mean "full of, abundant in"). Stephen Sondheim's lyric to "Send in the Clowns" begins "Isn't it rich," meaning "catch this irony" or "isn't this something to make you shake your head in amused dismay."

Although *rich* is a term wriggled away from by those in the moneyed class who are *loaded* (a slang term that carries a connotation of admiration), the same *rich* is mandatory in all commercials for coffee. Copywriters can leave out *full-bodied* and try any number of synonyms for *delicious,* but skip *rich* and the client is sure to invite in a new agency. (The Squad Squad will find "invite in" redundant, but it is an acceptable shortening of "to ask someone to come in and deliver a presentation to a client that expects *rich* in every commercial.")

Rich Soak

In our etymological dig for the coinage of the phrase *soak the rich,* one member of the Nitpickers' League argued that only words, not phrases, could be the object of etymology.

More helpful were two Lex Irregs who nailed down the coinage. Joe Klein of *New York* magazine cites Thomas Kessner's book *Fiorello H. La Guardia and the Making of Modern New York,* which reports that on March 10, 1932, the fiery Congressman from New York took the floor of the House to blast a tax bill and to add his own formula: "I am simply going to say, 'Soak the rich' "; he was denounced in *The New York Times* for those "wild and whirling words."

David Shulman, an avid phrasedick, comes up with the earliest known citation of the phrase as the compound adjective that populist politicians came to know and love, with this headline from the April 2, 1932, *Literary Digest:* "The 'Soak-the-Rich' Drive in Washington."

Re: Isn't It Rich?
Sam has fallen from his yacht and can't swim.

SAM: *Help, help!*
LIFEGUARD: *Hang on, hang on!*

Once ashore, the lifeguard props Sam up against the lifeboat.

LIFEGUARD: *Are you comfortable?*
SAM: *I make a nice living.*

Bob Gordon
Emerald Isle, North Carolina

Izationization

An ugly but necessary new noun is being floated out today: *izationization,* "the creation of lengthy nouns out of shorter words by adding *-ization.*"

Events in the Persian Gulf (CBS has stopped calling it "the Arabian Gulf," reflecting loss of prestige by Saddam Hussein or second thoughts by Dan Rather) have churned up a couple of *-ization* formations that need work.

One is *Lebanonization.* This tongue twister was coined in June 1983 by Shimon Peres, Israel's Labor party leader, on the analogy of *Vietnamization* as Israel removed its troops from Lebanon: "Our policy should be maximum Lebanonization of the territory and minimum permanent Israeli army presence." In that sense, *Lebanonization* was a good thing—returning Lebanon to the Lebanese, much as Americans wanted to turn the fighting of our 1960's war over to our South Vietnamese allies.

However, the Israeli withdrawal was followed by what seems to be a permanent state of civil war among the religious, ethnic and political factions within that unhappy country; as a result, the word gained a pejorative sense of "unending internal strife, fueled by arms sales from abroad." Speaking in San Salvador in 1985, Archbishop Arturo Rivera y Damas sadly said of his country: "Here is where we reach the theme of Lebanonization."

By 1989, Mary Curtius of the *Boston Globe* was using the changed sense in reporting from the West Bank of the Jordan River: "Israeli analysts now frequently refer to what they call the *Lebanonization* of the territories, a label that means that all semblance of restraint, of playing by rules, is breaking down." Mikhail S. Gorbachev joined in: "Let's be frank," he told a 1990 party plenum of his worry about Boris N. Yeltsin's calls for decentralization. "The country could really be threatened by Lebanonization with all the well-known consequences."

The postwar struggle within Iraq put the word in its negative sense over the top. In Washington last month, Laurie Mylroie (pronounced "mill-roy") of the Harvard Center for Middle Eastern Studies urged President Bush to establish contacts with dissidents in Iraq quickly: "The United States can constructively influence the situation in Iraq without settling for its Saddamization or Lebanonization." Otherwise, she warned, "Either Saddam will re-establish control, or you'll have a Lebanonization."

Bush Administration spokesmen used the word to justify a sudden hands-off policy, leaving vulnerable to Saddam Hussein the Kurdish and Shiite opponents that Mr. Bush had urged to revolt. (In a stunning double redundancy, President Bush said, "I do not want to see us get sucked into the internal civil war inside of Iraq." *Internal* made *civil* redundant, with *inside* doubling the redundancy; the Squad Squad is beside itself.)

"The new threat-word is *Lebanonization*," A. M. Rosenthal wrote in *The New York Times*. This term was not the same as *Balkanization,* a much older word. I asked my colleague for his differentiation.

"*Lebanonization* refers to the activity within a single country," he replied, "so riven with religious and other disputes that the country becomes impossible to govern. Lebanon was divided that way and became subject to foreign invasion by the Palestinians and then the Syrians.

"*Balkanization* means taking a country and splitting it into parts," Mr. Rosenthal continued, "into separate countries. In relation to Iraq, it means taking away areas to form Kurdistan and perhaps another country in the south. That would turn Iraq into three countries—they could make seven out of it, for all I care—but such *Balkanization* is not the same process as the internal struggle that causes *Lebanonization*."

(The historian Arnold J. Toynbee used the British spelling when he explained in 1922 that "The word *Balkanisation* . . . was coined by German socialists to describe what was done to the western fringe of the Russian Empire by the Peace of Brest-Litovsk.")

You may think this clearly pins down the meaning of *Lebanonization,* but a complication arises: Because the word is such a mouthful, posing a constant danger to broadcasters, a conspiracy is afoot to compress it. Bashir Gemayal, the President-elect of Lebanon who was assassinated before he could take office, spoke in 1982 of what was transcribed as "the re-*Lebanization*" of the mountainous area occupied by the Druse. Perhaps this was an error in transcription, but Zbigniew Brzezinski wrote in 1989 of "Iran even facing the danger of internal *'Lebanization.'*" After Saddam Hussein's military defeat, the Associated Press reported that Yemen's United Nations Ambassador, Abdalla al-Ashtal, complained that everybody said "they don't want *Lebanization* of Iraq," but actions were encouraging it.

Look, Excellency and Zbig, we're not talking about a country called "Leban"; if you are going to use the overused verb, it requires the full *Lebanonization.*

Now we take our leave of Beirut-causes and turn to the second example of izationization: What do we call the process of taking the salt out of water? The plants to do that were in the news when they were endangered during the recent hostilities.

"*Desalination* or *desalinization*?" writes Ben Bradlee, executive editor of *The Washington Post.* "Bush uses the former, Baker the latter. Lead us out of this minefield!"

We start with our gal *sal,* Latin for our noun "salt," and the adjective *saline,* the pronunciation of its first syllable switching to "SAY"; a *saline solution* is frequently a fancy way of saying "salt water." In 1904, when the notion of taking the salt out of sea water was first seriously bruited about, the verb was the simple *desalt.* In 1949, *desalinate* appeared, the function of a device called a *desalinator;* the author Arthur Koestler picked up the term and applied it to the purposely bland: "The blond, good-looking young man with his neutral, 'de-salinated' features."

People in the desalting dodge have named their trade group the International Desalination Association, and its director, Patricia A. Burke, says that when faced with the Bradlee question, "we prefer the shorter term *desalination.*"

I prefer the even shorter verb *desalt,* and would use the gerund *desalting* for the process, with the noun *desalter* to describe the machine or the person who operates it. We have no good reason to keep lengthening the terms from *desalination* to *desalinization* and ultimately to *desodiumchloridization.*

Must the *-ize* always have it? No; the *-ization* suffix, so readily used for turning a noun into the action, condition or result of making, should be resisted when a shorter route is at hand. Izationization is a bad habit; you can even forget the word.

Nervous broadcasters will have to negotiate the shoals of *Lebanonization* in all its stutter-inducing syllabification until a nation or region with a shorter name becomes the example of ceaseless hostility. And I suppose we'll have to prefer the familiar *decentralization* that Mr. Yeltsin seeks to an unfamiliar *decentraling.*

But if you don't like the *colorization* of old movies, complain instead about *coloring;* if you can't get your mouth fixed for needless extensions of brackishness, say *desalting.* (Become *desalinization-free!*)

"Look, Excellency and Zbig, we're not talking about a country called 'Leban,'" you say.

True, but we are *talking about a country called "Liban," which is both the French name and what the Lebanese had on their banner as their athletes marched into the Olympic Stadium.*

"Libanization" would therefore be echt, *so "Lebanization" isn't so far wrong. Furthermore, the inhabitants of that beautiful mixed-up country are Lebanese, not Lebanonese, thank God.*

> Arthur J. Morgan
> New York, New York

The Squad to Combat American Geographical Ignorance (SCAGI) is really beside itself this time.

Lebanon in reality is *also known as* Liban *by the French, who governed it by mandate between the two World Wars.*

Therefore, Libanization—or the Anglicized Lebanization—is perfect. Your apology is awaited by Zbig and His Excellency the Yemenese Ambassador.

> Bruce C. Haxthausen
> New York, New York

You suggest that the compressed form was perhaps "an error in transcription." A better hypothesis: Mr. Gemayel was a Maronite Christian, hence his language of wide intercourse was—I surmise—French. Now, Lebanon in French is le Liban. *The only way to express the term "Lebanonization" in French is to say* rélibanisation. *I do not know whether Mr. Gemayel spoke in French or in English at the time of his interview, but I bet that* le Liban *was at the back of his mind when he spoke to foreign journalists.*

The same hypothesis can be tried on Mr. Brzeziński. His Polish is very good indeed for a person who came across the Atlantic at the age of about 13 (if I remember correctly). Next time, instead of "Zbig," try "Zbyszku," "Zbysiu," or, if you want to be formal, "Panie Zbyszku" on him. Now, "Lebanon" in Polish is Liban. *This leads to the obligatory* Libanizacja; *and from there, there is but a step to the "Lebanization" of 1989.*

I fully support your suggestion that we should avoid -ization *whenever possible. I do it, however, with my heart. My head, and the experience of the last 2,200 years or so, tells me that we'll have to put up with the finalization of the hybrid suffix's victory. In Greek verbs, the suffix* -izō *has been the most productive one, certainly since the Hellenistic Period. Its cousin* -ismos *made a spectacular career (see* communism *and* sexism). *When* -izō *was adopted into imperial, and, later, Christian Latin (see* baptizo), *the whole semi-civilized world, in space and time, became its habitat. The hybrid Greek-Latin formation* -izatio *followed suit: We have* baptizatio *in an early manuscript of the Gospel of Mark (10:38), and in a fourth-fifth-century text.* Thesaurizatio *is attested in Pseudo-Augustine, that is, let's say, by the late fifth century. And so it goes. There is no hope. Not from the Russians (see* kollektivizacija). *Is it worth enquiring how one says* -ization *in Chinese?*

Still, I root for you, as one should for a defender of a lost, but just, cause.

Ihor Sevcenko
Department of the Classics
Harvard University
Cambridge, Massachusetts

I am strongly opposed to "desalinization." To me, the "-iza-" element implies a process moving in a particular direction—in the case of "salinization," the process is the addition of salt. "Desalinization" might be appropriate to describe an interruption or reversal of that salt-adding process, but using it to describe the removal of salt from a steady-state solution seems incorrect. There are other words that are often misused in the same way: One who gets off a vessel does not "disembark" but "debarks," and one who loses the right to vote is not "disenfranchised" but is "disfranchised." I vote for "desalting."

J. William Doolittle
Washington, D.C.

I am a "techie" according to my actuary lady-friend and her colleagues. That may be a new one for you. It means a scientist or engineer who can perhaps tie his shoelaces but is unlikely to balance a checkbook or prepare a proper tax return.

Be that as it may (or might), I know quite a bit about izations *and* izationization *(love that one!).*

Thus, when you come up with "desalting" versus "desalination" versus "desalinization," you are all wet (too much salt, obviously). These three terms, silly as it seems, are technically different.

"Desalting" refers to removing salt from something containing same.

"Desalination" refers to making something less salty than it was, not necessarily by removing salt (the salt could, for example, be chemically converted).

"Desalinization" refers to undoing or reversing a process by which something became salty, as opposed to merely making the thing less salty or just removing the salt.

> S. Berliner
> Sea Cliff, New York

Your preference for desalted *comes dangerously close to a* reduction ad absurdem. *Consider some other revisions in this vein. We could have: sanited, hogened, pasteured, mesmered, steriled, normaled, rationaled, customed, colinied, perhaps even realed.*

Admit it. Sometimes the ize *have it.*

> Peter A. Corning
> Palo Alto, California

Wasn't it after the "Destalinization" of Russia by Khrushchev that fewer people worked in "desalt" mines?

> Byron (Mike) Noone
> Garden City South, New York

Judge Crater Found, Vegged Out

"You ask about Marlin," George Bush wrote, kidding around earlier this year about his press secretary, Marlin Fitzwater. "He is a serious contender for the coveted Scowcroft Award. . . . He needs to improve his record on sleeping in important meetings. The Scowcroft Award gives extra points for he/she who totally craters, eyes tightly closed, in the midst of meetings."

This citation from *The Times* was sent in by Elizabeth N. Tate of New Haven with a shocked paraphrase of Little Red Riding Hood: "Grammar, what big teeth you got!" It was tucked in a file labeled "virgule" for its replacement of *one* with *he/she*. The President's jocular note was cross-filed under "slobject," my code word for "sloppy use of object," because the President should have used *him/her;* in the phrase "for him/her who totally craters," the slashed pronoun is the object of the preposition "for," which requires a *him* or *her,* and is not the subject of the clause "who totally craters," which would lead the misuser into *he* or *she.* But my filing system flopped because I was looking for the presidential use of *crater* as a verb. Took hours to find, a loss of time I am amortizing with this paragraph on virgules and slobjects.

The *crater* hunt was inspired by this sentence in Clifford Irving's novel *Trial:* "I've known enough liars so that one more won't *crater* me." (I would say this thriller makes a *good read* but recoil from that locution because every review now includes "a good *read,*" "a terrific *read*" or "spiritually edifying but not much of a *read.*" Here's a slogan to help you avoid reviewerese: "Better dead than *read* as a noun." I don't know if Irving's book makes any sort of *read* at all, but it's a far more satisfying courtroom drama than Scott Turow's second squeezing, and it includes slang verbs like *crater.*)

Our search begins in ancient Greece, where *kerannynai* meant "to mix"; from that root came *crater,* a bowl in which wine and water were mixed by Greek partygoers who wanted wine on the rocks but didn't know how to freeze water. The bowl's shape interested speakers of English, who began using it in the early seventeenth century to describe the bowl-shaped depression at the top of a volcano, and about a century ago to describe the holes caused by meteorites crashing into other heavenly bodies.

That gives us the noun *crater*, which was verbified by scientists studying candlepower in 1884, the verb meaning "to form a crater or hollow," in "This arrangement is found to have given a better light than the solid rod, which is apt to 'crater' or become hollow in its burning end." But whence the slang verb *to crater*, now freely used by Presidents and novelists?

My speculation is that *to crater* is an extension of the slang verb *to crash*, one sense of which is "to fall sound asleep." In his *Dictionary of American Slang*, Stuart Berg Flexner cited a 1973 usage from *Family Circle* magazine—"I heard about this place and hoped maybe I could crash here for a day or two"—and defined this intransitive *crash* as "to sleep or reside at a place, typically for a single night or just a few days without an invitation." Another sense was added by college students: "to pass out drunk," a synonym for *zonk out, cork off, get lost on the sauce.*

Thus, our search for Judge Crater (an obscure allusion to a New York jurist named Joseph Force Crater, whose disappearance in 1930 caused great media interest but remains unexplained) leads to this sense of the intransitive slang verb *to crater:* "to fall sound asleep," resulting in the presidential granting of the Scowcroft Award, a prize apparently drawn from a crisis-management occasion in which Brent Scowcroft, the national security adviser, did not impress his boss with a state of appropriate alertness.

In its transitive state (taking an object), as in Clifford Irving's "won't crater me," the verb can mean "destroy, devastate" or "cause to veg out."

That brings us to a related term that puzzles Barbara Levine, a teacher in Hastings-on-Hudson, New York. "I have been stewing over a certain expression—*vegging out*—and wonder why our noble vegetables are so maligned," she writes. "I suppose it comes from the term *to vegetate*, 'to exist with little mental and physical activity.' While I know that there are people who lead dull lives and sit on couches becoming potatoes, why the association with vegetables?"

Ms. Levine is apparently struck by the current perversion of the Latin word *vegetare*, "to animate," from *vegetus*, "lively," and *vegere*, "to rouse, excite." These reflect the opposite of the current meaning of *to veg out*.

Blame it on Colley Cibber, a spirited British playwright and actor unjustly deprecated by the literary biggies Pope and Johnson. Cibber turned the word's meaning around in his 1740 *Apology for His Life* by coining *vegetate* in this line: "The man who chuses never to laugh . . . seems to me only in the quiet state of a green tree; he vegetates, tis true, but shall we say he lives?" His meaning was "to be growing, but unthinking; to be alive but not lively."

That led to the current slang meaning of the noun *vegetable:* "someone who is mindless, out of it." The story is told of the young woman dining out with a group of much older men, who is asked by the waiter for her meat order and replies, "Roast beef." Waiter: "And for your vegetables?" "They'll just have to order by themselves."

Colley Cibber may be underrated, but he was no innovator. And if you're trying to give him credit for the modern meaning of vegetable, *you really should look further back. Think of Marvell's "My vegetable love should grow / Vaster than empires, and more slow," for example.*

As for your joke about vegetables ordering at the table, the far darker original joke is this riddle: "What's the hardest part about eating vegetables? The wheelchairs." But I realize that the Times *is a family newspaper . . .*

David Galef
University, Mississippi

Keep Your Shirt On

"Mild in public, but when the talk turned serious," reported NBC's John Cochran, "Mexico's President Salinas gave Vice President Quayle what one U.S. official called 'unshirted hell.' "

The subject was the abduction, or capture, of a Mexican doctor who is thought to be involved in the murder of a United States narcotics agent. "President Salinas expressed to me his strong displeasure" was the way Vice President Quayle put it; translated from the diplomatese, that is fair to characterize as *unshirted hell.*

Just what is this form of hell, and where does it come from?

In slang, a shirt—especially one in the process of being taken off—is a garment that signifies vexation or hot temper. In Hotten's 1859 slang dictionary, *shirty* is defined as "ill tempered or cross," with this explanation: "When one person makes another in an ill humour he is said to have 'got his shirt out.' " The earliest nineteenth-century uses are British, and P. G. Wodehouse in a 1934 Jeeves novel had a character say, "But don't tell me that when he saw how shirty she was about it, the chump didn't back down?" *Shirtiness* is close to *testiness,* far from *godliness.*

Somewhere—I cannot find it in my vast library of slang—there must be a link between *shirty* and *unshirted.* The first appearance of *unshirted* comes in modification of *hell;* The *Baltimore Sun* is cited by the *O.E.D.* supplement as the source, in 1932, of "When he proposed certain policies on prohibition ... he was given what is known in rural districts hereabouts as 'unshirted hell.' "

The picture comes to mind of a person tearing his shirt off to castigate another; a second possibility is to berate someone whose shirt has been taken off, as if to receive a whipping. The first picture is more likely the source; the unshirted one is angry and ready to give hell to the clothed recipient.

The phrase has more zing than *to give someone a hard time,* or *to give him what for* and has a populist connotation that *tongue-lashing* lacks. The rural American roots make it especially useful to political figures; one predecessor to the unidentified source on the Quayle staff quoted by the NBC reporter is Henry A. Kissinger, who wrote in Volume II of his memoirs: "I've been catching unshirted hell every half-hour from the President who says we're not tough enough." (I'm looking forward to Henry's writing the first unauthorized autobiography.)

In post–Civil War politics, the *bloody shirt* was a symbol of service in the armed forces, or an evocation of old sectional hatred; *to wave the bloody shirt* was to ask for a vote on the basis of wartime alliances or emotions. The origin may be in the account of the abolitionist James Baird Weaver in the 1850's, about how he acquired the stained and shredded linen of a preacher who had been flogged for inflaming slaves: "I waved it before the crowds and bellowed: 'Under this bloody shirt we propose to march to victory.' "

A shirt, then, is a kind of flag: that is why, in keeping calm, you keep your shirt on.

I have always thought "Keep your shirt on" referred to John L. Sullivan, who used to frequent the local saloon wherever he was, and invariably some potvaliant bystander would think he could take on the champ. Apparently it was the custom to fight bare-torso, so off came the shirt. If the would be-warrior had any real (sober) friends, they'd shout "keep your shirt on!"

Gay Bonollo
Mount Dora, Florida

Know-Nothing

Defending the National Endowment for the Arts from its critics, Senator Edward M. Kennedy declared that the American people would "reject the know-nothing censorship the right wing is trying to impose."

He may not have realized it, but in selecting *know-nothing* as his adjective, the Senator evoked an Americanism that has resonated with bitterness throughout the last century of American history.

In her fascinating and insightful biography of Anna Ella Carroll, *Neither Heroine Nor Fool,* published by Kent State University Press, Professor Janet L. Coryell traces the connections of the foremost female pamphleteer of the Civil War era to the American party, whose members styled themselves the Know-Nothings and later split to join the old Democrat and new Republican parties. (I used Anna Carroll as a character in a historical novel; this tempestuous and underestimated supporter of Presidents Fillmore and Lincoln deserves this scholarly treatment.)

In another recent book, *The Party of Fear,* the author, David H. Bennett, quotes Miss Carroll as excoriating "poll domination by drunken aliens, the intrigue and rowdyism of raw foreigners." This is Know-Nothingism at its purest and most troubling: reviling the immigrant, arousing the resentment of the majority against the minority.

Over the past century, the meaning of the adjectival phrase *Know-Nothing* changed from "anti-alien" and "nativist" to a less politically charged but equally insulting "stupid," which was probably what Senator Kennedy had in mind. For a while, it appeared that *nativist* would replace *Know-Nothing* in histories, but the emergence of *Native American* as a replacement for *American Indian* scotched that; we now see *Know-Nothing* used in scholarly circles, capitalized, to refer to anti-immigrant and racist movements in our Middle Period, and used by politicians today, uncapitalized, with only the "stupid, mindless" sense.

Why would any political party adopt such a name? The answer was in the signal given by members, when asked about their affiliation: With one index finger, the Know-Nothing would point to his eye, touch the side of his nose, and make a circle with his finger and thumb. That was Eye-Nose-Nothing, a refusal to reveal political leanings that was the mark of conspiracy, not of stupidity.

Larger Than Life

Charlton Heston was on the phone. "I'm having an argument with Michael Korda about the copy on the dust jacket of my book, *Beijing Diary*," he began, in the most sonorous voice you ever heard. Mr. Korda, author of *Success, Power* and other books (he hasn't used "Happiness" yet—presumably, a nonselling title), is editor in chief of Simon & Schuster, and not a man to lightly joust with on jacket copy.

"It's about *larger than life*," said Chuck Heston, a longtime Lexicographic Irregular. "He wants to refer to 'his *larger-than-life* personality.' I say that characters I've played—Michelangelo, Henry VIII, Cardinal Richelieu—are real people, dominant personalities certainly, but not 'larger than life.' The phrase carries a sense of unreality, of fiction."

I noodled that around. Did he ever play anybody that might be called larger than life?

"Long John Silver," he said, his voice taking on a piratical quality. "He was a legend—a larger-than-life figure."

Let's see how the alliterative attributive phrase is being used elsewhere. In the *Los Angeles Times,* Jonathan Freedman writes, "A larger-than-life Buddha image sits on an altar." That is a literal, unadorned use of the phrase: Buddha was a person; the statue is larger than *life-size,* the source of the phrase; hence, it is *larger than life[-size].* Same with the description in *The Independent* of London of a television presentation at the Richard Nixon Presidential Library in Yorba Linda, California: "ask any question and Mr. Nixon, larger than life on screen . . ."

Now extend the metaphor. A publishing executive, Linda Grey of Bantam Books, was quoted in 1985 in the *Los Angeles Times* (a publication especially fond of this locution) as saying: "I think [Hugh] Hefner is perhaps more controversial in some ways than [Chuck] Yeager and [Lee] Iacocca. And he is definitely larger than life." That uses the phrase to describe the aura of celebrity that seems to enhance the size of a living human being.

The Wall Street Journal, in a piece about the real estate developer William Zeckendorf Jr., used the term this way: "Mr. Zeckendorf's quiet demeanor stands in stark contrast to his larger-than-life father, with whom he apprenticed starting at age 14." The late Zeckendorf Sr. was a large man with a large vision and a large reputation, but was not a fictional character; evidently, the *Journal's* editors also believe that the phrase can be applied to real people.

Take a slightly different sense. Suzi Quatro, the singer and actress, told a *Chicago Tribune* interviewer that she puts all her "oomph and energy" into songs, "because being tomboyish and larger than life has always been me."

In that same sense, *Time* magazine described Grace Jones—bogus-titling her as "Media Diva"—in a music video as wearing "a 30-ft. by 60-ft. dress"; Jones later proclaimed: "The audience sees me as a larger-than-life image they can worship—like a hero." Here the show-biz vogue phrase is being used to mean "projecting an illusion of magnitude; heroic, epic, grand."

That's current usage; now to etymology. A version of the alliterative phrase was first used in an 1802 letter by Catherine Wilmot, a travel writer, in describing "a beautiful piece of clockwork representing Apollo with his lyre. . . . It was as large as life." Lady Wilton, in her 1840 *Art of Needlework,* wrote of "birds . . . being, in proportion to other figures, certainly *larger* than life, and 'twice as natural.' " The metaphor was extended by Margery Louise Allingham, a mystery writer, in her 1937 *Dancers in Mourning:* "A larger-than-life edition of his stage self."

Chuck, your Long John Silver character was *larger than life* (unhyphenated unless used as a compound adjective before the noun being modified) in the sense of "legendary, containing qualities exaggerating those found in human beings"; historical characters you have portrayed, including Moses, were real but are held in people's eyes as more imposing than most human beings—and are, to most beholders, endowed with an aura of power or fame that makes them figuratively *larger than life.*

However, don't let the jacket writer describe you that way, unless you want to be blown out of human proportion. You are neither your posters nor your persona. Keep in mind this humbling admonition: On a television screen, an actor playing a giant is *smaller than life.*

Lay Down Your Marker

"These politicians want Bush to *lay down a marker* for all the world to see," wrote the columnists Evans and Novak in their muscular style, "no matter how much discomfort it brings Gorbachev and his trading pals in Bonn."

Former President Jimmy Carter, just before the upset victory of the anti-Sandinistas in Nicaragua, dismissed as highly exaggerated the complaints of the forces of Violeta Chamorro about Sandinista campaign practices. Carter characterized this as "*laying down a marker* so if they do lose they can say, 'Well, there were some irregularities.'"

What is this *marker* that political figures are said to *lay down*? We have here a clash of slang meanings that cries out for clarification.

A *marker,* to a gambler, is an *I.O.U.* (I capitalize that fanciful abbreviation, which is a speedy way of writing "I owe you"; several stylebooks, including *The Times*'s, prefer *i.o.u.,* which looks like an abbreviation used by the anticapitalization poet e.e. cummings. This device of using letters that sound like words to create a phrase is the progenitor of license-plate messaging, from the net-leaping 10S-NE1 to the ultrapolite XQZE ME. The rule: When kidding around, capitalize.)

The gambler's definition of *marker* as "promissory note" appeared first in 1887, but was popularized in Damon Runyon's *Guys and Dolls* in 1932: "Now I am going to pay my landlady, and take up a few *markers* here and there, and feed myself up good." A 1934 film based on a Runyon tale about a little girl used as an I.O.U. was titled *Little Miss Marker*.

This sense—rooted in a mark made on a piece of paper to signify a debt, probably influenced by the scorecard in bridge and whist—has been extended beyond the promise of money payment. Sidney Zion's novel *Markers* deals with promises, loyalties and favors owed in a power network. In his blurb for the book, Frank Sinatra writes, "This book gives Sid Zion a royal-flush marker against all those people who thought they knew everything." I think Mr. Sinatra means *marker* there in the sense of "weapon" or "asset" and would appreciate hearing from him if I am mistaken.

A wholly different line of slang meanings exists. This is rooted in marking a boundary. "You are to employ . . . an assistant surveyor . . . and also proper chainbearers and markers," reads a 1743 New Jersey document. A *marker* is not only a person who marks boundaries, but also a stone used to mark that demarcation line. The military uses dyes and colored powders to mark targets or boundaries.

That military use may be the root of the political phrase *lay down a marker*. It issues a warning, or sets off territory that may not be challenged. It is akin to *draw a line in the sand,* but not as bellicose as *put a chip on your shoulder.* In 1970, "You left your calling card" was the way Yitzhak Rabin, then Israel's Ambassador to the United States, characterized an unsuccessful American attempt to rescue P.O.W.'s in North Vietnam.

In political usage today, *lay down a marker* ranges in meaning from "send a signal" to "announce a presence" to "issue a warning of 'this far, no farther.' "

Leavity

Children relate the sounds they hear to current words and meanings, often in a burst of originality that jars the rest of us.

In the Passover retelling of the story of the exodus of Jews from ancient Egypt, some irreverent Jews like to remind their seder companions of an "error" by Moses on the way to the Promised Land: If he had turned right instead of left, he would have founded his nation on top of a large pool of oil.

This petroleum fixation came to mind at the most recent seder dinner. That's the feast marked by the use of unleavened bread, or matzoh, in recollection of the flight from Egypt when the Israelites had no time to add the yeast, or leavening, that would cause the bread to rise. A child is called upon to ask the Four Questions about the significance of the symbols recalling the first exodus.

"Why, on this night," asked this ten-year-old, "do we eat *unleaded* bread?"

The "joke" was not on Moses, but on Abraham. Genesis 13:8 et seq—"And Abram said unto Lot, 'Let there be no strife, I pray thee, between me and thee . . . separate thyself, I pray thee, from me; if thou wilt take the left hand, then I will go to the right; or if thou take the right hand, then I will go to the left.' . . . So Lot chose him all the plain of the Jordan; and Lot journeyed east . . . [while] Abram dwelt in the land of Canaan . . ."

The "homily" goes on to say that if Lot had chosen differently, the Jews would have had the oil and the Moslems the Arab Bond Drive.

Reverting to the text, it was following the separation from Lot that Abram received the divine promise (Gen 13:15), "for all the land which thou seest, to thee will I give it, and to thy seed for ever." Consequently, when Moses led the Jews out of Egypt, he had no choice but to go generally in the direction of Canaan, now Israel.

David H. Fax
Pittsburgh, Pennsylvania

MAIL CALL (ALL CAPS)

If you were sitting there addressing mail all day, and you wanted a new sense of bureaucratic self-importance, what would you call what you were doing? You would call it "outputting addresses to mailpieces."

That's what the United States Postal Service calls it in its publication *Postal Addressing Standards,* which is "must" reading for those unfortunates born under the pound sign who cannot afford faxes and private delivery services.

In outputting addresses to mailpieces, we are told: "Uppercase letters are preferred on all lines of the address block." *Uppercase* is a large letter, taken from printers' lingo when such type was stored in the upper of a pair of stacked cases; small letters, you can readily assume, were stored in the typog-

rapher's lower case. *Capital,* from the Latin *caput,* "head," gained a sense in Chaucer's time of "large letter placed at the head of a page or line." Even today, when used in the plural to describe a group of large-style letters, the term *capital letters* comes more naturally than *uppercase letters* to native speakers, few of whom, it seems, work at the Postal Service; if more did, we would read an instruction like PLEASE USE CAPITAL LETTERS, with a reader-friendly explanation, "because it's hard to make out those little squiggles." Instead, we are advised: "Lowercase letters in various type styles are acceptable provided they meet the requirements of optical character reader (OCR) readability," which are said to be available in Chapter 4 of Publication 25, but my copy got lost in the mailpieces room.

Why is it necessary to standardize address blocks, formerly known as *addresses*? Because this will "reduce undeliverable-as-addressed mail, and provide mutual cost opportunities through improved efficiency," according to the National Address Information Center, whose address is listed in the booklet as "US POSTAL SERVICE (new line) 6060 PRIMACY PKY SUITE 101 (another new line) MEMPHIS TN 38188-0001."

The translation of "to provide mutual cost opportunities" is, I presume, *to save money,* or a sum of moneypieces, which would then be passed on to the consumer as a slower march upward of postage rates. As the model address in the previous paragraph indicates, no commas are to be put between city and state in the Postal Service's brave new mailpiece world, and no periods are to be used after abbreviations.

What and where, then, you may wonder, is PKY SUITE 101? In most of the U.S.—excuse me, US—that is pronounced "peeky sweet," and in the South, "peeky soot." Wait; close examination of the brochure's Appendix C (Suffix Forms) reveals that PKY stands for "Parkway"—not to be confused with MDWS for "Meadows" or PNES for "Pines"—which means we can place a mental period after the abbreviation, place a mental comma after that, and begin a new thought with SUITE.

But you and I rarely use *suite* or even *apartment number,* abbreviated to *Apt. No.;* most often, we use the crosshatch symbol for "number," which has come to be known as the *pound sign* (the origin and etymology of which I seek Lex Irreg help in finding). Aren't we allowed to use this simple signal, so dear to tick-tack-toe fans and sharp musicians, anymore? "If the pound sign is used," snaps the Postal Service, apparently irritated at the unsuite-ables, "there will be a space between the sign and the secondary number."

There will be? This construction may be considered the implied imperative, as in COFFEE GROUNDS WILL BE PLACED IN THE CONTAINER MARKED "INEDIBLE GARBAGE," a sign that has been fixed in my memory since KP days long ago. The tone of command is unmistakable: "You Will Report for Induction at 0800 Hours." In the same ominous tone, we are told by our masterful mailpersons, "There *will be* a space between the sign and the secondary number," with the clear implication that pound-sign miscreants who leave no such space will be prosecuted to the full extent of the law, like poor Bill Posters. This was no sudden surge of arrogance by a Napoleonic brochure-writer: We were also told in the 1989 version, "City names *will be* spelled out in their entirety" unless they run over 13 letters; in that case, "NEWBERRY SPRINGS becomes NEWBERRY SPGS." (The 1990 version, however, uses straightforward imperative: "Spell city names in their entirety.")

And all you people with beautiful words in your addresses: Cut 'em down. There's a bright golden haze on the MDWS; a fairy dancing in your GDNS; and a safe HBR past the happy LNDG at the XING, where no hope SPGS. Environmentalists are now GRN, as in how GRN was my VLY. PLZ stands for "plaza" (not "please"; that superfluous word needs no unpunctuated abbreviation in the postal lexicon). Is the language not lessened when words like *meadow, gardens, harbor, landing, crossing, green, valley*—even *islands* (*ISS*)—are disemvoweled?

We are permitted to spell out a few words of special interest to those in the Postal Service; they like to see GENERAL DELIVERY in all its glory, or perhaps some officials felt that GD looked like a shortening of the profane reaction of customers to the new postalingo. And don't go putting in useless names of streets when the computer code is enough: "Example: HC 2 BOX 18 BRYAN DAIRY RD becomes HC 2 BOX 18," its milk skimmed of all character.

The only punctuation permitted, except for a computer-friendly slash (which is what the USPS—an odious acronym, but officials insist on it—calls the virgule), is the hyphen between the "old" ZIP code and the additional four digits. The USPS diktat: "Hyphens are only printed as part of the box number when indicated as part of the address in the ZIP + 4 FILE." The misplacement of the *only* in that command makes it incomprehensible: If hyphens are only printed when the rest happens, are they scrawled by trembling hand when it does not? What's the punishment for hyphenating against postal regulations—forty backslashes?

"Use abbreviations for directionals," advises USPS (the way to get rid of a law is to enforce it, and that acronym *will* be used) in a recent news release. William F. Dwyer 2d of Beverly Hills, California, wrote back: "On what language authority are you allowed to cast an adjective, *directional,* in the role of a noun?" He sent a copy of his irate response to me, so an USPS-er in Washington, Paul M. Griffo, sent me a copy of his reply: "*Directional* is commonly used as a noun among delivery personnel within the Postal Service. It is used specifically to refer to the part of the address that gives directional information; e.g., '*S* BEVERLY DR, FOURTH ST *NW*,' etc." As a good sport, he adds, "Like any large organization or industry, we must continually be on guard against allowing specialized jargon to find its way into our external communications."

Fine, but that's not the central problem, which is stated by David Hochman, a longtime user of the mails: "In the age of artificial intelligence, it's more a scandal than ever that *we* must conform to the hardware, rather than the other way 'round."

Addresses are not codes, but expressions of place. *Bryan Dairy Road* means something to the people living there—to addressees and addressers—that HC 2 BOX 18 will never re-place. Same with Newberry *Springs* and Grover's *Corners*—Our Town wouldn't be the same as GROVERS CORS.

Standardization may be efficient, but regimentation is repugnant. Direct-mail marketers have led the way with computerized individualization; USPS should be able to design equipment to accommodate its customers' affinity for street or neighborhood. Let Current Occupants from all directionals rise and remind the crew: The SHP is built for the sake of the PSNGRS.

On the origin of the "#" or "pound" sign: It is a scribal variant of the abbreviation of the Latin for pound, libra, *and is thus a cognate to the British monetary pound sign, "£." Originally, the weight name was shortened, as it is today, to "lb."; but as was the calligrapher's habit, the abbreviation was marked with a horizontal line through the ascenders of the "l" and "b," (standing for the "r" of* libra, *as it did in the abbreviation of* per, *"p") yielding the sign "℔." Eventually this was written "℔" with a quick loop for the bowl of the "b," which was yet later omitted entirely, "#."*

Gary Munch
Stamford, Connecticut

L. L. Bean has equipment that will read handwriting and convert it into computer language. Why can't the Post Office?

If 600,000 Avon salesladies' written orders can be read by the computer with no human intervention, the Post Office should be able to do the same thing.

Leo R. Yochim
New York, New York

By now, computers are smart enough to accommodate themselves to people, and people should not be stupid enough to let themselves be accommodated to computers. (Kind of like governments, don't you think?) Only those who haven't updated their computer knowledge since their mother was scared by a mainframe in 1948 would miss the crucial fact this is one of the main points of the computer revolution (are those darn computers marching in the street— again—?).

I say this not as a computerphobe—quite the reverse.

The Post Office (oops, Postal Service—talk about your oxymorons) Doesn't Get It, as usual—which is why I'm not bothering to decide precisely how to show my independence by means of a really Luddite envelope address, but instead am cutting the Gordian Knot and sending this to you by fax.

Paul Bogrow
Glendale, California

Hit the Pound Sign

A sign of the times is the one-way caller. Person leans into the three-sided coop we used to call a telephone booth, squints to see what kind of machine it is, punches rather than dials a number, then waits. He or she fumbles for a pen and something to write on as a couple of rings go by. In a moment, the caller straightens to attention and receives instructions. Then the caller's fingers punch a few buttons; another brief wait; more punching, then a long listen, a smile or frown, and another punch. Not a word is spoken into the receiver.

The caller is either a K.G.B. agent under intense surveillance or your average user of a telephone message service. I have one, called Audix, or Unix, or Felix—there's an *x* at the end—and I no longer need other people. I just leave and get messages; I could be gone for years, and nobody would know.

The caller presses the numeric keys with his secret password, which is often the day and month of his birth, the easiest code imaginable to break, but it transmits a sense of confidentiality or satisfies some other message-service need. (Go memorize an irrelevant number; if you forget and have no mnemonic, you will be frantically banging on the numeric keys; it's a piteous sight.)

"Please enter your password," the synthetic-syrupy recorded voice directs, "followed by the pound sign."

"When was I born?" is my first internal question. The second, which I asked only once, was: "What and where is the *pound sign*?"

I always thought the *pound sign* was the symbol for the British pound sterling, a script capital *L* with a hyphen through it, a stylized representation of the Latin *libra*. (The Roman pound was several ounces lighter than the modern pound; some things stick in my mind, but numbers fade fast.)

No; the sign that the recorded Miss Syrup refers to is what some of us remember as the *tick-tack-toe sign*, or the *crosshatch*, or the *sign of the double-cross*, similar to the symbol Charlie Chaplin wore as a parody of the swastika in his 1940 movie, *The Great Dictator*. Willard Espy, the Valentino of word lovers, has built on this thought in *Harvard Magazine* to suggest *proditio*, Latin for "betrayal," or double-cross. Nice try; won't fly.

When #, as we shall call it here, is placed before a number, it is called a *number sign;* #1 pencils have a softer lead than #2 pencils, and nothing fits into a #10 envelope anymore. When a musician sees it, the meaning is "sharp"; doctors often use it as a symbol for "fracture."

When a proofreader uses the #, the meaning is "insert space here": Two words incorrectly runtogether are happily separated by a #. (When this copy comes to the proofreader, whose legendary name is Mr. Dunphy, that eagle-eyed worthy will circle *runtogether,* run a line out to the edge of the page, and put a # at the end. Another editor, with a profound sense of context, will write "stet" over that, meaning "leave as is," from the third-person present subjunctive singular of the Latin *stare,* "to stand." I get a lot of sweaters for birthday presents; think I was born in December.)

In internal memoranda, the telephone company (a locution left over from the days of AT&T monopoly; there are now hundreds of telephone companies) likes to use *octothorpe,* also spelled *octothorp. Octo-* is a combining form for "eight," as octogenarian octopuses know, and refers to the eight points around the outside of the symbol. But there are nine spaces in a tick-tack-toe game. The crosshatch has twelve line segments. Forget *octothorpe.*

Pound sign, however, is catching on. The origin may be from the use of # to mean "pound," as in "a 5# bag of sugar," written by someone unhappy with the abbreviation *lb.* to stand for "pound." (We know that *pound* is from the Latin *libra pondo,* "a pound by weight," which accounts for the *lb.;* not everybody knows that. The week before Christmas is when I was born.) This would not be the first time the weight of a *pound* was used to form a noun phrase; in *pound cake,* the original 1747 recipe called for a pound of butter.

A more remote possibility is that *pound* evokes a mashing of the desired button, as one pounds on a door, but I go for the 5#-bag theory.

Privacy Journal surveyed its readers in 1986 for ideas and discovered the symbol is called *bradgard,* or "lumberyard" in Swedish, because it looks like the mark for a lumberyard on maps for hiking and other outdoor activities. *Score* was also recommended, perhaps by a card player. The journal concluded that *thingamajig* was too general, *octothorpe* was most authentic, and *gridlet* was the most intriguing.

Ink-stained wretches, pounding the keys of long-ago typewriters, recall the # as a substitute for -30- written at the bottom of a story to signify termination, no pages or takes to follow. (Where does *ink-stained wretch* come from? Wait—I was born on December 17. My password is 1217. Now I can get my messages. The *pound sign* is the one on the lower right, not the one on the lower left, which is the *star sign.* Funny, it looks like an asterisk.)

Your delightful piece on the "#" button of the telephone inspires me to put a bit of history on the record.

In the late 50's and early 60's some of us in the data communications business at Bell Laboratories were planning the use of the ordinary telephone for data input and took advantage of the fact that a touchtone "pad" could be made to produce twelve different signals almost as easily as the ten that were in common use: The two extra signals (buttons) would be identifiers and punctuation for the data message.

People in my center built an audio response system and my secretary recorded phrases such as "you have reached ————" and "please enter your access code." My boss, W. T. Rea, had great fun at technical conferences around the country going on the stage with a speaker phone and calling back to our Holmdel, N.J. laboratories to demonstrate parts ordering by touchtone phone. We called the system DIVA, meaning Digital Inquiry (or Input), Voice Answerback.

The naming and labeling of the two new buttons was a challenge. It was fairly easy to agree on the asterisk. Happily, to my taste, the asterisk ended up sitting on two legs, the typewriter version, rather than one leg, the print version. People could call it a star or an asterisk as they chose. The great problem was the naming of the lower right button.

The final decision to use "#" was made by the two Executive Directors involved, Mike Wolontis (now deceased) in Systems Engineering and George Dacey in Development. I would have preferred a simple dot or period, but our professional human-factors people held strongly that a dot could be confused with an asterisk and did not have sufficient distinctiveness.

Way back then the many names we were aware of for "#" included octothorp(e) and lumberyard and, of course, pound mark and number sign. I was reluctant to go with the number sign (as I think of it) for three reasons: First, its name is a source of undesirable confusion. Second, for those people who do think of it as a number sign, the mind is pre-programmed to use it as a number sign; this may be different from the meaning in the particular protocol that is in use. Finally, thirty years ago I was deeply concerned with worldwide standardization, and I was concerned that some typewriters and keyboards around the world lacked the "#" symbol, thus denying their users the ability to type out the DIVA format.

So, there is some history. Again let me thank you for your delightful piece.

James R. Harris
Rumson, New Jersey

 # is used also in programming languages for the not-equal sign, which is more commonly handwritten by math types as an equal sign slashed by a virgule, ≠.

Richard M. Ball, M.D.
South Plainfield, New Jersey

What about scratch? *Were Mr. Dunphy's issues within user-friendly calling distance canvassed? Or do all proofreaders who have never worked with a copyholder simply not know of it? Or are you perhaps squirreling away examples from a dying proofreading practice for later use?*

One day in the late '80s—between stock market crashes and before the financial-printing company whose typesetting department I managed (as "Director, Electronic Composition Services") closed its doors forever—I was pressed into reading proofs with a journeyman Big 6 member. (Owing to gruesome business conditions, management had extracted from the ITU local the right for composing-room supervisors to perform "de minimus" work in the trenches.) My role was to check the proof by following the copy as read aloud by the journeyman copyholder.

The man employed an oral shorthand that nearly overloaded my capacity to coordinate eye and ear. The copy was straightforward, dreary, vanilla text— part of a proxy-fight proxy statement, I seem to recall—with nothing sexier than corporate officers' and directors' names, amounts of beneficial stock holdings, business affiliations and the like. But—oh!—the spoken, clipped geography of the text which streamed from the voice box alongside me and that I had to marry with the typeset proof: khaam *(,),* point *(.),* semi *(;),* et coe *(& Co.),* ink *(Inc.),* bucks *($—"bucks four point six nine mill" [$4.69 million]),* up *(proper noun or upper-case letter—"all up tee double-yew ay"),* balls *(%),* hyfe *(-),* syfe *(Arabic numeral not spelled out; used only when the context fails to settle it—"syfe ten hyfe year hyfe old"),* star *(*),* in the hole *(within* parens—*"three eye in the hole" [(iii)]). Jeez! Happily, it wasn't the proxy-fight letter—liberally peppered with italics ("ital... back to Rome"), boldface,* score's *(underlining),* bang's *(!) and* hook's *(?).*

Thus monosyllable scratch, *half the time of* crosshatch *(which surely predates pretender* pound*) and more akin to a printer's sensibilities than* sharp *(graphic vs. sound media—this despite a British industrial designer's failed attempt in the '60s [was it?] to develop a typesetting keyboard along the lines of a piano's).*

Keep up the good foot-pounds.

John W. Tutlis
Brooklyn, New York

I have also known the symbol to be called a name which did not appear in your column—the "hash" key.

I am bothered by one other artifact of our voice mail/computer era language. Anthropomorphic voice-mail narrators instruct one to "press" the pound key, which is sometimes mimicked by computer manual writers telling us to "press" a function key or other computer keyboard key. I do not know about you, but

I do not "press" keys on a keyboard (although I suppose I do on a telephone). I "type" the keys or more accurately when thrown back to my manual type-writer days "hit" and even "bang"—or even "pound"! But I am uncomfortable hitting or banging computer keys with their apparent and all-too-real fragility; "depress" just won't do. In earlier days (after I stopped being a daily reporter using the # key as a substitute for -30-), I actually wrote some computer manuals as a CEO of a software publishing company. It may have been retro-grade, but I could not bring myself to use any other word than "type" for the key-encounter.

Nicholas A. Ulanov
New York, New York

I am fairly literate, have B.A. and M.A. degrees but have been feeling like a perfect idiot since a telephone operator kept telling me to "hit the pound key! hit the pound key!" and I didn't know what in the world she was talking about. Then she changed to "the number key" and I said "which one?"
Thanks from an old fuddy-duddy who can't take too much progress.

Julia D. Weinstein
New York, New York

The recipe for pound cake was not named thus on account of a pound of butter: It contains a pound of butter, a pound of flour, a pound of eggs and a pound of sugar. The flavoring could be almond, orange or possibly lemon, but almond and orange were the most often used.
This recipe makes two loaves, and can be halved for one, if desired.

Dinah L. Foglia
South Huntington, New York

Mare Nostrum

"In your commentary," wrote Habib Ladjevardi to Dan Rather of CBS, "you said that the President would be speaking on the situation in 'the Arabian Gulf, also known as the Persian Gulf.' I believe this is the first time that any of the networks have referred to the Persian Gulf as the Arabian Gulf."

Mr. Ladjevardi, associate director of the Center for Middle Eastern Studies at Harvard, noted that the term *Arabian Gulf* was the choice of the late President Gamal Abdel Nasser of Egypt and is now commonly used by Iraq's Saddam Hussein. "I am puzzled," he wrote, "by the introduction of the term *Arabian Gulf* by an American broadcasting company at this particular moment in history, especially since it coincides with your return from a visit to the Middle East."

When a copy of this note was vouchsafed to me by one of my academic moles, I queried CBS News. The network researcher tried National Geographic, which lists only *Persian Gulf,* but hit pay dirt with *Webster's New Geographical Dictionary,* which lists both *Persian Gulf* and *Arabian Gulf* as the same body of water.

"Our position is that *Arabian Gulf* is acceptable," says a CBS spokesman, Tom Goodman, "as long as we also explain that it is the Persian Gulf that's being identified. *Persian Gulf* is the standard name, and it requires no further explanation."

That's odd; it's like saying "*Gotham,* also known as *New York City.*"

It strikes me that Saddam Hussein does not want to admit that the gulf in question has a special association with Persia, also known as Iran, a nation with which he just fought an eight-year war. The object of that war was access to that waterway; Iraq, having gained substantial access through Kuwait, has given back the narrow access it had won from Iran. By calling it the *Arabian Gulf,* Mr. Hussein (as *The New York Times* likes to refer to Saddam) lays linguistic claim to it on behalf of Arabs—and Iranians are Persians, not Arabs. Mr. Rather apparently did not want to take sides and introduced this note of confusion into the nomenclature.

If history is used to decide the name, CBS is aware of the ancient appellation: *Sinus Persicus,* for "Persian bend." In the interests of peace and amity, I have a suggestion: how about *the Gulf of Kurdistan?*

Marriage Lines

This department tries to stay on top of the proper pronunciation of words in the news. In the gossip arena, the word most often mangled is *nuptial.*

"After the tumult surrounding the playing of the celebrated trump," writes Stephen Gutkin of Jersey City, "I've yet to descry your voice on the subject of *prenuptial*—namely, 'Whence the pronunciation *prenupchewal?*'"

There may be bite but no *chew* in *prenuptial agreement.* The word *nuptial* is from the past participle of the Latin verb *nubere,* "to marry," which is also the root of *nubile,* "marriageable," or at least "apparently fully developed sexually," which is not the same thing. Use the plural to refer to a wedding ceremony, as in "I cannot make it to the *nuptials,* but I hope to be at the festive signing of the first postnuptial agreement."

Pronounce *nuptial* "NUP-shul," just as you pronounce the warlike *martial* "MAR-shul." They are not "NUP-chill" or "MAR-chill", and they are certainly not pronounced as if spelled "nuptual" or "martual." (On the other hand, you can pronounce *victuals* "VIT-els," because this synonym for food is used only in dialect form.).

Ivana may be pronounced to rhyme with the old Ipana toothpaste, if you pronounce *Ivan* the American way, "EYE-vun"; however, if you accept the Russian pronunciation, the masculine is "ih-VAHN" and the feminine, "ih-VAHN-uh."

Mavenhood Spreading

The language dodge is booming. Here is proof—hard, commercial data— that the market for etymology, usage, style and grammar is burgeoning (in that word's two senses of "increasing" and "blooming").

James J. Kilpatrick, who invented the conservative syndicated column, is also the author of "The Writer's Art" each week. Watch for Kilpo's annual review of crotchets: misuse of *partially* when *partly* is intended, and substitution of *like* for *such as.*

A regular feature titled "Glossary" appears in the *Boston Globe,* written by Michael Kenney. Columnist Jack Smith has long commanded the language in the *Los Angeles Times.* Humorist Dave Barry writes an irregular "Ask Mr. Language Person" in *The Washington Post Magazine,* and recently reported a new sense to *per se:* "if you catch my drift."

In *The Atlantic Monthly,* lexicographer Anne H. Soukhanov's word-watching alternates with Craig M. Carver's etymologies from the *Dictionary of American Regional English* (Anne came up with a slang interjection, *quux,* an expression of mild disgust used by hackers). Bar journals and legal newspapers have been running regular features on legalese, as lawyers are learning that solecisms are at least as serious as torts.

Jeffrey McQuain, the educator who researches this column (and is, of course, solely responsible for all errors), has launched his own daily word column, "Our Language," distributed by United Media's Newspaper Enterprise Association, in which he provides catchy definitions, answers reader questions on grammar and usage, and offers "ad-vice" to errant copywriters.

A. P. Newsfeatures distributes "Word for Word," an etymological cartoon strip by Australia's Michael Atchison; I never knew that *ice cream sundae* came about as soda-parlor operators circumvented laws against selling flavored sodas on the Sabbath.

Read 'em all, wherever you are; instead of bemoaning the state of language, dive into the pool of language mavens. We'd have a convention, but everybody is afraid to make the first speech.

Humor columnist Dave Barry writes for the Miami Herald *and is nationally syndicated to hundreds of newspapers, including* The Washington Post.

Janet Chusmir
Executive Editor
The Miami Herald
Miami, Florida

Merry Month of Might

"What happened to *may?*" inquires Timothy B. Blodgett, executive editor of *Harvard Business Review.* "Quite often these days, I find *might* used where *may* is correct. Obviously the distinction is becoming blurred in the public mind."

He enclosed the clips that made his point: Some of our best copy editors and headline writers are doing the blurring.

"Miniscribe might have to write off as much as $200 million in bad inventory and uncollectable receivables," said an article in *The Wall Street Journal.* A headline at the top of the front page of *The New York Times* stated, SOVIETS AND CHINA MIGHT BE ALLOWED INTO TRADE GROUP.

In both cases, *may* makes right. In the lexicon of iffiness, and setting the past tense aside, the two words show different degrees of possibility. When the possibility is real, sometimes verging on probability, we say *may;* when the likelihood is remote, or when we state a condition contrary to fact, we should say *might.*

You may not like being told to preserve the distinction; you might even be inclined to throw a shoe at your friendly neighborhood usagist; but the difference is real and may not be ignored (or you might get zapped by a thunderbolt from the Voice of Authority).

Here is advice for weathercasters, or as they like to call themselves, meteorologists. (I *may* need to know the weather; I *might* need to know if a meteor is headed this way.) When the chance of precipitation (what happened to rain?) is more than 50 percent, tell me, "It *may* rain"; when that dread possibility diminishes to 10 percent, tell me, "It *might* rain."

Mnemonic: I'm mighty uncertain.

When Mr. Blodgett of the Harvard Business Review *asked, "What happened to 'may'?" he might (sic) equally have asked, "And what happened to 'might'?"*

The two words are inextricably bound: "Might" is both the past tense and the subjunctive form of "may."

When the baseball announcer says, "If he'd played closer to third base, he may have caught the pop fly," he hurts my ear. This is a case where the condition-contrary-to-fact requires the use of "might," and it comes up in ordinary conversation quite often, but in sports broadcasting all the time.

Tim McCarver, take notice.

> Arthur J. Morgan
> New York, New York

Mickey Mouse

"The lines between children's television and the Federal Government are blurred," Anna Quindlen wrote in *The New York Times*, ". . . and if people get the government they deserve, are we all Mickey Mouse?"

Whence *Mickey Mouse* as a symbol of childishness, and its use as a slang adjective with a meaning ranging from "cockamamie" to "rudimentary" to "unsophisticated"? The *Oxford English Dictionary* defines the Americanism as "something small, insignificant or worthless," but that misses the nuance of dismaying oversimplification.

The cartoon character with the alliterative name was created by Walt Disney in the late 1920's, and George Orwell turned the name into an adjective in 1936, writing of "a sort of Mickey Mouse universe where things and people don't have to obey the rules of space and time."

Mickey was a mouse, and mice are small; a *Mickey Mouse spot* became the smallest spotlight in a motion-picture studio. The phrase was used in World War II British military slang to describe complicated machinery, but this sense soon atrophied; the use of the cartoon character on inexpensive children's wristwatches gave it an added meaning of cheapness.

To go to the mouse's mouth about the source for the current sense of simplism, I shot a query to Dave Smith, the archivist for Disney Studios in Burbank, California.

"Carl Nater, who worked on our educational films during World War II, had an explanation," said Mickey's historian. "He said the Government once sent its accountants to the studio, and they were dismayed by the way we kept the books—they found overhead charges for the office in New York, scribbled notes, that sort of thing. One of the accountants exclaimed, 'What a Mickey Mouse way of bookkeeping!' and that's how that sense of the phrase was born."

Dear Bill,
Your column about Mickey Mouse reminded me of a troublesome American political question: Why, since the Boy Scouts of America is such a symbol of rectitude and American decency and honor, is it one of the worst things to say about a politician that he is "a Boy Scout"? Has our cynicism level always been so high?

Frank [Mankiewicz]
Washington, D.C.

Microwave of the Future

Jimmy, the most noteworthy item about electronic communication today is the fixation on viewer-avoiding transitions. This thought hit me upon receipt of a few items of the latest dialect from Lexicographic Irregular T. Brokaw of New York and Riyadh, after a brief sojourn in Montana.

Microwavable, as label-readers know, is not new; this low-tech word, found on the labels of food packages, means "able to be subjected to the subtle intensities of a microwave oven." The verb *to microwave,* however, has developed a second sense, using the "fast zap" of radiation to stand for decision-making: "to glance at a long list of options and make a quick decision."

This new sense of the locution was only the first of three items spotted by Mr. Brokaw. He also passes on *riding for the brand,* a modern cowboy term meaning "staying loyal to your employer," a practice that's disappearing like the cowboy from the corporate range.

The third Montana item is an especially exciting dialectical find: *hot quit.* This last term may turn out to be the much-needed alternative to the belabored *blinking* after an eyeball-to-eyeball encounter. According to Mr. Brokaw, *hot quit* is used to refer to "a sudden backing away from a confrontation."

Because it has such an impact on American speech, the language of news broadcasting deserves periodic review, something that I am now impelled to do.

The news, Jimmy, is that newscasters (journalists on wheels) are simultaneously compressing and inflating the language; that is, whatever they save in the swings of delivery they lose on the roundabouts of transition.

I have this letter from Dr. Alan G. Cole of Natick, Massachusetts: "Tonight on the news, the anchor signed off 'For Garrick Utley, I'm Faith Daniels. Good night.' For Tom Brokaw, is she Vanna White?"

A profound question, that. Her meaning is surely not to be construed as "I am Faith Daniels for Garrick Utley, but who knows who I'll be for a slightly shorter and much more hirsute anchor." Rather, her sign-off means "On behalf of my partner, Garrick Utley, I am Faith Daniels, saying good night."

In some minds, the compressed message is received as intended; in some, other meanings lurk in Rorschachean complexity. (Most people look at a Batman logo and see a black bat on a field of yellow; doctors see a yellow pair of tonsils. In the same way, many children hear the first line of the Pledge of Allegiance as "I led the pigeons to the flag.")

The shrunken sign-off is symptomatic of electronic journalism's pressing problem of compression.

A half-second on network television, worth an indeterminate sum often described hyperbolically as "tons of money," is saved by this telescoped form. The term for the omission of words that are intended to be "understood" by the reader is *ellipsis.* Its extreme or irregular form has a name in Greek rhetoric: *brachylogy,* relying on the listener to supply the missing words, much as I relied on the reader to put a verb in the sentence fragment "A profound question, that."

But how laconic can language get? "And now, a word from our sponsor" has been pared down to what seems to be its nubbin: "Now this." Before long, some cost-effective type will ask: Why stop there?

The syllable count could be reduced by 50 percent, saving a dozen milliseconds (which, multiplied by its number of network usages, would amount to $376,000 per year) by the simple expedient of saying, "Now . . ." or "This!" Perhaps some other word or sign—a wink, a nose twitch or a roll of the shoulder—would best build a bridge from editorial copy to commercial message.

Curiously, while this compression using ellipsis is on the march on the air, a reverse trend is simultaneously taking place: Proper nouns (also known as *proper names*) are being inserted where they are not necessary. Syllables are added to all news broadcasts by the requirement—evidently etched in stone—that correspondents address the anchor by name before, or instead of, addressing the home audience.

Only the central newscaster has the franchise to communicate directly with the viewer; reporters on the scene are required to begin, "Peter [or Dan or Tom or Faith-for-Garrick] . . ."

The reporter forced to use this friendly salutation thus appears to be reporting to him, or through his good offices to us. This time-wasting deference to the anchor is intended to give a unity to the program by making the star of the show the spine, a more accurate metaphor than *anchor*.

Of course, this is merely a dramatic device; the reporters are standing in front of some sandy tank not to communicate with an intermediary, but to touch base with the anchor by acknowledging his or her permeating presence through the use of a first name.

On occasion, the device has a function when the anchor follows up with questions about the report, though these are often prearranged. But in most cases the salutation is for show-biz reasons, similar to looking at hand-held notes as if the copy were not printed on the TelePrompTer in front of the lens.

Though we might lose the happy-family feeling of journalists who are addressing each other by first name (and I always admire the interviewee who uses a dignified honorific in answering a reporter), the snipping off of "Dan" from "Dan, the story here is . . ." would save thousands of milliseconds per year.

Add these to the milliseconds to be saved by the dropping of the Obsequious Concluding Interrogatory: ". . . which remains to be seen. Peter?" The incessant use of the first name with a rising inflection serves little purpose, as it can mean anything from an inquisitive "You want anything more from here?" to a crisp "Over to you" to a wheedling "Did I do good?"

Whenever I hear the O.C.I., as the Obsequious Concluding Interrogatory is known in the trade, I wonder how it would sound if directed at me instead of the anchor: ". . . and that's all from here. Audience? Viewer?" My reaction would be "Just sign off with your name and place, and don't ask me to rate your performance; I'm not into interactive video."

What if the pendulum swings back toward direct reporting? The disintermediation of the anchor would save precious time, which could be traded off (not merely "traded") for the continuance of the relaxed, discursive "Now this."

This piece began with an unnecessary word—a salutation to my editor, James Greenfield—which interferes with my usual intimacy with you, the reader. Why should an editor intrude his personality between writer and reader? Why should a television anchor come between reporter and viewer?

If microwaving board chairmen join this crusade to eliminate the salutation to the anchor, we may see a great many familiar faces that have been riding for the brand doing a hot quit.

Jimmy?

The Militant Mitigator

In a column headlined "A Chat With Jesse," my colleague A. M. Rosenthal revealed that Jesse Jackson was unlikely to run for mayor of Washington, D.C.

The world-renowned political figure (nobody assumed the first name applied to Jesse Helms or Jesse James) explained that "the mayoralty of Washington has zero political leverage." Mr. Jackson said he was honored to be considered and added, "But logic and politics *mitigate* against it."

Mr. Rosenthal's readers were ahead of the news—Mr. Jackson subsequently announced his mayoral noncandidacy—but were subjected to solecism. *Mitigate* for *militate* is one of those mistakes made so often by so many of us that resistance is crumbling. *Mitigate* means "to soften," from the Latin *mitis,* "soft," which may also be the root of *mignon,* the tenderest steak; *militate* means "to be directed, to work (against)," from the Latin for "serve as a soldier, fight," which is also the root of the adjective and noun *militant.*

Let us not permit either logic or politics to *mitigate* our resistance to error: Instead, let us—politicians and pundits all—*militate* against confusion.

Misplaced Mod

"Avoid confusing readers with misplaced modifiers" is a fumblerule; the reader cannot tell if *misplaced modifiers* refers to *confusing* or *readers.*

The best example in the past year was in a *New York Times* caption, sent in by George E. Burns of New York with the captious comment "I think this is a record." The caption quoted "a program participant who is expecting her sixth child in two weeks."

The Mood of 'Tude

To most of us, an *attitude* is something a person has: a cheerful frame of mind or a negative outlook. The word is neutral, requiring some modifier to tell us what kind of attitude we're talking about.

To some, however, *attitude*—not preceded by the article *an*—has lost its neutrality and gained a new sense: pugnacity, sullen defiance, self-confidence tipping over into arrogance. This attitude has a hostile modifier built in.

The first inkling of the new sense in the *Barnhart Dictionary* files comes from *The New Yorker* in 1978, about a car-rental agency: "We have a very good atmosphere here. We enjoy our work. We don't have an *attitude.*" *Vanity Fair,* in 1990, recalled how the actor Marlon Brando "rode into town, like Elvis with an *attitude.*"

Lewis Beale in the *Detroit Free Press* reports that *attitude* "is a uniquely post-modern way to look at the world. It's cynical, cool, a bit detached. . . . In the male of the species, it can include macho posturing; in the female, it's called bitchiness."

He provides a table for the age of attitude: Mickey Mouse needs it, Bugs Bunny has it, Bart Simpson has too much; John le Carré needs it, Elmore Leonard has it, Norman Mailer has too much; in the animal world, gerbils need it, cats have it, ferrets have too much.

The same linguistic phenomenon was noted concurrently by Tony Gabriele in the Newport News (Virginia) *Daily Press,* who had a character explain: "You don't have to be rich or famous to attitudinize; the lowliest street-corner lout can give you attitude just as well." The politeness and lack of affectation of the residents of Newport News made it an "attitude-impaired region."

To cop an attitude was prison slang for "to adopt a complaining demeanor" or "to whine," similar to the Yiddish "to kvetch"; it later changed to a more assertive "to project haughtiness" or "to stand up to the Man." Clipped to *'tude,* it is black English (which may have been its original source) for "confident posture."

Language is playing one of its cyclical tricks. The Latin *aptitudo,* "fitness," root of "aptitude," is also the source of *attitude:* The meaning has to do with the fitness of the arrangement of a body or figure. In the fine arts, this is expressed by sculptors or painters as "the disposition of a figure; the posture given to it to show a mood, humor or spirit."

From this physical positioning, *attitude* came to mean the mental or emotional state that the posture represented. Rodin's *Thinker* was in the physical position, with chin in hand, of being ultrapensive; the artist's intention was to show that as his mental attitude. By figurative extension, the word took on the sense of "opinion": In 1837, Thomas Carlyle wrote (prophetically) "the attitude of the Right Side is that of calm unbelief."

The slang sense in such vogue today reaches back for that original sense of fitness: What's suitable these days, according to those who seek just the right *'tude,* is a mixture of sassiness, brassiness, cockiness, self-assurance and defiance—in terms of posture, standing tall. Too much of this, of course, leads to the hostility and sullenness that is now called *an attitude problem.*

Attitude, with the emphasis on the last syllable, is a position of the body in ballet dancing. The Concise Oxford Dictionary of Ballet, *by Horst Koegler, describes it as "inspired by Giovanni da Bologna's statue of Mercury, and codified by Blasis. The body is supported on one leg with the other lifted behind, the knee bent at an angle of 90 degrees, turned out, with the knee higher than the foot. The corresponding arm is raised above the head, while the other arm is extended to the side. The various national schools have developed different variants." Attitudes are further differentiated by the position of the body in relation to the audience, but that takes us into thickets of ballet French for no good reason.*

Lou D'Angelo
New York, New York

Rodin's Thinker *does not have his chin in his hand. He is chewing his fist, as one might before the Gates of Hell.*

Philip Lancione
New York, New York

Moving the Goalposts

"These conditions are clear-cut and are not open to reinterpretation," said President Bush, explaining his criteria for opening trade with South Africa, "and I do not believe in *moving the goalposts.*"

There's a term that has been popping up of late. "The Japanese . . . can no longer rely on localization as a means of satisfying Europe's requirements," complained a Japanese lobbyist in London. "This is a classic case of moving the goalposts."

A few years ago, following the Reykjavik summit meeting, a British diplomat at the United Nations objected to the way "the Russians have withdrawn from that understanding. . . . They have moved the goal posts."

The first use I can find is in 1978, when Albert V. Casey of American Airlines used the phrase while keeping a stiff upper lip about deregulation. *The Washington Post,* in quoting him, used a revealing verb: " 'They keep moving the goal posts,' he lamented."

You *lament, complain, gripe* and *whine* about moving the goalposts (which I write as one word, contrary to *Times* style, to settle the issue). That is because the phrase refers to an example of unfairness, a useful shortening of "changing the rules in the middle of the game."

"This term is British," says Peter Stothard, United States editor of *The Times* of London, "and means 'changing the terms of a debate or a conflict after it's been started.' I expect it's more from children's playing, where the sticks marking the goal can be moved, than from organized football. It's a very common term now, both in politics and in social conversation. A child, for instance, who's been told to keep his room clean for an extra 50 pence a week, and then doesn't get the extra money, may say, 'Hey, you've moved the goalposts.' "

The term is always accusatory; nobody boasts of moving the goalposts. But a right-wing commentator who was surprised by the scope of change in the Soviet Union, and then set new criteria for the success of perestroika, pre-emptively struck at told-you-so criticism by asserting that he (O.K., *I*) had indeed moved the goalposts "to reflect the basic changes in the game."

In 1974, the ("all-powerful") National Football League Competition Committee did indeed move the goalposts from the goal line to the back of the endzone. Although the committee's stated purpose at the time was to "open up the passing game" (i.e., by eliminating the post as an obstacle), what the move accomplished in concrete terms was to tack an additional 10 yards on to every field-goal and point-after-touchdown attempt.

Thus, your definition of "moving the goalposts" as "changing the rules," while not untrue, strikes this (sports)writer as entirely too vague. Rather, I suggest that "moving the goalposts" means "suddenly making the original objective more difficult to attain."

Eli Spielman
Senior Writer
CBS Sports
New York, New York

Mutt-aphor

I had this great idea of using a comic-strip metaphor to describe tall Boris Yeltsin and short Mikhail Gorbachev as "Mutt and Jeff." In a recent polemic, I wrote about "President Gorbachev (hereinafter known as Mutt for metaphoric purposes . . .)."

Small problem: It turns out Mutt was the tall one in Bud Fisher's strip. In a pre-emptive correction next time up, I admitted breathlessly that "My entire essay was built on a metaphoric lie."

"You now have Mutt and Jeff sorted out," writes Louis Jay Herman of New York, "but not *metaphor*." He argues that *metaphor* has a precise meaning: "a figure of speech containing an implied comparison, in which a word or phrase ordinarily and primarily used of one thing is applied to another," citing as examples *the long arm of coincidence* and *food for thought*.

"The fact that *metaphor* currently enjoys cachet among the semi-literati," he says, "and is being used to mean everything from *symbol, analogy* and *simile* to ham on rye is no reason why you, of all people, should join the parade."

I am tired of admitting error. In olden times, *analogy* was the general term for "comparison for effect"; *metaphor* was an implied comparison ("long arm of the law"), and *simile* a direct comparison ("eyes like limpid poolrooms"). The umbrella term covering these two figures of speech, *analogy,* also had a specific meaning: "the illuminating of a likeness by use of a parallel structure," like explaining a complicated war in terms of a simple football game.

Guess what: The umbrella has changed. Usage has relegated *analogy* to its specific senses, including linguistic patterns (*empathize,* from *empathy,* by analogy of *sympathize,* from *sympathy*). Usage has elevated *metaphor* to umbrella status, meaning not only "implied comparison" but also "a figure of speech that explains by comparing different things with certain unexpected likenesses."

I resisted this switching of umbrellas for years, while awaiting the vogue use of "this is a metaphor for" to fade; it has not. Nobody says even "this stands for that" anymore. (Brother, can you paradigm?) So here I stand, my ultimate cave-in on this a metaphor for (no longer *analogous to*) my approach to politics: Stand up for what's right until it stops being right.

Mr. Herman is right to resist vogue words; he and I have hooted at the abuse of *vulnerable,* and his crusade against the pretentious overuse of *resonate* and *frisson* has my support. (Lex Irregs who believe that vogue words and phrases are *out of control* are invited to send them in, with citations, for a Vogue Word Watch.) But there is a time to loathe and a time to cave, and *a metaphor for* has driven *analogous to* from the tip of the tongue. I just have to remember that Mutt was the tall one.

Dear Bill:

Your mistake about the relative heights of Mutt and Jeff is a tribute to your superior sense of words—superior to that of their creator and also in the absolute sense. For the sound, look, and connotation of Mutt *is shortness: a poor little mutt of a stray dog; while* Jeff *is inescapably tallness: Geoffrey, Jeffery—giraffe!*

I think every philosophical mind must have felt the wrongheadedness of the fellow who baptized them. Even as an adolescent, soon after I came to this country, I noticed the inversion and remembered which was which by the mnemonic device of "it's the opposite of what you think."

Yours,
Jacques [Barzun]
New York, New York

As for simile, analogy, etc., I must say that I've never metaphor I didn't like.

Herman Gross
Great Neck, New York

The New Contras

"It's a great day," enthused Dr. C. Wayne Bardin, one of the developers of Norplant, when the Federal Drug Administration approved the contraceptive device to be implanted under a woman's skin. (You wonder about the use of *enthuse,* a verb back-formed from *enthusiasm*? I have just approved it; these things sometimes take years.)

"There are going to be a significant number of women who really like this," Dr. Bardin went on to say, construing *a significant number* to be plural. "Whether it is 2 percent or 10 percent of *contraceptors,* I can't say."

Those of us in the language dodge were startled—and some troubled—by the implantation of a new *agent noun,* one of those words that describe a person performing an action. (Following Dr. Bardin's lead, I construe "one of those words" to be the plural antecedent of "that.") Some agent nouns—*writer, actress, firefighter, activist*—raise no eyebrows, but *contraceptor* is new.

It begins, as so many things do, with *conception,* a fourteenth-century term for "the state of being conceived; the act resulting in pregnancy." In 1886, a social scientist, E. B. Foote, wrote: "Where it becomes a necessity to decide between lawful abortion and unlawful contraception, they prefer to break the manmade law against *contraceptics* rather than the natural law against abortion."

Foote's coinage was partly followed; *contra* was used, and the *con* in *conception* was dropped, but the ending was changed within five years from *-ics* to *-ives,* and we had the noun *contraceptives.*

But what do we call one who uses contraceptives? What is the agent noun? If a *reception* is handled by a *receptionist,* is not a *contraception* to be done by a *contraceptionist?*

That's what the *Boston Pilot* thought in 1917, sternly editorializing: "The *contraceptionist* would take from the Almighty all power over life and dispose matters after his own whim and liking."

But that word died aborning. *Reception,* for example, required an agent noun other than *receptionist* (which was limited to an office worker) and *receiver* (largely limited to a leaping football player); as a result, *receptor* was born, on the Latin analogy of *deceptor,* "deceiver," *inceptor,* "beginner" and *praeceptor,* "teacher."

Here we go, then: From *contraception* was back-formed the verb *to contracept* (it's O.K. to use backward constructions only in describing back-formation), and finally—rejecting *contraceptionist* as unwieldy—the innovative language gives birth to the new term *contraceptor,* "one who practices contraception."

If an idea conceived in the brain is a *concept,* wouldn't a good word for an opposing idea be a *contracept?* No. Geddoudahere. *Contracept* has already been taken.

I am now applying for the position of Latin and Greek secretary to the column. I urge you to disapprove "enthuse" as soon as possible for any discourse above the level of whimsy. The "-iasm" in the corresponding noun and the "-iastic" of the adjective derive from a verbalizing ending that Greek has to resort to because it is too highly inflected to function shift a word without changing its form, which English can do because it is a more sequential language. The only acceptable derivation would be "enthusiasticize," which you will agree is hopeless. How about "Dr. C. Wayne Bardin asserted enthusiastically" or "gushed Dr. C. Wayne Bardin"?

> Thomas J. Snow
> New York, New York

My Aching Back-Formation

The verb *to back-form* was back-formed from the compound noun *back-formation.* To many of us in the language dodge, that observation of a new circularity is proof of the inexorable working of justice, the symmetry of feedback and the existence of God.

Back-formation is defined by E. Ward Gilman in *Merriam-Webster's Dictionary of English Usage* as "a word formed by removing an affix—real or supposed—from an already existing word." To understand that, it's helpful to know that an *affix* is something added to a word at the beginning (prefix) or at the end (suffix) or in the middle (infix, as in *absobloodylutely*). The linguistic surgery can be as minor as a single letter: From the field of *statistics,* Merriam-Webster says, we clipped off the final *s* to backform a single *statistic.* (I do not hyphenate the verb *backform* because I do not *backdate* checks to the gym where I alleviate my *backache* by doing *backbends;* I hyphenate the noun *back-formation* because the dictionaries do and I don't want to backslide.)

"Less is more" applies to language, because the subtraction of an affix leads to the addition of a new word. From a nice medieval bowl of *pease,* some finicky eater fished out a single unit he mistakenly called a *pea,* just as the person today receiving *kudos,* meaning "applause," thinks he can get one hand to clap with a single *kudo.*

Hold on, now: If a single *pea* is acceptable, how can the panjandrums of the usage mafia hold that a single *kudo* is a mistake—an egregious solecism, an example of what Americans can do to Greek when they don't understand that language? This eat-your-peas diktat seems inconsistent, but give a panjandrum a break: We resist the trendy (not formed, I suspect, by adding to *trend*, but backformed by subtracting from *trendiness*) and like to make a word work long and hard before granting it standard status.

Gangle strikes me as a wonderful verb, describing a loose, graceful awkwardness of a lanky person, or the posture of a basketball player when he's just standing around; it is backformed from *gangling*. Same as *burgle* from *burglar*, with its nice distinction in meaning from *rob* and *robber:* Although legal definitions vary, you *burgle* a place, but you *rob* a person. On the other hand, *dangle* is not a back-formation from *dangling;* the verb probably came first, from the Old Scandinavian. The dangling participles we have come to know and love are described by the present participle of the verb *dangle*.

Because we knock the nonce, usage mavens look askance at back-formations like *liaise:* Instead of discreetly developing a deliciously dangerous *liaison*, too many promiscutarians freely *liaise* with anybody they want to hop into communication with. We heap ridicule on the new word to see if it will slink away; if it sticks around and fills a linguistic need, we will eventually liaise with it. Maybe we'll accept from *laser beams* the new verb *to lase*—"See if you can lase out a few of these stupidity cells in my brain, willya, doc?"— and this will conflict with *liaise* as well as with *laze* as in *laze around*, backformed from *lazy;* in that case, the three sounds will fight it out in the marketplace of the mouth. (I'm free-associating here, but madness-methodology is involved.)

Are we right to resist the invitation to the bacchanalia of back-formation? Of course; that's our job. When do we cave in and join the party? Some sooner, some later, which brings me to the chief of the Burning Deck Brigade, Jacques Barzun, Prescriptivist Emeritus.

"I see that you took advantage of the holiday spirit of riot and revelry," he writes, "to indulge in the use of *enthuse*. But I think I also detect a twinge of guilt in your aside that here is a back-formation you have judged acceptable at last."

He's right. I use *enthuse*, in the sense of "to show enthusiasm for," because I can't get the right meaning out of *gush, excite, emote* or any of its other near synonyms; no other verb does the trick. I know that the poet Robert Frost used *enthused* in a letter in 1894; still, the usage gives me a frisson of furtiveness.

"A back-formation it certainly is," writes Professor Barzun, one of my octogenarian mentors, "but have you wondered why it has not been accepted long ago like several others? The reason is, it does not backform properly. People do not consciously work out the backward step, but they have a sense that *burgle* is to *burglar* what *sail* is to *sailor*, *laze* is to *lazy* what *craze* is to *crazy*. They do not know or worry about the fact that *sail* precedes *sailor* and *craze, crazy*. Even the dubious *frivol* sounds legitimate because of *desire, desirous; covet, covetous*. The seeming models seem to fit."

Ah-hah. Watch out for that "seeming." We approach the source of my guilt: "Now the relation of *enthusiasm* to *enthuse* is not like the others," Professor Barzun writes. "It's not a verb snatched from a noun or an adjective supposedly born of a verb. Is there a parallel? With *phantasm* we have its original twin, *phantasy,* and by extension *phantasize.* But we have no *enthusy* and nobody would cheer for *enthusize.* Try getting a verb out of *dynamism, orgasm, patriotism, pleonasm, tuberculosis, seismic,* and the like. You can't, because they have no cognate in common use and no 'model,' right or wrong.

"It was possible to work back from *diagnosis* to *diagnose,* which was instantly accepted, because we had *gnosis, gnostic* and the absurd *agnostic.* . . . After *diagnosis,* I understand, lab workers use the verb *osmose*—fair enough."

But isn't there some linguistic way to get around the lack of a snippable affix? Can't we have *enthuse* even if it's not a legitimate back-formation?

"The only way out for your baby," offers this sage of Scribners, "is to say that *enthuse* starts fresh with *en* (in) and *thuse* (god) to mean 'bring in the god,' like *enlist, entrain, involve,* etc. In that case what we have is a neologism, not a back-formation, and the choosy will find it 'colloquial only,' because nowhere around is there any *thuse* (*theos*) to work up from. Now if you used *Zeus,* which is the same thing, I'd be with you; I'd *enzeus* or *enzuze* heartily at your side."

Bring in the god; send in the clowns; but let me have *enthuse.* In return, I'll swear off *liaise* for the rest of the millennium.

You are one super human being, but I was exceptionally impressed by your discussion of the "infix"—halfway between a suffix and a prefix. The example you used abso-bloody-lutely was unfuckingbelievable.

Arthur B. Laffer
La Jolla, California

Like you, I think enthuse *is an OK word, even though it doesn't pass the Barzun Test. However, those who simply must have a properly formed verb to keep company with* enthusiasm *and* enthusiast *need look no further than Greek, which provides not a back-formation but a full-fledged, perfectly kosher front-formation. Greek* enthousiasmos *and* enthousiastes *are formed from the verb* enthousiazein, *which can easily be Englished into* enthusiaze *(not pretty, but etymologically correct). By the same token, Greek* gymnastes *goes back to a verb* gymnazein, *so that there's nothing to prevent you from saying that the gymnast went over to the gym and gymnazed around for a while. Not only that, but an orgiast* (orgiastes) *can orgiaze* (orgiazein) *at an orgy, and, once you're on this kick, analogy permits iconoclasts to iconoclaze and (for the privately printed edition of your next book) pederasts to pederaze. (Incidentally, -asm, -ast, -aze are parallel with -ism, -ist, -ize:* antagonism, antagonist, antagonize.*)*

An etymological note for them as likes etymology: Just as the Greek source of enthusiastic *meant "inspired or possessed by a god* (theos),*" that is also the generally accepted underlying meaning of English* giddy, *which appears to be related to the word* god.

Louis Jay Herman
New York, New York

On First Looking into
Merriam Webster's English Usage

Henry Fowler, William Safire,
Noah Webster and E. B. White
Thought that they knew all the rules
On how to say and write things right.

H. L. Mencken, Ambrose Bierce,
Like Johnson, Sam, and Jonson, Ben,
Declaimed at length their snobbish views
On what to say, and where and when.

William Zinsser, Bergen Evans,
Emily Post and Joseph Priestly
Hesitated not a whit
To tell us what was couth or beastly.

Teddy Bernstein, Edwin Newman,
Stephen Leacock and William Strunk
Confidently sneered at phrases
We thought fine, but they said stunk.

But now comes Webster's "English Usage"
To tell us not to fear for error.
They'll cite someone who said it first—
Like President Bush or Yogi Berra.

D.B.C.
2/9/91

D. Bret Carlson
Fairfield, Connecticut

The New New World Order

"The old order changeth," said the dying King Arthur in Alfred Lord Tennyson's 1842 poem "Morte d'Arthur," "yielding place to new."

He was right. "As I look at the countries that are chipping in here now, I think we do have a chance at a *new world order,*" President Bush told a news conference on August 30, 1990.

He liked the sound of that phrase. In his address to the United Nations General Assembly a month later, he used it again in urging a worldwide ban on chemical weapons and a redoubling of efforts to stem the spread of nuclear and biological weapons. (The Defense Department lumped *nuclear, biological* and *chemical* together under the letters NBC, which is causing great pain at the National Broadcasting Company.) "It is in our hands to leave these dark machines behind, in the dark ages where they belong," Mr. Bush said, "and to press forward to cap a historic movement toward a *new world order,* and a long era of peace."

As the phrase caught on, Mr. Bush gave it a context of cooperative action to stop aggression. In his 1991 State of the Union Message, he called upon the world "to fulfill the long-held promise of a *new world order*—where brutality will go unrewarded and aggression will meet collective resistance."

Where did he get it from? Possibly from James A. Baker 3d, his Secretary of State, who must have heard it often when he served as President Reagan's Treasury Secretary. At a 1985 meeting in Seoul, South Korea, when Mr. Baker lectured countries that "attempt to go it alone," the Peruvian Minister of Finance, Alva Castro, responded with a plea for a *"new world order"* to replace the International Monetary Fund and assume the debt of third world countries. On May 22, 1986, the *Financial Times* headlined a story on banking that grew out of this meeting "Towards a New World Order."

Another possible source was Mikhail S. Gorbachev, who told a conference of the World Media Association in the Kremlin on April 11, 1990, according to the Tass translation, "We are only at the beginning of the process of shaping a *new world order.*" For months, the Soviet leader had been using phrases translated as "unique world order" and "integral world" as well as *new world order.* Eight months later, he returned to the phrase in rejecting ideas of a loose confederation of Soviet republics, insisting instead on "our remaining a great country, one of the pillars of the *new world order* that is being built."

For the first time, the leaders of both superpowers were pushing the same phrase. (The closest previous pass at this phenomenon was when Richard Nixon tentatively titled his 1971 economic package the New Economic Plan but was stopped in the nick of time by my own vague recollection that this was the name Lenin used in 1921.) No wonder NWO (pronounced "new-oh") caught on; if you resisted the phrase, you were out of order.

But our etymological dig is just getting started on this: Where did the leaders of the U.S. and U.S.S.R. pick up the phrase?

It's United Nations diplolingo. In 1974, the General Assembly advanced a plan to redistribute wealth from rich to poor nations it called the New International Economic Order. That turned out to be a nonstarter (a word originating in British racing terminology) and led linguistically to the New World Information and Communications Order, a plan sponsored by Unesco to sanction government control of news organizations. Although the substitution of *world* for *international* helped the phrase, that notion was seen in the Western industrialized countries as a censorship scheme and faded away by the late 1980's.

Meanwhile, third world diplomats in the 70's had been pressing for a Law of the Sea Treaty; this was headlined in the May 5, 1975, *U.S. News & World Report* as "New Order of the Sea." The magazine reported that "American officials would prefer to negotiate a treaty establishing a *new world order* by general consent." However, this treaty was opposed by the Reagan Administration, and its demise was helped by right-wing pundits who kept harping on its unfortunate acronym, LOST. *U.S. News* liked the phrase *new world order* and pioneered its use frequently throughout the 70's, although it wrote in that same May 5 issue: "You hear less and less talk these days of 'a *new world order.*' "

Henry A. Kissinger, as Secretary of State in the mid-70's, was hoping to build what he called "a new structure of stability, a new order of peace." That structural metaphor was picked up later by both Mr. Gorbachev—*perestroika* means "restructuring"—and James Baker, whose "New Architecture" never made it out of the basement. But any use of the term *new order,* without the interceding word *world,* is insensitive, because it has connotations that should cause diplomats to shudder.

Die neue Ordnung was Hitler's language for imposing a National Socialist regime throughout Europe, much as *co-prosperity sphere* was the Japanese phrase for their imperial plan. During a visit to Berlin in 1940, Foreign Commissar V. M. Molotov asked Hitler, "What does the new order in Europe and Asia amount to, and what part is the U.S.S.R. to play in it?" Two years later Stalin was saying, "They have turned Europe into a prison of nations, and this they call the 'new order' in Europe."

But wait—years before, at the 1932 Democratic convention, F.D.R. pledged "a new deal for the American people." His next line, drafted by Samuel I. Rosenman or Raymond Moley: "Let us all here assembled constitute ourselves prophets of a new order of competence and of courage." The newspapers (led by a political cartoonist, Rollin Kirby) chose *new deal* over *new order.*

The last spadefuls of the dig turn up a hyphenated *world-order,* meaning "an organized existence in this or another world," used by Archbishop Richard Trench of Ireland in 1846: "There is a nobler world-order than that in which we live and move," and finally, the Latin root *ordiri*, "to lay the warp," or to prepare the loom for the beginning of weaving.

All this digging shows how a famous phrase is not "coined," but rather updated or reconstituted or adapted. This one is worth watching; it may fit the same sort of linguistic need that enshrined *cold war* and *Iron Curtain*, which were popularized (but not coined) by Bernard Baruch and Winston Churchill.

The question "Where does *new world order* come from?" is easy enough to answer, as we have seen; the nice double meaning of *new world* and *world order* has yet to be remarked, as if the orderliness of the world is to be the responsibility of the New World, or Western Hemisphere. The next question is "What does *new world order* mean?" Sorry, that's beyond the phrasedick paygrade. For the definition, we political lexicographers must defer to political leaders; President Bush has not yet made his *"New World Order* speech."

Gotcha! Safire,

New World Order is the doing of Adam Weishaupt in Bavaria on May 1, 1776. This world conspiracy slipped Novus Ordo Seclorum onto the great seal, and fellow-travelling Henry A. Wallace got it put on the currency having duped Morgenthau into thinking it was Latin for New Deal. *CFR member Richard Nixon was part of the undercover follow-up.*

A Concerned and Patriotic Citizen,

> *Daniel P. Moynihan*
> *Senator, New York*
> *United States Senate*
> *Washington, D.C.*

The phrase has recurred many times (a 1987 book by Gary Allen, titled Say "No" *to the New World Order, is devoted to a conspiracy of Communists and bankers to bring America under the domination of a world government). But in its current use by President Bush, it can be traced back to a speech by Gorbachev to the U.N. General Assembly on December 7, 1988, in the presence of President Reagan and President-elect Bush.*

Under the subheading "Toward a New World Order," Gorbachev said, "Today, further world progress is only possible through a search for universal human consensus as we move toward a new world order."

Indications are that N.W.O. figured in summit conversations in Malta, and the idea came up strongly to refer to the emerging coalition in the Gulf. Thus, Bush, at his August 30, 1990, news conference, "As I look at the countries that are chipping in here now, I think we do have a chance at a new world order . . ."

Marlin Fitzwater on September 5, 1990, talking about the impending Helsinki summit: "A new foundation for a New World Order is being built and the spadework begins in Helsinki."

President Bush, arriving in Helsinki September 8: "We have entered a new era in world affairs . . . the actions we take can shape this new world for years to come."

Before a joint session of Congress September 11: "Out of these troubled times, our fifth objective—a new world order—can emerge."

Secretary Baker, in Moscow September 13 for a meeting with Gorbachev: "This (Soviet-American cooperation) offers an immense chance for creating a new world order."

During the Fall campaign, Bush referred to N.W.O. dozens of times. Thus, September 19, at a Wilson for governor rally: "Ours is the generation to finally see the emergence of a promising exciting New World Order which we have sought for generations."

And, on October 1, 1990, President Bush brought the N.W.O. home to the U.N. General Assembly, where he had heard about it from the lips of Gorbachev twenty-two months earlier: "It is in our hands . . . to press forward to cap a historic movement towards a new world order and a long era of peace."

As you suggest, we still don't know what it means, except that it's what is supposed to happen "beyond containment."

> *Yours,*
> *Dan [Daniel Schorr]*
> *Washington, D.C.*

P.S. It may be "NBC" to the Pentagon now, but for years it was ABC (atomic, biological and chemical) including during the Nixon Administration. Fairness dictates that, at some point, it should become Chemical, Biological and Savage weapons.

I may have the satisfaction of doing a documented gotcha on the Pharaoh of the Phrasedicks.

For all its chilling Nazi connotations, I believe the phrase new order, in its political sense, can be traced to the Latin novus ordo seclorum, which appears on the unfamiliar obverse of the Great Seal of the United Sates (see any one-dollar bill). My mother always told me that this should be translated as "a new order for the ages" and, if so, would bear a striking resemblance in meaning and political connotation to the current buzzword.

> *Philip T. Weinstein*
> *Miami, Florida*

This afternoon the Bancroft Library yielded up a copy of Great Seal of the United States *(U.S. Dept. of State 1986), and a comforting validation of my thesis that "new world order" is traceable to this nation and its 18th-century origin, and ultimately to Virgil.*

According to State (vested by the United States Code with custodianship of the Great Seal, see 4 U.S.C. sec. 42), on 20 August 1776 Franklin (chair), Adams, and Jefferson were tasked to formulate the seal of the new nation. Almost immediately they agreed on the obverse design of an eagle and the motto e pluribus unum. *But in a manner more typical of contemporary legislative deliberation, the Congress did not complete this task for six years. Then, remarkably, the job was done in a fit of seven days.*

On 13 June 1782, the Congress charged its secretary, Charles Thompson, to recommend a final seal design. Seven days later he presented his design of the reverse, featuring the pyramid and the two Latin mottos annuit coeptis *and* novus ordo seclorum. *State translates the latter "a new order of the ages," but more relevantly, Thompson's report, adopted by Congress on 20 June 1782, stated, "The date underneath (the pyramid) is that of the Declaration of Independence and the words under it signify the beginning of the New American Aera, which commences from that date."*

As a lawyer and law professor, I'd argue that translates into "new world order," a translation consistent with the dual derivation from the Latin sæculum, either "of or pertaining to the world," or "of or belonging to an age or long period."

Antonio Rossmann
School of Law
University of California
Berkeley, California

Enclosed please find a copy of a passage from The Visit, *a play by Friedrich Dürrenmatt. I thought perhaps the phrase "new world order" might interest you. Patrick Bowles did the translation from the German (Grove Press, Inc.)*

CLAIRE ZACHANASSIAN: *Feeling for humanity, gentlemen, is cut for the purse of an ordinary millionaire; with financial resources like mine you can afford a new world order. The world turned me into a whore. I shall turn the world into a brothel.*

Karen Payne
Berkeley, California

Nice, Bossy

Soda jerks (now called *fountain attendants*) know that a *black cow* is a root beer float. What of *cash cow*? "It is apparent that [Mortimer] Zuckerman has improved the magazine during a very difficult period for newsmagazines," wrote Eleanor Randolph of *The Washington Post* about the owner of the competing *U.S. News & World Report*. But, "On the business level, the magazine is no longer the *cash cow* it once was."

Writing about Time's merger with Warner, *Newsweek* observed, "Cable companies can be *cash cows,* but they periodically dilute earnings while constructing their cable networks." Note the nice adverbial play on *periodical* in that sentence—journalists enjoy covering each other—but the writers may not have been sensitive to the latest and slightly larcenous connotation of *cash cow.*

This financial slang term, which popped up in the early 1970's, at first meant "a dependable source of profit," with this refinement: "a subsidiary company producing funds used to finance other investments or to nourish divisions of a corporation that do not produce current income."

In the 1980's, however, our innocently bovine locution gained a second sense of "company being abused by predators," as in this angry comment quoted in the *Los Angeles Times:* "Diamond International used United

States Playing Card as a *cash cow,* siphoning money to other areas. . . ." *The Washington Post* wrote of a savings and loan officer "accused of illegally milking First Maryland as 'their own *cash cow*' from 1982 to 1985, squandering millions of depositors' dollars on themselves, insider loans, kickbacks and risky commercial ventures."

The root of the metaphor is the pejorative use of the verb *to milk,* in its sense of "to draw off money or assets as if by milking." (The associated *to bilk,* or defraud, may have come from an amalgam of *to balk* and *to milk.*) Stuart Berg Flexner of Random House thinks the new noun phrase was influenced by *cash crop,* and may even be associated with the biblical *golden calf;* I suppose *cash flow* belongs in that network of roots.

Be careful of the changing meaning of this phrase, and guard against the herd instinct in stretching the metaphor: *Forbes* was stampeded into quoting a businessman in 1977 saying, "As a *cash cow* turns into a *dead horse,* it's going to be gotten rid of."

In a related development (a journalistic phrase that means "might as well stick this on here"), *U.S. News* recently zapped its better-selling rival in this advertisement: "According to *The Wall Street Journal, Time* magazine is about to reduce their rate base by another 300,000. Which means you'll be hearing a lot of the familiar excuses . . ."

An institution or group is not plural, except in England; the English say *the audience are* and *the public have,* but Americans construe the group as singular. Thus, in referring to a magazine, it is incorrect to write of "their" rate base; it's *its.* (I would add that the next sentence should have begun with *that* rather than *which,* but that would be flogging a cash cow.)

You stated that "a black cow *is a root beer float." According to the enclosed excerpt, however, "to the root beer and vanilla ice cream in an ordinary root beer float, add a little cream and chocolate syrup—and what you've got is what your grandmother called a* brown cow*" ("Informed Source"/by L. M. Boyd/ Houston Post/Feb. 1, 1989).*

It seems to me that adding chocolate syrup to a root beer float would turn it from brown to black, more or less, and therefore the most sensible use of these terms is to call a root beer float a brown cow and to call it a black cow only if chocolate syrup is added to it.

Charles D. Poe
Houston, Texas

No Leading Role

"The most important weapon in my arsenal," Joseph Stalin was quoted as saying, "is the dictionary."

Maybe Old Joe said it and maybe he did not: It is on the cover of Raymond S. Sleeper's 1983 *Lexicon of Marxist-Leninist Semantics,* and the source the author cites is Stalin's book *The Word.*

Apocryphal or not, the Stalinist hosanna to dictionaries is intended to show his respect for linguistic manipulation. As Humpty Dumpty demonstrated, meanings can be assigned to words to suit the speaker, corrupting communication and derailing intelligent discourse.

Take the *leading role* of the Communist party.

To most of the world, that phrase comes from the theater and means "the most important part to be played"; the *leading role* does not mean "the only role" or even "the position that runs the show," as most theatrical producers and directors will heatedly point out. Perhaps originating in navigation's *leading light* or *guiding light,* the phrases *leading man* and *leading lady* entered the language in 1827 and 1874, with both phrases now clipped to the nonsexist *lead; leading role* and *title role* date back at least to the beginning of this century.

However, in Communese, "total control" is what *leading role* is intended to mean: domination, mastery, command. The "role," or part, is a euphemism for central authority.

Now here comes the mystery: Why does the Western world refer to the leading *role* of the Communist party? That word does not appear in the Soviet Constitution's notorious Article 6, adopted in 1977, reading:

"The Communist Party of the Soviet Union is the leading and guiding force of the Soviet society, the nucleus of its political system. . . . The Communist Party determines general prospects for the development of society and the lines of . . . domestic and foreign policy."

The Russian phrase transliterated into our alphabet is *rukovodiashchaia i napravliaiushchaia sila.* The word *sila* does not mean "role," which would be transliterated into the similar *rol'.* Instead, *sila* means "force," a word that also has the sense of "strength, physical power" and the legal sense of "in power, in effect."

Let's face it: *Force* is a stronger word than *role,* much closer to "power" than mere "participant."

"In Stalin's time," says Professor Robert Sharlot of Union College in Schenectady, New York, a student of the Soviet Constitution, "they referred to themselves as 'the vanguard of the proletariat,' playing a 'leading role,' but the word adopted in the 1977 Constitution is definitely the Russian word for *force.*"

Because this explicit statement of party domination was a Brezhnev-era codification of Stalinist practice, it can be changed without challenging the Lenin heritage; recently, a move to amend Article 6 was narrowly defeated in the Supreme Soviet. Curiously, most Western coverage of this attempted change referred to the *leading role,* making the empowerment of the party seem more gentle than Leonid I. Brezhnev's Constitution-writers probably intended.

Does *the leading and guiding force* mean what it says? No constitutional court exists in the Soviet Union to do the interpreting, as our Supreme Court under John Marshall assumed the right to do.

Let's keep an eye on Article 6 and on similar articles in the constitutions of satellite states (soon to be called "neighboring states"). *Role* or *force*? *Leading* or *guiding* or merely *significant*? A movement is afoot to use words that mean what the rest of the world accepts them to mean.

Now let's consider a favorite term of perestroika. (I do not use italics for that word; it has entered the English language now and is on a par with the Russian and English *troika,* a word that replaced the Latin-based *triumverate.*) The term is *neobratimy*—in English, "irreversible."

Are the changes being made under perestroika permanent? Mikhail S. Gorbachev called a party conference in 1988 specifically to make his wide-ranging reform program *neobratimy.* West German Chancellor Helmut Kohl said about helping East Germany, "Economic aid will be in vain unless there is an irreversible reform of the economic system. . . ." Recently, the Tass correspondent Alexander Sorokin asserted, "Changes taking place in the U.S.S.R. are positive and irreversible."

Not everybody agreed that the clock could not be turned back: "All these welcome changes we are seeing in the Warsaw Pact countries," wrote Caspar W. Weinberger, "are neither irreversible nor cause for concluding that the West and NATO can reduce their military strength now." The former Defense Secretary derided the word by putting its adverb form into quotation marks: "Less than six months ago, China . . . was 'irreversibly' launched on the road to free market economics and more democracy, or so most people believed and hoped."

"I think that the changes in Eastern Europe are now essentially irreversible," Joshua Muravchik of the American Enterprise Institute told a Heritage Foundation panel, adding, "That's a funny word that's come into our political vocabulary."

Why funny, in the sense of odd? "Because, of course, in politics nothing is irreversible. . . . In using this word, we should assume that we don't really quite mean it." When Mr. Muravchik used the word, he limited his meaning to "the sense that I don't believe that conservative forces within those Communist parties have it in their power any longer to effect a reversal and a re-establishment of their authority by means of force."

The closest synonym to *irreversible* is *unrecallable*, but that is rarely used; the more familiar *irrevocable* is available, but connotes specific laws rather than a movement or tide; *unstoppable* does not have the backward-turning sense; *unalterable* and *unchangeable* also miss the point of continuing change.

The word was carefully chosen, both by Mr. Gorbachev and by his translators, but has been used by different politicians in other circumstances. Delaware Senator Joseph R. Biden Jr. in April 1987 told an audience that, in the 1988 election, "the country will be set on an irreversible course, and once the genie is out of the bottle, there's no way to put her back in."

That brings us to the figures of speech used to illustrate irreversibility. Mr. Biden's *genie out of the bottle* is a reference to Aladdin and his Magic Lamp, from an ancient Persian folk tale. My copy of the Aladdin story in Richard F. Burton's translation of *The Arabian Nights' Entertainments* does not have a passage showing the reluctance of the genie to go back into the lamp. (I am now rubbing my word processor in the hope that an expert in Persian folk tales will magically materialize, but it doesn't work.)

A twentieth-century trope for the same idea is *there's no putting the toothpaste back in the tube,* which was used sometime after 1895, when that dentifrice was first put into the container.

A third metaphor, *turning back the clock* or *setting back the clock,* can be tracked to 1635; perestroika-shocked cold warriors like to say that their favorite moment of the year comes in October, when daylight saving time ends, and "you actually get to turn back the clock."

I had only three years of high school Latin, and that was forty years ago, but if, as you say, the word you are using is "Latin-based," it has to be triumvirate, *rule by three men, each of whom is a "vir."*

> Walter Nugent
> Granger, Indiana

Transforming the word triumvirate *into (ugh!)* triumverate *is the most shocking thing you have done since that day of infamy when you wrote* androgenous *instead of* androgynous.

I detect a definite pattern here. First of all, you seem to be suffering from an e-fixation. (This can be analyzed from a psychophonetic standpoint, but I won't go into it at this time.) More important, there seems to be latent sexism at work. Last year, you neutered the Greek root gyn *"woman" into* gen *"race, kind, species." Now you have turned upon your own sex (gender, whatever) and attempted to disguise the fact that the third syllable of* triumvirate *contains the Latin word* vir, *"man," to which we are also indebted for* virile *and* virtue. *(If you'd like a native English cognate, there's the first part of* werewolf.*) Enuf said.*

> Louis Jay Herman
> New York, New York

This is doubtless the 2000th letter you will have received noting your original rendering of the word "triumvirate." Nevertheless, I need to point out that by spelling it "triumverate," you have emasculated a highly virile word. This would be so alien to your normally robust approach that it must be assumed you were sabotaged by a solo, duo or possibly even troika of liberal proofreaders.

> Lincoln P. Bloomfield
> Professor of Political Science
> Massachusetts Institute of
> Technology
> Cambridge, Massachusetts

With the Light Brown Hair

Irreversible is the big word in perestroika these days. What's a good figure of speech to suggest irreversibility? I recently tried two of the best known: the modern *to put the toothpaste back in the tube* and the older *to put the genie back in the bottle.*

When I confessed an inability to find the genie episode in the Aladdin story in *The Arabian Nights' Entertainments,* Lexicographic Irregulars rushed to the rescue. "The reference is not to Aladdin and his lamp," writes Patrick J. O'Connor of West Redding, Connecticut, "but to King Solomon, who, according to legend (a legend that Richard F. Burton, in a footnote to the 836th Night, says is 'often mentioned in the *Nights'*) sealed *jinn* in bottles and cast the bottles into the sea. Anyone finding such a bottle and breaking the seal of Solomon thus released a *jinni* imprisoned for many centuries and understandably reluctant to return to the bottle." (This legend of Solomon does not appear in the Bible; however, Solomon, the "Son of David," is mentioned frequently in this tale of a fisherman who found a bottle and opened it, releasing an evil spirit.)

Peter Wagner of Scarsdale, New York, picked up the story: "The imprisoned *jinni* had sworn he would kill the person who freed him. Our fisherman was not exactly pleased by this prospect and tried a trick. He told the *jinni* [nine pieces of mail, three different spellings] that he could not believe that such a huge being could have been in such a small bottle. The *jinni* [so spelled in the singular from the Arabic word in Muslim folklore for "demon," often confused with the Latin *genius,* "guardian spirit," in French *génie,* causing the English spelling of *genie,* and this is longer than any interpolation should be in brackets] was foolish enough to demonstrate how he could get back in the bottle, which the fisherman closed again very quickly."

That's curious: The story of the fisherman and the genie illustrates the opposite of irreversibility. You can, if you're shrewd enough, get the *genie* (*jinni, jann, djinn,* sometimes called the *ifrit*) back in the bottle. Most writers think the opposite: "After Lowth and Priestley had let the genie of disapproval out of the bottle, however tentatively," writes *Merriam-Webster's Dictionary of English Usage* in the entry on *whose,* "there was no putting it back." (E. Ward Gilman, its editor, would explain that usage makes it correct; he's wrong.)

Genies, by the way, used to be illustrated as male; in the 1960's, a sitcom titled *I Dream of Jeannie* starring Barbara Eden switched that assumption to female. The title was a play on the song by Stephen Foster that begins "I dream of Jeanie with the light brown hair," and the pun further confused the spelling of *genie/jinni.* However, the TV Jeannie was often tricked back into the bottle in accordance with the original legend.

If it is the nature of genies to be tricked back into bottles, where is a suitable ancient reference to irreversibility? Aha! Try the Greek myth of Pandora's box. That receptacle contained all forms of human evil; once it was opened, there was no way to recapture the evils released.

Fortunately for mankind (renamed nonsexily *humankind* by global warmers), Pandora's box also contained Hope, which is what keeps alive Mr. Gorbachev's belief that the toothpaste of perestroika cannot be pushed back into the Stalinist tube.

Genie is a male, Genniah is a female. Ifrit is a male, and Ifritah is a female.

Heskel M. Haddad
New York, New York

You, at one point, used the word djinn *interchangeably with the word* efreet. *The djinn were, in ancient mythology, enchanted creatures from the Elemental Plane of Air, which appeared in the form of humanlike beings surrounded by clouds. Efreet were creatures from the Elemental Plane of Fire, which appeared as giant men surrounded by fire. Efreet and djinn were mortal enemies.*

David Alvaro
Westfield, New Jersey

You say, "Fortunately for mankind (renamed nonsexily humankind *by global warmers)...." "Nonsexily" is wrong. In fact, no such word exists in* Webster's Ninth *edition.* Sexily *is the adverbial form of the adjective* sexy. Nonsexily *then would be the opposite, meaning not sexually stimulating or attractive. I presume you mean nonsexist or non-gender-specific, in which case you would need to recast the sentence, since nonsexistly not only doesn't exist, but sounds horrendous.*

Gigi Marino
University Park, Pennsylvania

The way the nuns of St. Vincent Ferrer School explained it half a century ago was that "in" or "on" pertain to a situation of being, whereas "into" or "onto" denote a change in location of someone or something. Thus, "The girl ran into the room," not, "The girl ran in the room," unless of course she was already in the room and perhaps running in circles. Similarly, "He put The New York Times Magazine *onto the table," not "on the table."*

I find that the almost universal surrendering of this distinction actually makes reading more difficult, as it is often necessary to reread a sentence after the "in" interpretation didn't seem to make sense.

In your column we see "... put the toothpaste back in the tube ...," "... put the genie back in the bottle ...," and, later, no less than twice, "... back in the bottle." But all is not lost! We also see "... cast the bottles into the sea ...," then twice "... tricked back into the bottle ...," and best of all in the closing sentence, "... pushed back into the Stalinist tube."

One of the pleasures in *reading your column is your willingness (if not pleasure) at being challenged. These comments are submitted in that spirit. Perhaps they will find their way into your column.*

Eugene R. Ganssle
Skillman, New Jersey

No Use of Forceable

Jimmy Carter, stung by criticism of his human-rights silence while a visitor to Syria, fired off a letter of complaint to *The New York Times:* "What would your columnists' policy be if an Arab leader was taking Jewish mothers and children away from their homes and husbands, and forceably deporting them to a foreign country?"

Louis Jay Herman of New York cites another story in the newspaper about "the forceable seizure of territory" and writes, "What gives here? Are these people Greshamizing the correct spelling, namely *forcible/y?*" He notes that the word *forceable* exists, meaning "capable of being forced," as in "This door is forceable" (not to be confused with "This door is alarmed"), but its meaning is not the same as *forcible.* He adds, "The superpermissive *Webster III* did accept *forceable* as a variant of *forcible,* but I'm glad to see that it's been dropped from *Webster's Collegiate.*"

Forcible is worth preserving just the way it is. As noted, *forceable* is useful in describing what can be forced; *forceful* means "strong, powerful, potent, puissant," which is far more general than *forcible,* which means "using physical force." A *forceful entrance,* like that made by politicians bent on comeback, is not a *forcible entry* undertaken by burglars.

Of "Of"

"Dear Ace," begins a note from an old friend.

Ace, rooted in the Latin *as,* "unit," "single item" and the ancient Roman unit of weight—originally about three-quarters of a pound—has a variety of modern meanings. In Amslan, the American sign language of the deaf, the sign for No. 1 is sometimes used as the sign for the playing card ranked higher

than a king; the noun *ace* means a lone, brave pilot with a record of shooting down many enemy planes, and in tennis, the verb *to ace* is to blaze a serve past an opponent on the first shot.

As a name, the word has a less heroic quality: Sid Zelinka, the comedy writer for the Marx Brothers and other zanies, told friends that whenever he wanted to spoof a company, he would name it the Ace (Whatever)—the Ace Detective Agency fell asleep on the job, the Ace Laundry lost the pillowcases, and so on. In current parlance, the word has a nicely dated raciness, interchangeable with the nickname *Sport.*

Now to the body of the letter and the topic for today: "I see in my favorite sports section this morning the following, 'How big *of* a deal was Princeton's near upset of Georgetown . . .'" (The citation is presumably from *The Washington Post,* of which my correspondent is executive editor.)

"Everywhere I go I see that *of,*" continues Ben Bradlee, "and I hear it even more on radio and television. Is this something that you might find worthy of comment? Or am I making all this up?"

His editorial ear is keen as ever: The use of the infixed *of* in casual speech has been growing despite the efforts of language mavens to slap it down. "He's not that good *of* a blocker," says the TV sportscaster. "How big *of* an issue will the federal deficit be?" asks the nation-facer.

When I demand, in Standard English, "Gimme a slice *o'* that salami," the proprietor of the famed Hole in the Wall delicatessen in Manhattan responds, "How big *of* a slice do you want?"

That is nonstandard (the usage, not the salami, which is unsurpassed). An adjective (like *big*) modified by an adverb of degree (like *how*) should not be followed by a preposition (like *of*) in modifying the noun that follows (in this case, *slice*). Standard English requires "How big a slice?" and the response "Not that big a slice because I'm having Miriam's Special." Poets can get away with *fair of face,* but that's archaic.

What about such phrases as *much of a muchness,* a Britishism meaning "similar," or the Americanism *too much of a good thing? Much,* unlike *big,* has also been used as a noun, dating back to the fourteenth century; however, *much* is primarily an adjective or adverb, and may be qualified by an adverb of degree, like *too.*

How long until the infixed *of* becomes standard—that is, deemed correct by those of us who make a living in syntax? The usage is halfway there; *not that big of a deal* is heard and accepted in speech to the point that it has achieved unassailable idiom status. However, the inserted *of* still looks funny in writing, and is a long way from being accepted as "formal." If you work for Ace Copy Editing, cut it out—unless it is in a quotation, where the inserted *of* can remain as a transcription of common speech.

This is not the only case of an unneeded *of.* Consider "Where did you get that hat?" "I got it off of the hatrack." "Well, get your cotton-pickin' hands off of my chapeau." James Shriver 3d, formerly of the Gallup Poll, sent in a citation from *The Wall Street Journal:* "One complex case began in March 1973, when the wings broke off *of* a Hercules cargo plane . . ."

Here is a case for the Squad Squad. The word *off* started out as a variant of *of,* in the sense of the Latin *ab,* "away, out from," expressing removal or derivation; by 1600, *off* gained its own adverbial sense ("the head flew off") and that detachment sense was applied in a preposition ("off his rocker"). Although *off* and *of* now have separate lives, *off of* is still as redundant as it was when Shakespeare used it. Get *off* it; never get *off of* it.

Another case of *of*-abuse is in *could of* and *should of.* That's misinterpreting a pronunciation: When you want to say "I shoulda stood in bed," you mean "I should have stayed in bed"; the *should have* is often clipped to *should've,* which is then spelled mistakenly as *should of.* This is widely accepted as a rendering of dialectal speech, but not by me: The *'ve,* pronounced "uv," is just as faithful a rendition of the sound and does not misinform the reader. One of my favorite advertising bloopies was an ad that read: "Our Store Hours Were Stated Incorrectly and Should of Read . . ."

Where do these flying *of*'s come from? I have a theory: They are refugees from two orgies of *of*-napping. When *New York Times* reporters wrote of a mayor "swearing in a couple dozen new transit police officers" and "with the tournament offering that size purse," what happened to the words that should have separated *couple . . . dozen* and *size . . . purse?*

Similar *of*-napping takes place in Yiddish English: "Have a piece fruit" with a "nice glass tea." The *of*'s are snatched out and sent over to the dealmakers, who press them into service for *not too big of a deal.*

Dear Bill,

Your column on of *was more interesting than I suspect that you realize, even if you did leap back and forth among several unrelated topics. I call your attention to three noteworthy characteristics of* how big of a deal *and* not that good of a blocker: *(1) in such combinations the* of *is always followed by an indefinite article and a singular noun (i.e., no one says* how big of deals *or* not that good of the third baseman*); (2) the adjective phrase that comes before* of *is semantically a modifier of the noun that comes after* of a *(i.e., the expression refers to the extent to which something is* a big deal *or someone is* a good blocker*); and (3) even if you omit the* of, *the word order doesn't conform to the otherwise general "Article Adjective Noun" order of English (a* very big deal, *but instead of* a how big deal *one must say* how big a deal*). I conjecture that ". . . Adjective of a . . ." expressions occur only in those combinations in which a more specific rule overrides the normal rule that the adjective follow the article (e.g.,* You aren't going to get any better (of) a deal*), and I suspect that the* of *that Ben Bradlee alerted you to functions simply to make expressions like* how big a deal *look more like ordinary English noun phrases: An article in the middle of a noun phrase usually is possible only when a preposition introduces a smaller noun phrase that is part of a larger one (as in* a story about a princess*). I find that hypothesis more plausible than your suggestion of hypercorrection based on* Have a piece fruit, *etc., since that common Yiddicism is restricted to cases in which the relevant noun* doesn't *have an article.*

Fair of face *has nothing to do with Bradlee's* of *(here, I follow the terminological model of "Hansen's disease"): it is an adjective phrase, not a noun phrase, and it occurs in the same contexts in which adjective phrases otherwise occur (*Lucy is fair of face; Any woman fair of face fascinates him*). The adjective* fair *is the "head" of the phrase (the item of which the other parts of the phrase are "dependents"), unlike* how big (of) a deal, *where the noun* deal *is the head and* big *is dependent on it. A much more apposite comparison is with* a bitch of a problem *or* that swine of a manager, *where a word that functions semantically as a modifier of a noun is camouflaged to look as if it were the head of the noun phrase and the noun were dependent on it.*

Jim [James D. McCawley]
Department of Linguistics
University of Chicago
Chicago, Illinois

I was especially glad to see your column on the intrusive of. *The easiest way I have found to show students why it is intrusive is simply to reverse the word order: When "He was too good of a man" is rephrased "He was a man too good," they can see that the* of *serves no purpose.*

Richard Knowles
Department of English
University of Wisconsin
Madison, Wisconsin

You are right in much of *what you said, but there are a* couple of *points on which I must disagree. You mentioned the archaic or poetic "fair of face" as if it were analogous to the modern "how big of a deal." But in "how big of a deal,"* big *is modifying* deal, *and the whole phrase serves as a noun. In "fair of face," I would say that* of face *is modifying* fair, *and the whole phrase serves as an adjective, as in "She is fair of face." The meaning is close to "fair [when measured in terms] of face." We may want to distinguish different types of fairness: King Solomon was fair of judgment, but likely not fair of face. This use is surely archaic, but substituting* in *for* of *can make it sound more modern.*

You mentioned some examples of missing ofs *in Yiddish dialect and from the* Times. *I don't agree, however, that there should be an* of *in "with the tournament offering that size purse." What size* of *shoe do you wear? I wear simply a size 11 shoe. I will (if I do more shopping) own a couple* of *dozen pairs of shoes, and they will be shoes* of *size 11, but not size 11* of *shoes. (Just as the tournament had a purse of some size, but not that size of purse.)*

Mathematics is full of such examples of a noun followed by a number functioning together as an adjective. A curve of length 1 can also be described as a "length 1 curve." A manifold of dimension 2 (a certain kind of surface) is also a "dimension 2 manifold." In this case we also have an adjectival form of dimension, *and can rephrase this as a "2-dimensional manifold." ("Eleven-sized shoe" is also perhaps possible, but I don't think "one-lengthy curve" has any chance.) In addition, recognizing the etymology of* manifold, *sometimes the surface is simply called a "2-fold."*

John M. Sullivan
Department of Mathematics
Princeton University
Princeton, New Jersey

There are, besides meaningful of *(as in* speak of*), a number of dummy* of's *in English; these are mere grammatical particles that link items. For example, we (and the French) say* City of Washington *or* University of Washington, *where a Germanic language would have no word linking* City *or* University *with*

Washington. *This dummy* of *also follows quantifiers in English (and French), where German would often have nothing; e.g.,* a glass of beer *(cf.* ein Glas Bier*). We say* many of *as well as simply* many, *though* few *and* few of *carry different connotations. Nowadays, speakers of English tend more towards parallel* all of *than simply* all *(except with vocative* you*). English has a special rule for the verb to agree with the noun following* of—*except when the quantifier is* one—*whereas the verb in German agrees with the quantifier; e.g.,* one- *in* one-third of *the apples, where the English verb agrees with* apples. *Cf.* two-thirds of *the sugar, where English has a singular verb. Similarly, dummy* of *follows two kinds of prepositions: (1) compound ones from the Romance languages like* in front of *(a few of these have contentful* in, to, *or* with*) as well as the type,* inside of; *(2) others like* out of. *Why Safire objects to* off of *simply because historically (etymologically) it is redundant—or was before* of *became today's grammatical dummy—*of—*is unintelligible to me; for it's the same thing as* out of.

There are also expressions like He's a great bear of a man. How big of a deal *seems to be modeled on these. One may or may not wish to accept it, but it is quite understandable in origin and in sense—and it's coming in.*

Charles-James N. Bailey
Professor of English and
General Linguistics
Technische Universität Berlin
Berlin, Germany

Why is "that size purse" incorrect, yet "that size shoe" is not? One certainly would not say, "What size of shoe do you wear?" even if he were a shoe salesman.

Paul Hoffman
New York, New York

The other chord struck by "of-napping" had a sonorous rather than contextual resonance: "off." The word "off" is sometimes used as "on" remarkably as in the phrase "the alarm went off*" where its meaning is identical to the phrase "the alarm went on." I would prefer "the alarm rang, sounded, buzzed, blared, blasted," etc., all to avoid the* off*-on paradox. After all, with "the alarm went* off*," did it really go "on" or did it "go* off*"?*

Sidney Pestka, M.D.
Piscataway, New Jersey

To "ace" someone in a game of tennis is slang; the correct expression, as any real aficionado could tell you, is "to serve an ace," which makes it clear that the point is gained by means of a service rather than any other stroke. Ask President Bush, he ought to know.

An ace is not necessarily scored on first service. It can also be done on second service although this happens infrequently.

John Perry
Dully, Switzerland

Off the Record

"The statement was never made on the record, off the record, in any way," insisted Speaker of the House Thomas S. Foley. He had been reported by the *Washington Times* to have told a group of foreign journalists that "the President is like a mad dog after a bone on this capital gains cut."

This department is only mildly interested in the "mad dog" flap: The metaphor, if used, was contradictory. A healthily purposeful dog goes after a bone with gusto; but a mad, or rabies-afflicted, dog would be as likely to go after any object in its path. If the Speaker merely said that the President went after his capital gains cut "like a dog after a bone," that would have meant "determinedly, single-mindedly," well within the bounds of political discourse.

Of more concern here is the Speaker's subsequent use of *off the record,* a phrase whose meaning is fraying at the edges. Time for a new look at the lexicon of quotability.

Mr. Foley met with the group of reporters *privately;* that is, it was agreed beforehand that the fact of the meeting would not be publicly revealed. This protects the confidentiality of the relationship between journalists and *source,* the widely accepted term for "fount of information."

By speaking with them on the understanding his words would not be quoted at all, or at least not with attribution to him, the Speaker was engaged in the hallowed Washington tradition of *backgrounding.* (In German, this form of transmitting news or opinion without accepting responsibility is called *Hintergrundgespräch;* Soviet spokesmen, including the handsome Gennadi Gerasimov, call it *bekground.*)

If one of the reporters under the seal of the background agreement faithlessly tells another, who was not present, of the session, that second reporter can expose the whole charade. The second reporter will be treated as a pariah at press club bars, but that reporter cannot be said to have acted unethically; it is the first reporter, the one who confided the name of the source, who broke the rules of engagement.

Such a meeting is intended to treat the source, but not the information, as *off the record.* What does this phrase, born in the F.D.R. era, mean? Bob Pierpoint of CBS News called me about that the other day: "I always thought it meant 'Not to be used in any way,' but now some sources are using it to mean just 'Don't quote me.' Is the meaning changing? Do you remember *the Lindley Rule?*"

I not only remember the rule, but have it in writing from the rule-giver himself. Ernest K. Lindley, the Washington reporter for the New York *Herald Tribune* during the New Deal and later a pundit for *Newsweek,* noted that *off the record* was covering too wide a spectrum of unquotable comments, and laid down a stricture for *nonattribution.* In 1968, when he was an aide to Secretary of State Dean Rusk and I was writing a political dictionary, he vouchsafed it to me:

"The Lindley Rule was laid down early in the Truman Administration to enable high ranking officials to discuss important matters—especially those involving international and military affairs—without being quoted or referred to in any way. It was, and is, a rule of *no attribution*—thus differing from the usual 'background rule' permitting attribution to 'official sources' or 'U.S. officials,' etc."

I quoted the journalism critic Ben Bagdikian describing the Lindley Rule, under which "no meeting took place so far as the public is concerned. If reporters want to use something the nonspeaker has said at the nonmeeting, they must paraphrase the nonspeaker and attribute his ideas to their own intuition or some nameless source."

"The paragraph you quoted from Bagdikian is not quite correct," replied

Lindley. "Attribution to a 'nameless source' is not permitted under the Lindley Rule."

Can't argue with Hoyle himself, if you're going according to Hoyle: *Not for attribution,* in its strict interpretation, means not for attribution to anybody or anything. It has to seem to spring out of the writer's brain, stated as a flat truth inspired by the muse of punditry or the spirit of John Peter Zenger.

For example, if Mikhail Gorbachev whispered to me at a Kremlin cocktail party, "World War III starts tomorrow, just after the kickoff of your Army-Navy game," I could not write "According to an informed Soviet official, World War III will start tomorrow." Instead, under the Lindley Rule, I would have to lead with a sprightly "The nation's military leaders, assembled at tomorrow's Army-Navy game, will not be around for half-time festivities . . ." The news would have to come on my personal authority, not from my source.

Faced with this prospect, I might turn to a Moscow bureau colleague and tip that reporter to what had been said, permitting the filing from Moscow that, "According to a hawkish American pundit, the Soviet leader today hinted, perhaps jocularly, that World War III could be expected to commence tomorrow at 1:00 P.M. Eastern Standard Time." I would be breaking the rules, just as the reporter did who blabbed to another journalist what Speaker Foley did or did not say about mad dogs and Yalemen.

The new name for *the Lindley Rule,* and a synonym for *not for attribution,* is *deep background.* When a source says only, "This is *background,*" it means attribution can be made to "an Administration official" or "a law-enforcement officer," or whatever fairly but fuzzily identifies the source; however, if he or she insists, "This has to be *deep background,* really *graveyard,*" then the understanding of the Lindley Rule for nonattribution applies.

Or does it? Here we come to the weakening of linguistic standards that has led to the confusion about degrees of off-the-recordness. Some sources now say "Off the record" as gossips say "Don't tell a soul," meaning "Pass it on, but don't say I told you." Others will use *off the record* to mean "attribute it to somebody else," or *fuzz it up,* which means "talk to a bunch of other people to cover my footprints." What of, "We're talking *between friends,*" or "This is a *social occasion*"? That means "I am not speaking to you in your capacity as journalist," and is a particularly insidious form of *deep background.*

The reporter has the responsibility to make the rules clear. Everything is on the record unless specifically restricted. The columnist Philip Geyelin, who first enticed me onto an Op-Ed page, says, "There's no such thing as 'off the record,' especially if it's about something that happened. Are you supposed to forget about it? Of course not. Your first job is to work out the circumstances under which you can use it."

Writing as a prescriptivist seeking to avoid misunderstandings rather than a lexicographer describing confusion, let me suggest these meanings:

On the record means "for quotation by the named source" and is the most honest and responsible sourcing; a sophisticated "you can clean up my prose" is a grant of permission to print journalists to reduce verbosity in transcription without having to use ellipses.

Background is for direct quotation with the source muddied, such as "a source close to the investigation" for the United States Attorney's talkative paramour. When a background briefing is given to a roomful of reporters, the source seeking anonymity invites a derisive description that identifies him to the cognoscenti. ("A smooth-talking official with White House experience, traveling on the Secretary of State's plane . . .")

Deep background and *not for attribution* mean "This is your idea, not mine"; good reporters try for an upgrade into *background*.

Off the record? Spoken casually, it means "between us" or "use with discretion"; spoken ponderously, it means "not for publication," in Russian *ne dlya pechati;* when these words are spoken, a good reporter turns around and walks away.

As I recall the Lindley Rule on non-attribution—I think from him—it is defined as "compulsory plagiarism." Your source's thoughts become your thoughts, presumably with benefit to both sides.

"Off the record " has gone through considerable devaluation, in part because journalists have come increasingly to suspect that persons who don't want something known keep it to themselves, and those who whisper information "off the record" really want it out, consciously or unconsciously.

What is an appropriate use of Lindley Rule information? A hypothetical case:

President Bush tells a few trusted columnists and bureau chiefs, "Look, fellows, don't keep asking me about no-new-taxes because that makes it harder for me to slide into a new policy that I am considering because of the recent natural disasters. For your guidance, I'm going to duck the question as best I can from now on, and I may come up with a new tax policy in a few weeks. But not if I don't have some wiggle room. And that's off-the-record."

Wrong way to use that: "Sources close to President Bush say he is reconsidering his no-new-taxes policy in the light of recent natural disasters. One reliable source said that, while reassessing his policy, the President intends to avoid repeating his pledge not to raise taxes."

Wrong, because it gives the game away.

Right way: "President Bush has recently appeared to be more reticent when asked about his no-new-taxes pledge. Budget experts say that the pressures for new expenditures resulting from Hurricane Hugo and the California earthquake are being felt in the White House. It would be no surprise, observers believe, if the President should find himself obliged to reconsider his pledge on taxes."

Many journalists dislike the whole game of compulsory plagiarism to protect a source. Fair enough—don't play. If you play, play by the rules.

Dan [Daniel Schorr]
Senior News Analyst
National Public Radio
Washington, D.C.

Having spent many years playing Washington's "background-deep background-off the record" game for NBC News and CBS News, I long ago devised a couple of formulations to break the code, at least for news junkies.

When a source refuses to budge from deep background into the more readily identifiable role of "senior administration official" or "subcommittee member," the reporter needs a mechanism for using the information without having it seem to spring from his or her overly active imagination.

My solution is to enter the "It is understood here that . . ." mode. That abstract construction is a useful device for communicating the essence of a policy trial balloon or intelligence report without having to actually quote anyone or cite a document. Variations include the overused "CBS News has learned . . . ," "It can be reported that . . ." and "Officials won't say so on the record, but it's safe to say tonight that . . ."

Of course, all of this still lets the talkative deputy assistant secretary and the junior senator maintain their CYA deniability. But, as a last journalistic resort, it does get presumably vital information before the public in a reasonably understandable form and without doing violence to Brother Lindley.

Bill Lynch
Dobbs Ferry, New York

While I was covering the so-called war agencies for the Times *in Washington, I attended a news conference by Paul McNutt, who was chairman of the War Manpower Commission from 1942 to 1945.*

At one point he was asked a question he chose not to answer.

"No comment," he said. "And that's off the record."

The ultimate in caution, we figured.

Walter H. Waggoner
Pittsboro, North Carolina

O Little Town of Plugsville

The holidays advance inexorably; trite phrases like *'tis the season* and *Yule-tide cheer* come out of the attic along with the old tinsel, and readers of this column demand specific advice on language books to prevent those on their gift lists from facing the Nifty Nineties at a loss for words.

Not all books that deal with language come under the language-book heading. The best of this cushion-shot genre is *Miss Manners' Guide for the Turn-of-the-Millennium,* by Judith Martin, which is a bargain at $24.95. She deals, for example, with telephonic identifications. When you pick up the phone and say, "Hello," and the calling party says, "Who is this?", what should you say?

"The answer to the question, 'Who is this?' ", writes Miss Martin, often called Miss Manners, "is another question: 'Whom are you calling?' " Note the correct *whom,* which is a put-down in itself. If you don't want to make the caller feel like an intruding fool, Miss Manners offers the way out: "The method of polite instruction is to say, 'I'm so sorry, but I'm terrible at guessing voices. Who is this, please?' "

Millennium is a hot word that we will see in many titles of books and movies. (Why does *-ennium* have two *n*'s and *enema* only one? Because *enema* is rooted in the Greek, while *millennium* is rooted in the Latin—specifically, the word for "year," also the root of *annual.*) It is dealt with in *The World*

Almanac Guide to Good Word Usage (Martin H. Manser and Jeffrey McQuain, editors, $19.95), and is highlighted in Edwin Newman's introduction: "The first century began January 1 of the year 1 A.D. It follows that the 20th century will not end until December 31, 2000, and that the 21st century will begin on January 1, 2001. Not, repeat not, January 1, 2000, as the common assumption has it."

These guys are going to miss all the parties. Language mavens and bean-counting calendar-watchers can prove their case to their hearts' content, but the big ball is going to drop in Times Square at midnight of December 31, 1999. (The time you let out a whoop—"Hey, look, Pops, the old buggy has just gone ten thousand miles, time to trade it in!"—is when the numbers all change on your odometer, not when the last one moves to 1.) Such linguistic and mathematical correctness gets tromped on and flattened by the hooves of the happily inaccurate herd, leaving a small knot of hard-faced language protesters holding a sign that reads "Not Yet" amid the cork-popping celebrants of the new millennium.

Both the above books are published by Pharos Books. It struck me as nice that the old kings of Egypt, after millenniums of derogation, were getting together to put out some publications, but it turns out that Pharos is a division of Scripps Howard, which has a lighthouse as its corporate symbol. One of the seven wonders of the ancient world was the lighthouse at Pharos, situated at Alexandria, city of the first great library, making the choice of this book publisher's name an apt one.

Waterhouse on Newspaper Style (Viking/Penguin Books, in Canada, $19.95) contains the world's best dictionary of tabloidese from Keith Waterhouse of London's *Daily Mail.* Here are a few words with translations into the lingo of headline hype: avoid, *shun;* attempt, *bid;* difficulty, *snag;* fire, *blaze;* quarrel, *feud;* vital, *key;* exclude, *bar;* possibility, *threat;* restrict, *curb;* reprove, *rap.*

The New New Words Dictionary (Harold LeMay, Sid Lerner and Marian Taylor, editors, Ballantine paperback, $2.95) has *happenin'* as an adjective, meaning "stylish," as in "those are happenin' pants"; this and *tentpole movie,* "a sure-fire hit to help support the entire season schedule," were new to me. However, the authors root *the whole nine yards* in tailoring, as the use of a lot of fabric in a suit; the etymon that I consider authoritative is the contents of a cement truck (called by construction purists a *concrete* truck).

Pop etymologists will dig the roots in David Feldman's *Who Put the Butter in Butterfly?* (Harper & Row, $15.95). Not much new here about *butterfly*— the English butterfly is the brimstone, which is the color of butter, and that may be the source of the name—but I have long been scratching my head about the origin of *cooties,* and am glad to note that it comes from the Polynesian word for a parasite, *kutu.*

For language mavens, of course, there is the explanation of *maven* in Leo Rosten's latest, *The Joys of Yinglish* (McGraw-Hill, $29.95). It's from Hebrew for "understanding," the plural in Yiddish *meyvenim.* He attributes the English *bottom line*—one sense of which is "the minimal commitment required to conclude this deal"—to a metaphrase from the Yiddish *untershte shure.* (*Metaphrase* is a useful word, meaning "direct, word-for-word translation," in contrast to *paraphrase,* a loose interpretation.)

Mr. Rosten has a great ear for the nuance of word emphasis on meaning; one of his entries is "Casting doubt on the sanity of another by stressing one word in a sentence repeated as a question." The example: "You expect *her* father to pick up a *check?*"

A nonlanguage book, *Jewish Folktales,* by Pinhas Sadeh (Doubleday, $24.95, and Anchor paperback, $12.95), has other such nuances. (I have a rising inflection?)

English teachers will be well instructed by *Growing Up Writing,* by the educator Arlene Silberman (Random House, $18.95), which takes a serious look at the link between writing and straight thinking. And though it gripes me to plug the politically tilted National Council of Teachers of English, that outfit has published a superb paperback, *Declining Grammar and Other Essays on the English Vocabulary* by Dennis Baron of the University of Illinois. He says, "A few usage critics veer dangerously toward the idiosyncratic in their judgments," and I think he means me. (Send $14.20, including postage, to the National Council of Teachers of English, 1111 Kenyon Road, Urbana, IL 61801.)

If you're willing to take the trouble to write away for a book, also try *Words &C* (meaning "Words, Etc.") by John F. Gummere, the late language columnist for the *Philadelphia Inquirer.* In one of his essays, he shows the way languages can shorten words down to a nubbin: *Mea domina,* five syllables in Latin for "my lady," is cut to three in Italian's *madonna,* two in French's *madame.* In English, one more letter is clipped in *madam* and one more syllable goes in *ma'am.* Finally, there's a vocalic consonant of one letter in *yes'm.* (Send $14—Pennsylvania residents add 75 cents sales tax—to Words &C, Box 411, Haverford, PA 19041.)

Lawyers! You have two new chances to make sense of your briefs: *The Lawyer's Guide to Writing Well* by Tom Goldstein and Jethro K. Lieberman (McGraw-Hill, $19.95) skewers such locutions as *it would seem that* as fearful hedge words, and urges attorneys (a word that implies the passing of the bar, while *lawyer* may not) to avoid the Latin *arguendo* as "pomposity." In *The Writer's Lawyer* (Times Books, $19.95), Ronald L. Goldfarb and Gail E. Ross list those words that courts have ruled as acceptable and not actionable name-calling: *screwball, lousy agent, stupid, senile, bum, meshuggener.* (For that last, see Rosten.)

If you have somebody down on your list for a $2,500 gift, skip the fur coat and ship the Second Edition of the *Oxford English Dictionary.* If eclectic reference is your bag, try the new *New York Public Library Desk Reference* (Webster's New World, $29.95). It has lists of oxymorons (*pretty ugly, rolling stop, working vacation, deliberately thoughtless, bad health, cardinal sin, justi-fiably paranoid*) and overlapping acronyms. DAM, for example, stands for both Denver Art Museum and Dayton Art Museum. (I would add Mothers Against Dyslexia.)

Edwin Newman to the contrary, I'm with you on when the 21st century begins, and the point is easily proved.

The fallacy lies in the assumption that the Christian era began on January 1, 1 A.D., implying that the previous day was December 31, 1 B.C. However, simple arithmetic tells us that minus one plus one is zero, not one. Thus viewed, the 1st century began on January 1, 0 A.D., and the 21st will begin on January 1, 2000, as everybody knows.

E. Parker Hayden, Jr.
Princeton, New Jersey

If you were able to obtain a car directly off the assembly line in Detroit (or Japan, as the case may be), the odometer would be set at zero and would not move to "1" until you had driven one mile. When the odometer turned to 100,000 you would, in fact, have driven 100,000 miles.

If the measurement of time begins on January 1 of year 1, the end of the first year is December 31 of the year 1, and the end of the 2000th year will occur on December 31, 2000, not 1999.

Saul Freedman
Rydal, Pennsylvania

You made mention of the expression "the whole nine yards."

The Hon. Robert Cameron McEwen, former member of the House of Repre-sentatives and most recently chairman of the Joint Commission of the United States and Canada, has given me permission to bring his explanation to your attention.

Mr. McEwen, descendant of Highland Scots, feels that the expression is related to the wearing of the tartan and the kilt. He says that the official kilt of British and Canadian regiments, such as the Seaforth Highlanders, measured precisely nine yards. He has confirmed this with several Canadian friends who served in kilted regiments during World War II.

Constance Peterson
Ogdensburg, New York

Dear Bill,
I think "metaphrase" is a lousy term for what linguists have usually called a
"calque." If you really insist on a Greek-derived word, "epiphrase" would make
more sense: meta- *is an odd prefix to have on a word with that meaning.*

Jim [James D. McCawley]
Department of Linguistics
University of Chicago
Chicago, Illinois

You cite The New York Public Library Desk Reference *as referring to the*
phrase pretty ugly *as an oxymoron. When I was growing up in South Carolina*
in the '50s, we often used the word pretty *as an adverb to alter the strength of*
the following adjective—as in "He's a pretty nice guy," or "That's a pretty ugly
sunburn you got there, son." This usage must be less than formally acceptable,
but my dictionary does list "considerably" as one meaning for pretty. *The*
phrase pretty ugly *is pretty peculiar, I admit, but to call it an oxymoron is to*
infer a clash of meanings that isn't there—no more than in "A new generation
of Olds."
    In my mind, the adverb pretty *(used to strengthen an adjective) is somewhat*
stronger than somewhat, *but not quite as strong as* quite. Rather *might be a*
good approximation, but all these distinctions are pretty subjective. Pretty *has*
one advantage over these other words: Its meaning can vary with pronunciation.
If you pronounce the two syllables distinctly, it becomes even more potent, and
may carry a hint of suspicion: "That's a pret-ty big insurance policy you took
out on your wife, buddy!"
    Another example of an apparent, but not genuine, oxymoron might be fairly
ugly *(or* fairly swarthy*), although I doubt that that one appears in the* Public
Library's *list. Incidentally, I've always liked the phrase* disgustingly beautiful,
which does represent an incongruity—and fairly drips with envy. I've also heard
the expression "He's an extremely normal fellow." Is this an oxymoron, or is
it ain't?

Robert Moore
Tuscaloosa, Alabama

The plural of oxymoron *is* oxymora, *not* oxymorons.

Captain Haggerty
New York, New York

On "One"

The intellectually meatiest and most thought-provoking speech of the first half of 1990 was "Keeping America First: American Romanticism and the Global Economy," delivered at Harvard by our director of the Office of Management and Budget, Richard G. Darman.

Now for the knock. This readable, trope-studded speech contains a line that brought me up short: "If one asks where in America's cultural establishment is there visible representation of American Romanticism, one is hard pressed to come up with an answer."

How about the pronoun *one*? The writer William F. Buckley Jr. can get away with it, because he delights in a self-mockingly lofty style, but is it—as one might posit—off-putting to the average highbrow?

I think *one* is stuffy. It strains to avoid the self-confident *I* and the cozy *you*.

Partisans of *one* point to its asexuality, formality and neutrality. *One does one's best,* they argue, is more forceful than the breezy *You do your best.*

We disagree. (That's the royal, or editorial, *we;* it goes with the style of *one.* Actually, the person disagreeing is me, not a milling herd of anonymous mavens.)

"When one is very old, as I am," said George Bernard Shaw, ". . . your legs give in before your head does." That illustrates one of *one's* problems; it cannot be replaced by the pronoun *you.* To be correct, he would have had to go on with "one's legs give in before one's head does," which is stuffy to the point of suffocation. A better fix: "the legs give in before the head does."

Having fixed Shaw, one gets the courage to fix Darman. "Where in America's cultural stuff-stuff-stuff? I'm hard pressed to come up with the answer." Or "If we want to ask where . . . we're hard pressed for an answer." Or "If you . . . you'd be hard pressed, etc."

I hope that helps. One does one's best.

Open the Door

Our much-abused Attorney General, born Richard L. Thornburgh, prefers that people call him *Dick,* even in print. Our director of Management and Budget, Richard G. Darman, who has never run for public office, likes *Richard,* and that's how he is addressed.

Defense Secretary Cheney leaned toward *Dick,* but the Pentagon brass resisted. "Stuff is coming across my desk signed *Richard B.,* but I'm still signing *Dick,*" he said. That caused Dick Thornburgh to send this limerick:

> To be "Richard" or "Dick," my friend,
> Is a quandary that seems not to end.
> But opting for "Dick,"
> You'll learn very quick,
> Reinforces your streamlining trend!

That advice from counsel did it; Mr. Cheney's formal name is no longer *Richard,* but *Dick.* (His friends call him *SecDef.*)

O Solecism Mio

At the biannual meeting of the Judson Welliver Society, the association of former White House speechwriters, the Kennedy Administration's Ted Sorensen rose to assail my use of *biannual* in the invitation: "This word means 'twice a year,' not 'every two years'; either Mr. Safire has erred and should have said *biennial,* or I have not been invited to all the meetings."

Kill *biannual;* the word causes more confusion than it's worth. If you mean twice a year, or twice a month, use *semiannual, or semimonthly,* or better yet, *twice a year, twice a month*—that avoids confusion. If you mean every other year, go with *biennial* as an adjective, or the universally understood *every other year* if you want to avoid having people show up on the right date but the wrong year.

Let us not correct ourselves out of fear, but let us never fear to correct ourselves.

Outing

In the January 29, 1990, issue of *Time,* William A. Henry 3d was among the first to note "the spread of a phenomenon known as *'outing,'* the intentional exposure of secret gays by other gays."

The language is dexterous in giving sinister meanings to familiar words. *Outing* comes from "coming out of the closet," which has meant the public assertion of previously secret homosexuality.

"*Outing* we used to call 'telling on,' " writes an anonymous Irregular, "and *an outing* was what the family took in the car on weekends."

Lexies take note: We are witnessing the birth of new meaning to a gerund. *Outing,* as a noun, has meant "excursion," from "going out"; now it also means "exposure," from "forcing out."

Panama's Operation

The United States faced a similar problem in Korea in the 1950's: If only the Congress can declare a *war*, what was the military struggle that the U.S. conducted in the name of the United Nations to be called? President Harry Truman liked *police action;* the Congress, which had to appropriate money to pay veterans' claims, settled on an official short-of-war moniker: the Korean *conflict.*

What took place recently in Panama? Let me tell you about our *operation.*

When the decision was made to name the action Operation Just Cause, the effect was to cause others to use the first word as a description of the event. The harsh word *invasion* was used by many newscasters—and a military *invasion* it indisputably was, though the invasion was invited by the elected government—but the White House and Defense Department held to *operation.* The State Department floated out *consented intervention,* but that sank rapidly. Nobody tried *incursion,* a term for hostile but temporary entry into another's territory, because of its use to explain our penetration into Cambodia in 1970. The size of the force that was put into the field inhibited the use of *raid* or *foray.*

By far, the preferred term was *operation*, as the Administration had hoped; thus was a *war* avoided.

What military jargon was churned up by the shooting engagement? A verb tossed about a great deal was *reduce.* "The headquarters has been *reduced,"* said General Colin L. Powell, chairman of the Joint Chiefs of Staff, in his initial briefing. This is correct military terminology; according to the strategist Edward N. Luttwak, "You *raze* walls, you *slight* fortifications, you *reduce* fortresses."

Although the most widely understood sense of *reduce* is "to diminish, lessen" (just as the desperately intransitive "I gotta reduce" is well known to dieters), a more destructive sense has long existed. "To bring to (or into) order, obedience, reason, etc., by constraint or compulsion" is an *Oxford English Dictionary* definition with a citation for 1490, and "to pulverize, to grind down to powder" entered the scientific language about a century later; this sense led to the cliché "reduced to rubble."

The military adopted *reduce* to describe the "busting" of a noncom: *To reduce to the ranks* meant "to degrade a noncommissioned officer to the rank of private." In 1951, Frank Gaynor's *New Military and Naval Dictionary* defined the verb as "to wipe out enemy resistance at a certain point."

Lieutenant General Thomas W. Kelly, director of operations for the Joint Chiefs of Staff, took this meaning a bridge too far in his briefing: He said that our forces had "engaged the cavalry squadron and *reduced* it" and that "the naval infantry company . . . has been *reduced."*

No; speaking with military precision, one does not *reduce* people, either individually or in companies or armies. You *kill, destroy* or *wipe out* the enemy, but you *reduce* places and things. You *overcome, subdue, overwhelm* or *force the surrender of* troops or small units, and *defeat, conquer* or *vanquish* a larger conglomeration of people—but you *demolish, annihilate, bring to ruin* and *reduce* enemy positions, weapons, cities.

The distinction between people and places as the target of *reduce* is worth preserving; the phrase *to reduce casualties* means "to lessen the number likely to be killed or wounded," not "to wipe out the already wiped out."

This postcard came from Robert F. Gibson of Thornville, Ohio: "General Powell talked about the critical nature of the Panama military operation using the word *criticality.* Later, in responding to a question about when the American troops would return to their bases in the U.S., he said when the operation was concluded they would be *retrograded* back home. Did General Powell catch this language from General Haig?"

Don't be critical of *criticality.* The state or quality of being critical—not in the sense of offering criticism, but in the sense of approaching a point of crisis—has been used by atomic scientists for a generation. The noun is preferred to *criticalness,* much as *specificity* is preferred to *specificness.* As Al Capone might have said, *ness* has had it.

Retrograde, if the general used it as a transitive verb, was a mistake. In Latin, *retro* means "backward" and *gradi* means "to go or to step." In synonymy, *retreat* implies withdrawal while *retrograde* implies a movement that just happens not to be forward; in the military, however, a *retrograde movement* has long been a euphemism for *retreat.* General George B. McClellan took much derision when he used such a word and "a change of base" to describe his withdrawal from the neighborhood of Richmond. General Powell probably meant *rotate,* in the sense of "bring home" without the imputation of *replace.*

Was any euphemism used? When *The Washington Post* reported that a Stealth bomber had been used in Panama, it added that the plane had missed its target. "Pentagon spokesmen confirmed that the plane had been used," wrote William Branigin and Joanne Omang in a follow-up story, "but said its mission was to bomb a field near Panamanian military barracks, rather than the barracks itself, to disrupt and confuse any would-be defense against invading Americans."

The reporters added that "a senior military officer, who asked that his name not be used, told *The Post* that *bombing a field* is a euphemism for *missing the target.*"

I am unable to locate an Air Force official who will confirm that the phrase used for a Gross Bombing Error is *bombing a field,* but mock-jocular descriptions of minor disasters are traditional in military lingo: Artillerymen who shell their own infantry troops have been known to shrug off the horror with variations of "Too bad they can't take a joke."

Press and congressional criticism of the *operation* was muted; success has a thousand fathers (as John F. Kennedy said, quoting "an old proverb" that nobody has traced). However, during a news conference a few days before the move into Panama, President Bush was being criticized for sending two envoys to China despite a continued crackdown on dissidents by Beijing.

"To those suggesting that I have normalized the relationship with this power because of one visit," the President said—an earlier, secret visit by the same envoys had not then been revealed—"they simply are wrong, *off the reservation* on this point."

He made an arm gesture accompanying the phrase *off the reservation* to emphasize how far away from the truth the critics were.

This suggests that the President has a tin ear when it comes to colloquialisms. *Off the reservation*—grounded in a reference to Indians who leave their assigned space—was given an extended sense by George Ade in 1900 to mean "beyond acceptable limits."

In politics, to go *off the reservation* has a specific meaning: to refuse to support a party's candidate without *taking a walk* or *bolting* the party. To use an ecclesiastical analogy, it means *in schism* but not *in error;* the political phrase has more to do with organizational loyalty than with factual accuracy.

To use *off the reservation* as a synonym for *wrong* is incorrect; in this, the President was *off base,* which was probably the phrase he meant.

I thank you for coming to my defense on my use of the words "reduced" and "criticality." I regret that you did not feel it appropriate to defend my use of the word "retrograde." Most of my friends assure me that getting two out of three from Bill Safire is an enormous achievement in and of itself. Nevertheless, being greedy I researched my use of the word "retrograde" to see if I could possibly call you to account. Unfortunately, the closest I could get to a defense was contained in the dictionary of the United States Army military terms— hardly a worthy reference—and my case was much too unconvincing.

At the same time I choose to challenge your suggestion that the proper word was "rotation." Rotation suggests replacing one unit with another. Upon reflection, a better word would have been "redeployed." I am hopeful I will not have to give another similar press conference, but if I do, I will try to keep all of this straight.

> *Colin L. Powell*
> *Chairman*
> *Joint Chiefs of Staff*
> *Washington, D.C.*

Might the senior military officer have told The Washington Post *reporters that "bombing afield" [i.e., astray] is a euphemism for "missing the target," only to have the euphemism reported as "bombing a field"?*

> *Guy R. Fairstein*
> *Scarsdale, New York*

While reading the definition of bombing a field, *I was reminded of an Underground newspaper story in France.*

At the time the Allies were bombing the Renault factories in Boulogne-Billancourt; the official German paper said that only a cow in a field *had been hit.*

The Underground paper quoted this verbatim and added: "The cow burned for three days."

> *Felix Schnur*
> *Yonkers, New York*

Al Capone would not have said "Ness has had it." "Had it" is a British expression that did not come into use by Americans until WWII.

> *Charles Broxmeyer*
> *McLean, Virginia*

One Hundred Dads

"Success has a thousand fathers," I carelessly wrote, adding that the quotation was from John F. Kennedy, who said it was an old saying, but nobody knew the source of the adage.

All wrong. "J.F.K. said 'victory has a hundred fathers,' not 'success has a thousand fathers,' " writes Arthur M. Schlesinger Jr. "When I asked him where he had come upon this interesting thought, he said vaguely, 'Oh, I don't know; it's just an old saying.'

"The 'old saying' has been traced. On 9 September 1943," writes the historian (he uses that military style of dating, and does not capitalize "jr."), "Count Ciano noted in his diary, 'As always, victory finds a hundred fathers but defeat is an orphan.' This felicitous thought was incorporated in the film *The Desert Fox* (1951), which was no doubt where J.F.K. picked it up."

That is the main contribution to history of Count Galeazzo Ciano, Benito Mussolini's son-in-law and foreign minister. It is a good line, and if original, bestows credit on a diplomat otherwise known as being the butt of one of the most vivid derogations of his time. When a British diplomat asked Churchill if he should negotiate with Ciano or his father-in-law, the British Prime Minister, using what might now be considered an ethnic slur, is said to have replied: "Never deal with the monkey when the organ grinder is in the room."

If that's not accurate, I'll hear about it, as will you.

Parley in the Foothills

The *summit* used to be 'way up there, at the top, the peak, the zenith. From the Latin *summus,* "highest," the word offered a view that was breathtaking.

Winston Churchill was displeased in 1950 at what his friend Bernard Baruch called *the Cold War* (coinage claimed by Walter Lippmann but actually made by the Baruch speechwriter Herbert Bayard Swope). The British statesman recalled the cordial wartime meetings he had with Roosevelt and Stalin and called for a "parley at the summit." Such a top-level meeting of a few leaders, he said, would better bridge the international gap than a gathering of "hordes of experts and officials drawn up in a vast cumbrous array."

So started *summit* in diplolingo, followed in the late 1950's by *summitry* (on the analogy of *telemetry*) and *summiteer* (on the analogy of *pamphleteer* and *profiteer*). For more than a generation, this coinage and its derivatives held the definition to a meeting at the very top; with currency, however, the Churchillian coin has been debased.

President Bush has just met with the nation's governors for what was billed as an *education summit;* schoolchildren from Gorky held what Tass designated a *youth summit;* last year, President Reagan and congressional leaders held hands at what was labeled an *economic summit* to reduce the deficit; then delegations from New York and New Jersey met at the World Trade Center in Manhattan for what they insisted was a *regional economic summit.*

If a bunch of guys from neighboring states can call their subway series a *summit,* anything goes: Conservationists in conclave call their motel brunch an *environmental summit,* and in the competition between Sony and Philips, *Newsday* reported: "Both the hardware and software people have discussed a possible 'summit' meeting later this winter to talk about alternatives to the Copycode technology."

We are reaching the point where you can hold a summit of nobodies in the basement. (*Basements,* by the way, have disappeared, along with *cellars;* these glitzy temples are now *lower levels, ground floors* and *underground colonnades.*) With the zing gone out of a parley at the summit, what's a poor Sherpa to do?

Apex sounds like a foaming cleanser; *apogee* is too often confused with *apology* and *acme* with *acne; crest* is toothpaste and *zenith* a laptop; *crown* is too royal; *vertex* would be good, the highest point (which is properly the turning point), but it would get spun into the middle of *vortex. Big Two* would offend multipolar bears and be derided as *Big Toe. Pinnacle* sounds too much like a card game.

How can the language cope with the lowering of *summit?* Same way, I suppose, that it did with the diminution of *stars* and *great powers:* We now speak of *superstars* and *superpowers.*

You clerks, drawn up in vast cumbrous array, can have your piddling little summit down the hall; I'll see the other world leader at the *supersummit.*

Since there is no word telemet *to which to attach a* -ry, *it is the height of absurdity (absurditry?) to suggest that* summitry *was formed from* summit *"on the analogy of* telemetry." *The suffix* -ry *actually started in such words as* ribaldry, revelry, banditry *and* artistry.

Louis Jay Herman
New York, New York

Peacework

The lingo of war provided this column with a target-rich environment; now for the mopping up.

"He is not *withdrawing*," George Bush said of a statement by Saddam Hussein soon after the ground war (a retronym) began. "His defeated forces are *retreating*. He is trying to claim victory in the midst of a *rout*."

In previous usage, *withdrawal* had been a euphemism for *retreat*, along with *retrograde movement, pullback, pullout, adjustment of front, declination of engagement* and *redeployment*. General George B. McClellan even brazened it out with *change of base*.

In this case, however, the President wanted to narrow the definition of *withdrawal* to "voluntary evacuation of troops." In his meaning, *retreat* meant "fighting while running away," while *withdrawal*—the centerpiece of a dozen United Nations resolutions—had been available to the Iraqis as the requirement for a cease-fire.

Saddam Hussein caught that nuance and, after his troops were in full retreat from Kuwait, announced their *withdrawal* as if it were a voluntary act, or at least one that met United Nations standards. But Mr. Bush was not about to let him get away with appearing to have complied voluntarily or even honorably.

Was this an attempt to *humiliate* an enemy? (The root of that verb is the Latin *humus*, "earth," and an early meaning was "to pound into the earth," which can happen in a ground war.) I think not. The pretense of leaving on his own accord put up by Saddam (deliberately mispronounced "SAD'm" by Mr. Bush) invited clarification; hence, the United States President's careful new distinction between *withdrawal* and *retreat*. The first is done peacefully, the result of negotiation; the second is done as the direct result of military pressure. That's how new senses are given old words.

BUSH RELAXES EFFORT TO ABASE SADDAM was a subsequent *Washington Post* headline, after the President declared Kuwait liberated and suspended offensive combat operations (a rare pre-ceasefire, showing the extent of the distrust of the enemy).

That was a literate headline-writer at work (one who had no room for *humiliate*); *abase* is from the Old French *abaissier*, "to bring lower," and can be heard today in French in the cry *à bas Saddam*, "down with Saddam." Though not as strong as *humiliate*, it is a more forceful transitive verb than *dishonor;* another synonym, *defame*, is directed more to the reputation than to the person, and *belittle* and *demean* are much weaker.

In the general abasement, care has been taken in print and on the air by those of good taste to avoid a play on the tyrant's first name. On *This Week With David Brinkley*, George Will caught himself just in time from falling into the *sodomize* pun and was then forced into the awkward phraseology of "de-Saddam Husseinize Iraq."

Before we leave this war, do we agree on what historians are to call it? Some support exists for the "Six-Week War," a play on the 1967 "Six-Day War," but that assumes the war began on January 16, 1991, and not on August 2, 1990, when Iraq attacked Kuwait.

Foot soldiers may call it the "Hundred-Hour War," since that was the exact length of time chosen by the President for the ground war, but that derogates the contribution made in softening up enemy forces from the air. (Everybody who remembers "A Thousand Days" by Arthur M. Schlesinger Jr. will race for "A Hundred Hours"; we'll see which publisher wins.)

The word humiliate *is indeed derived ultimately from the Latin* humus, *"earth," but the meaning did not develop in the way you suggest.* Humus *gave rise to the adjective* humilis, *meaning "on the ground," hence "low," hence "humble." The Latin verb* humiliare *(from which we get* humiliate*) thus means "to humble" or—to use a semantically analogous word to which you refer in* *your column—"to abase." (Our humble comes from humilis by way of Old French.)*

Louis Jay Herman
New York, New York

Pop Me No Pops, Pop

What word, of onomatopoeic origin and more than six centuries of use in English, has been taken to the bosom of ballplayers and bakers, warriors and drug abusers, cartoonists and concertizers, each group having its own special sense of it? What unappreciated little word deserves the honor of scholarly examination on this day?

Pop, of course—the clip of *poppa,* a variant spelling of *papa,* a reduplicative sound echoing a small explosion that you have been using from infancy to signify and demand attention from your sire.

Do not be misled by the Latin *populus,* meaning "people," root of *popular.* As an adjective, *pop* with this meaning began by modifying *concert;* in 1862, the novelist George Eliot wrote, "We have been to a Monday Pop, to hear Beethoven's Septett." That led to *pop music,* more recently to *Pop Art,* and finally to its pinnacle, *pop grammarian,* which describes my Sunday role. Dismiss this entire line of inquiry; we are more interested in the word-tree of the explosive *pop.*

"At a poppe, down they descende into hell," wrote Sir Thomas More in 1534, using the word to express the suddenness of an explosion. "Popping or smacking with the mouthe" was the way the translator Thomas Newton used the term in 1576. Within a century, the sound applied to the firing of a gun, and later to the figurative shot: "Prestige, you know," wrote a historian in 1881, "I always like to have a pop at."

We have the etymology of *soda pop* from no less an authority than a British poet laureate, Robert Southey, who wrote in 1812: "A new manufactory of a nectar, between soda-water and ginger-beer, and called *pop,* because 'pop goes the cork' when it is drawn."

Pop up popped up in a sixteenth-century translation of Ovid—"up their heades they pop"—and the same sense of a sudden thrust, as if abruptly or involuntarily propelled, appeared a couple of centuries later in *pop the question,* to propose marriage. *Pop off,* a Britishism for "to die," has softened in this century to a less final "to leave," and has recently acquired the sense of "to remonstrate loudly; to let off steam." The opposite idea, *pop in,* means "to arrive unexpectedly," and is probably the source for the last name of Mary Poppins.

Baseball fans, munching their *popcorn,* recognize a *pop fly* as a ball hit high, as if cast up by an explosion, providing an easy catch; oculists avoid the expression *popeyed,* preferring *exophthalmos* to describe the protuberance of the eyeball. Grocers today sell *Pop-Tarts* for use in *pop-up toasters,* and bakers still sell *popovers.* (Latin mavens suspect a connection here to *papaver,* "poppy," but that is the etymon of the flower, which is apparently connected neither to the explosive sound nor to the popularity series.)

Almost every great word has its dark side; for *pop,* it is the sense of "an injection of a narcotic drug." In 1935, a slanguist spotted the noun in a verb phrase, *take a pop;* from this came *skin pop,* which means an injection into the skin rather than *mainlining* into the vein. The synonym for "hit" or "dose" is used in pricing—"fifty dollars a *pop*"—which has crossed over into general slang, meaning merely "each," and we now buy theater tickets for nearly fifty smackers a pop.

As a verb, according to the new *U.C.L.A. Slang, to pop* includes senses of "to punch; to deflower; to bust" (the last as in "Uh-oh, we're going to get *popped*"). Paul Dickson's *Slang!* gives us the military *pop smoke,* "to ignite a smoke grenade," and the automotive *pop the clutch,* "to engage the clutch suddenly." Abruptness pervades all these usages, from the figurative root of an explosion.

Do weasels pop? Let us examine the original lyrics of that English song:

> Up and down the City Road,
> In and out the Eagle,
> That's the way the money goes,
> Pop goes the weasel!

City Road was a famous street in old London; the Eagle was a public house, perhaps a brothel as well, in Shepherdess Wall, where money was spent boozing and wenching. Now come the hard parts: First, *pop* had a slang meaning of "pawn, borrow against"; next, in Cockney rhyming slang (where "trouble and strife" is the code phrase for "wife"), a "weasel and stoat" is a code for "coat." (A *stoat* is a furry animal similar to a weasel.) *Pop goes the weasel* could mean "off comes the coat," to be pawned for money to spend on more carousing. (Other speculations will be entertained if you'll get off yer plates of meat, guv.)

We have controversy about *Pops,* as in the 1920's bandleader Paul (Pops) Whiteman; is its root sense in popular music, like some of that played by the Boston *Pops* Orchestra, or in fatherhood? Most evidence points to the latter: In jazz usage, *Pops* was "a form of address to an elderly man, or an authority figure." According to the *Oxford English Dictionary* supplement, the *s* in *Pops* is "a shortened form of the hypocoristic diminutive suffix *-sy.*"

Got that? No? Further thumbing through a dictionary reveals that *hypocoristic* means "adult use of baby-talk endearments" such as *tootsy, babsy* and—here we go—*popsy.*

Drop the *y* or *ie* from *tootsie*—the baby-talk word for "toe"—and you have *Toots,* as my Aunt Dorothy was called after the language said goodbye to *Toot-Toot-Tootsie.* In the same way, drop the *y* from *popsy* and you have *Pops*—a happy discovery on this Father's Day. (Not *Fathers Day* or *Fathers' Day*—let's punctuate properly, Pops.)

Dear Bill:
Are you aware of yet another use of the word "pop" brought about by the introduction of cellular telephones: that industry, and Wall Street, use "pop" as shorthand for "population" in order to define the value of the cellular telephone system, for example, company "A" buys a cellular telephone system for X dollars a "pop"—or a person. Thus, this growing industry evaluates its potential on a census basis.

"Pop" might also refer to the explosive growth of the cellular stocks over the last few years, the recent decline notwithstanding.

> *Best,*
> *Ed [Edward Bleier]*
> *New York, New York*

A British reader living in France, I could add "pop round to the pub, pop up/down to my neighbours, pop out for a bit of air, etc."

As for popping the weasel in the old London song, I have another version, told me by my grandmother (born 1858 in Hollywell Street, Shoreditch), daughter of merchants. She explained that the City Road quarter used to be full of bespoke tailors. That they spent their money on beer at the Eagle, and had to pawn the weasel—that is, the smoothing iron, which got its nickname weasel from its shape, as it ran quickly up and down the cloth, its nose ferreting out creases. Of course, it was a great tragedy to pop the weasel, for how could one finish the clothes without the iron?

There is another version of the song that I learned at school:

> *Half a pound of tuppering rice,*
> *Half a pound of treacle,*
> *That's the way the money goes*
> *Pop goes the weasel.*

As for the weasel meaning "weasel and stout-cout," I have never heard this in rhyming slang. Perhaps because cockneys didn't wear coats, but waistcoats only. I've often used "take your Charlie Prescot" (waistcoat—it rhymes in cockney) and "yer titfa (tit for tat = hat)." But I am no authority on rhyming slang, knowing only the most common terms.

I expect you know that "Up and Down the City Road" is a song and round dance, sung to a skipping measure where the "weasel pops out" after each refrain, leaving the dance.

> *Philippa Griffith-Hentges*
> *Vallauris, France*

The right interpretation of "plates of meat" is not "seat" as the context implies; "feet" 's the dicky bird "plates of meat" stands for; you want the reader to get off his or her bottle and glass. I've collected examples of Cockney rhyming slang over the years, and I send along [some entries from] my list. (I've featured Cockney rhyming slang in two stories: "Voiceover" in Sherlock Holmes Through Time and Space, *edited by Asimov, Greenberg, and Waugh [Bluejay, 1984], and "The House that Jack Built" in* The New Adventures of Sherlock Holmes, *edited by Greenberg and Waugh [Carroll & Graf, 1987].)*

apples and pears: stairs
Aristotle: bottle
army tank: Yank
babbling brook: crook
bees and honey: money
bug and flea: tea
dicky bird: word

elephant's trunk: drunk
give and take: cake
I suppose: nose
the lady from Bristol: pistol
lean and lurch: church
lump of chalk: talk
mutton pie: eye
one another: mother
rats and mice: dice
sorrowful tale: jail
storm and strife: wife
twos and threes: knees
you and me: tea

Edward Wellen
New Rochelle, New York

Pronunciation Drill

I do not often err in the pronunciation of *salmon.*

"How come people seem to now be saying *air* when I say *er?*" asks Alexandra Moffat of Oxford, New Hampshire. And Marlene Kuntz of Baltimore adds, "What about the pronouncing of the *l* in *salmon* and the *t* in *often?*"

The *l* in *salmon* should be silent. Why, if the most likely source is the Latin *salire,* "to leap," which pronounces the *l?* Because that's the way it's been since the days of Robert Nares, a lexicographer, in 1784. The three things to remember about salmon are: they leap waterfalls upstream to spawn, they are delicious when smoked as *saumon fumé,* and their name contains a silent *l.*

Pressure to pronounce the *l* comes from two sources. First is the pathogenic bacteria *salmonella,* cause of food poisoning. Pronounced with an *l* at both ends, that word is derived not from the fish but from the name of a veterinarian, Daniel Salmon, who apparently pronounced his name with the *l.* That brings us to the second source of pressure: the name *Solomon,* which may be a variation of *shalom,* Hebrew for "peace," or may be derived from *salma,* "strength," or *zalmon,* "ascent."

Names not only make news, but also influence pronunciation. The *l* is articulated in the name of the novelist Salman Rushdie, author of *The Satanic Verses,* suggesting that we do the same with the name of the fish.

Resist. Split that baby: Solomon, Salman and similar names get the *l* pronounced, and *salmon,* the name of the fish so happy on a bagel with cream cheese, retains its silent *l.* Pass the *sammon,* Salman.

Many a time and oft we pronounced the *t* in *often,* until most of us dropped it in the seventeenth century; about fifty years ago, it began to reappear in the speech of la-di-da types. So is it "correct" to put the *t* in *often*? Because of that archaic usage, it is not as incorrect as putting it in *soften, listen,* or *moisten,* but it still sounds like an affectation to most listeners. If it worries you, try *frequently.*

"To err is Truman," cracked Martha Taft, pronouncing it *ur* because she was not one to put on airs. In his lively book on pronunciation, *There Is No Zoo in Zoology* (that's "ZO-ol-o-gy"), Charles Harrington Elster writes: "*Air* for *err* is right up there in the competition for the Great Beastly Mispronunciation of All Time." However, among the sources now preferring *air* are the *NBC Handbook of Pronunciation* and *Merriam-Webster's Ninth New Collegiate Dictionary.* What to do? I prefer *ur,* same as the name of the ancient city in Iraq, because (1) it is closer to the first syllable of *error* than *air,* and (2) I like to swim upstream. The majority of the population seems to be floating down with *air,* and in pronunciation more than grammar usage is king, so *air* for *err* is no mistake.

As for me, I do not offen ur in the pronunciation of *sammon.*

Relatedly, the Conseil Supérieur de la Langue Française, in yet another ludicrous attempt by the French government to keep its language pure, has decreed that all English words ending in *er* are to be spelled *eur,* causing *le speaker* to become *le speakeur.* However, *les mavens de la langue* also decree that when *er* is pronounced *air* (as in *mer,* the word for "sea"), that word will keep its *er* ending. *Quel nonstarter.*

Finally, this Anglo-American pronunciation flash from *Eye-rack,* pronounced by the British *"Ih-rawk":* much confusion between what Murkens call "PATE-ri-ot MISS-els" and what the Brits call "PAT-ri-ot miss-AILES."

"Perhaps the most boggling usage encountered so far," wrote Simon Heffer in the (London) *Daily Telegraph,* "was uttered by an American . . . discussing 'antie missel missels' with an American interviewer.

"Neither batted any eyelid when, in mentioning the 'I-racky' capability of dealing with 'Paytriot missels,' the expert ruled out the possibility of any 'I-racky an-tie an-tie missel missel missels.' "

Often is reasonable because of oft, where the T must be pronounced. But you overlook that delicious pun in Gilbert & Sullivan's The Pirates of Penzance *where, asked piteously "Have you ever been an orphan?" the chorus trolls back repeatedly "Yes, orfen."*

Kenneth R. Lake
London, England

Proofreading

When the news media get on your case, nothing you do is right.

Marion Barry Jr., the beleaguered Mayor of Washington (I prefer *beleaguered,* "besieged by encirclement," to the more general *embattled,* the other adjective now appended to his title), was the recipient of a pop first from *City Paper* in Washington and later from *The Washington Monthly* in the form of its "Memo of the Month." This feature presents for public ridicule the best bureaucratic effluvia it can find.

In the current issue, a letter purported to be from Mayor Barry to the head of a citizens' association is pictured, letterhead, signature and all. Mr. Barry thanks the committee for its "hands on [sic—should be hyphenated] participation in issues which [sic—should be 'that'] effect the city [sic—should be 'affect']. . . ."

The letter writer, trying to be helpful, goes on: "I am providing you with a copulation of answers to several questions raised. . . ."

Presumably the writer meant *compilation,* a collection or gathering-together, from the Latin *compilatio,* "pillaging" (an unfair derogation of anthologists). Did Mayor Barry really make the mistake?

Lurma Rackley, his press secretary, insists that the letter was prepared by someone no longer at the Office of County Affairs, was never sent to the Mayor's office for proofreading or approval, and was not signed or even read by the Mayor. But having delegated the authority to sign his name, he was responsible for the error.

It wasn't until after the letter was delivered to the citizens' association that the mistake was spotted (not the lack of hyphenation in *hands-on,* but one of the others) and sent back for revision. Too late; photocopies of the as-delivered original were sent around to much giggling and snickering.

Proofreading, as this episode shows, is an undervalued endeavor. Never trust your own copy; get somebody else to look over your words with fresh eyes. "The word we look for most these days is *public,*" says the forthright

Ms. Rackley. "The word *public* is in every other paragraph of every state-ment, and the *l* has a way of dropping out."

This item is written in the hope that typographical errors will be forgiven and that the blame for unreviewed letters will not fall on nonsignatories; it is brought to you as a pubic service.

Pundit-Bashing

A useful linguistic scapegoat or whipping boy has been created in time for the presidential campaign of 1992.

"The seven million votes I got didn't come from no *pundits*," the Reverend Jesse Jackson told Paul Taylor of *The Washington Post*, when asked for a reaction to press critics who charged him with a "descent into triviality" because he chose not to run for Mayor of Washington, as many columnists and editorial writers had urged.

Mr. Jackson, savoring the word that characterized his would-be tor-mentors, used it again in the same interview: "When I was talking to a 27-year-old Perdue worker last week who has bursitis in her wrist from pluck-ing 50 chickens a minute and no health insurance, she didn't ask for no *pundit*."

The Democratic noncandidate (a locution meaning "one who has not yet officially announced his candidacy for tactical, equal-time or fund-raising reasons, but is widely presumed to be a candidate") twice placed the target word within a double negative. I suspect that Mr. Jackson, a skillful user of the language and soon to become a talk-show host, committed this solecism deliberately, even defiantly, to firmly dissociate himself from such users of Standard English as political commentators. (I just firmly split an infinitive to show I ain't no elitist.)

His second usage—"she didn't ask for no *pundit*"—is an adept turnaround of a technique used by supporters of local police forces in the 1960's, whose cars sported bumper stickers reading IN TROUBLE? CALL A HIPPIE.

The choice of this breed of media representative as a target for accumulated political resentment is not new; President Eisenhower denounced *sensation-seeking columnists and commentators,* and Adlai E. Stevenson lashed out at *the one-party press.* The historian Arthur M. Schlesinger Jr. turned a mouth-filling phrase in blasting the "panjandrums of the Opinion Mafia." However, Mr. Jackson's selection of the word *pundit* suggests that a bit of journalism jargon has had enough currency to make it worthy of easily recognizable derision.

Pandita is Sanskrit for "scholar, learned man"; the Hindi word based on it is *pandit.* The word was occasionally given as a kind of title: In India, Jawaharlal Nehru was often called "Pandit" Nehru, with the pronunciation falling between "pun" and "pan" for the first syllable. "That this pandit (i.e., 'wise man') has become Prime Minister," observed a writer in the magazine *Encounter* in 1953, "is one of the caprices of history."

The word has long been used to mock pretension. "For English pundets condescend" appeared in 1816, and in a *Saturday Review* of 1862, a writer noted "a point upon which the doctors of etiquette and the pundits of refinement will differ." The novelist C. E. Montague in 1924 warned against judgments taken from "some aesthetic pundit or critical mandarin."

At the end of World War I, a group of Yale undergraduates founded a club, sponsored by Professor William Lyon Phelps, called, with elitist self-derogation, The Pundits. Henry R. Luce was a member; after he started *Time* magazine in 1923, he applied the phrase as a courtesy title to such savants as the playwright Thornton Wilder and the columnist Walter Lippmann. (Also to the American language he applied a curiously Germanic notion of locating phrases ahead of verbs.)

As long as *pundit* had a self-mocking connotation, writers of opinion in journalism could apply it to themselves with impunity; however, in recent years, some of us have taken to using it without the necessary disrespect, and as a result have given political figures a handy term with which to castigate us.

This brings us to the lexicon of opinion-mongering, a field of locutions rarely the subject of synonymy because the usual students become shy and stammer. If Jesse Jackson's poultry worker can denude fifty chickens of their feathers in one minute, however, I can try to differentiate among six terms in six lightning paragraphs:

Editorialist means "newspaper or periodical editorial writer, usually anonymous." He has a steadier job than his countervailing force, *frequent Op-Ed contributor,* whose work appears under such titles as "Another View," "My Turn," "Taking Exception," et cetera.

Columnist applies to "an individual writer or a team producing regular, signed opinion," and sometimes gains the circulation status of *syndicated columnist.* In *Pundits, Poets and Wits,* a new anthology of columns gathered by Karl E. Meyer, a *New York Times* editorialist, the anthologist notes that the term *columnist* has an "association with the I-shaped pillar from which the columnist can harangue the populace—as was literally the case with Simeon Stylites of Syria, who spent thirty years preaching from a column until his death in A.D. 459. He has come to be the patron of an unruly calling."

Commentator connotes "one who expresses opinion on radio or television" (and the verb is not merely *comment,* but the more specific *commentate*).

Analyst is "one who professes objectivity in reviewing the origin of a controversy and dissecting its possible outcome" but who often sneaks in prejudices of his own.

Bigfoot, or *media biggie,* is a celebrated byline writer who is despised for stepping on the assignments of his workaday betters. Although this person is not necessarily a writer of commentary, sometimes what he or she has to say is news itself.

Pundit is an expert on nothing but an authority on everything, a harmless nudge.

Mr. Jackson has found a means of riposte more succinct than Spiro Agnew's *nattering nabobs of negativism,* a phrase I originated in my attempt to update Adlai Stevenson's antipessimist *prophets of gloom and doom,* but was soon narrowed to scorn at adversarial journalists. *Pundit* (much like another Hindi term, *guru,* "spiritual adviser") began as a title of respect or reverence, and then was turned into a term of derision when applied to leaders of opinion.

I am a language *maven,* a word with a range of senses from "aficionado" to "enthusiast" to "scholar" to "connoisseur"; in another incarnation, I am a political *pundit,* variously defined as "opinion-molder, sage, seer, controversialist, invidiator, vituperator."

The word *pundit* lends itself to alliterative attack—"petty, petulant, Pecksniffian political pundits, preying in packs on protectors of the public"—and if it is to be a target in 1992, we will be tempted to defend our glorious calling.

The danger in that, of course, is that we might forget that *punditry* is self-denigrating; in using the term as we have been, we poke fun at our own pretensions of sagacity. Should the term become a scapegoat, we might lose our perspective and embrace it without today's gentling mockery—and who knows, perhaps voters in need will turn from what Lyndon B. Johnson called "chronic campaigners" to their helpful local pundit.

Whatever its links to the Sanskrit Pandita, *the word "pundit" undoubtedly entered the English language as an Anglo-Indian term for a knowledgeable spy, probably through reports from farflung correspondents of* The Times, *back in the days of the Great Game.*

Peter Fleming (Ian's brother, he of "News from Tartary" fame) describes the original pundits in Bayonets to Lhasa, *his 1961 account of Colonel Francis Edward Younghusband's ill-fated 1904 expedition (incursion?) to Tibet, which has recently been reissued by Oxford Press:*

> *There was, finally, a small but important category of explorers in the shape of the "Pundits." These were native agents who, from 1866 onwards, were sent into Tibet by the Survey of India to carry out clandestine reconnaissance, mainly of a topographic nature. They were known by code-names or initials and travelled in disguise. Nain Sing, the first of them, measured distances along his route with the help of a rosary [sic—this would have been a string of Buddhist prayer beads] which, comprising 100 beads instead of the statutory 108, made it easier to pace out the miles; and his successors used a variety of simple expedients, such as compasses hidden in prayer-wheels, to facilitate their formidable task.*
>
> *Loyal, brave, patient and conveniently inexpensive, these humble spies covered thousands of miles of Tibetan territory, and thanks to them the main geographical features of Central Tibet were recorded with a general accuracy by the Survey of India. One at least—Sarat Chandra Das, on whom Kipling based the character of Huree Chundor Mookerjee in* Kim—*reached the capital (Lhasa); and Sven Hedin paid a compliment (which he probably meant to be backhanded) to the native agents employed by both sides in the Great Game when he wrote: "Truly it was a crazy project to risk so much, my life included, mainly for the pleasure of seeing Lhasa, a city which, thanks to the descriptions of Indian Pundits and Russian Buryats, their maps and photographs, is far better known than most other towns in Central Asia."*

—Fleming, Peter, Bayonets to Lhasa, *(Oxford) Oxford University Press, 1961, pp. 53–54. The sub-quote is from Sven Hedin's* Central Asia and Tibet *(London) 1903.*

What may be of further interest is that Younghusband's expedition was prompted by rumours that Russian agents were active in Tibet, and even that Russia had concluded a secret treaty regarding Tibet with China's Manchu

rulers. These rumours, though eventually proved ill-founded (and which origi-
nated in diplomatic circles in Peking and Russia, not from the Pundits), led
Lord Curzon to push for the expedition as a means of countering the supposed
Russian influence.

Robert Delfs
Bureau Chief
Far Eastern Economic
Review
Peking, China

In reference to the historical use of the term in this country, you note the
formation after World War I of an undergraduate club at Yale called The
Pundits. I wonder if you are aware of a substantially earlier use of that name
for a scholarly and literary club formed in Rochester, New York. The Pundit
Club of Rochester was organized in 1854 by Lewis Henry Morgan, a resident
of that city, who is known today as the "Father of American Anthropology."

Morgan, who pioneered the comparative study of kinship and the political
systems of American Indian cultures, was also the author of a nineteenth-
century classic on social evolution entitled Ancient Society. *He was the founder*
of the Anthropology Section of the American Association for the Advancement
of Science, and he brought many of the ideas and people encountered at the
AAAS back to the Pundit Club in Rochester. While I do not know this for a
fact, I suspect the club and its name were well known in scholarly circles of the
late nineteenth and early twentieth centuries. I do know that the Pundit Club
carried on well into the twentieth century.

Jeffrey L. Hantman
Associate Professor of
Anthropology
University of Virginia
Charlottesville, Virginia

In describing a pundit as a "harmless nudge*," you revealed that you ain't no*
pundit in the area of Yiddishisms adapted into the English language. I state my
case:

Webster's dictionary defines nudge: *"to push, gently shove with the elbow,*
etc."

Thus it could be justifiably assumed (there, I split it!) that you probably
meant to put pundit *in the class of* bore *or* pest, *and used the Yiddish term,*
which in Uri Weinrach's Yiddish-English dictionary is "nudnik," a noun. He
also cites the verb as "nudyin" or "noojin." Yiddish has no letter for "J" and
uses the combination of its equivalent of "dz" for that sound.

And so you come to the abbreviated version of "nudnik" popularly referred to as "nooj," the "oo" as in good.

If you find this all too boring, you can yell, like my mother used to do so often: "Stop noodzin (noojin) already!"

Riki Englander Kosut
Astoria, New York

Readout

"Is a written *readout* a handout?" asked my colleague David E. Rosenbaum of *The New York Times.*

At about that time, Richard E. Cohen of *National Journal* was being told by a staff member of the House Appropriations Committee that his question would be answered as soon as a *readout* could be prepared. Troubled by this locution, the reporter found a citation in writing and sent it to me: a transcript of a White House press briefing that began, "Welcome to the pre-brief—or *readout,* excuse me—on the visit of President Ben Ali of Tunisia."

A quick phone call to the horse's mouth (which is an expression of authenticity, not a derogation of President Bush or his spokesman) for an explanation of current usage:

"*Readout* is a colloquial conjunction of two separate expressions," says Marlin Fitzwater, the presidential press secretary, obviously consulting notes in his hand. "The first is 'to *read* your notes,' which is what we do in reporting to the press about a meeting we attended. The second part, the *out* part, may be from 'to speak *out*,' as in telling the press about what happened."

Date of coinage? "I've heard it since I got here in 1983," recalls Mr. Fitzwater, which pushes its time of origin back to the early Reagan or late Carter Administration. The meaning? "A *readout* is a report on what happened at a meeting."

The derivation is computerese. The first sense in the *Oxford English Dictionary,* which prefers the hyphenated form, is "the extraction or transfer of data from a storage medium or device."

For a more hands-on definition, let us turn to Pete Cottrell of the University of Maryland's computer science department: "*Readout* refers to instrument panels or video displays. It's human interface with the machine conveying information, as opposed to *printout,* which is the output of the machine that you can carry away in your hand."

Thus, an answer to Mr. Rosenbaum: In journalese, a *readout* is not a handout; it is a public recitation of information from which notes may be taken or, if permission is given, pictures may be transmitted.

Revanche Is Sweet

"German Nazism marched under the standards of *revanchism*," Soviet Foreign Minister Eduard A. Shevardnadze told the United Nations. "Now that the forces of *revanchism* are again becoming active and are seeking to revise and destroy the postwar realities in Europe . . ."

The Times of London noted the usage: "For decades, the Kremlin used *revanchism* almost as a synonym for West Germany," wrote Charles Bremner, "but Mr. Shevardnadze's words appeared to encompass the nationalist movements erupting across the Baltic region as well as Bonn's policy of welcoming the flood of refugees from East Germany."

Here's an old term we'll be hearing more from. *Revanchism* is rooted in the French *revanche*, "revenge"; in diplomacy, it is the determination of a state to regain territory lost in war or through a treaty signed under duress.

Queen Victoria first used the French word ironically in English in an 1858 letter: "She never allows a word to be said against Leopold who in revanche is much kinder to her than he was." In 1926, *The Scots Observer* gave it the political twist: "It is France's policy [toward Germany] that the sores be kept open even if they give a handle to Monarchist revanchists."

After World War II, Soviet speakers picked up the word to reapply to Germans who wanted the reunification of their country. "Far from being an instrument of either 'American aggressors' or 'German revanchists' (as Soviet propaganda would picture it)," wrote *The New York Times* in 1955, "the North Atlantic alliance is entirely a defensive organization."

The word is usually pronounced by Americans to rhyme with *ranch* ("meanwhile, back at re*vanch*ism"), rather than the French "rih-VAHNSH"; that's curious, because we do not pronounce *détente* "dih-TENT." It has always been used pejoratively, since vengeance is supposed to be left to the Lord. Nobody identifies himself as a revanchist, because we attribute higher motives to our policies than merely getting even; *self-determination, ethnic pride* and *nationalism* are tossed about, but for an upbeat connotation and scholarly cachet, see your *irredentist* twice a year.

Irredentism, from the Italian *irredenta*, "unredeemed," has associations with theology—"not in a state of having made amends to God"—but redemption was the political motive of Italians in the nineteenth century who wanted to incorporate certain regions like Trieste (*Italia irredenta*) into the mother country.

Neither word can properly be applied to advocates for the Baltic nations, which are seeking the re-establishment of their previous independence, but that might not stop Soviet officials.

Queen Victoria was not being ironic in her use of revanche *in 1858. She was merely using the ordinary French expression* en revanche, *which means "in return"—with no irony at all. The phrase was current as far back as the 16th century in games such as cards, where the player is bound to give "a return match."*

As for revanche *in the sense you rightly describe as a nation's resolve to win back territory, it dates only from the Franco-Prussian War of 1870–71, which cost the French Alsace-Lorraine. Thereafter, until 1914, a large party of militarists and others kept calling for* la revanche *without further specification. Everybody knew it meant getting back the two provinces.*

From that usage the term was extended to other nations' similar passions, just as the Italian terra irredenta *("unredeemed") gave the noun* irredentism *with the same meaning.*

Jacques *[Barzun]*
New York, New York

Trieste is a city, not a region. Grazie.

Giancarlo Neri
New York, New York

Right On, Dead-On

"For a bravura example of deadline reporting," reads the citation to Linda Greenhouse, "and dead-on analysis as the Supreme Court ended its session . . ." That's the wording of one of the coveted publisher's awards posted on the bulletin board in the *New York Times* Washington bureau.

What stopped me was not the subsequent reference to "abortion rights of teenagers," using *teenagers* unhyphenated as I have been urging (and contrary to *Times* style); it was the use of the compound adjective *dead-on*, meaning "exactly right."

Barrere and Leland, in their 1889 *Dictionary of Slang*, were first to define the term: "A rifle-shot talks of the aiming being dead-on when the day is so calm that he can aim straight at the bull's eye instead of having to allow to the right or left for wind. He is said to be dead-on himself when he is shooting very well."

The word worked especially well following the award citation's use of

deadline (from the Civil War prison-camp boundary, beyond which a prisoner would be shot; now that punishment is inflicted when copy is filed late). *Dead-on* is a variation of the British *dead steady,* although a closer parallel is the British *bang-on,* literally "bang on target," the meaning extended to "precisely as planned."

A synonym is *spot-on,* which first appeared in 1920, also a shooting term. This may be a rewording of *on the spot,* which means either "immediately" or "at the very place," as in "Unexpectedly paid on the spot, he died on the spot."

I can find no connection of the British *spot-on* to the Vermont expression cited in 1856, *to knock the spots off,* originally used in a horse-breeding context for "to be in the vanguard." For a time, this competed with a term coined a dozen years earlier, *to knock your socks off,* meaning "to impress, bedazzle, overwhelm." One pulls, jerks or strips socks off; nobody uses a mallet to knock them off. What happened, I think, was this: *Knock your spots off* didn't get widely adopted because the pronunciation of its two key words conflicted, not quite rhyming; the rhyme of *knocks-socks* demonstrated the staying power of a rhyme. (Use it or lose it.)

Because Ms. Greenhouse, whose name generates environmentalist jocularity in the bureau, was cited for her abortion-rights coverage, this is a good place to deal with an objection to my account of how the coinage of *pro-choice* preceded the coinage of *pro-life.*

Logically, it should have been the other way around: *anti-abortion* would lead to *pro-abortion;* people who held that view would want to change that harsh term to a more accurate *pro-choice;* people who disagreed with them, but who did not want to be "anti-choice," chose the positive *pro-life.*

Language does not always follow logic. Fred R. Shapiro, a librarian at Yale Law School, takes the logical view and says I have my facts backward: "The truth is that *pro-life* came first, a clever slogan presenting a negative position in a positive light. . . . According to *Webster's Ninth New Collegiate Dictionary,* Merriam-Webster's files record the use of *pro-life* as early as 1972 but do not document *pro-choice* until 1975."

In linguistic and propaganda history, this is no nitpick; I asked Fred Mish at Merriam-Webster to show the cards in his hand. Yes, the *pro-life* citation is dated 1972, but it's in a phrase about "anti-war and pro-life articles"—the meaning had nothing to do with abortion. Indeed, the *Oxford English Dictionary* has a 1961 citation of *pro-life,* meaning "life-enhancing" and not about abortion; you can track *right to life* back to George Bernard Shaw's 1916 *Androcles and the Lion,* but in a different context. In the coinage dodge, we're interested in the phrase used in its current sense.

Logic, shmogic; the first evidence of the existence of the word *pro-choice* was in a *Wall Street Journal* article by Alan L. Otten on March 20, 1975, when this political analyst reported with great prescience: "Both right-to-life and pro-choice forces agree the abortion issue is going to be around for a long time." The first use of *pro-life* came more than nine months later, on January 18, 1976, in a *New York Times* quotation of a "pastoral plan for pro-life activities."

That's it, until somebody comes up with an earlier citation of the new words used in their current meaning. And I suspect somebody will. To him or her, I say, *"Right on!"* (an interjection first used in Odum and Johnson's 1925 songbook, *The Negro and His Songs,* in the phrase "Right on, Desperado Bill!," which sounds like one of the postcards I get).

When I was young, my father always told me that a safe bet regarding a quotation was either the Bible, Shakespeare, or Pope. It seems he was correct.

In Julius Caesar *(Act III, SC. II), during Antony's speech to the people, he says, "I only speak right on, I tell you that which you yourselves do know . . ."*

For 24 years, I've been pointing out to 9th-grade English students just how contemporary the Bard still is.

James M. McMahon
River Vale, New Jersey

Ro v. Ru

Romania, says the A.P. stylebook. "Not *Rumania.*" The *New York Times* stylebook is just as unequivocal: *Rumania. Time* magazine goes along with *The Times.*

Webster's New World Dictionary and Merriam-Webster both list the spelling with the *o* first, with the *u* spelling a variant. The embassy in Washington lists itself as *Romania,* and the State Department, as usual, will spell it the way the country wishes. People from Bucharest, knowing my longtime interest in this issue, have sent in photocopies of birth certificates with the *Act De Nastere* using *Romania.*

Some citations of the *u* spelling can be found, as in *Simpson's Contemporary Quotations* and the *NBC Handbook of Pronunciation,* which gives different pronunciations for *Romania* and *Rumania.* For a combination of *o* and *u,* try the cynical Dorothy Parker's poem:

> Oh, life is a glorious cycle of song,
> A medley of extemporanea;
> And love is a thing that can never go wrong;
> And I am Marie of Roumania.

The Times bottoms its decision on the *Columbia Lippincott Gazetteer of the World,* which prefers *Rumania* because its editors thought that was how the people over there pronounced it. The French thought so, too, spelling it *Roumanie.* In fact, the pronunciation is neither a simple English *o* nor *u,* but a mixture leaning toward the *o.*

The name is rooted in "Roman," another term for Latin. For a time, the Soviets preferred their puppet state to be known as *Rumania* because that seemed less Western and more Slavic; the Ceausescu regime, then considered in the West more maverick than monstrous, made a political point of spelling it with the *o.*

Will *The Times* and *Time* cling to the minority spelling? Will the next edition of the *Times* stylebook, ever sensitive to the subtle changes in language, dig in its heels in this case and prescriptively refuse to go with the flow of common usage? Sure it will, and I am Marie of Romania.

Ro, Ro, Ro Your Boat

You think powerful institutions are incapable of drastic change? You think the people are powerless to bring about fundamental reform in entrenched bureaucracies?

Consider this Editors' Note in *The New York Times*, reprinted here in its entirety:

"The Times today adopts the country name *Romania*, spelled with an *o*, in place of *Rumania*. The *o* form is preferred by many Romanians as a reflection of their Roman origins and has been favored in recent years by most English-language publications.

"Until now, in using the *u*, The Times has been guided by its main geographic reference, the Columbia Lippincott Gazetteer of the World. The gazetteer editors apparently believed that *u*, better than *o*, conveyed the Romanian pronunciation of the name.

"The gazetteer was revised most recently in 1961, and its publishers have no current plans for a new edition. The Times is shifting now because *Romania* has become more familiar to Americans than *Rumania*."

The "Rum" spelling of "Romania" is probably derived from the Arab "Rum," later adopted by the Turks, referring originally to the Byzantine Empire, and later to Europe in general. The Byzantines considered themselves to be Romans ("Rhomaioi" in Greek), since their Empire was a direct descendant of the eastern half of the Roman Empire. The Byzantine spelling always used an "o," but the Arabs and Turks used the "u" ("Rum" was pronounced like the English "room"). This is the origin of "Rumelia" (Turkish-speaking province of Bulgaria), and it is likely that the Ottomans in the 19th century would have referred to the emergent state as "Rumania," regardless of how the locals spelled or pronounced it.

What I'm not sure of is how the Romanians came up with their own name. They are, I believe, descendants of the Vlachs, a people who settled in the region in the later Middle Ages. They spoke a Latin-derived language, but I don't know if they called themselves "Romanians" at that time.

Jim Smither
Allendale, Michigan

Lest you become too smug over the NYT's change in the spelling of Rumania, *you should know that the paper has been had by Transylvanians (not even Wallachians or Moldavians) living in Cleveland and Detroit, whose purpose in clamoring for the change was to stick it to the Hungarians. By emphasizing that they have been in Transylvania since Roman times, they feel they are making the point that the province should belong to Rumania, not Hungary.*

Whatever that poor benighted Ceausescu's reasons for wanting to change the spelling, his successors may well want us to change it back. Then what do we do? Keep changing? What if the Germans want us to call their country Deutschland, because that's the way they spell it? Do we do that too?

Can you imagine how far this little band of not-quite-Rumanians would have got telling the French, say, how to spell their own language?

Marilyn Minden
The New York Times
New York, New York

Screwing Up

After these pieces are written, a researcher in Washington laboriously checks the facts and grammatical judgments; then a copy editor in New York, eyes narrowed and fine-toothed comb in hand, sifts and weighs each word, checks every spelling and challenges every controversial usage for style, taste and libel. Before the presses roll—(*O.K., we use Motter gravure press with 33-pound supercalendered paper*)—the printout is reviewed by someone known to me only as "Top-ed."

Despite this reverence for taste and accuracy, in my political pieces as well as in the scholarly articles, screwups (*CHECK hyphenated?*) occur. In a recent polemic, I wrote that Governor Mario M. Cuomo, unless he headed the New York delegation to the next Democratic National Convention, "could count on no automatic deliverance of delegates"; as Louis Jay Herman, *capo di tutti capi* (*CHECK use of Italian phrase, ethnic slur?*) of the Gotcha! Gang pointed out: "For shame! The verb *deliver* has two basic meanings: 'to hand over, transfer' and 'to set free, liberate.' However, the noun *deliverance* reflects only the second of these meanings. The noun for the first meaning is *delivery*." I meant *delivery,* which made this a mistake, but slipped the religiously freighted *deliverance* past my editors in a subliminal jab at the bishop who said Governor Cuomo might be in danger of going to hell for his abortion position. The end result (*CHECK redundant?*) The result can now be elevated to screwup.

In the foregoing, the noun *screwup* was used twice. In this space a few weeks ago, I defined what NASA officials call a *major anomaly* as a "massive screwup." (*CHECK Maj. Anomaly first name?*) As the reader can see, the word was challenged today only on my decision to eliminate the hyphen, which I base on the frequency of the noun use, contrary to the decision of hidebound Associated Press editors and *New York Times* editors, who prefer the old-fashioned *screw-up.* Thus, when the President of the United States was asked about our soldiers' search of the Nicaraguan Ambassador's residence during the invasion of Panama, he was quoted as replying, "It's a *screw-up* and they have expressed their regrets that it happened."

The locution as a past participle is also a presidential favorite. In another setting, Mr. Bush kiddingly told students at the University of Tennessee that while he was delivering the State of the Union address, they were watching the Vols playing Vanderbilt in basketball, and "some of you had your priorities all *screwed up.*"

Some people are shocked, shocked. (*CHECK too obscure an allusion to Casablanca?*) Frank Mankiewicz, a bluenosed public relations executive in Washington, writes: *"Screw up, it must be noted, is the euphemism for the eponymous SNAFU."* (*CHECK he doesn't mean "eponymous"; he means "acronymic," which he uses later—O.K. to change incoming letter without permission to save writer from looking silly? Also, acronym longer than four letters should not be all-capped.*) "You are too young to remember World War II," continues Mr. Mankiewicz, "but surely your older brother must have told you about the acronymic *frisson* that *snafu* gave otherwise proper men and women to use the word." (*Review whole graph, borderline tasteless.*) (*Sorry, entire tier of eds in meeting will last all week, say let copy-ed handle, but be sure double-check spelling "Mankiewicz."*)

Newspapers and news agencies now use *screw up,* both as noun and verb, without blushing. According to Reuters, Bette Fenton, communications director of the Minneapolis *Star Tribune* (*CHECK not Star and Tribune anymore?*) (*Sorry, that's how Reuters writes it*), was asked about a hoax perpetrated on the paper: "At the time, we had no reason to suspect the person was not legitimate," she said. "We screwed up." In *The New York Times,* Peter T. Kilborn reported the words of a former marijuana smoker: "That's how drugs screwed me up." Nor is the usage limited to the news pages: The straightlaced (*CHECK tight is spelled "strait"*) the straitlaced editorial board of *The Times* seemed to enjoy using the formerly taboo term when it wrote, "President Bush is much too cavalier when he dismisses Friday's raid as a mere 'screw-up.'" (*CHECK if we have been using this so often that we have a style decision to hyphenate, why doesn't the bigfoot language maven go along?*)

Screw began as a noun in the fifteenth century, from the Old French *escroue,* "female screw, nut," which came from the Latin for "sow." (*CHECK I know this is straight from the O.E.D., but I don't like the direction this is taking.*) In 1605, *screw* first appeared as a verb in Shakespeare's *Macbeth,* as Lady Macbeth urges her husband not to lose courage before killing King Duncan: "screw your courage to the sticking place, / And we'll not fail." That carpentry metaphor reappeared recently in a *Times* article about a computer hacker who jammed a network: "Mr. Morris said he went to sleep and the next day 'screwed up his courage,'" in a meaning wholly different from the modern "befouled, blundered, went awry."

In World War II, the particle *up* used in combination with a verb made an impact on slang. *Louse up, ball up, gum up, mess up, foul up* were among the less offensive forms meaning "to botch, to make an egregious mistake, to bungle, to err repeatedly." *Screw up,* in this sense, is first found in a December 1942 issue of *Yank,* and was further popularized in the 1951 *Catcher in the Rye,* the famed novel by J. D. Salinger: "Boy, it really screws up my sex life something awful." The verb is both transitive (*screw up my sex life*) and intransitive (*I really screwed up*).

Another famous American novelist, John Steinbeck, used *screw* with another particle, *around,* joined to the verb (*When does that meeting break up?*) in *The Grapes of Wrath:* "Goin' all over the world drinkin' and raisin' hell and screwin' around." This form may have started with *playing around* and *fooling around,* both coming to mean "sexual promiscuity" and now both used as euphemisms for the still-taboo *screwing around.* (*CHECK get higher-ups to look this over fast; I'm d----d if I'll let this screw up my pension.*) (*If it's still taboo, how come we're using it?*)

The adjective *screwy,* perhaps a synonym of "twisted" or taken from "to have a screw loose," has never been taboo; however, the taboo on the transitive verb form of the noun continues.

In sum, the presidential use of *screw up,* in conjunction with frequent newspaper quotation of the term with no concern for its sexual etymology, has legitimized *screw up* as verb and *screwup* as noun; this in turn may one day lessen the sting of the slang meaning of the central word without its gentling use of *up,* but let's let a generation go by. (*O.K., meeting's over. What's all the fuss about?*)

Dear Bill,
I am not mad north-north-west; and when the wind is southerly I not only know a hawk from a handsaw, but I also know eponymous *from* acronymic. *I used* eponymous *in connection with SNAFU, pushing the envelope only by deviating from the meaning of "the original person" to mean "the original reference."*

As I read your entire screed, it seems to me you are coming out just about where I did, that we have another Republican president who wants to ingratiate himself as a regular guy by using locker-room language.

Frank [Mankiewicz]
Washington, D.C.

The only thing worse than an ethnic slur is an incorrectly expressed *ethnic slur: The phrase should have read "capo di tutti i capi," with the definite article used for generic emphasis. ("Boss of all the bosses," and not just "of the bosses.")*

Anita Dente
Brooklyn, New York

You committed a minor error—notice that I did not say you "screwed up"—in your use of the expression "capo di tutti capi." Since this expression is seldom, if ever, written correctly, I thought that I would bring it to your attention. The word "tutti" (all) requires the use of an article whenever it is followed by a noun. Thus "tutti i giorni"—literally "all the days"—and, of course, "tutti i capi."

> Gaetano Cipolla
> Professor of Italian
> St. John's University
> Jamaica, New York

You use the term "capo di tutti capi."

You may be interested to know that the grammatically correct version is: capo di tutti i capi. When these words are spoken the two subsequent i's are pronounced like one, so the expression sounds the way you have written it, but when it's written it must be written with the article before "capi."

You don't want to screw up with mafia words, do you?

> Angelo G. Gurrieri
> Pleasantville, New York

You described the difference between delivery *and* deliverance. *Of course, there are other uses of these words. Melville actually used both in a single sentence, illustrating another common use of the former.*

Tashtego was trapped within the sinking head of a sperm whale. Queequeg dove into the briny, cut a hole in the head, reached in, pulled out a leg [a breech no less], pushed the limb back in, and finally pulled the Indian out by the hair: "And thus, through the courage and great skill in obstetrics of Queequeg, the deliverance, or rather, the delivery of Tashtego was successfully accomplished . . ."

> Walter Sussman, M.D.
> Bellmore, New York

Was the bit about sticking place/carpentry intended for all your fans to write in? If so—the more obvious reference that surely Shakespeare had in mind is to music, *turning and pushing a peg on a violin etc. to the sticking place.*

> David Roessler
> Guilford, Connecticut

I am not sure Lady Macbeth's exhortation to her husband to ". . . but screw your courage to the sticking place, and we'll not fail" is a carpentry metaphor.

Rather, I believe the image is held to be taken from archery, where a cross-bow string was screwed back to the "sticking place," the point at which the weapon was "cocked" and ready to fire.

Peter Seares
Brooklyn, New York

Send in Sovereign for Socialist

It's name-changing day in the socialist Eden. Leningrad's officials told for-mer Senator Gary Hart, who now represents American businesses active in the Soviet Union, that they expect the name of their city to be changed back to Petrograd. (Built by Peter the Great and named after the Christian Saint Peter, it was called at first "St. Petersburg," but in Russian merely "Petro-grad," or "Peter's city," thereby fuzzing the honoree.)

But there is this reason for the referendum's delay: It will cost millions of rubles to remove the signs, fill in the granite and marble chiselings, print new guidebooks and maps, and buy new government stationery. Residents al-ready refer to the city as "Pete"; as soon as they get the money, they'll change the name officially.

Mikhail Gorbachev, however, is harder pressed to change the name of the Soviet Union, which in English is officially the "Union of Soviet Socialist Republics," or U.S.S.R. He is willing to scrap the word *soviet* or *socialist* to save the Union.

With socialism in disrepute and the notion of the sovereignty of the con-stituent republics on the rise, a delegation from Kazakhstan told the Soviet legislature that it preferred "Union of Soviet Sovereign Republics," sub-stituting *sovereign* for *socialist*.

Other deputies were willing to adopt *sovereign* so long as they could keep the ideologically unifying *socialist*. They preferred to jettison *soviet,* a Rus-sian word for "council" long associated with the Bolshevik Revolution, and put forward "Union of Sovereign Socialist States." This does not have the advantage of keeping the old initials, but seems to copy the American use of *states* as being less sovereign, or independent, than *republics.*

Socialist is obviously under fire; that word first appeared in print in 1827 in England's *Co-operative Magazine,* which compared the stand of "Political Economists" with "the Communionists or Socialists" on whether "capital should be individual or in common." In 1840, *communism* was coined.

Soviet nomenclature (not to be confused with *nomenklatura,* or "elite") has not been finally decided. The Congress of People's Deputies voted down the changes—for now. But if you plan to open an office in the Soviet Union, it might be a good idea to postpone the engraving of expensive stationery with "Leningrad, Union of Soviet Socialist Republics"; the post office may soon insist on "Petrograd, Russia."

The fight over these words reflects the struggle going on in the Kremlin over the meaning of *sovereign*. Mr. Gorbachev apparently feels he can live with the word so frequently used by his rival, Boris Yeltsin, provided it is hedged in with a word like *states* in the limited American sense, and follows the key word *union*. This is resisted by Mr. Yeltsin in Russia and other nationalist leaders in Soviet republics like Georgia and Ukraine (don't use *the* in front of *Ukraine*, say Ukrainian nationalists—it's a nation, not a region). They want little or no mention of *union* and the devolvement of *sovereignty* from the Kremlin to the republics. Their sovereignty message: devolution to avoid revolution.

The word *sovereignty* is treated with such respect because it describes the distribution of power in the crumbling superpower. That's a word sure to be at the heart of dissension in international affairs elsewhere, too.

"The new partition threatening Europe," writes Flora Lewis of *The New York Times*, "is not just between rich and poor, comfortable and desperate. It is also between countries that have learned to pool some sovereignty, for mutual benefit, and those determined to assert sovereign separatism."

Let's pull the word up by its roots and try to find the meanings: *Sovereign* is from the Middle English *soveraine*, in turn from the Old French *soverain*, from the Latin *super*, "above, over."

The meaning of the noun in English began as "acknowledged leader" in this citation circa 1290: "For, sire king, thou art mi souerein." Then different senses emerged for the adjective *sovereign*: one took the road of "supreme" in the sense of "excellent, none better than," but that faded in time; another connotes "above all other authority" as in "a sovereign leader," reflecting the use of the noun form for "the king, queen or ruler." A third sense developed out of the second, as the personal tie binding vassal to leader became a territorial tie binding people to territory, with such synonyms as "independent, autonomous, autarkic, self-governing, free from external control." (I hesitate to include a fourth meaning, "of a husband in relation to his wife," which is as obsolete as meanings get.)

In its most famous use in United States political history, *sovereign* signified local decision-making without separation. *Pop-sov* was 1860 Democratic presidential candidate Stephen Douglas's position on the extension of slavery to the territories: *popular sovereignty* was used as we use *local option* today, to mean local or state decision-making on difficult issues. Republican candidate Lincoln, though no abolitionist, opposed *pop-sov* and advocated instead the limitation of slavery to where it then existed.

Can *sovereignty* be diluted or pooled and retain its meaning? Yes; *The*

London Gazette reported in 1712 that "The Canton of Berne [Switzerland] shall be admitted into the Co-Sovereignty of the common Bailliages." In 1793, Thomas Jefferson wrote that a leader "proceeds . . . to act as co-sovereign in the territory," and in 1820 wrote that the United States Constitution "has wisely made all the departments co-equal and co-sovereign between themselves." (Today's usage frowns on *co-equal* as redundant and prefers *among* to *between* with more than two, but now I sound like carping John Adams.)

A related term, from the same Old French root, is *suzerain,* originally "a feudal lord to whom fealty is due from a vassal," which has now come to mean "a nation that controls the foreign relations of a vassal state but permits self-government in internal affairs."

George P. Shultz, one of Mr. Jefferson's successors as Secretary of State, noted in an etymologically dramatic speech "On Sovereignty" in October 1989 that "The Declaration of Independence places sovereignty in the people," which is "exercised on behalf of the people by both Federal and state authorities." Similarly, as nations bound themselves in international associations, they "have accepted limitations on their sovereign rights to act as they choose . . . affected powerfully by technology, by the way borders are becoming porous, almost irrelevant, in more and more areas of sovereign importance: money, ideas, information, missiles."

In the Shultz definition, "the concept of absolute sovereignty is long gone." He sees "divided sovereignty" as today's fact (much as Jefferson glommed on to "co-sovereignty"), and suggests to Middle East policy makers that "a little creativity about new mixes of sovereignty might help right now."

As it turns out, that is what Mikhail Gorbachev is looking for, but what other Soviet leaders are working against. People who insist on political recognition of their long-submerged national identities, as in the Baltic states, are derogated as *disunionists* and *separatists* or hailed as *freedom fighters* and *patriots;* a more neutral term is *nationalists.* When *sovereignty* becomes a fighting word, peacemakers tend to turn toward a word that directs itself to free behavior rather than to territorial ownership: *autonomy.*

Dear Bill,

*You've probably had a hundred letters about Petrograd by now, but in case you didn't, permit me to do a gotcha. The city was St. Petersburg from its founding until World War I. Germans were esteemed in Russia, many were hired at court, and several married into the imperial family. It was only after Russia and Germany became enemies in World War I that the city's name was de-Germanized (*burg *means town, just as* grad *does.) In the same way, and for* *the same reason, the British Royal Family's name was changed at that time from Battenberg to Mountbatten, which also means the same thing.*

Warmest regards,
Flora [Lewis]
The New York Times
Paris, France

St. Petersburg (Sank Peterburg in Russian) was renamed "Petrograd" at the beginning of the First World War when anti-German sentiment was rampant in Russia at that time. "Petrograd" has a more Old Slavonic ring to it. It was renamed Leningrad after Lenin's death.

Misha Allen
Toronto, Canada

Leapin' Lenins!
You write that the proposal to rename the USSR the "Union of Sovereign Socialist States . . . does not have the advantage of keeping the old initials but seems to copy the American use of states *as being less sovereign, or independent, than* republics.*"*

However, in Russia there are two words used for state. *The American states are referred to as* shtaty, *while for State (as in "the union of the two German states) the word* gosudarstvo *is always used—this is the G in KGB.* Gosudar' *is an old word meaning sovereign (the person), and* Oxford's *says that it also translates as "Your Majesty." The proposals to which you refer are for the use of the word* Gosudarstvo. *The union republics are formally recognized as these in the Soviet constitution, and it was the nationalists who first called attention to this and insisted that their republics were indeed* States *whether in captivity or in voluntary union.*

Jeff Zelkowitz
Westport, Connecticut

Sex in the News

In a tirade leveled at Mikhail S. Gorbachev in my daily occupation, I denounced him for sending Western *newsmen* out of Lithuania before his economic crackdown.

"I'm one of those female 'newsmen' who was denied permission to stay in Lithuania," writes Alison Mitchell of the *Newsday* Moscow bureau. "So are Esther B. Fein of *The New York Times,* Anne Imse of the Associated Press, Penny Fishlock of the *Daily Telegraph,* Bridget Kendall of the BBC and Pilar Bonat of *El Pais.*

"Now, I'm not a stickler on getting gender out of language," Ms. Mitchell advises. "I don't like *chairpersons* and *Congresspersons*—but it does strike me as unnecessary and even inaccurate to use *newsmen* in such circumstances when there are perfectly good words around like *journalists, reporters* or *correspondents.*"

Right; *newsmen* may be used to refer to male reporters, but leaves uncovered female reporters; the sexist *newshens* has been banned, and the breezy *newsies* belongs in an informal category with *media types.* Using *newsmen* in that instance seemed to assume that only males were on the journalistic job in Lithuania, which is obviously untrue.

Ms. Mitchell is one of the reporters who *were*—not *was*—denied permission to stay. When the pronoun *one* is followed by a prepositional phrase (*of the reporters*), we must decide whether the relative clause (starting with *who*) refers to the one or to the many.

In this case, the *Newsday* reporter is not seeking to separate herself from the crowd to assert her singularity; on the contrary, she is expressing solidarity with her fellow female journalists, stressing the collective. Since the clause refers to the many, we use the plural verb *were.*

I am one of the newsmen who try not to offend journalists who are female.

Shnorring the Burden

The topic was *burden-sharing,* a locution used in the past to describe the allocation of reimbursement of some of the cost to America of the defense of Europe. This year, however, the compound gerund is applied to the distribution of the cost of the campaign against Saddam Hussein.

"I do think it's a little degrading," said Representative Les Aspin, chairman of the House Armed Services Committee, who appeared on *This Week With David Brinkley,* "to have the Secretary of the Treasury and the Secretary of State *shnorring* around looking for funds. . . ."

"Shnorring?" Mr. Brinkley asked.

"Good word, isn't it?" said the Congressman, pleased at getting this valuable *face time* to display his breadth of linguistic vision.

"If you know Yiddish," said Mr. Brinkley, who evidently does. However, he did not go on to give the translation, which is left to me.

Shnorrer (sometimes spelled *schnorrer*), originally rhyming with *snorer* but now slipping toward rhyming with *demurrer,* is related to the German *schnorren,* "to beg," and is perhaps derived from the sound of a beggar's small pipe or whistle. As a noun, *shnorrer* means "beggar, panhandler," but carries a connotation of effrontery, sometimes a shrewd dignity. The lexicographer Leo Rosten points out in *The Joys of Yiddish* that the "*shnorrer* was not apologetic; he did not fawn or whine. He regarded himself as a craftsman, a professional. . . . He expected recognition of his skill, if not encomiums for his character."

Nowadays, the verb used is "to shnor." I have a large, dignified-looking Bernese mountain dog that occasionally is drawn to the dinner table in looking for handouts. When I say, sharply, "Don't *shnor!,*" he withdraws to a nearby doorway to look hungry and offended, with an expression that ill befits a multilingual animal and causes his owner to cave.

On the international diplomatic scene, *burden-shnorring* is a new term for an old appeal.

As a self-appointed member of the Squad Squad, I feel compelled to draw your attention to your "large, dignified-looking Bernese mountain dog." The mature weight of the Bernese easily exceeds 100 pounds (in males) and approaches that in females. To describe a mature Bernese as large is as unnecessary as describing a Chihuahua as small.

> Michael Roth, DVM
> Saugerties, New York

P.S. Table scraps aren't good for any dog.

Sign Here

Welcome, semiotics fans, to lit-crit's glorious new era of *post-deconstructionism.*

This epoch, which could last six months to a year, has been named here today. *Post-deconstructionism,* which I will define in due course, is coined on the analogy of *post-modernism,* the label that architects and decorative artists put on their complex and classic shapes evocative of historical periods, as they rejected the stark International style of the first half of the twentieth century, with its Cubist art and wasteland poetry and twelve-tone music suitable for the elevators of the World Trade Center buildings. (That sentence was written in post-modern style, with dependent clauses and recherché four-syllable words, self-consciously free to go on and on. The previous, modernist style was a combination of Hemingway and James Joyce: *did the earth move for you yes yes yes yes.*)

Post-modern art is on the way out, of course, and the newer wave is, for lack of an original idea, being called *post-post-modernism,* which sounds more like a stutter than a style.

What happened to plain old *modern*? That dated adjective came into English in 1585, from the Latin *modo,* "just now," and became a popular synonym for *contemporary* or *up-to-date;* the term *Modern English* covers the development of our language since roughly the mid-fifteenth century. As a style, however, *modern* seems passé. The current exhibit at the I.B.M. Gallery of Science and Art in New York is "What Modern Was," a look at design from 1935 to 1965.

Paul Goldberger, cultural news editor of *The New York Times,* thinks modernism may never have died, and tells me that the current trend—less dogmatic and rationalist than modernism—might be called *Late Modernism,* or *Romantic Modernism,* or even (for those who like oxymorons) *Romantic Pragmatism.*

These terms have more of what deconstructionists call *jouissance* than the other candidates for architect-designer nomenclature like *New Romanticism* or *New Historicism* (terms also used by literary critics and historians). My vote is for *Romantic Modernism* because it can be shortened in headlines as *Ro-Mo,* on the analogy of *lit-crit* for "literary criticism."

Whether it's the catchy *Ro-Mo* or some dreary monicker like *double-post-modernism,* the new label will be featured alongside Cold War II in those timetable-of-history books in the years running up to the third millennium.

Leap from "decorative arts" over to the politic arts: For a few weeks, the corresponding political era was called *post-cold-war,* a posting that turned out to be premature. *The Second Cold War,* or *Cold War II,* was coined by Richard J. Whalen as a chapter title in his 1974 book, *Taking Sides.* This parallel to World Wars I and II did not take hold until recently, when a chinpull of pundits began to use it. Now it bids fair to challenge the New World Order, which could be the name of an era to come if the *Second Cold War* turns out to be the brief interlude between Gorbachev and Yeltsin.

Now leap from politics to the humanities, where *modernism* has also been posted. This world of linguistics, semiotics and literature likes to quote Ludwig Wittgenstein sighing, "The limits of my language mean the limits of my world." The high life of the mind in this world was roiled in the 70's and 80's by the rise of *deconstructionism,* which we will henceforth call *decon* because it is suitably irreverent. Although the word has a root in the existentialist philosopher Martin Heidegger's use of the word *Destruktion,* it does not mean "destruction" so much as "detailed disassembly."

This is the philosophy that makes the reader more important than the author, placing the interpretation higher than the text. That word *text* is central; in the old days, a flesh-and-blood author created a *work;* nowadays, a critic studies a stand-alone *text.*

Decon is a way of analyzing literature by denying the traditional meanings of words, breaking their link with real things and insisting that they have significance only in relation to other words or signs. Author's intent, agreed-upon meanings of words, historic or cultural settings all go by the board. (I started to write *by the boards,* but that mistakenly points to the plural *boards* of a theater. The singular *board* has been used for the past millennium as a nautical term meaning "the side of a ship," as in the right-sided *starboard.* Since 1630, the seagoing *by the board* has been used to indicate loss or disappearance.)

In decon, only the interaction between the text and the critical reader counts. This delights the regimented legions of professional iconoclasts, but upsets communicators who like to fix meanings with some precision; it also infuriates academics who don't want to join a club with no clubhouse. Some decon, particularly in biblical exegesis, has revealed meanings in scripture heretofore unknown, and the questioning of long-held interpretation is refreshing, but the kick in the philosophy is more in taking apart than in putting back together. *Annihilate* and *nihilism* have the same root.

Today's heavy lifting is occasioned by the reading of the most lucid and controversial lit-crit book of 1991, *Signs of the Times* by David Lehman. The author is a poet and critic (and, incidentally, a precinct captain in the Poetic Allusion Watchers division of the Lexicographic Irregulars).

Mr. Lehman derides Jacques Derrida, French founder of the movement; he zaps Roland Barthes, author of *The Death of the Author,* and really gives a hard time to the late Paul de Man, high priest of the decon school in the United States, a temperate and beloved Yale professor who, it was recently discovered, happened to have embraced the tenets of Nazism in his youth in Belgium.

Everybody in this dodge doubleplays around; for both decons and their opponents, the pun is mightier than the word. Professor Geoffrey Hartman calls his hard-squeezing colleagues "boa-deconstructors" and the surreal philosophy "Derridadaism"; Mr. Lehman subtitles his book *Deconstruction and the Fall of Paul de Man,* playing on the fall of Man, and labels the past-forgetfulness of his subject "Waldheimer's disease."

The name of the decon game is that the game's name means something different every time. That language philosophy is provocative, but it goes nowhere and cries out for a more satisfying theory to refute it. How can I be Saussure? Because the pressure that many of us in the language dodge get from average users is not "free us from rigid meaning" but "give us moorings"; Norma Loquendi is discontent with explanations that words can be ambivalent (and is of two minds about my using *ambivalent*).

That's why we are certain to see the rise of *post-deconstructionism.* That word assumes that decon will be remembered as important enough to rate a *post,* as *modernism* was. I think it will; some of its terminology resonates. (You cannot write anything on this subject without using the vogue verbs *roil* and *resonate,* and citing Wittgenstein and Ferdinand de Saussure.)

Take *jouissance,* for example: The common meaning is "sexual ecstasy," but Roland Barthes uses it to mean "the pleasure of the text." That sure beats *a good read.*

You mentioned "post-post-modernism," and I thought you might be interested in the following, just in case you were starting a stuttering file. Psychologists who study verbal learning have a task or procedure known as Modified Modified Free Recall, or MMFR for short. If a subject had studied two lists of word associations, asking the subject to recall a set of associations would be free recall; asking for recall of one or the other list is modified free recall; and asking for recall of both is modified-modified free recall.

> W. Scott Terry
> Charlotte, North Carolina

Please do not use "Ro-Mo" to describe Romantic Modernism. It sounds too much like "Ro-Ro," which is a roll-on, roll-off cargo ship (it carries cargo on trucks and trailers, rather than in containers—these roll on and off the ship at the port. Other similar ship types are the "Flo-Flo," which floats cargo barges on and off, and the hybrid "Flo-Ro," which carries both barges and trucks.)

> Larrie Ferreire, PE
> Naval Architect
> Alexandria, Virginia

I am personally partial to the term "Neo-Modernism" because it can be short-ened to "N'o-Mo."

> Wally Jones
> Marathon, Florida

Squad Squad Report Report

When you spot a redundancy, do you shrug your shoulders? Not if you are John Hersey. "Have you noticed the redundant *is,*" writes the author, a member of the Squad Squad, "with which we're being bombarded these days?"

Examples: "The-bottom-line-is is that . . ." and "The-point-is is that . . ."

We are grouping words in our minds just as shorthand transcribers grouped frequently used assemblages of words into "brief forms." This should be resisted, if only on the grounds of redundancy, like "START talks."

Other members of the Squad Squad are on the alert for repetitive repetition. Michael J. Saxton of Davis, California, forwarded a memo from the chancellor of the local University of California that created "an ad hoc task force," as if all task forces were not by their nature *ad hoc,* Latin for "to this," meaning "for this task only."

I was taken to task for referring to "the Negev desert"; Wallace Alcorn of Austin, Minnesota, points out that *Negev* means "desert" (as well as "south") in Hebrew. The writer aware of meanings uses only "the Negev," unless thinking that readers do not know it's a desert; same thing with the *Sahara,* rooted in the Arabic for "desert."

Years ago, the Wall Street firm of Salomon Brothers had "Cold Gazpacho" on its menu, but that sent a chill through fastidious diners: All gazpacho is cold.

Refer back (No!), if you will, to the opening sentence of this item. When I wrote that not a few of us were shrugging our shoulders at the use of *litotes,* the double negation, Ed Cashin of the Bronx objected: "*He shrugged* means 'he lifted his shoulders,' so *he shrugged* is correct and adding *his shoulders* is incorrect."

A *shrug* was originally a shiver or shudder, but became a lifting or drawing up of the shoulders in an expression of indifference, distaste or puzzlement, sometimes accompanied by a sound approximating "Ih!"—"You're asking me?"

The-point-is is that only shoulders are for shrugging; you cannot shrug your eyebrows, even though you can lift them. When shrugging, I side with the Squad Squad. As the couturier Claude Montana would say, with an eye to the 1990's, drop *the shoulders.*

You wrote, "We are grouping words in our minds just as shorthand transcribers grouped frequently used assemblages of words into 'brief forms.'"

Shorthand writers, not transcribers, group words into "phrases," not "brief forms."

"Brief forms" are special Gregg outlines which shorten words and do not include all the sounds in the word. For example, "can" is represented by "k," and the "an" are not written; this builds speed. In Pitman these shortened words are now called "Pacers." Formerly they were called "Short Forms" or "Grammalogs."

Goodwin W. Gilson
Brooklyn, New York

I disagree with your conclusion that the phrase "shrugged his shoulders" is redundant. One may not be able to shrug one's eyebrows, but one can shrug "it off."

When one says, "He shrugged his shoulders," we assume he is referring to a physical activity, as opposed to "shrugging it off"—a mental exercise.

Please advise the Squad Squad to focus its forces on "tuna fish" sandwich instead.

> Mary Klotz
> Jersey City, New Jersey

Looking Askance

We all thought John H. Sununu, the White House chief of staff, had at last been cornered. The official presidential position on the dread subject of tax increases (*hikes* in journalese) in budget talks was *no preconditions*. Governor Sununu had been caught off base when he told reporters, not for quotation or attribution, that a tax increase was not in the works—that the Democrats at the "budget summit" might seek that way to reduce the deficit, but that President Bush would say no.

Albert R. Hunt of *The Wall Street Journal*, his target in sight on *Meet the Press,* closed in on the meaning of *no preconditions:* "You said, according to the reports, that it meant, and I'm quoting now, 'The Democrats could propose tax increases, but the White House would veto them.' "

Mr. Sununu could not deny having been the source of the story, but denied having said what *The Washington Post* quoted "a senior official" as saying. "That is not the quote. I never used the word 'veto.' I indicated that the White House would be likely to *look askance* at it . . ."

He had slipped out of the corner with a near-archaism of obscure origin. What is a *look askance*?

The literal sense—"obliquely, with a side glance"—is no longer germane. The figurative sense of that sideways look has become "with scorn, doubt, suspicion, disapproval or distrust."

"Scorn" belongs right up there. Although *askance* first appeared as *a scanche,* two words, in Palsgrave's 1530 book on French grammar, meaning "sidewise, obliquely," the first use of the single word in literature was by the poet Edmund Spenser two generations later: "That scornfully looks askaunce."

Shakespeare tried to make the adverb into a verb meaning "to turn aside" in his poem "The Rape of Lucrece"—"That from their own misdeeds askaunce their eyes"—but that never took hold in the language. It was a good try, though; *askance* may be related to the Italian verb *cansare,* "to turn aside."

Etymologists clash on the source. The *Oxford English Dictionary* says the origin is unknown: "There is a whole group of words of more or less obscure origin in *ask-.*" These include *askew, asquint* and *askance,* and all have that cocked-eye connotation. *The Barnhart Dictionary of Etymology* disagrees with that don't-ask attitude, pointing instead to a 1395 Chaucer use of a conjunction *ascaunce,* to mean "as though, as if." This conjunction predates the adverb *askance* and may be derived from the Latin *quasi,* "as if."

All this must have flashed through the mind of John Sununu (a quasi-genius, reportedly with an intelligence quotient of 180) as he turned aside the direct challenge of the word *veto* and went back to the undefined and indeterminate *no preconditions.*

This brings up a related question: Why *pre*conditions? Aren't plain *conditions* conditional enough? Does this belong with *preheat, preplan* and *pretest* in the concatenation of redundant *pre-* prefixes?

No. Not all *conditions* are *preconditions,* Fred Mish, editorial director at Merriam-Webster, once told me: "Hard work is a necessary *condition* of success, but it is not a *precondition* because the condition is met in the process." The words are not interchangeable; *precondition* stresses the element of time. The Squad Squad can relax; no redundancy here.

However, a curious redundancy appears twice (yes, that's four usages) on a close reading of the transcript of Governor Sununu's appearance. "Well, the fact is is that the reporters were assuming there would be taxes," he said.

Later, he again doubled the *is:* "would be likely to look askance at it, and the fact is is that we would look at each issue as it came forward."

This is a vivid illustration of a construction known as the Hersey Double-Is, named after the author John Hersey, who wrote in last year to wonder about such usages as "The bottom line is is that . . ."

My theory was that this was a grouping of words into a phrase, followed by a treatment of that phrase as if it were a single word. Its reach into the corridors of power, however, requires further analysis. For this we turn to a lively British publication calling itself *English Today,* which published a paper by Dwight Bolinger* on the double *is* in 1987.

Reached in Palo Alto, California, Mr. Bolinger points to a nineteenth-century usage in a letter by Charles Darwin: "My excuse and reason is, is the different way all the Wedgwoods view the subject . . ."

Mr. Bolinger believes that the phenomenon has blossomed in the past generation. What causes it? "The reduplication of *is,*" he speculates in his article, "must respond in part to the speaker's uncertainty as to the affinity of the copula." Hunh? A *copula* is a verb that couples, or links, a subject with the rest of the predicate; would he run that by us again? The speaker, Mr. Bolinger explains, does not know if the *is* belongs "with what precedes or with what follows," and "seems to want to make sure that neither half of the sentence is deprived of its *is.*"

The Hersey Double-Is, then, is probably the speaker's subconscious way of making certain that both the subject and the predicate have a verb. Mr. Sununu, in being hypercautious about avoiding error, has erred. A double *is* may be his way of insuring that both his subject and predicate are firmly verbed, but in most cases, what the double *is* is is a mistake.

You allow the word "preconditions," without which the Republicans promise to meet the Democrats to discuss the possibility of an increase in taxes. I wish that you would reconsider your position regarding that word.

The Oxford English Dictionary *says that a "condition" is "something demanded or required as a prerequisite to the granting or performance of something else," and "something that must exist or be present if something else is to be or take place," and "that on which anything else is contingent."*

Since both the prefix "pre" and the word "condition" refer to something which happens previously, the preceding "pre" in "precondition" must be considered redundant.

Furthermore, I believe that you were careless in your selection of examples: "Does this belong with 'preheat,' 'preplan' and 'pretest' in the concatenation of redundant 'pre-' prefixes?" Clearly, "preplan" belongs in the trash heap, with

*Mr. Bolinger died in 1991.

"precondition," for the reasons stated above. "Preheat" and "pretest," however, although ambiguous because they don't explain to what the action is previous, may define something which was pre(viously) heated (before applying, for example), or previously tested (before the potentially embarrassing public test?). Unlike "plan" and "condition," "heat" and "test" do not imply prepatory action. The prefix "pre-," therefore, is not redundant.

Finally, contrary to what you, or Fred Mish, whom you quote, say: All conditions are established prior to that which is conditional. The example which you quote: "Hard work is a necessary 'condition' of success, but it is not a 'precondition' because the condition is met in the process" doesn't make any sense. That statement, along with "preplan" and "precondition," belong in Wonderland with Alice, in a time warp just previous to the past.

Ted Scott
Toronto, Canada

Your triple is comparable to a hole-in-one on the links.

Arthur Gray, Jr.
New York, New York

While usage of the double is in everyday speech may very well be improper, it fails to draw the undue attention, or even confusion, one senses it may have elicited when it was first heard. Not so in writing, where such usage continues to provoke a curious sense of jamais vu—recognizability of a grammatical usage in writing as new and unique when the same usage in speech has been experienced before and gone unnoticed.

When observed by me in news copy, the fact is is that I consider it anathema and what I do do is edit it out.

Humayun J. Chaudhry
News Writer/Newscaster
Third World Broadcasting
New York, New York

Dear Bill:
William Steinkraus, Chairman of the U.S. Equestrian Team, Doubleday author, amateur grammarian, and Lexicographic Irregular, suggested the following conclusion for your column on "is": "What I'm saying is 'is is' is always to be frowned upon."

For a future column, he hoped that the following might inspire you: "Tom, where Jack had had 'had,' had had 'had had.' 'Had had' had had the approval of the examiner. Eleven "had"'s in a row! I couldn't resist passing this on.

Joel E. Fishman
Editor
Doubleday
New York, New York

The Double Is

We have been observing the increased reduplication of *is,* as in the locution of John H. Sununu, the White House chief of staff: "The fact is, is . . ." This construction, more prevalent than linguists suspected, is an unnecessary attempt to give a verb to both ends of a sentence.

Members of the Squad Squad immediately complained about the word *reduplication,* contending that should mean "three or four usages," or a repeat repeated.

Sorry, this is not like *iteration* and *reiteration;* in linguistics, logic does not always prevail.

Reduplication is the word used to describe the formation of words like *willy-nilly, higgledy-piggledy, hocus-pocus* and *razzle-dazzle.* (Those are second-order reduplications, because the second part of the term rhymes with but does not exactly duplicate the first.) Pure redupes are the perfectly repeated *tom-tom* and the slang term for "hurry," *chop-chop.*

Is is is both a reduplication and a mistake. Mauritz Johnson of Delmar, New York, writes with the suggestion that the White House chief of staff may be signaling the positive in Spanish: "The real explanation is simply a sibilant palindrome, viz., '*Is is* is Sununu's *Si! Si! Si!*' "

Summer Reading

Summer reading is a phrase that means "the sort of book that you take to the beach, which can be suntan oil-stained and sprinkled with sand without making the reader feel anything worthwhile has been destroyed; escapist pap."

Not always true. Summer vacations or long weekends offer time for reflection and regeneration of the mind cells. Here is a sack of ten books I have been setting aside for reading on holiday, especially suitable for language mavens with a foreign-policy bent.

The trick is to mix the light and heavy, but to stick to the literate or at least provocative—by elevating your reading, you improve your writing or at least tickle your thinking.

One, by One, by One by Judith Miller (Simon & Schuster, $21.95), a stunning report on the ways six countries are handling the memory of the Holocaust.

The Sooner Spy, a breezily comic spy novel narrated by an Oklahoma politician, by Jim Lehrer, the only television anchor who writes funny novels (Putnam, $19.95).

The Impoverished Superpower, this year's bible for foreign-policy hard-liners, Henry S. Rowen and Charles Wolf Jr., eds. (ICS Press, San Francisco, $29.95).

Jubilee Jim and the Wizard of Wall Street by Donald Porter (Dutton, $19.95), a historical novel about Jim Fisk and his partners in greed, power and good fun—a must for today's Trumpniks.

The Bible and Us: A Priest and a Rabbi Read Scripture Together by Andrew M. Greeley and Jacob Neusner, a not-so-odd coupling of prolific iconoclasts who team up to offer a lively entrance to exegesis (Warner, $24.95).

On Liberty and Liberalism by Gertrude Himmelfarb, how the conflicting views inside the head of one man—John Stuart Mill—foreshadowed today's political argument ($10.95 from ICS Press—that's two for these guys, and I never heard of them before).

Business Buzzwords by Michael Johnson, from *golden hello* to *gorbasm,* the tough new jargon of British business, published in London by Blackwell; pick one up if you get over there, and achieve a high *pass-along rate.*

The Road to a Free Economy by Janos Kornai (Norton, $16.95), a plan for taking Hungary from socialism to a market system, timely enough to enable me to drop the ideas on the heads of visiting apparatchiks.

Conflicts Unending by Richard N. Haass, about the need for ripeness in negotiation by a current National Security Council member (Yale University Press, $22.50).

Why Blacks, Women and Jews Are Not Mentioned in the Constitution by Robert A. Goldwin, who has a Locke on our political history (A.E.I. Press, Washington, $16.95).

Some of these authors I don't even know. Clifford Irving has a new novel I want to see, and Letitia Baldrige is taking the fiction plunge, too. But that's for the fall; this bag of ten will do the trick on the beach. (*At* the beach? No; the idiom is *on* the beach, *at* the shore and *in* the mountains.)

With reference to my summer reading, since I live in northern New Jersey, my bag of 10 will be read down *the shore. That is the proper idiom here.*

Leonard J. Felzenberg
Livingston, New Jersey

Supa Japanese

The languages of East Asia seem disoriented these days. Bouncing about what is no longer called the Far East, where I found China Airlines (two words) more reliable than Japan Air Lines (three words), the traveler is jarred by the adoption of American terms: *Teribi* is Japanese for "terrible," and *supa,* for "super," is superseding the ancient Japanese borrowing, "O.K."; the pronunciation of *supa* mimics the American "soop-a." This signifies a rough balance of trade in words: We have adopted *honcho,* their word for "squad leader," as a verb meaning "to be straw boss over."

All around the world, however, language follows life. As work habits change and living styles shift, we form new words to describe people in new roles.

In the United States, a word was needed for a man who does the housework and looks after the kids while his wife pursues a career outside the home; the coinage was *househusband,* based on *housewife,* which was formed in parallel over the past eight centuries with the German *Hausfrau.*

Many housewives now prefer the sexless *homemaker;* few househusbands adopt that term, preferring—cheerfully or defiantly—the specifically male identification. In time, as the need to assert sexual identification declines, that term may be replaced by *domestic economist* despite objections from learned practitioners of the dismal science.

Househusband is an analogue, coined by analogy; the Japanese usually prefer to coin a new lifestyle word by applying a new sense to a word already familiar in another area.

Example: What do you call a man who retires and pokes around the house, getting in the way? In the United States, he's called a *retiree,* and in Britain, a *pensioner*—both neutral terms, with the adjective *aimless* or prepositional phrase *at loose ends* tacked on fore or aft to modify them pejoratively. (If anyone has a good term for "active, involved retiree, creatively contemplative, and a real pleasure to have around the house," as most of my retired readers surely are, send it in.)

In Japan, the word for a bored retiree, as viewed by his soured spouse, is *nureha.*

"*Nureha* are wet, fallen leaves," writes C. Alton Robertson in *The Japan Times*. "And anyone who has tried to sweep wet, fallen leaves off their steps or street (as any Japanese housewife has) knows how impossible it is. They are well and truly stuck.

"*Nureha* is now used to mean a retired man who sticks to his wife like a wet, fallen leaf. . . . He watches her cook; he watches her do the laundry; he goes shopping with her. *Nureha.*"

A cruel term, but life is unfair, and language follows life. They keep moving the goalposts.

"Nureha" does not sound like a legitimate Japanese word to me. A moment later I recall "Nureochiba," which did recently acquire the meaning you described in the article; wet, fallen leaves or an obnoxious retired husband. "Nureha" means just wet leaves, which may very well be still hanging on to the tree. A metaphor for a disagreeable male retiree should be messy fallen leaves, wet or dried, so we should not eliminate "ochi" here. My guess is that "ochi" has fallen off somewhere during the transpacific flight. Or is it a simple confusion? There is another word pronounced "nureha," though it has a different meaning and different manifestation. We have long had a phrase "Karasu no nureha iro," which literally means "color like a wet raven's plume" and figuratively means beautiful shiny jet black hair.

One other thing I do not quite understand is that "teribi" is Japanese for "terrible." Is this true? I have never heard of it. "Teribi" seems to me very close to "terebi," which is for television. Well, I admit Japanese TV is, all in all, terrible. Isn't it too farfetched? Could you kindly enlighten me?

Junko Deguchi
Mt. Prospect, Illinois

Japanese

infure—inflation
depato—department store
apato—apartment

and even more

mansion—a (very small) apartment, probably a condominium
romance car—a limited express train.

Robert Anthony Myers
New York, New York

Terrible Television

The Japanese are engaged in maven-bashing, some justifiable. The loan-word *teribi*, mistranslated in this space as "terrible," means "television." Charles Fleming, of the show-business publication *Variety*, sets me straight on this and adds: "If they think things are terrible, and want to say so in English, the Japanese of my acquaintance generally use *baa-do*."

Good-o. Comes now Japan Airlines, which says its last name is the one-word *airlines*, not, as I reported, *air lines*. Although it made this change to *airlines* last year, and pouts about "*The New York Times*'s inexplicable refusal to accept the change," the airline retained the initials "JAL" in its logo. Sorry, fellas—you can't have three initials for two words.

The company is unlikely to change its acronymic lettering to conform to its new name, because that would make it "JA," which would be a fine name for a German airline with a positive attitude. The officials have backed themselves into a linguistic corner; no wonder they feel so television.

The scolding you gave JAL was well deserved, but I think you should know that JA is also a Japanese word. It means "well, then" or "in that case" and is also used as an auxiliary verb for the verb aru, to be. In fact, a very common Japanese expression, "Ja, ne" (So long or See you later), would make an excellent running slogan for a JAL advertisement. It would translate as "Jal it is" or "Jal, of course." A baa-do pun.

Linda Elisabeth Laddin
Tokyo, Japan

Tar Baby

Nobody joined Representative Charles E. Schumer, a Brooklyn Democrat, when he charged that internal bickering within the government had contributed to the savings and loan scandal.

"It's regarded as a tar baby," said the legislator about the scandal. "Nobody wants to get ensnarled in it."

Jon von Zelowitz of San Francisco clipped the Congressman's quoted comment and wondered: "I thought *tar baby* was a dated, racist term—did he mean *tar pit*?"

Tar baby is defined in Merriam-Webster's *Ninth* as "something from which it is nearly impossible to extricate oneself" and adds no racist caveat; to most minds, the phrase is innocent of slur. Mark Twain, an early antiracist, used the phrase in his 1910 autobiography: "For two years the *Courant* had been making a 'tar baby' out of Mr. Blaine, and adding tar every day—and now it was called upon to praise him."

The origin is in an 1881 Uncle Remus story by Joel Chandler Harris: A doll is covered in sticky tar to entrap Brer Rabbit. (No apostrophes in *Brer;* the contraction of *brother* is the character's first name.)

The common colloquial sense today of *tar baby* is "a sticky problem, one better left untouched." However, the *O.E.D.* supplement adds a second definition: "a derogatory term for a Black (U.S.) or a Maori (New Zealand)." The lexicographer, Robert Burchfield, is a New Zealander, and should know. Also, the novelist Toni Morrison, who is black, titled a 1981 novel *Tar Baby,* probably a play on both senses.

Although most people do not use it with a slur in mind, apparently some think the tar baby is not a doll covered in pitch, but a black child. What do you do in a case like that? Insist on the author's original intent and refuse to be waved off by a perhaps-mistaken sensitivity—or recognize that the phrase has gained a racist connotation in some minds?

Professor Richard Spears, author of the 1981 *Slang and Euphemism,* believes "there are many contexts in which *tar baby* may be used that have no racist sense at all." He's right—but if I were a politician, I wouldn't touch it.

Brer *is NOT a first name. It is a title of respect. It is not used in the biological sense. Members of the same congregation, at least in the South, addressed each other as "Brother" and "Sister" plus their last name—"Brother Jones," "Sister Smith." Probably the custom extended to close friends in the community. In fact, there are some places where this courtesy is still observed.*

ANYWAY—Brer was not ANYONE's first name. Had it been, just imagine the stampede in the "settlement" when the spouse of Brer Fox, Brer Bear, Brer Wolf, Brer Rabbit, Brer Tarrypin, Brer Turkey Blizzard, Brer Bull, Brer Coon, Brer Possum or any of the other woodland residents went to her door and called, "Come to supper, Brer!"!!!!!

Betty Timmerman
North Augusta,
South Carolina

It may interest you to hear that the "Tar baby" folk tale, so far as I recollect my readings here and there, goes back to India. The arrogant peasant (or child) sees the straw-covered figure in the road. Demands that it get out of his way. No answer. Slams with the right hand, and sticks fast; slams with the left, and sticks fast, kicks with the right foot, and sticks fast, kicks with the left, and sticks fast. What to do? Butts with the forehead and sticks fast. The meaning? The five senses, attacking this world, which yields no answer but its own obdurate silence, each stick fast in attachment, the head coming last. It is about Maya or delusion. The ego never gets free by attacking this world, but indeed is lodged in it.

The moral therefore is to avoid sticking to the world altogether, and not to try to overcome it as it blocks the path towards freedom from attachment and delusion. It is a secret wisdom tale, and the tar baby is indeed a stage of baby attachment of the senses, etc.

Jascha Kessler
Professor of English and
Modern Literature
University of California
Los Angeles, California

I wonder if you are familiar with a boxer named Sam Langford. Sam Langford was a contemporary of John L. Sullivan (1880's–1890's) and was considered by many to be the best boxer of his time. Sullivan refused to fight him and he never got a chance at the heavyweight title. Sam Langford was known as the "Boston Tar Baby." Since Langford's heyday followed "Uncle Remus" by only a relatively short period of time, it is understandable that the term could easily acquire both meanings, although Langford probably used it to suggest that he was difficult to subdue.

Edmund L. Cogburn
Houston, Texas

That Shifty Functional

"There's a *disconnect* between Baker and the White House on this one."

I heard that phrase while prowling the corridors of power. It was a hallway remark, an exchange between political appointees, hardly suitable as a citation for lexicographers, but its recording here will have to suffice.

The overheard conversation had to do with a disagreement between the Secretary of State and the White House National Security Council staff.

Apparently the communication between these centers of power was broken, and what was termed a *disconnect* had taken place. But it was not a *disconnection;* the word *disconnect* has a sense beyond the physical breakage of contact.

The earliest modern citations for this noun use of the verb *disconnect* were nonmetaphoric, purely physical: "Most of our citations have to do with phone-company usage," says James Rader, etymologist for *Random House II.* "In the November 1982 *Maclean's* magazine, this appeared: 'The number of *disconnects* for nonpayment is no higher than usual.' " The obvious meaning of the noun was "the cutoff of telephone service because the subscriber didn't pay" (followed by a Darth Vader recorded voice informing the caller that "That number is no longer in service," a euphemism for the previous "That number has been disconnected").

When did *disconnect,* a noun for a cutoff of slow payers, make a connection with a meaning of "breakdown of communication between people or policies"?

The earliest citation in the Random House files credits the pollster and political analyst Pat Caddell (famed for his "national malaise memo" in the Carter era). Mr. Caddell, backing the nuclear-freeze movement in 1984, was described by *Mother Jones* magazine as "steaming over the intellectual and moral bankruptcy of the Democratic Party—its 'disconnect,' as he put it, from the vast forces for sweeping social change that are waiting to be mobilized: 'Look at the energy that is out in this country that is not being coalesced and put together!' "

Mr. Caddell's use of *disconnect* as a noun caught on; in diplomacy, it means "the breaking off of discussions or negotiations," and in politics, I find that it has gained these meanings: "1. out-of-touchedness, or the failure to perceive the direction of a movement; 2. misunderstanding based on lack of communication; 3. outright disagreement."

Thus, we have witnessed what grammarians call a *functional shift*—a change in the use of a word from its customary status to another part of speech. The word itself doesn't change, but its function does; if you cannot stomach this, stop using the noun *stomach* as a verb; on the other hand, if you get a kick out of it, enjoy the verb *kick* in its functionally shifted form, as a slang noun meaning "surge of pleasure."

In the spoken language, we often signify these shifts with a change in pronunciation: if you obJECT to being Her Majesty's SUBject, become an OBject lesson in refusing to subJECT yourself to the Queen; to make up, preSENT her with a PRESent.

Edmund Burke, the English political leader, would be pleased at the functional shift that turns the verb *disconnect* into a noun with such nice political nuances. Writing in 1769 of "the Present State of the Nation" (a phrase that was picked up by Americans writing the Constitution as *State of the Union*), Burke used *disconnexion* much as *disconnect* is being used today in warning of "a spirit of disconnexion, of distrust, and of treachery among public men."

Given his Irish birth, Edmund Burke ought not to be described as "English," even though admittedly England is where he made himself famous.

> Richard W. Lyman
> Director, Institute for
>   International Studies
> Stanford University
> Stanford, California

Those Defining Moments

"The Iraqi invasion of Kuwait," testified Secretary of State James A. Baker 3d, "is one of the *defining moments* of a new era. . . ." Lest anyone miss the import of the phrase, he came back to it a moment later: "We must respond to the *defining moments* of this new era. . . ."

The phrase is not yet in the dictionaries, something that is curious because lexicographers are sensitive to words like *defining*. "It's not the sort of thing that gets recorded in citation files," says Cynthia Barnhart of Barnhart Books, "because it's a collocation—two words put together with a straightforward sense."

Before pinning down the meaning and its grammatical repercussions, let's consider some usages:

In January 1988, soon after Vice President George Bush confronted the CBS anchor Dan Rather in an exchange Mr. Bush called "tension city," the manager of the Bush presidential campaign, Lee Atwater, hailed it as a "defining moment." The *Los Angeles Times* editorialist noted that Mr. Atwater chose the phrase over another possibility, *shining hour.*

During the 1988 Democratic convention, the columnist Mark Shields used the phrase in a reflexive sense, not as "a moment that defines" so much as "a time for defining oneself." Speaking of Jesse Jackson's forthcoming convention speech, the pundit told MacNeil-Lehrer: "It's a defining moment politically . . . he's going to be talking to 50 million plus Americans, and I think he has to define what he's about."

In a sense of "action that illustrates character," Howard Phillips of the Conservative Caucus earlier this year called Mr. Bush's signing of a trade agreement with Mikhail S. Gorbachev during the Soviet crackdown on independent-minded Lithuania "the defining moment of the Bush Administration."

The increasing frequency of the use of the phrase in a political context made it prey for ironists. Maureen Dowd of *The New York Times,* in a story about the recall of Perrier bottled water after impurity was discovered, wrote: "As yuppies poured their Perrier down the drain and debated the merits of

Pellegrino water versus Ramlosa, they wondered whether the recall might be a *defining moment.*

"Would they finally learn," she asked, "that life, despite all attempts to control it, can never be risk-free? Would image and status cease to be of such overriding importance in their lives?"

We may have a major coinage here; the term is crossing over from politics to the general language. This is a job for the Phrasedick Fraternity. (Relax, we also have a Solecism Sorority; the nomenclature is determined by alliteration, not sex.)

Who coined *defining moment,* and at what moment? This etymological dig was in my own backyard; all I had to do was stroll through the noiseless city room of the Washington bureau of *The New York Times.* The earliest citation in our Nexis files is a November 13, 1983, article in *The Times* by Howell Raines—now the Washington editor—titled "John Glenn: The Hero as Candidate."

"Confronted by Glenn and his 'constituency of the whole' candidacy," Mr. Raines wrote, "Walter Mondale has rallied the Democratic establishment. It is a *defining moment.*"

People in Washington kill to be recognized as the originator of anything, but Mr. Raines, a modest man, declined to claim coinage: "The phrase was in the political air that year. I heard it around, and decided to use it. No, I can't claim it as my own."

Rarely does one find a writer, confronted with evidence of his first use in print of a term, with the natural humility to disavow coinage. "I did coin *redneck Riviera* to refer to the Gulf Coast of Florida," he said. Funny, the things you remember and the things you forget.

I offered him the historic opportunity to define his term. Here it is, from the horse's mouth: "*Defining moment* is that point at which the essential character of a candidate or campaign stands revealed to the individual or political organization and to the external world."

Now let's get to an important decision. I will surely be asked to take a stand on this issue: Is *defining* as used in this phrase a gerund (an -*ing* form of a verb used as a noun, as in *swimming pool*) or a participle (an -*ing* form of a verb used as an adjective, as in *swimming children*)?

In other words, is this a job for the Gerund Jerries, who claim even *lovemaking* as an example of their favorite category? They hold that *defining,* in *defining moment,* is a gerund—a noun ending in -*ing*—rather than a participle. Let's examine that claim.

Consider the difference between *moving target* and *moving van:* A target actually in motion may be properly called a *moving target,* with its *moving* a participle defining the noun *target.* But a van used for a move, even when the huge vehicle is double-parked and causing gridlock for miles around, is a *moving van,* with its *moving* a gerund used as an attributive noun, modifying another noun. It is a van *for* moving, not a van *that is* moving, illuminating the linguistic landscape with the difference between a participle and a gerund.

Now apply that to *defining moment.* You could argue that the moment does the defining; it is not a moment set aside for defining, because nobody knows exactly when that moment will occur (although George Bush had Dan Rather in his sights when he came on the show). In that case, *defining* would be a participle.

But you could also argue that it is a moment *for* defining, just as a moving van is a van for moving—with the moment itself not doing the defining—in which case *defining* would be a gerund, causing much shouting for joy among the Gerund Jerries.

Before deciding, we may entertain a friend-of-the-court brief from historical etymologists. Nobody disputes the root: from *definire,* Latin for "to terminate, to bound"; the noun *definite* means "with clear boundaries," or in modern vernacular, "hard-edged." To the controversy: The participle form of *defining,* defined as "that defines," was first used by the author James Ross in his 1773 hit, *The Fratricide,* presumably a musical about phrasedicks: "Defining ears, which idolize/The dignifying climax of thy verse." Nice try, Jim; however, *defining* first appeared in gerund form almost four centuries earlier, in John Wycliffe's commentary on Ezekiel 43:13 about "the diffynyng, or certeyntee, therof . . ."

I reject the participilian argument: A *defining moment* is not, in my view, a moment that defines anything. I say that *defining moment* uses *defining* (or *diffynyng,* if you prefer—I'm no stiff on spelling) as a gerund, in this way: A *defining moment* is a moment for defining a person's character, a moment for defining a policy's purpose, a moment for defining an era's quality.

This means, of course, that *moment of truth* is facing its moment of truth. This is from a Spanish bullfighting term (*el momento de la verdad,* for the final thrust of the sword into the dying bull's neck), which was introduced into English by Ernest Hemingway in his 1932 *Death in the Afternoon* and defined by him as "the actual encounter between the man and the animal." This meaning was extended within a decade to "a crisis, turning point, crucial test."

With *defining moment* at hand, is there any need for *moment of truth*? I think we should hang on to it; like *point of no return,* from the World War II aviation term to set a point from which planes could not turn back without running out of fuel, Hemingway's phrase—though overused—has a brave and noble and true resonance.

In the synonymy of confrontation, a *moment of truth* emphasizes the painful necessity of decision-making (like lovemaking, a gerund); a *point of no return* connotes decisional irrevocability; a *turning point* stresses the point in time at which change was made, and a *defining moment* centers on the expression of character, or lack thereof, in a person or organization facing a crisis.

My Sprachgefühl *keeps telling me that a defining MOment is not a deFINing moment. It's like the moving VAN that may hit a stationary MOVing van. It's a matter of stress distribution or, as some linguists would put it, suprasegmental phonemes. A defining moment is indeed a moment that defines, not set aside for defining, preordained like the quitting time in "GWTW." I thus come down on the participilian side!*

Louis Marck
New York, New York

I am amazed that you consider the "defining" of "defining moment" a gerund. I believe you have ignored the most reliable criterion for such a determination, namely the pattern of vocal stress.

A noun phrase compounded of noun elements (including gerunds) has one primary stress; if the collocation includes verbal elements, such as participles, there may be more than one primary stress. To take your examples, using caps to indicate primary stress and an accent mark for secondary stress: Do you not hear a difference between MOVing TARget *and* MOVing van? *And suppose you wanted to indicate that a pedestrian was hit by a small, half-ton Ford van, unsuitable for the transport of a houseful of furniture. Surely you would say (if you happened to choose these words): "He was hit by a MOVing VAN." Another example: A WHISTling swan is a particular species of bird* (Olor Columbianus), *and an individual of the species may be so called even at a moment when it happens to be silent; a WHISTling SWAN might be a swan of another species that had learned to whistle and was doing so.*

Now, have you really ever heard, and would you really ever say, "deFINing moment"? I myself believe I have heard only "deFINing MOMent."

Nils Ekfelt
Canton, New York

This, I would suggest, is the water-tight test of a true gerund: its ability to stay in place regardless of its noun's circumstance or the perspective of the observer.

Examine the phrase sinking reputation, *however. For a reputation to be a* sinking reputation, *it must actually be sinking at the moment of discussion; once an observer judges the attitude of descent to have reversed itself or stabilized, the modifier* sinking *immediately detaches from the noun* reputation, *revealing a participle rather than a gerund. As integral as the notion of descent is to a* sinking reputation, *it is the concept of* reputation *which survives all transformations, whereas* sinking *is wholly dependent on the continuous action of the modified noun, or at least the continuous* perception *of action.*

And this is the crux of the problem with categorizing defining moment *as a gerund. Ask yourself if a defining moment remains a defining moment if it no longer defines the person or thing it was once purported to define? Is George*

Bush's decision to turn a deaf ear to Lithuania any longer the defining moment of his administration, now that we have seen the invasion of Panama and the impending war with Iraq? Obviously not. Was it ever, at least to anyone but a few conservative Republicans? We can hardly remember what all the fuss over Lithuania was about, much less see it as the beginning of an overall pattern of appeasement. That particular moment is no longer a defining one, even in memory.

Conrad Goehausen
San Rafael, California

You mobilize a Phrasedick Fraternity to ferret out the first use of "defining moment." Nice alliteration cum gumshoe, that. But let me offer a gender-neutral alternative: Fearless Phrasedicks. *This gets you alliteration (admittedly one letter less . . .) and also gets you a double sleuthing image from "Dick Tracy."*

Saul Rosen, M.D.
Bethesda, Maryland

*There is no "el momento de la verdad" (moment of truth) as introduced by Ernest Hemingway or anyone else. The correct term—*la hora de verdad*—is defined in Barnaby Conrad's* Encyclopedia of Bullfighting *as "the time of truth; the kill." Also called the moment of truth by novelists.*
    There is no "final thrust of the sword into the dying bull's neck." Initially, the estoque *or curved sword (is) "driven in where it should go high up between the shoulder blades (*Death in the Afternoon, *page 235). If the bull has not been killed after at least one thrust, the* dercabello *or* puntella *may be used to sever the medulla.*

George Rattner
Kings Point, New York

Tickety-Boo and NASA, Too

"Enclosed is an article from *The Houston Post* of February 12," writes Andrew Hero, the kind of specific citator that lexicographers like, "which uses the expression *tickety-boo*."

The Associated Press story dealt with a difficulty aboard the Jupiter-bound *Galileo* spacecraft: A camera on board was taking too many pictures and wasting film. Engineers at the National Aeronautics and Space Administration's Jet Propulsion Laboratory in Pasadena, California, were able to gain control of the camera, which was acting like a solar-system tourist, and a spokesman was quoted: "There's no repeat of the incident . . . no problems. Everything has gone *tickety-boo.*"

"I thought I had found a new expression," my Texas citator added, "but my wife informs me that the actress Maggie Smith used this word in the 1982 movie *Evil Under the Sun,* based on a Hercule Poirot mystery novel by Agatha Christie. Can you shed any light on this strange expression?"

Its first use in my world was by the columnist George Will in 1977, projecting ahead: "The morning after the 1978 elections Republicans were feeling *tickety-boo.*" A few years later, an A.P. correspondent, Hugh A. Mulligan, recalling the early days of space flight, wrote of "the supercool British correspondent whose mastery of the Queen's English enabled him instantly to translate 'Shorty' Powers's historic 'A-O.K.' to *'Tickety-boo.'* " (Mulligan noted that the reporters covering the pioneer right-stuffers called themselves *fruit flies.*)

Apparently the word found its way into song in the early 1960's. James Isaacs, a music historian, recently recalled his appearance on a 1963 *Ted Mack Amateur Hour,* when "I lost out to the Decatur Women's Kitchen Band—50 housewives playing 'Everything is Tickety-Boo' on pots, pans and kazoos."

I called the source of the recent usage at the Jet Propulsion Lab. *"Tickety-boo* just sort of slipped out when I was being interviewed," says Bob MacMillin, the spokesman. "I picked it up from an old colleague of yours at *The New York Times.* Richard Witkin used it in a story in the 1960's, back before John Noble Wilford was covering space, when Witkin was writing about the *Mariner* mission. We were tired of hearing 'A-O.K.' from Houston, so we decided to try something new, and *tickety-boo* seemed to fit."

Was it, then, a NASA coinage of about three decades ago? No; further digging turns up this 1947 comment in the journal *American Notes and Queries:* "Lord Mountbatten, now Governor General of India, is credited in *The New York Times Magazine* with 'giving currency' to the phrase *tickety-boo* (or *tiggerty-boo*). This Royal Navy term for 'O.K.' is derived from the Hindustani."

Hmm. The supplement to the *Oxford English Dictionary,* where the earliest citation is a 1939 use by the author Noel Streatfeild, labels the etymology "obscure," but speculates, "Perhaps from Hindi *thik hai,* 'all right.' "

I wonder. This outmoded British colloquialism, meaning "in order, in good shape," equivalent to the American *hunky-dory* or, as NASA engineers would now say, *all systems go,* seems to me (and to *Webster's New World* etymologists) to come from the expression "That's the ticket!"

That British expression may have been based on the American Colonial use of the word to mean "names of candidates on a list to be voted on." In 1766, Benjamin Franklin's daughter, Sarah Bache, wrote, "The old ticket forever!"

Thus, we are presented with a choice: either a Hindi root, picked up by the Royal Navy and transferred to Americans during or soon after World War II, or the Colonial Americanism *ticket*. (The American sense of "political list" was sent over to England to be used in "That's the ticket!" and the subsequent, nonpolitical *tickety-boo*, which migrated to the United States for popularization by the two NASA spokesmen, "Shorty" Powers and, later, Bob MacMillin, as a synonym for "A-O.K.")

And that, Mr. Hero, is the closest I can get to the answer to your query; it's been a worthwhile *flyby*. At NASA today, incidentally, *liftoff* is still preferred to the sci-fi *blastoff*, and a "massive screwup" is referred to primly as a *major anomaly*.

Dear Bill:

"Hunky-dory"—well, well—I was going to ask you: "Whatever happened to hunky-dory?" I well remember when the "latest" bits of American slang were gobbled up by the more modish of the BBC staff—in the mid-Thirties—"hunky-dory" was an early favorite. But, as often happened, they tended to get it the wrong way round (cf. "a bomb," which then, and now, came to mean in England a smash hit). The radio critic of the Evening Standard, *one Eric Dunstan as I recall, once issued a warning: "In the next ten days, short-wave reception is likely to be hunky-dory. The trouble is due to sunspots."*

As ever,
Alistair [Cooke]
New York, New York

From 1937 to 1940 I was a young seaman in our Asiatic Fleet (in the South China Patrol Gunboat Asheville*), and one of our favorite liberty ports was Yokohama. It was, at that time, the only Japanese port open to our warships, and was also the first, and for many years, the only one allowed our merchant ships.*

Prior to the Great Japanese Earthquake the street which led from the dock straight up the hill to the bars and geisha houses was the main street, and was named the Honcho-dori; it still, in 1937, led nearly to the "Red Light District." I was told this is the origin of our "hunky dory"—brought back by sailors from both our warships and merchantmen.

Charles E. Griffin
Stinson Beach, California

Dear Bill:

For what it's worth, there's no doubt in my mind that "tickety-boo" is of Anglo-Indian origin, since one says in India almost every day such things as "Everything tik hai?" (pronounced "tickeha").

Steven R. Weisman
Tokyo Bureau Chief
The New York Times
Tokyo, Japan

Once again, your column prompts a shoot of useless information to sprout from the mulch that passes for my brain.

Having collected memorabilia on Danny Kaye since 1953, I immediately remembered a song from his MGM movie Merry Andrew. *In the role of a British schoolmaster, he sings a song called "Everything Is Tickety Boo" by lyricist Johnny Mercer and composer Saul Chaplin. (Capitol's soundtrack album uses no hyphen.)*

The lyrics go, in part: "Everything is tickety boo on such a dreamy day. . . ."
This sort of optimistic ditty makes my back teeth hurt.

Marie Shear
Brooklyn, New York

Tick-Tock

Right behind my bulging file on *tickety-boo* is a slim folder labeled *tick-tock.* This is journalistic jargon, inside baseball stuff, of little interest to the general reader until it is broken out into common discourse by a nonjournalist.

"I think it was a good trip," said President Bush, defending his tour of defense installations at a time of disarmament talk, "and I've read some *tick-tock* inside here, but it doesn't bother me a bit."

Tick-tock, an onomatopoeic noun evoking the sound of a clock without a quartz movement, is newsmagazinese for "chronology of events leading up to a major news development." One example is the listing of meetings and phone calls on the President's calendar, interspersed with the time of developments outside; the headline is often "Anatomy of a Crisis," "Toward the Fateful Decision," or some such doom-laden copy stripped along the corner of the cover.

This President is misusing the term; what he should be complaining about is (or *are*—the number of a verb that links a *what*-clause and a plural predicate nominative is a matter of fierce dispute among grammarians) *think pieces, dope stories, thumbsuckers*—analyses, often critical, but not detailed or based on a minute-to-minute schedule. (When one pundit asks another what he is working on, and is answered with a thumbs-up signal, that is not a sign of elation or encouragement; it is a coded admission that the current piece is to be based on rumination, introspection and the wisdom of a lifetime rather than fatiguing "shoe-leather" reporting.)

If the President is unhappy about the lead article of a newsmagazine, one that sets the tone for the national or international coverage of the week, he should mutter insidedly about the *violin.*

Toughlove

"I would characterize this summit," said the White House press secretary, Marlin Fitzwater, "as a demonstration of the kind of *toughlove* working relationship that we were able to develop with the Soviet Union in four or five previous summits."

USA Today headlined "TOUGH LOVE" APPROACH KEY TO SUMMIT, and the *Washington Times* promptly dubbed the forthcoming meeting the "Toughlove summit."

Both newspapers were in error. *Toughlove* is a single word, no hyphenation. This I have from the horse's mouth: "When we started our group in 1977," says David York, a cofounder of Toughlove, a network of more than two thousand support groups for parents of difficult teenagers, "a friend of ours who ran a bookstore listened to our concept and said, 'You have to call it toughlove.' "

In a gentle but hard-nosed way, Mr. York declined to identify the creative bookseller to whom he attributes the coinage. However, he described the purpose of the organization as "to counter the type of love promulgated in our time by psychobabble—the notion of tender loving care and the effectiveness of 'active listening' to how your kid feels. Instead, we wanted kids to know that love has a value, and it's earned from the parent when the kid is cooperative.

"And by the way," the Doylestown, Pennsylvania, editor and author notes, "our group's name is one word: 'Toughlove.' "

Is it an oxymoron, a felicitous contradiction in terms? No; the opposite of the adjective *tough* is the adjective *tender,* much as the antonym of the noun *love* is *hate.* However, another sense of *tough*—one that dates to the seventh century, rooted in the Old High German *zahi*—is "durable, able to last, hard to break."

Tough has both a phony-strong sense and a mean sense, but a likable overtone crept in with the American tough-guy novel. The writer Raymond Chandler compared actors who portrayed his tough detectives: "[Humphrey] Bogart, of course, is . . . much better than any other tough-guy actor. . . . [Alan] Ladd is . . . a small boy's idea of a tough guy."

In diplomatic negotiation, *tough* is a compliment: A *tough* negotiator is associated with words like *tenacious* rather than the pejorative *stubborn* or the impossible *intransigent;* few negotiators want to be known as *flexible,* which has acquired a connotation of "overly accommodating," or even "loving."

To Wherever in a Handbasket

"Harry and I have been wondering," writes Lois Reasoner of Westport, Connecticut, "about the origin of the phrase *going to hell in a handbasket.* We have heard it used in conversation five times in the past few months."

I have the vision conjured in my mind of the genial inquisitor of *60 Minutes* [he died in 1991], counting the times his Connecticut neighbors use this phrase, and finally exploding, "Five! That's it, Lois—roust out Safire and find out why."

Lexicographers call this "Old Slang"—a figure of speech used by people who stopped picking up the latest slang about two generations ago. *To hell in a handbasket* means either "to one's doom" or—if used mockingly to describe a small dissipation—merely "mildly indulgent."

The origin is believed to be *to heaven in a handbasket,* a locution that *Dialect Notes* spotted in 1913 in Kansas, where it was taken to mean "to have a sinecure." One who was nicely ensconced in an untouchable job was said to be on the way *to heaven in a handbasket.* When used in Wisconsin a decade later, the term was defined as "to do something easily."

Then the direction changed. The alliteration remained the same, but the first stage of this rocket dropped off and was lost in the sea of archaic phrases; the second stage, with *hell* substituted for *heaven,* took us to where we are today: The meaning is "to degenerate rapidly; to fall apart suddenly." The final stage? We cannot tell; *down the tubes in a handbasket* uses modern surfers' lingo but lacks the alliterative zing.

What is it about a *handbasket*—a word rarely used now outside the hellish phrase—that makes it so useful in talk of decadence, degeneration, declension and downfall?

The key quality is portability; the basket is small enough to be carried in one hand, and anything in it is little or light. From a couple of centuries after its coinage, the word lent itself to belittlement in phrasemaking: In the play *Juliana, or the Princess of Poland* by John Crowne in 1671, a character says, "I can see when I see, surely; I don't carry my eyes in a hand-basket."

Most people who use old slang are *long in the tooth,* a folk metaphor of uncertain age first used in print by William Makepeace Thackeray in an 1852 novel: "She was lean, and yellow, and long in the tooth; all the red and white in all the toyshops of London could not make a beauty of her."

The term is current: "For New Yorkers long in the tooth," wrote Donal Henahan in a *New York Times* review of an opera, " 'Il Pirata' is probably best recalled as a concert vehicle for Maria Callas . . ."

The phrase was originally applied to horses. As a horse ages, its gums recede, making the teeth look longer; the term as applied to humans as well as horses now means "aging, getting on in years" and is taken as a slur by anti-agists.

While dishing out this fodder for phrasedicks, I will now turn to the mysterious *dressed to the nines,* subject of many queries.

As artists know, the number of Muses is nine; some fanciful originicists see that as the source for the fashion term. A more respectable etymologist, W. W. Skeat, recalled that the old plural for *eye* was *eyne* and speculated that *to the nines* was derived from *to then eyne,* but at that stage of his life, the great wordsmith was long in the tooth and his work was going to hell in a handbasket.

Nine is the highest single-digit number; it stands for "the best, the highest, the nearest to perfection." In 1787, the poet Robert Burns wrote, " 'Twad please me to the nine." The phrase *up to the nines* had this meaning of excellence, and in Hotten's 1859 dictionary of slang was defined as "up to the dodges and 'wrinkles' of life"—what we would now say is a state "capable of coping with stress." Hotten also included *dressed up to the nines,* defined as we use it today: "in a showy or recherché manner."

The fashion phrase was temporarily replaced in the 1890's with *dressed to kill* (and even now, women yearn for that *drop-dead dress*), but numerals have largely replaced mayhem in dressessment, and *dressed to the nines* is again with us. I counted its use five times in the past few months. I like the old slang.

Thank you for opening up the problem of "to hell in a wheelbarrow."

I grew up in New York City in a Protestant Ulster Irish culture, and as a child I had often heard the phrase "to hell in a wheelbarrow" and a variant "to hell in a handbarrow." When I retired after teaching chemical analysis of pharmaceuticals for thirty years in a college of pharmacy, I decided to keep myself busy learning more about the wall paintings in the churches of medieval Denmark. Since there was nothing on this subject in English, I was forced to develop my own resources from the available Danish information. In 1983, I took a trip to Denmark and returned with about 3,000 slides taken in 220 village churches in Denmark.

Among those slides, I found that one group of painters, the Isefjord Workshop, who worked about 1450, had painted sinners being pushed into hell in a wheelbarrow in four churches. In Ottestrup there is a painting of a devil carrying sinners to hell in a handbasket. Banning [Knud Banning, ed., A Catalogue of Wall-Paintings in the Churches of Medieval Denmark 1100–1600 Scania, Halland Blekinge, *Akademisk Forlag, Copenhagen, 1976] reports two churches showing the damned going to hell in a wheelbarrow, and two showing devils taking souls to hell in a handbasket.*

While looking for parallels between the Danish church wall paintings and the English mystery plays, I found that visual representations of the damned going to hell in a wheelbarrow were known in England. The earliest dated picture that I found was in the Holkham Bible Picture Book, *page 42v, dated 1325 plus or minus 10 years. [W. O. Hassall, ed.,* Holkham Bible Picture Book, *London: Dropmore Press, 1954. 42v Above—Bishop, king, priests to hell. Below—soul on wheelbarrow to hell.]*

While only a few would have been familiar with the picture in the Holkham Bible Picture Book, *hundreds, if not thousands, would have seen the carvings and the window in the churches showing the damned going to hell in a wheelbarrow. It is my feeling that "to hell in a wheelbarrow" was, as T. Adams said, a "byword" much earlier than it appeared in his sermon.*

James Mills
Glen Head, New York

You write that the phrase "long in the tooth" is of uncertain origin. I believe I know the original phrase but unfortunately not its transmission into English.

Like your name, the phrase is of Arabic derivation. "Tawīlu sunna" means "long of years," and "tawīlu sinna" means "long in the tooth." As you have noted before, Semitic languages don't inflect short vowels. Therefore, in reading a normal text and coming across one of the standard phrases denoting "old," it would be a common mistake for the beginning reader to vocalize the Arabic "s" "n" "n" as "sinna" instead of "sunna." Hence the pun in Arabic is embedded in the peculiarities of the Arabic writing system, and is one of its many longstanding linguistic jokes.

Frederick Schultz
New York, New York

I wonder how many horse lovers have written to you about your explanation of "long in the tooth." The way I learned it, it is all a matter of relativity; the gums do not recede any more than ours. The teeth just keep growing longer than in most animals, but eventually they stop. This can lead to trouble, for the natural diet of horses is abrasive; grasses contain little blobs of silica called phytoliths. If a horse lives long enough on such a diet, the teeth wear down to the gums. Rodents have a different problem. Their teeth keep growing for life, and they get into trouble if they do not keep them worn down.

W. T. Edmondson
Professor of Zoology
University of Washington
Seattle, Washington

The alert student knows that "dressed to the nines" refers to seating arrangements in Elizabethan theater. The rabble stood on the floor in front of the stage, cheaper seats flanked the sides, and the nine rows in front, in raised tiers of three, were reserved for the middle-class gentry. There, these young Republican yuppies of their day could show off their fineries, safely separated from their inferiors below, and under the elite eyes of the lords in their boxes above, whom presumably were also above ostentation.

Can I substantiate? Alas, no. As with everything else Shakespearean, theater seating is sketchy and controversial. Blast it if I could not find my original source from lo these many years ago. But it sounds good, and certainly it is better than this weak bit about nine being an ultimate number.

Peter D. Johnston
Houston, Texas

I, too, like the "old people's slang." They're so wise. So here are a few that might bring memories of irascible old relatives.

"He's a snake of the first water." (Why first?)
"It's just a stone's throw from here."
"It'll be done in two shakes of a lamb's tail."
"I'll just give it a lick and a polish."
"We were on the porch spinning yarns."
"He's out in right field in my book.*"*
"He thinks he's a little tin god on wheels" (this must come from the British Empire).

Nina Lockwood
Rochester, New York

Trick or Treaty?

We all remember the names of old battles and wars, but few of us are attuned to the nomenclature of peacemaking. "Faraway Places With Strange-Sounding Names," as the song had it, form the basis of much of the language of treatying. Worldly economists and geopolitical scientists—the sort of people who begin their questions with *given* and begin their answers with *absent*—like to stud their argot with pact-impact.

When the Soviet Prime Minister recently announced a five-year plan that sounded like recycled Old Thinking, the Soviet economist Pavel G. Bunich rose in Moscow to denounce the compromises as an "economic Brest-Litovsk."

They all shuddered at the recollection in the Supreme Soviet, but only a relative handful of diplolinguists outside the Soviet Union caught the allusion: In 1918, at the town of Brest-Litovsk in eastern Poland, Germany and the other Central Powers took Russia to the cleaners, forcing the new Bolshevik regime to sign a treaty surrendering a vast area, including much of the Ukraine. After the Allies in World War I (which was at first called the Great War, not pessimistically numbered World War I) defeated the Central Powers with no help from Russia, Lenin abrogated the humiliating treaty with the beaten Germans; Stalin later justified an arms buildup to avoid "another Brest-Litovsk."

At a time of tectonic shift in world affairs, foreign-affairs types like to spice up their analyses with references to old treaties.

The more arcane, the better. *Another Munich* is much too widely under-stood by average people as the symbol of appeasement, just as *another Yalta* carries overtones of "secret agreements" to suspicious newspaper readers everywhere. The trick in diplolingo, city-name division, is to refer to unfamiliar places or events far back in history.

I caught myself pulling this stunt the other day, suggesting that worried Europeans hold "another Congress of Vienna"; that was the meeting in 1814–15 dominated by Francis I of Austria, Alexander I of Russia and Frederick William III of Prussia to decide the fate of the nations of Europe.

"Risking a Second Rapallo" was the headline over a *Washington Times* column by Patrick Buchanan. My old speechwriting colleague used the word in this attention-grabbing way: "Rapallo! Inevitable consequence of Germanophobia." Whenever you have the need to describe a diplomatic end-around by a couple of losers at the expense of the would-be winners, try "another Rapallo"; that was the treaty signed in Italy by Germany and Russia (you remember them from Brest-Litovsk) in 1922 recognizing each other and renouncing war claims. France and the other Allies were outraged at the deal between the two pariah nations, in effect ending the isolation imposed upon them since the *Treaty of Versailles*. (That was the treaty that ended World War I, and the harshness of its terms was later claimed by some Germans to be the reason for resentment and the rise of Hitler; "another Versailles" is now a treaty whose severe terms motivate the loser to ven-geance, or *revanchism.*)

How about a sweeping deal to deal comprehensively with all the problems of the continent? Try "another Locarno pact," a confabulation in the Swiss Alps that was hailed in 1925 by Aristide Briand, French Foreign Minister, as "the first concrete step toward a United States of Europe." (They're still leaving footprints in that concrete.) This gathering was noted for *the spirit of Locarno,* perhaps the first conjuring of "the spirit of" at international confer-ences. In the pact, Germany waived claims to Alsace and Lorraine—long a sore point with France—and this led to Germany's admission to the League of Nations; Locarno was renounced by Hitler in 1936, and "another Locarno" is an example of an idealistic scheme soon to be shattered.

Want to sow the seeds of long-range trouble? Try "another Potsdam," which split up Germany after World War II, and then recognized the Polish and Soviet occupation of German territory east of the Oder and Neisse Rivers, pending a peace treaty that has never been signed. When East and West Germany unify, Europe's attention will be fixed on the border that now separates East Germany from Poland; many Germans will turn what the Soviets will call *revanchist.*

Potsdam could be said to have produced *another Peace of Tilsit,* in which Napoleon and Alexander I forced the Prussian leader to give up much of the land west of the Elbe. Think about that: Do we want another Peace of Tilsit? Just asking the question intimidates your interlocutors.

Uncertain Tocsin

"I'm not trying to sound the tocsin of war," said President Bush at a news conference called to balance what some felt was a bellicose note in his previous day's "I've had it." (Slanguists differ on the origin of "had it"; some say it's a clip of "I have had it up to here"; others think the "up to here" is an intensifier that came later; the origin is probably from "I have had enough.")

One reporter called me to ask, "What do *toxins* sound like?"; another called from the President's traveling entourage to ask if tocsins were like trumpets, and could sound uncertain. One reporter heard "dachshunds of war" and wondered if this could be an allusion to "let slip the dogs of war."

A *toxin* is a Greek word for "poison," especially the poison in which the tips of arrows were dipped by unscrupulous archers.

A *tocsin* is from the Old French Provençal *tocasenh,* "to touch (or strike) a bell," a bell rung to sound an alarm; hence, a signal of warning. The poet Longfellow liked the word, and the poet Byron used it in a gentle way in *Don Juan:* "That all-softening, overpowering knell, the tocsin of the soul—the dinner bell."

Words that are pronounced the same but are spelled differently are called *homophones,* a specific form of *homonym* that especially pleases punsters.

Toxin-tocsin has led to confusion before. I recall an evening in 1969, in Henry Kissinger's kitchen, when a call came in on an unsecured line from Secretary of Defense Mel Laird. "Yes, I understand," Henry, then national security adviser, said, and then began talking cryptically about the destruction of certain toxins. The answering message sounded confused; Henry's brow furrowed more than usual. The conversation led nowhere, both men wondering what was wrong with the other's comprehension of important issues.

Next day, they discovered that Mel was trying to talk about a secret project named Operation Tocsin. Lesson: Never use a code word with an unlisted homophone.

Erik L. Hewlett, M.D., also alludes to the word's origin from the Greek toxikon, *a poison placed on arrows by Greek warriors. Furthermore, he refers to an 1888 French article by microbiologists Roux and Yersin wherein the term was first used in the scientific literature to describe the factor released by* Corynebacterium diphtheriae *that eventuated in the death of recipient animals.*

B. Vittal Shenoy, M.D.
Department of Pathology
Mercy Hospital
Charlotte, North Carolina

Unify or Reunify?

"An agreed, managed process of German *unification*," wrote Henry Kissinger, "would ease an otherwise festering crisis."

"*Reunification* means many different things," Representative Lee H. Hamilton of Indiana told *Europe* magazine.

"Stopping *unification* is like trying to hold back a wall of water," editorialized *The New York Times.*

"A senior State Department official [that's how James A. Baker 3d is identified when he is trying to act like Henry Kissinger] . . . today endorsed a West German plan for German *reunification*," reported Al Kamen in *The Washington Post,* who quoted the unidentified former White House chief of staff from Texas as saying that "*unification* is taking place on the ground right now."

Well, which is it—*unification* or *reunification*? Are the terms interchangeable, or do they contain a subtle difference known only to diplomatic nuancists?

Chancellor Helmut Kohl of West Germany blithely used *Wiedervereinigung*—"reunification"—in his ten-point plan for getting together again, but he has been avoiding the *wieder* ("re") ever since. "Now the politicians are making discriminations in their use of *unification* and *reunification*," says Thomas Mouillard, a correspondent in Washington for the German Press Agency. "Some people say that *reunification* would implicate the borders of 1937."

Aha. That is why these two words were called to my attention by David

Binder, roving correspondent of *The New York Times,* who speaks fluent East European.

This big little difference is illustrated in this interchange between Michael Lucas of *World Policy Journal* and Karsten Voigt, a spokesman for the West German socialists: "How do you assess the prospects for German reunification?" "I don't like to speak about *re*-unification, because we are not talking about going back to an old state of affairs."

That old state can be construed to contain a slice of Pomerania, Silesia (from which we get the derogation *sleaze*), East Prussia and even Czechoslovakia's German-speaking Sudetenland, all once called by the Nazis "Grossdeutschland." ("Greater New York City" spreads over Connecticut and a Brooklyn-accented portion of New Jersey.)

As might be expected, Germans are highly sensitive to reactions to the *re-* because it contains a reminder of expansionism, *Lebensraum,* and reopens "the German Question." The American economist Pierre Rinfret, irritated at what he considered the arrogance of German politicians who insist that the merger is a matter for Germans alone to decide, dubbed the coming amalgam "the Fourth Reich"; he knew this would annoy them.

The very thought of the prewar borders incenses many Europeans, who are thinking only in terms of a combination of the present East and West Germany that stops at the Oder-Neisse line drawn at the end of World War II. "In France, most of the press and the politicians use the word *réunification,*" reports Daniel Labrosse, press secretary of the French embassy in Washington. "Certainly it points to the problems that came when Germany was previously united."

To skirt the controversy over the *re-,* French and German officials have begun to drop the *-cation,* talking instead about German "unity"—*unité* or *Einheit.*

President Bush's aides are apparently unaware of the fuss. In a written statement presumably cleared with, or run by, the State Department, the White House announced that this weekend's visit of Chancellor Kohl will provide a chance "to exchange views about prospects for German *reunification. . . .*"

The astute reader will note the unexplained phrase *German Question* above. I am told it came into use in the mid-1930's, but none of the usual suspects have a printed citation to nail it down.

The even more astute reader will find fault with Dr. Kissinger's phrase "festering crisis." My erstwhile colleague's syndicated column has grown more purposeful and forceful of late (unification of subject has been a boon), and his audience now extends beyond members of the Conceptual Frameworkers Union.

However, even those of us who can take instruction from him on the cultural contradictions in German history know that *festering crisis* is an oxymoron. The nature of *crisis* is the state of having come to a head, not the contrary state of festering (from *fistula,* a pus-filled sore that has not come to a head and burst in its moment of crisis). A *crisis* can be said to continue, but only a chronic problem, issue or question can lay claim to *fester*.

The distinction between Vereinigung *(unification) and* Wiedervereinigung *(reunification) was very interesting. But did you know that in the mid-1930s the term* Wiedervereinigung *was specifically used to refer to Germany and Austria? The term* Anschluss *(annexation) was not coined until about 1937. It seems probable that* Wiedervereinigung *was originally used in the very first paragraph of* Mein Kampf. *In case you do not have it handy, I am copying below the first few sentences together with my free translation.*

Als glueckliche Bestimmung gilt es mir heute, dass das Schicksal mir zum Geburtsort gerade Braunau am Inn zuwies. Liegt doch dieses Staedtchen an der Grenze jener zwei deutschen Staaten, deren *Wiedervereinigung* mindestens uns Juengeren als eine mit allen Mitteln durchzufuehrende Lebensaufgabe erscheint!

Today I count it as a fortunate arrangement that destiny has assigned me particularly Braunau on the Inn as my place of birth. After all, this little city is located at the border of those two German states whose reunification, *at least for us younger ones, appears as our life's task to achieve by any means possible!*

As one who has lived through that period and escaped, only to have to return a few years later and fight against the aggressors, the current events give me a sad feeling of deja vu!

Fred R. Homburger
Lancaster, Pennsylvania

You defined fistula *as "a pus-filled sore that has not come to a head." That is an* abcess. *A fistula is a tract between two internal structures, or an open communication to the skin or the gum. An abcess is usually painful, and is incised and drained when it comes to a head/crisis. A fistula allows for drainage (like the Vistula?) and is not painful because it merely festers. A fistula is abnormal, usually pathological. If it is normal, it is called a duct.*

Michael C. Wolf, DDS
Hackensack, New Jersey

I assume (presume?) that I am not the only surgeon festering about your definition of "fistula."

While the dictionary refers to the Latin root of "fester" as being "fistula," the definition following, that you quote, is of "fester." It wants you to look up "fistula" when you have more time, and then you will learn that it is an abnormal connection between two hollow organs or skin and one organ.

Surgeons don't like them, and patients like them even less.

I'll not pester you about "fester" any more this semester.

Louis W. Kaufman, M.D.
Bloomfield Hills, Michigan

Unwordability

Robert Penn Warren, the novelist and poet, died recently at the age of eighty-four. In an appreciation written soon afterward, Colman McCarthy of *The Washington Post* recalled a telephone interview in which he had asked the Poet Laureate about a most unfamiliar word used by Warren: *appallment.*

"Speaking like a gourmet chef over a kettle happy to spoon flavorings of some fresh-simmering vocabulary," McCarthy wrote, Mr. Warren had this to say about the word he thought he had coined: " 'If you're writing and a word is needed, you create it. This is a word that ought to exist. I've invented several other words. *Appallment* is my latest.' "

A search of the *Oxford English Dictionary* turns up *appalment,* with a single *l*, first used in a French-English dictionary in 1611. But this noun is rarely used, and is not found in any other dictionary; Warren had reached into his own mind and come up with it on his own.

Same with *unwordable,* a more specific form of *inexpressible,* which Warren used: "The merciless grasp of unwordable grace. . . ."

Unlike *unutterable,* the word *unwordable* also applies to writing. The term was first used in theology; its original application, in 1660, was to "holiness," not far from Warren's use of the adjective to modify "grace." In 1882, it appeared in a travel story as "an unwordable calm, an indescribable tranquillity."

Poets should stretch the language and renew its roots, reinventing or coining words that open new vistas. Robert Penn Warren did his job.

You commend Robert Penn Warren for "reinventing or coining" the word unwordable. *I have no objection to reinvention or coinage where necessary, but I wonder whether* ineffable *would have served Mr. Warren's purpose in the passage you quote. It has the same number of syllables and the same accent as* unwordable. *Moreover, like* unwordable, *it is more specific than* inexpressible *and broader than* unutterable. *In short, its meaning seems to be identical to that of* unwordable.

Donald S. Dowden
New York, New York

Usage, Shmusage

"Re the enclosed," writes Lexicographic Irregular Edward M. Kennedy of Capitol Hill, "the know-nothings are falsely shouting quotas!"

He encloses a clipping from *The Wall Street Journal* about a civil-rights measure passed by the Senate despite the threat of a veto by the President. A circled paragraph beings: " 'Quotas, schmotas,' said Sen. Edward Kennedy (D.-Mass.), floor manager of the bill, adding that the 'false cry of quotas' is a 'disreputable tactic.' "

Although Senator Kennedy's punctuation needs work (his note should have read "the know-nothings are falsely shouting, 'Quotas!' "), he is an ace at spelling; I presume he sent in the clip to protest the newspaper's incorrect insertion of a *c* in what should be *shmotas.*

The reduplication of a word, substituting *shm-* for the beginning of its first syllable, is Yiddish. According to Sol Steinmetz of Random House, "I recommend the *sh* spelling because the German *sch* is misleading."

The earliest citation of this derogation in English listed by the *Oxford English Dictionary* is from a 1929 novel, *The Five Books of Mr. Moses,* by Izak Goller, who felt called upon to explain the usage twice: " 'Crisis-shmisis!' mocked Barnett disparagingly."

The punctuation of this type of expression has been changing. At first, almost all usages were hyphenated, as in *fancy-shmancy;* this gave a singsong effect, however, which did not reflect the shrug of studied indifference implicit in the phrase's meaning.

At present, the proper punctuation is a comma, as in *quotas, shmotas,* unless the term is used as a compound adjective, as in *fancy-shmancy linguists.* The *shm-* play is always on the first syllable, even of a proper noun or phrase: *Senator, Shmenator;* Wall Street Journal, *Shmall Street Journal.*

Vilna-Vilnius

The British call the islands the *Falklands;* the Argentines call them the *Malvinas.* Palestinians call the territories in dispute on the western side of the

Jordan River *the West Bank;* Israelis call that land by its biblical names, *Judea* and *Samaria.*

What you call a place has a great deal to do with what you think about its political sovereignty. Consider a capital in the turbulent Baltics, where most of the people believe they are or ought to be independent nations, and Russians think the nations are part of the Soviet union of republics:

"My grandfather used to tell me of his childhood in *Vilna,*" writes Steven D. Heller of Washington. "This was *Vilna,* Lithuania. Now Soviet tanks are parked in *Vilnius.* Same place?"

Same city, different ideas about its sovereignty. The traditional Russian name for the city is *Vilna,* pronounced "VEEL-na," though that is used less often now; the Polish name is *Wilno,* pronounced "VEEL-no," and still used because many Poles still think of the city as essentially Polish. (See your irredentist twice a year; if Churchill were to update his Iron Curtain speech, the most famous passage would now begin: "From Szczecin on the Baltic . . ." The Germans still call it Stettin.) With these growling throwbacks understood, the Lithuanian name for the city is *Vilnius,* formerly spelled *Vilnyus;* one of the small but significant triumphs of the Lithuanian patriots who resist Soviet rule has been the promulgation of the Lithuanian name.

If your travel agent books your trip from "the Malvinas to Judea to Vilnius," he's not issuing a ticket, he's making a statement.

You write that "promulgation of the Lithuanian name" Vilnius is "one of the small but significant triumphs of the Lithuanian patriots who resist Soviet rule." In fact it was the Soviet annexation of Lithuania in 1940 that was responsible for promulgating the Lithuanian version of the name.

The city that had been known in the Russian Empire (and hence internationally) as Vilna, and later Vilno, was ceded to independent Lithuania in the 1920 peace treaty between that country and Soviet Russia. It was, however, occupied by Polish forces in October 1920 and, together with the surrounding territory, annexed by Poland. Until the outbreak of World War II it was officially the Polish city of Wilno.

The Ribbentrop-Molotov pact of 1939 contained an article recognizing Lithuanian interest in the city, and after the Soviets occupied what had been eastern Poland in September 1939, they signed a treaty with Lithuania (October 10) on the transfer of the city and province to Lithuania. Vilnius did not become the capital of Lithuania until ten months later. On August 25, 1940, shortly after the Soviet annexation of Lithuania, the newly established Lithuanian S.S.R. adopted a constitution (modeled on the 1936 "Stalin Constitution") that provided for moving the capital from Kaunas to Vilnius. On the next day Tass and the Soviet media started using the form "Vilnius" rather than "Vilno." This was presumably in keeping with Stalin's doctrine that the culture of each

Soviet nationality was to be national in form and socialist in content. Although the United States did not recognize the annexation of the Baltic republics, the official Russian toponym (derived from the Lithuanian version) became the basis for using the name Vilnius in English.

Robert A. Rothstein
Professor of Slavic Languages
and Literature
University of Massachusetts
Amherst, Massachusetts

Wilna, as it is listed in the "Lexikon des Judentums," was a center of Jewish learning, as was Lemberg-Lviv-Lwow-Lvov. The scholars in Vilnius were "Litvaks," those in Lvov "Galitzianers."

Louis Marck
New York, New York

Virile Women Target Tobacco Men

My heart goes out to the R. J. Reynolds Tobacco Company. Taken over in a leveraged buyout; junk bonds sinking; publicly blasted into dropping its plan to make a pitch to sell its products to blacks. Nobody seems willing to walk a few steps, much less a mile, for a Camel.

"When sorrows come," says Claudius in *Hamlet* as the king recounts his troubles, "they come not single spies, but in battalions." The newest trouble for the tobacco giant is centered on a word: *virile.*

A faithless employee of an outside contractor of RJR, currying favor with the healthy-lung crowd, leaked a proposal by Promotional Marketing Inc. not yet submitted to the tobacco company. The embryonic idea was to help launch a new brand, Dakota, by aiming a message at women—not the sort of feminists attracted to Philip Morris's Virginia Slims, with its slogan "You've Come a Long Way, Baby," but the kind of women who smoke that competitor's masculine-oriented brand, Marlboro.

What sort of women are attracted to the cigarette touted by the strong, silent, mustachioed, tattooed Marlboro Man? The answer, according to the anonymous leaker: *virile females.*

"I went to high school with girls like this," wrote Tony Kornheiser in a *Washington Post* column about the marketing idea. "We called them *hitter*

chicks, because they liked to hit people, and I adored them for their wild ways. . . . They all dyed their hair either black or blond, and did it up in a rattail bouffant piled high enough to hide a sharp comb inside that they could use as a weapon. They were very big on chewing gum, often grape gum; they'd pop it so loud, it sounded like an air rifle." He fantasized about taking one to Palisades Amusement Park for a weekend, "knowing if anything went wrong with the car she could fix it."

Apparently the woman in the market segment we are cruelly disparaging here—using the attributive noun *hitter* to modify the down-putting *chicks*—enjoys events like tractor pulls and rodeos, fiercely but tenderly stands by her man, dresses like Dolly Parton on a fine day in the country and smokes Marlboro.

Now to my department: Is it accurate to call her *virile*? Would it be fair to require the manufacturer to carry a message on the side of the pack that reads "Warning: Women smoking this are in danger of becoming *virile*"?

That word is rooted in the Latin *vir,* "man, male." A virile person is endowed with what men like to think are manly characteristics: strength, force, dynamism, vigor, potency. The most frequently used synonym for *virile* is *masculine.*

Here we are at the critical issue: Can you use *virile woman* without committing an oxymoronic act? Do adjective and noun absurdly conflict?

No. *Masculine woman* is an acceptable phrase, as is *effeminate man;* what is meant here, however, is different from a female who acts like a male. A *virile woman,* as I interpret the promotional message, is "a woman who associates herself with activities and images formerly considered of primarily male interest."

I confess to never having attended a tractor pull, which is presumably less painful to participants than a tooth pull, but do not consider this a fair test of virility. (I gave up smoking not for health reasons, but because I could never get the hang of lighting two cigarettes simultaneously, the way Paul Henreid did with such manly grace in *Now, Voyager.* Burned a lot of holes in my pants while trying that.)

Etymologists will support the use of *virile woman* because the first appearance of the adjective, in William Caxton's 1490 translation of a French romance based on Virgil's *Aeneid,* was in the phrase "O the fortytude viryle of wymmen." That reference to "virile fortitude" suggests the writer considered gutsiness to be a male attribute, but that is no longer the case; you've come a long way, virility.

What is the equivalent modifier to apply to men? If you can call a woman *virile* without impeaching her femininity, what is a noneffeminate word for a man who has the attributes of womanliness?

Sensitive. That word, the primary meaning of which used to be "keenly susceptible to stimuli," changed to a primary "easily offended" and later to a bureaucratic "one cut above top secret"; now it most often means "sympathetic to minorities' and women's concerns." Jacques Barzun, a member of my Board of Mentors, hates this: He calls this "voguery to eschew" and urges us to use *sensitive* only for "skin, plant, soul." (Other members of the Board of Mentors are Frederic G. Cassidy, editor of the *Dictionary of American Regional English,* Alistair Cooke, the noted linguist and interpreter of Britain to America, and Allen Walker Read, famous for tracing the origins of *O.K.;* you have to be octogenarian, and not only in possession of all your marbles but also able to differentiate among *pureys, cat's-eyes, aggies, glassies, marididdles, steelies, boulders* and *snotties.*)

A related controversy involved *to target.* This verb started as a noun, from the Germanic *targe,* meaning "lightweight shield" (an apt designation for the next phase of the Strategic Defense Initiative). The shield became the object at which to aim, and the noun *target* was verbed by 1837; a century later, economists began using it for "planning to attain an objective." In 1948, this sense was recorded by *The Observer* of London: "Even herrings have targets now: 175,000 tons of fish are being 'targeted' to yield 17,000 tons of oil a year."

Targeting was an innocent, if manipulative, advertising term until it ran into the antismoking campaign. Suddenly, a market segment was being *targeted* with a health hazard; that revived the early object-of-arrows meaning of the noun, and now everybody is denying any effort to target anybody except a newly sensitive Marlboro Man and the virile hitter chick repairing his wheezing engine at the tractor pull.

"Sensitive" as an adjective for effeminate men is both ambiguous and unnecessary when the English language offers a precise, if somewhat awkward (and arcane) word, muliebrile, *which my trusty* Concise Oxford *defines to be the opposite of* virile. *No more weak-kneed and ignorant abuse of "sensitive"!*

Your gentle, though hardly muliebrile reader,

Ramesh Venkataraman
Princeton, New Jersey

I was surprised that you did not mention the term "virago," from the Latin vir, *defined as a woman of great stature, strength, and courage. As might be expected given our cultural heritage, this complimentary term for women is undermined by its second sense, a loud overbearing woman: termagant.*

I agree that "sensitive" is a poor choice for an equivalent modifier to apply to men. In psychological circles the term I hear most often for a man who has positive attributes of womanliness is "nurturant."

J. Steven Reznick
Assistant Professor of
Psychology
Yale University
New Haven, Connecticut

Vogue Words of 1990

Grammarians of tomorrow, in whatever swinging lingo they choose to converse, will be talking about 1990 as the Year of the Present Participle. As Duke Ellington would have put it, "It Don't Mean a Thing If It Don't End in *-ing.*"

In a recent piece in this space, readers were asked to send in words that have gone *out of control*—as *vulnerable, resonate* and *frisson* had done in the 80's. Lex Irregs responded with an outpouring of participles: Here are a few of the most inescapable words of the past year—all formed from verbs and used as adjectives or as parts of the hot verb phrases.

Rosie the Riveting

"*Riveting* testimony" was what NBC's Andrea Mitchell called the evidence presented by Edwin Gray, a federal regulator, in the investigation of the "Keating Five."

"A slick, *riveting,* viscerally scary film" was Janet Maslin's review of a recent horror hit in *The New York Times.*

"A woman absorbed in a *riveting* private vision pulls her room around her like a spectral cloak" is the description by Cathy Curtis of the *Los Angeles Times* of pastel drawings by Robin Palanker. Taken with the term, she adds, "Palanker's are the most immediately *riveting* of the works by seven Los Angeles artists."

The French verb *river* means "to attach." In metalwork, fastening can be done by putting a headed pin or bolt through two pieces and then beating the plain end so as to make another head; that's what Rosie the Riveter did, and the figurative extension is "to attach one's attention." (No, there's no connection between *fasten* and *fascinate.*)

Peach Cobbling

"Have you noticed journalism's new obsession with *cobbling?*" Steven Zousmer writes from Scarsdale, New York. He notes "*cobbling* together a budget agreement" and "*cobbling* a Mideast settlement."

Jack O'Shaughnessy of Columbus, Ohio, sends a clipping of a *New York Times* article by Michael Oreskes that leads with "Congressional leaders *cobbled* a new deficit-reduction plan *together* today." The reader takes exception: "My dad took my shoes to a *cobbler.* My mother used to make *peach cobbler.* Tell Mr. Oreskes that the word *together* after *cobbled* is redundant because *cobble* means 'to put together hastily.' "

In its sense of "to pave with cobblestones," *cobble* may be used alone; however, in its shoemaking sense—"to mend or patch coarsely"—I consider the joining together of *cobble* and *together* to be acceptable. (*Joining together* is redundant.) I prefer to drop the *together* when cobbling an agreement, but will not berate Mr. Oreskes, widely admired as a shoe-leather reporter, for tossing in the extra word; however, in the verb phrase *cobble together,* the particle *together* would have been better placed immediately after the verb, as "Congressional leaders today cobbled together a new deficit, etc."

A *whisky cobbler,* by the way, may be derived from *cobbler's punch,* which John F. Mariani in his *Dictionary of American Food and Drink* speculates "had the effect of 'patching up' the imbiber." (Dissolve a packet of diet sweetener in a big shot of cheap bourbon and pour into a glass of shaved ice with a slice of lemon and whatever fruit is lying around for Safire's Cobbler; "riveting," say barkeeps.)

Rules of Engaging

"It is time now to *engage* in a dialogue," Secretary of State James A. Baker 3d likes to say, using the verb *engage* to mean "to take part in." However, when the Estonian Prime Minister, Edgar Savisaar, urged him "to *engage* Moscow on the Baltic situation," as the words were paraphrased in English, the meaning of *engage* was "to involve, to draw in," bordering on "to confront"; an extreme extension of this meaning leads to a "naval engagement" or exchange of fire.

In Old French, *gage* was a pledge, some valuable token deposited to insure performance; en-gaging led to the ring used to mark the promise of marriage.

Monica Borkowski, my colleague in the *Times* Washington bureau, points to the increased frequency of the use of *engage, disengage, re-engage* and the present participle *engaging.*

"For all its faults," goes a Peter Biskind book review in *The Times,* "this survey is an *engaging,* if not particularly provocative, read." The meaning here is "involving, drawing in," as in the original sense; an *engaging* smile is infectious, like the nouning of *read.*

Nothing Daunting

Riveting and *engaging* as adjectives, *cobbling* as a verb—none of these vogue words of 1990 come close to (I construe the *none* in this case as plural, "not any," calling for *come,* not *comes,* so save your postage) the most unnerving, consternating present participle of the year: *daunting.*

Will the deposed British Prime Minister, Margaret Thatcher, influence her chosen successor, John Major? The columnist Peter Jenkins told ABC: "She will be a *daunting* presence."

"A *daunting* task" was how the introducer of Henry Kissinger described his assignment to a group of newspaper editors. "During another segment of the meeting," writes an Iowa journalism professor, Gilbert Cranberg, "former U.S. Senator Gaylord Nelson proposed that George Bush put a question to Mikhail Gorbachev: 'What is the most *daunting* environmental issue facing us?' Everywhere I turn, it seems, *daunting* is haunting discourse. Why is everybody all of a sudden flaunting *daunting*?"

One of the many layers of nail-nibbling copy editors who review this column in New York and live in dread of the Gotcha! Gang is named Michael Molyneux. (He is responsible for all errors herein; I am innocent.) I will ignore what will surely be his stricture that, in the above paragraph, the verb *writes* should come after, rather than before, the name of the person identified; somebody way up top is worried about falling into the backward *Time*-style. Most of the time, I agree—*he said* is less labored than *said he*—but when I put a long title or identification before a name, I prefer to stick the verb up front to help the reader know what is happening while the identification is marching along.

When it comes to *daunting* as the Vogue Word of 1990, however, I happily accept his submission of proof that this participle is booming. He crunched *The New York Times* through his computers and discovered that the usage had grown from 172 times in 1985 to more than 380 in 1990.

Sign of the times: *Daunt,* from a French alteration of the Latin *domitare,* "to tame," meant "to cow, to instill fear in." For centuries, *undaunted* and *dauntless* were the most common ways the word asserted itself; H.M.S. *Dauntless* was a British light cruiser that fought in two wars, and the Douglas *Dauntless* was a U.S. Navy dive bomber in World War II. Now fearlessness is out, and the word bursts forth in its intimidated state.

Basically, the use of vogue words is linguistic laziness. ("Have you heard how often *basically* is used to begin sentences these days?" Evangeline Bruce of Washington writes. "As an adverb to start a sentence, *basically* is a nonstarter.") A vogue word is the mark of a writer who has not yet found his voice. (Daniel B. Payne of Newton, Massachusetts, writes, "*Found his voice,* now in vogue, seems to mean 'to speak persuasively and with conviction.' ") You can expect such terms to be excoriated every year in this space.

"Newspaper columnists have adopted *in this space* as a replacement for the editorial 'we' " is the painful observation of Janet Rosenblatt of Boston. "They confuse their 'space' with themselves."

I am currently looking for an appropriate way to rivet a copy of your column to my wall.

Robin Palanker
Culver City, California

The Walls Have Orejas

Orejas, Spanish for "ears," is the word used by peasants in El Salvador and Guatemala to describe government informers. *Inside Central America,* the Guntherian new Summit book by my *New York Times* colleague Clifford Krauss, also informs us that roving bands of Sandinistas that broke up opposition demonstrations in Nicaragua were called *turbas divinas,* or "divine mobs."

Why *divine?* This was a description from the French Revolution of two centuries ago; it was meant to give some spiritual authority to the rule by angry crowds that led to the Reign of Terror. Phrases like *les foules divines* leap languages and centuries to put down new roots in unexpected places.

Same with slang, but dialects produce curious differences in meaning. In the United States, *to stretch your legs* means "to go for a walk, to get a breath of air"; it is akin to baseball's *seventh-inning stretch,* a chance for fans to stand up en masse without the guy behind yelling, "Down in front!"

Georgi Arbatov, a Kremlin Americanologist, was telling ABC's David Brinkley and other correspondents about a letter read in the Soviet Parliament: "It said that you boys—it means Gorbachev and Yeltsin—better stretch your hands toward each other, or the country will stretch its legs."

To blank looks from the American interviewers, Mr. Arbatov explained: "You know, it is an idiomatic expression. *To stretch legs,* it means 'to be dead.' "

Which figure of speech will triumph in a multipolar world? Will leg-stretching symbolize rejuvenation or the opposite? *Orejas,* keep us informed; there's a divinity in dialect.

In Colombia, and I believe in most of Latin America, estirar la pata *("to stretch the leg"), has long meant "to die."*

However, it is not necessary to reach so far for an equivalent, since in this country, "kick the bucket" conjures up the same knee-jerk image.

I always assumed estirar la pata *was an allusion to the final shudder of a person or animal in which an involuntary jerking of the extremities occurs at the moment of death. We have all seen this mimicked in silent movies and cartoons, where the legs of a cowboy, horse, or other animate being in extremis histrionically jerk straight and fall slowly to the ground to demonstrate the subject's demise. Incidentally, but not coincidentally, the expression* sacar la mano *("stick out a hand"), means "to die," or "cease to function," in Colombia.*

Albert Talero
Bayside, New York

War of Nerves

One phrase we may be seeing a lot of in coming weeks is *war of nerves,* meaning "the use of propaganda or symbolic actions to undermine an enemy's morale or induce him to acquiesce." The target is not so much the enemy's territory as its hearts and minds.

The coinage belongs to a faceless but talented bureaucrat writing in Britain's Annual Register of 1939: "The British public . . . did not allow the 'war of nerves' organised by the Nazi government to interfere in the least with its August holiday."

For a time after World War II, the phrase was used to describe the tensions building between the United States and Russia, as the U.S.S.R. was popularly known. On receipt of George F. Kennan's memorandum urging a containment policy, Secretary of State James Byrnes stated, "We must not conduct a war of nerves to achieve strategic ends," but that was the best phrase to describe what went on until Herbert Bayard Swope came up with *cold war* in a speech he wrote for Bernard Baruch.

A parallel expression to *war of nerves* is *war of words,* usually favored by government propagandists who called themselves *psychological warfare operatives,* or *psyops* for a time, then turned milder with *public affairs specialists* and *communications consultants* and now adopt the style of *public diplomatists.* That has distinguished provenance. Alexander Pope, in his 1725 translation of Homer's *Odyssey,* wrote this ringing put-down to the hyperarticulate teenagers of his day: "O insolence of youth! whose tongue affords / Such railing eloquence and war of words."

War Words

"Naked aggression," President Bush called the *blitzkrieg* seizure of Kuwait by Iraq; the United States, he said, had to *"draw a line in the sand"* to defend Saudi Arabia. News analysts called the presence of American troops in the path of Saddam Hussein's *"megalomaniacal and hegemonic"* ambitions a *tripwire.* Lexicographers donned their battle gear.

Naked Aggression

"Iraq, having committed brutal, naked aggression," President Bush said, "ought to get out."

Aggression means "forceful attack," from the Latin word for *attack;* in modern usage, the noun has the connotation of an *unprovoked* attack. Therefore, "unprovoked aggression" would be redundant.

The adjective wedded to the noun *aggression* is *naked.* These words are as tightly fused in cliché as *brutal murder, unmitigated gall* and *stark naked.*

Why *naked*? This word, its meaning ranging from "free" to "unconcealed, bare, plain," has another sense of "stark" (which also means "bare," making *stark naked* redundant) but has the connotation of "shocking, stunning" or even "ghastly, appalling." Although *naked* looks like a past participle—a verb form ending in *-ed*—it was not formed from the verb "to nake"; its earliest use can be found in *Beowulf,* written about 725, as *nacod.*

Why *naked* and not *nude*? Shock is the key to the word: not the fact of being unclothed, but the surprise and perhaps embarrassment in the eye of the beholder of the plain sight is what gives this adjective its impact. A blade is *naked,* never *nude,* when it is unsheathed. "For the human body," writes J. N. Hook in *The Appropriate Word,* "*naked* is the more frank, honest and shameless word." Robert Graves dealt with that difference in his 1957 poem "The Naked and the Nude": "For me, the naked and the nude stand as wide apart / As love from lies, or truth from art."

Naked aggression, then, means "unprovoked, shameless attack," denuded, or stripped bare, of any pretense to legality.

Draw the Line

"A line has been drawn in the sand," said the President in a televised speech to the nation.

To draw the line is to set a limit; its figurative origin may have been in plowing a boundary line between farms in England or in establishing dimensions for a court in early tennis games in France in the fourteenth century. First recorded use was in the trial of Fyshe Palmer in 1793, not in defiance but in puzzlement: "It is difficult . . . to draw the line."

During the siege of the Alamo in San Antonio in 1836, legend has it that William Barret Travis drew a line in the ground (some say sand) with his sword and said, "Those prepared to die for freedom's cause, come across to me" (189 of 190 Texas defenders did; the 190th provided the story).

In what material is the line drawn? Mr. Bush was referring, of course, to the sands of the Arabian desert. However, the addition of *in the sand* recalls a children's game on the beach, in which the drawing of a line in the sand was a dare to come across. That could not have been what he meant. However, the usage by a President in a crisis may have overridden the "dare" connotation; a *New York Times* headline read WORRIED NATION BACKS U.S. LINE IN THE SAND.

Tripwire

A British soldier writing home in World War I described a facet of trench warfare: "He walks forward, he has found his landmark. . . . He is coming to the Hun trip wire. He has cut the German trip wire."

From that literal meaning—a wire strung to set off a trap or alarm—came a figurative sense of "a small force used as a first line of defense, less to stop an invading force than to trigger the intervention of reinforcements."

"The German electorate are baffled," wrote *The Observer* in 1957, "as to whether NATO is meant to defend their soil, or provide the tripwire for a Soviet-American suicide pact." By 1969, this idea spread to the Middle East: "[King Hussein] is anxious to make a separate peace with the Israelis," wrote

The New Statesman, "on the basis of a demilitarised West Bank, with an Israeli military tripwire on the Jordan."

The meaning is firmly set as "self-activating commitment to deeper involvement," more automatic and less self-challenging than the older *tossing your cap over the wall.* Throughout the pre-post-cold war period (only yesterday), the American troops stationed in Berlin knew that in the event of hostilities, they were destined for internment; other troops in NATO knew they were expected to struggle until reinforcements arrived, or until their loss of life caused a nuclear retaliation. *Tripwire* troops are in position to be saved or avenged. The larger the force, the less frequently it is referred to as a tripwire.

Blitz

During the Vietnam War, doves derided *the Munich analogy,* an attempt by hawks to draw a parallel between the defense of South Vietnam and the failure of the Allies to stop Hitler after he first showed his expansionist intent.

For at least a year before Saddam Hussein's attack across the Kuwaiti border, his critics had little luck establishing a Munich analogy. Subversive sobriquets like "The Butcher of Baghdad" and "The Hero of Halabja" (a reference to Saddam's use of poison gas against Kurdish civilians in Halabja, Iraq, killing at least five thousand) did not persuade policy makers or the American public that a new Hitler was in the making. Neologisms like *Todeskrämer,* literally "peddlers of death," were coined to derogate those Western nations who sold arms to Saddam and to Libya's Qaddafi; the use of a German word was intended to call attention to the Federal Republic's participation in the Mideast military buildup as well as to the Hitlerite nature of the arms buyers.

However, after the Iraqi invasion of Kuwait and the threat to U.S. oil supplies, President Bush took an interest in the Munich analogy and used a key word from World War II to make his point: "When you plan a blitzkrieg-like attack that's launched at two o'clock in the morning, that's pretty hard to stop . . ." For emphasis, he repeated *blitzkrieg* in his statements.

The German word has been so absorbed into English that it is no longer capitalized. It means "lightning (*blitz*) war (*krieg*)"; its first use in English was on October 7, 1939, in *The War Illustrated:* "In the opening stage of the war all eyes were turned on Poland, where the German military machine was engaged in *Blitz-Krieg*—lightning war—with a view to ending as soon as possible."

Another World War II reference was apt: In discussing possible ways of stopping Saddam, the phrase *the von Stauffenberg solution* was used. Count

Claus von Stauffenberg was the Wehrmacht officer who led the plot to assassinate Hitler in 1944.

Meg & Heg

Deploying U.S. forces was necessary, said Frank J. Gaffney Jr. of the Center for Security Policy (an organization entitled to wear the coveted Anti-Saddam Before Kuwait button), if the Iraqi dictator "is to be prevented from indulging still further his megalomaniacal and hegemonic ambitions."

Megalo- is a combining form for "abnormally large"; a megalopolis is a metropolis gone too far. *Megalomania,* according to Dr. Kay Redfield Jamison of the Johns Hopkins medical school, coauthor of the definitive work on manic depression, means "a mental disorder characterized by delusions of grandeur."

Hegemonic—properly, *hegemonistic*—is an adjective for *hegemonism,* with the emphasis on the *gem,* meaning "a policy of dominance over other nations."

Using both adjectives in a single phrase is called *overkill.*

I remember hearing that one of the Macedonian kings of Syria (I think it was Antiochus the Great) attempted to invade the Ptolemaic kingdom of Egypt, only to be met by a solitary Roman envoy. This Roman senator, undeterred by the massed ranks of the Macedonian phalanx, demanded to know if the king, as a "friend" of Rome, would agree to abort his invasion. When it appeared as though the king was hedging, the Roman drew a circle in the sand around the nonplussed monarch. The envoy demanded an unequivocal answer to his demand before the king stepped out of the circle. Antiochus, apparently, did not take long to decide on the proper response; he turned around and marched, at the head of his army, back to Syria.

I'm not sure that I have the details and particulars of the story right, but I can vouch for its general shape. If this incident did not serve as the inspiration for the phrase "draw a line in the sand," then the contextual similarity between the anecdote and the situation to which the phrase is currently being applied (power-hungry and aggressive Mideast ruler plans aggression, is opposed by foreign interventionist power) is quite remarkable.

Justin D. Abelow
New York, New York

I thought I should drop you a line about "line in the sand." The earliest known instance of this gesture is in connection with an event in Rome's march to domination of the eastern half of the Mediterranean. In 168 B.C. Antiochus Epiphanes, badly in need of funds, moved against Egypt (then a Roman protectorate). He was met on the approaches to Egypt by a Roman senator, Popillius Laenas, who had been dispatched as envoy to deal with the unstable conditions in the area. In a face to face meeting with Antiochus, Popillius Laenas drew a circle in the sand around King Antiochus ordering him to agree to the orders of the Roman Senate to withdraw his army into Syria before he left the "line in the sand." The story of Popillius's diplomatic coup enjoyed a great vogue among the Romans. You will find it described in Livy's History of Rome *Book XLV, chapter xii, and in Polybius,* History *Book XXIX, chapter xxvii.*

This Antiochus Epiphanes, king of Seleucid Syria, is the same Antiochus who, driven to desperate measures, in 169 B.C. plundered the treasury of the Temple in Jerusalem and sought to end the cult of Yahweh and transform it into a pagan cult. You know the sequel: the revolt of the Jews led by the Maccabees, the success of the war of national liberation, and the rededication of the Temple to Yahweh and the commemoration of this event in Chanukah. Antiochus Epiphanes, by the way, was called by some Antiochus Epimanes ("Lunatic"), and died soon after.

> *Meyer Reinhold*
> *Professor of Classical Studies*
> *Boston University*
> *Boston, Massachusetts*

In 168 B.C. the Roman Senate sent the consular Popilius Laenas to Alexandria to halt an invasion of Egypt by Antiochus V of Syria.

When Antiochus equivocated, Popilius Laenas drew a line in the sand about the monarch and ordered him to give him an answer to carry home to the Senate before stirring out of the circle.

> *Arthur D. Kahn*
> *Brooklyn, New York*

In 169 B.C. Antiochus Epiphanes, the Seleucid King of Syria, attempted to invade Egypt. He was met near Alexandria by the Roman envoy, C. Popilius Laenas, and informed that such an invasion would not be in Rome's interest. When the King attempted to procrastinate, Popilius drew a circle around him with his staff and demanded a definite answer before he stepped out of the circle. Antiochus yielded. (See Livy, 45.12, Polybius, 29.11).

R. H. Stacy
Professor Emeritus
Syracuse University
Syracuse, New York

The most accurate testimony about the Alamo siege was provided by Mrs. Susannah Dickenson. She was in the fortress with her daughter and her husband, who was killed in the fighting. The "man from the Alamo," celebrated in at least one Hollywood B movie, was Louis Rose, a drifter and veteran of the Napoleonic wars. Rose's testimony was influential in land commission hearings on behalf of men killed in the Alamo, but he never elaborated on his departure. According to Mrs. Dickenson, as hope of survival waned Travis simply urged those who wished to leave to do so, and one man stepped from the ranks. The famous sword line in the sand was the 1873 invention of promoter and yarn-spinner William Zuber. But the imagery is still powerful and may well have inspired President Bush's comment.

Mrs. Dickenson was a woman who combined exceptional strength and the most traditional sort of outlook—a point worth stressing in a New York City publication.

Arthur Cyr
Chicago, Illinois

The lead editorial in a Sunday New York Times used a phrase which sounded strange to my ear. After reading your column, however, I think I understand the usage.

The editorial contains a list of terms for resolving the Iraq crisis. The first term calls for Iraq to withdraw from Kuwait, "but its territorial claims could be adjudicated by the World Court." Such an adjudication would "afford Saddam Hussein a fig leaf."

A fig leaf? I would have expected a "bone," or a "sop," or a "means of saving face," but not a fig leaf. What does the adjudication cover up?

I read your column, and the scales fell from my eyes. Saddam, as you point out, is charged with (and guilty of) "naked aggression" against Kuwait. By withdrawing and seeking a World Court adjudication, Saddam's aggression would be reversed, and its nakedness covered up. Voila! A fig leaf!

W. Peter Burns
Hendersonville,
North Carolina

Aux armes, *lexicographers!*
What about STARK NAKED AGGRESSION??

John M. Anspacher
Naples, Florida

Well, Bite My Ankle

Asked by *Defense News* if he had a message for American forces stationed in his country, Saudi Arabia's Ambassador to the United States, Prince Bandar bin Sultan, replied in part: "Don't let the *ankle-biters* get to you. You are not there to defend material things. . . . You are defending your national interest and also you are defending great principles."

Who are these *ankle-biters?* A few weeks after Prince Bandar's interview appeared, the word popped up in a controversy between Wayne Berman, a lawyer at the Department of Commerce, and F. Michael Maloof, director of technical security for the Department of Defense. The Commerce official was embarrassed by charges that his bureaucracy had approved shipments to Iraq that might have helped its production of weapons of mass destruction; he lashed back at the men who had opposed such shipments, criticizing Mr. Maloof as a "low-level clerk" who was part of a group of *"ankle-biters."*

Slang dictionaries offer little help. Eric Partridge's classic work defined the term as trousers fashioned after the pants worn by Hussars, the Hungarian light cavalry of the fifteenth century, with bottoms tucked inside the stockings to avoid contact with the stirrup. This cannot be the current meaning.

In the recent revision and abridgment of Partridge's *Dictionary of Slang and Unconventional English,* Paul Beale dispenses with the Hussars and defines the term simply as "young children," noting the usage to be "widespread Canadian and U.S.: since circa 1960."

That is one sense of the term, noted also in the *Collins Concise Dictionary* as an Australian term for "young child." For example, in a piece on Teenage Mutant Ninja Turtles, *The Toronto Star* reports that "the Turtles were never really intended as *anklebiter* fare"; the editor of *Skiing* magazine used two words when she wrote in 1980, "We adults are going to be seeing more and more of those endearing *ankle biters* on the slopes"; and *People* magazine also noted the term as two words in British usage, defining it as "a small Sloane, an heir. 'Julia? She's too busy with those two *ankle biters* of hers.'"

But that is surely not what the annoyed Commerce techno-pusher had in mind. An extended meaning has developed, first noted in the military; Lieutenant General Andrew J. Goodpaster, as West Point superintendent, was described by James Feron in *The New York Times* in 1981 as "able to make the changes because he had enough prestige to 'keep the *ankle-biters* away,' according to an aide on the administrative staff."

The legal profession seized the new term of derision. *Inc.* magazine noted in 1984 that law firms often made huge fees in extended arbitration cases "particularly if they latch onto an *'ankle-biter'*—a client who wants to chew up a baited partner no matter what the cost."

Politics, ever sensitive to derisive neologisms, was not far behind: when Representative John D. Dingell of Michigan criticized the Lockheed Corporation as having slipped past accountability checks, *National Journal* quoted an unidentified industry executive berating Representative Dingell as an *ankle biter* (two words).

The recent *Washington Post* account of the Commerce-Defense contretemps drew mail centered on the new usage: "I'd like to bite Mr. Berman's ankle, too," wrote Irmie Bellman of Springfield, Virginia. Stefan A. Halper of Great Falls, Virginia, added, "The nation owes a great debt to this *ankle-biter* for gnawing away at the 'clay ankles' of those at Commerce."

This means that we have a replacement at last for the *weenie.* That locution of the 80's, related to the reduplication of *tiny* as *teeny-weeny* and influenced by *Wiener wurst,* small sausage first produced in Vienna, was also first applied to a child; later it came to mean "small-minded" as an adjective and "petty bureaucrat" as a noun.

Late in the Reagan Administration, the *weenie* was given competition only in the plural, as *mice*—meaning "the quick-footed, small-minded, negative aides to people in power who justified their staff salaries by nibbling at bold approaches and big ideas submitted by outsiders until the proposals were reduced to a size that would not discomfort the entrenched." In her Reagan memoir, the speechwriter Peggy Noonan deplored the "White House mice" who chewed up her prose. This locution, too, has a parallel meaning of "children" among producers of television programs.

In the Nixon, Ford and Carter years, the derogation of these careful public servants who did not want their principals embarrassed by principles was *munchkins.* These were the little people in L. Frank Baum's 1900 book, *The Wonderful Wizard of Oz;* even today, *munchkins* is sometimes used to mock pretentious staff members; perhaps a connection exists between the chewing, munching connotation of that word with the nibbling of the mice and the biting of the ankles.

In the early 70's, when I was engaged in a series of tirades at a Senatorial cover-up of investigations into Kennedy Administration excesses, a good writer—maybe it was Murray Kempton—came to a Senator's defense by pitying him for having "the tiny teeth of Safire sunk in the bottom of his pants leg."

Apparently I never got through to the ankle, but this vivid image illustrates the dual nature of the derogation: It is a bite or chew or nibble—not enough to hurt but enough to annoy or eventually to debilitate—and it is the work of someone of small stature who cannot rise above the target's ankle. It is akin to, though not synonymous with, the much older phrase *nipping at the heels of,* about a dog following aggressively, now used to mean "catching up to" or in the sense of "giving alarmed impetus to."

Small children are also referred to as *rug rats, crumb catchers* and *curtain climbers,* though these have not yet been applied to small-minded, idea-watering, prestige-diminishing *ankle-biters* (one word, hyphenated).

Alas, your discussion of the origins of "ankle biter" could have benefited more from entomology than etymology.

As most people who've lived west of the Rockies know, an ankle biter is a species of mosquito indigenous to the Great Basin and nearby desert areas. It gets its name because it rarely flies more than a foot above the ground and packs a painful bite that frequently swells into a huge, red, itchy welt.

Because these pesky varmints tend to travel in clouds, especially in moist years, they're a particularly vexing plague upon the ankles of anyone hapless enough to stroll into their territory. I've seen grown men hop yelping in their midst, as wildly as if a gunslinger had ordered them to dance and started firing at their feet.

Cary Groner
Berkeley, California

On ankle-biting, you could have gone back further than 1960—re our common religious heritage.

"Dan shall be a servant by the way, an adder in the path, that biteth the horses heels, so that the rider shall fall backward." Genesis 49:17.

Philip Goorian
Cairo, Egypt

The Talmud in Berakoth 33a discusses when the leader of the davening can interrupt his repetition of the Amidah (silent prayer said standing). The Mishna says: "ah-fi-lu na-chash kaw-rooch ahl ah-kay-vo . . . lo yaf-seek" . . . And even if a serpent be wound about his heel, he is not to interrupt."

Lawrence H. Goldberg
Atlanta, Georgia

In Genesis 3:15, the serpent is addressed: "I will put enmity between you and the woman, and between your offspring and hers; he will strike at your head, while you strike at his heel."

Robert J. Kovacs
Livingston, New Jersey

The Wetlands Fox

Francis Marion, an American general in the Revolutionary War, bedeviled the British with his surprise attacks from the marshy areas of South Carolina. The short, sickly-looking fellow was among our earliest partisan fighters, pioneering guerrilla tactics against regular troops in skirmishes at Tearcoat Swamp and Halfway Swamp. Because he and his small force would strike and then disappear into seemingly impenetrable bogs, through brambles that tore the red coats of his pursuers, the elusive Marion was given the sobriquet "the Swamp Fox."

Today he would be called the *wetlands* fox. *Swamp* is out; this soggy companion of ours for more than three centuries, perhaps from the Greek *somphos,* "spongy," is considered unscientific and slightly pejorative; the new word put forward by environmentalists and galoshes-equipped journalists is *wetlands.*

The Army Corps of Engineers, in chorus with the Environmental Protection Agency, begins to define *wetlands* as "those areas that are inundated or saturated by surface or ground water." But that area must be capable of supporting "vegetation typically adapted for life in saturated soil conditions," which means plants ranging from cattails and bulrushes to willows and mangroves, which can grow at least part of the time in ground that lacks oxygen. These wetlands include *swamps, marshes, wet meadows, wet tundra* and *bogs.*

As a longtime muckraker, I have been trying to unearth the moment when all this muck was upgraded in our vocabulary. Although *wet land,* as two words and even one word, has been kicking around for centuries, the first citation in the plural is in *The New Scientist* of June 17, 1965: "*Wetlands* are defined to include marshes, bogs, swamps and any still water less than six meters deep."

Twenty years later, the plural word was being construed as both singular and plural: *A wetlands is* is just as accepted as *the wetlands are.*

Last month, a *New York Times* headline read OVER E.P.A. PROTEST, WHITE HOUSE ALTERS WETLAND AGREEMENT (using the plural *wetlands* in the copy), while *The Washington Post* preferred the plural modifier and a zippier style: WETLANDS AGREEMENT WATERED DOWN.

"Twenty years ago," says Jon Kusler of the Association of State Wetland [singular] Managers, "almost all discussion of wetlands involved waterfalls and fisheries. Now there are concerns for water quality, flood storage, food-chain support and especially birding."

How do we wade into the differentiation that will help us make a splash in synonymy? A *marsh,* a word that may share a root with *marine,* is wet land characterized by nonwoody or herbaceous plants like cattails and similar tall grasses; these include an herb of the mallow family once used in preparing a confection called the *marshmallow.* (Hardly anybody uses real marshmallow root anymore; only a few old swamp foxes remember the taste.) A *mire,* from the Old Norse, is synonymous with *marsh,* but is used more in Europe than in the United States.

Bog, from the Gaelic word for "soft," is spongy ground that is acidic; that's where gardeners turn for peat moss. The British like the synonyms *heath* and *moor.*

A *swamp* is land permanently or periodically saturated by water but featuring trees. The term subsumes marshes and bogs, but is not as moist-embracing as *wetlands,* which spills over to bottomland forests, pocosins, pine savannas and lands that the engineers say "are not easily recognized, often because they are dry during part of the year or 'they just don't look very wet' from the roadside."

What's the opposite of *wetlands?* No, not *drylands*—at the E.P.A., it's *uplands.*

In a related terminological development, the controversy over the term *ground water* continues. The water in the ground that supplies wells and springs is written as two words in *Webster's New World Dictionary,* and as one word in Merriam-Webster's *Ninth New Collegiate* (because, says its editor, Fred Mish, "the preponderance of citational evidence shows it as one word").

Joe D. Winkle, in 1988 a deputy regional administrator of E.P.A. based in Dallas, sent a memo with twelve pages of attachments to his colleagues in which he complained that "we are seeing numerous documents presenting *groundwater* as *ground-water* or *ground water,*" and requested that the two-word style be adopted. This was sent to me by a whistle-blower within the agency with a disgusted notation: "Our tax dollars at work!"

Winkle style has been adopted by most bureaucrats at E.P.A., but the single word appears in the agency's news releases. "*Ground water,* two words, is what is used in the name of the Office of Ground Water Protection," says John Kasper, press aide to chief William K. Reilly, "but the *Ninth New Collegiate* uses one word. That's the style I prefer to use in press releases." So the ground rule is to use *groundwater* outside, *ground water* inside.

Bogged down in details? *Mired* by memos? *Swamped* by work? Try explaining to your with-it boss you've been *wetlanded.*

Beachcombers down here on Long Beach Island have been digging into the muck of the wetlands in marshy backyards for quite a while. The first reference to wetlands as one word in The Beachcomber—*that's a weekly newspaper published since 1950—appeared on August 9, 1956:*

"Initial plans call for purchases of some 5,000 acres of wetlands over the next ten years."

> Margaret Buchholz
> Publisher
> The Beachcomber
> Surf City, New Jersey

The lowlands of the Adirondack Park are full of wet places—from cedar and spruce swamps to quaking bogs. As in the Catskills, German and Dutch words, vlaie *and* vlie, *were applied to wet places. These words were corrupted to* vly—*and* vlys *are ubiquitous: Dead Vly, Crystal Vly, Twin Vly, Burnt Vly, Vly Lake, and many others. Perhaps because* v *is pronounced as* f, vly *became* fly. *Locals still refer to Burnt Fly, Racker Fly, and so on, and this corruption is recognized in Fly Pond, Fly Creek, and Fly Brook. Upstate the common name for wetlands remains* vly *or* fly.

> Barbara McMartin
> Croton, New York

In England a heath *is typically a* sandy *tract of upland where heather grows. Presents a chicken and egg puzzle for linguists. Most inland English golf courses are built on heather—the land is worthless for agriculture, and the sand traps are already in place.* Bogtrotter *is an English term for an Irishman, not necessarily complimentary.*

Hubert Hall
Lecompton, Kansas

You still fail to appreciate the absolutely fundamental distinction, in linguistics, between a derivative and a cognate. English swamp *is not "perhaps from" (i.e., a derivative of) the Greek word* somphos *"spongy." It is akin to (i.e., cognate with)* somphos. *What this means is that both* swamp *and* somphos *are derived from a common Indo-European root (or base, to use the equally valid terminology of* Webster's New World Dictionary*).*

Indo-European, which existed as a more or less unitary language until circa *3000 B.C., is the parent language not only of the Germanic group (including English) but also of Greek, Latin, Sanskrit, Balto-Slavic, Celtic, etc. For that reason, many (perhaps most) everyday English words have clearly identifiable Greek cognates; very few of them, however, are "from" Greek. Thus, English* mother *is cognate with (not "from") Greek* meter, *as is English* three *with Greek* treis, *English* moon *with Greek* mene, *English* mouse *with Greek* mus, *English* eat *with Greek* edmenai, *etc.*

Louis Jay Herman
New York, New York

How does one grind water?

Julian S. Herz
Indianapolis, Indiana

Who's Counting?

Peter Norton, the computer-software genius, sends in a clipping from *The New York Times Book Review.* Usually, the number of pages in a book is (I construe "the number" to be singular) listed right after the author's name, but in this case the word *unpaged* appears.

"I shudder to think what *unpaged* might actually mean," Mr. Norton word-processes and laser-prints, "but whatever it does, surely your colleagues meant *unnumbered.*"

Publishers have been using *unpaged* to mean "having no page numbers" since 1874, but there may be an uneasiness about possible confusion with "having no pages," which is why *unpaginated* should be preferred.

When one edits a document using word processing or desktop publishing software, adding and removing text often changes where each page ends and the next begins. Adding a paragraph on page 2, for example, may push the last paragraph on page 2 to the top of page 3. Pagination *is the process of adjusting the position of these* page breaks *for the best visual appearance before printing the document.* Most software provides automatic pagination, *though some of the more primitive products still require* manual pagination. *To say that a book has been published* unpaginated, *then, suggests no one has taken any care with the page breaks, probably resulting in a visually unappealing presentation. I suspect, however, that this care has been exercised, and that the publisher has merely omitted the numbers from the well-paginated pages. I think Mr. Norton's suggestion,* unnumbered, *comes closer to the mark.*

David A. Knopf
San Francisco, California

Word of the Year: Freedom

In his recent meeting with President Bush, Mikhail S. Gorbachev was reported to have suggested that the American stop using the phrase *Western values,* as in "the triumph of *Western values.*" This hint that the West had won the cold war smacked too much of gloating.

Mr. Bush, an ardent antitriumphalist, agreed to change his rhetoric; he and his Secretary of State immediately switched to *democratic values,* a concept that his Communist counterpart professes to share.

That adjective was inoffensive to Mr. Gorbachev because *democracy* is a word long adopted by Communism, along with *people.* Many Marxist-Leninist regimes styled themselves *democratic peoples' republics,* though this is redundant: *Demos* is the Greek root for "people." (*Kratos* means "strength" or "power.")

A *democracy* is a system of government in which the power comes directly from the people; past mislabeling is tacitly recognized in the Soviet Union today, which is undergoing what Mr. Gorbachev calls the process of *democratization.*

One word, however, is generally recognized to be a Western value, to use the provocative term, which orators often use with the phrase *Judeo-Christian heritage.* The key word is *freedom,* certainly 1989's Word of the Year.

In a curious but longstanding agreement, speechwriters of the left and right have come to respect each other's primary rhetorical turf: Communists call their countries and allies *peaceloving* (not hyphenated); conservative ideologues call their countries *freedom-loving* (hyphenated).

Many Westerners hasten to add *peace,* as in "to live in freedom and peace," often adding Abraham Lincoln's adjectives "just and lasting," but their emphasis differs from the Communists'. Few would accept Picasso's symbol of a dove of peace as their own. The West's appropriation of the word *freedom* is apparent in a Communist spokesman's reference to "the so-called *free world*"; that phrase, now used mainly by unreconstructed cold warriors, has effectively cast aspersions on the state of liberty in Communist-dominated nations.

Freedom has even triumphed over *liberty.* The two words are synonyms, but resonate differently.

Liberty, from the Latin *liber,* "free," taken from the Greek *eleutheros,* is a product of the Romance languages—in French, *liberté;* Spanish, *libertad;* Rumanian, *liberdade.* In American English, the revered word has the happy connotation of a Liberty Bell with its invocations to "proclaim Liberty throughout the land" and calls up images of the pre–Civil War liberty poles ("What's liberty without a pole?" asked William Seward, defending the idea of a proclamation of emancipation).

Perhaps because of recent bicentennial celebrations, the word *liberty,* unmodified by the controversializing *civil,* has gained a historical connotation; we tend to associate it with a symbolic spread eagle, and think reverently of *liberty* as the remembered goal of the philosophy of self-government.

Freedom is a hammer of a word, without a Greek or Latin pedigree, from the proto-Germanic *frijaz* that came into Old English as *freodom.* These Germanic words are punchier than their Romance-language counterparts: *Rich* and *hard* are more telling than *affluent* and *arduous.*

The root *freo,* in Dutch *vrij,* was among our earliest English words, making its appearance in the eighth century. The first meaning was "dear, beloved, close," to identify family members in contrast to servants or slaves; the Indo-European *prei-,* "to be fond of," is the root of "friend," and is related to the Sanskrit *priyas,* "beloved."

Loved ones had privileges: One held in freedom by the authority of the house had fewer restrictions on speech or movement. The free had the capacity to act without the many constraints imposed on those in bondage, and that ability came to be valued highly. "I remember a proverb said of old," wrote John Lydgate in 1430. " 'Who loseth his freedom, in faith he loseth all.' "

In time, *freedom*—the state of the loved ones—came to mean more than a guiding principle of householding or government; in its passionate political sense, the thundering word now means a way of life unbounded by arbitrary power.

Freiheit was the word shouted at the opening of the Berlin wall. (Metaphorical problem: A wall does not "open" like a gate; a wall falls, crumbles, or is climbed over, breached or torn down. That did not happen as movement within Berlin was permitted, leaving commentators straining for a suitable verb. Orators pray for a tearing-down, with remnants left standing as reminders and platforms.)

In Prague, Czechs call for *svoboda,* which is also the word in Russian and Bulgarian. In Warsaw, you hear *wolnosc,* pronounced "VOL-nosch." In Budapest, Hungarians say *szabadsag,* pronounced "SAH-bahd-shag," and in Riga, Latvians demand *briviba,* pronounced "BREE-VEE-ba." In Albania, there's not much *liri,* but it will come one day. Same with *azadi* in Afghanistan, *laisve* in Lithuania and *zi uyou* in China.

Diplomats still talk carefully about *peaceful change, measured reform* and *progress toward self-determination,* but the blunt and thrilling words for *freedom* can be heard in the streets, bouncing off satellites to television screens and inspiring others to hit the streets around the world. (And if a T-shirt manufacturer would print all these words for freedom on single shirts, machine washable, demonstrators everywhere would buy them.)

"Sir," said Robert Young Hayne of South Carolina in the Senate more than a century and a half ago, "there have existed, in every age and every country, two distinct orders of men—the lovers of freedom and the devoted advocates of power." The year 1990 may see *order* or *stability,* the euphemisms for the imposition of power, come roaring malevolently back; but in 1989, at least in most places, *freedom* was the rallying cry.

I was saddened to see that you have fallen for the simplistic Anglo-Saxon chauvinism of Strunk and White. You write that "these Germanic words [like freedom*] are punchier than their Romance-language counterparts:* Rich *and* hard *are more telling than* affluent *and* arduous.*"*

More telling in which context? Should John Kenneth Galbraith have titled his famous book The Rich Society *instead of* The Affluent Society? *You seem to betray your own high standard, that is, an unremitting attention to the context of individual words—merely to make a misleading point about Anglo-Saxon words.*

Is it an unfair ad hominem *to allude to your public confession of a failure to learn Latin in high school? You might take heart from I. F. Stone, who learned classical Greek in old age.*

Mario S. De Pillis
Amherst, Massachusetts

On the various words for freedom, *the Romanian form is* libertate, *not* liberdade, *which is the Portuguese form. The Romanian form is not an inherited
word, but part of the re-Latinization process of the Romanian lexicon in the
19th century when French forms like* liberté, *combined with Latin* libertas
(specifically the oblique forms like libertatem, *etc.), formed the basis of
Romanian* libertate.

Interestingly, the corresponding Latin verb liberare *is the basis of Romanian*
A *(preposition meaning "to," as with the English infinitive also)* Ierta, *meaning
"to excuse, forgive."*

Charles Carlton
Professor, French and
    Romance Linguistics
University of Rochester
Rochester, New York

The Latin word liber, *"free," is not "taken from" Greek* eleutheros *any more
than (for example) English* free *is from German* frei *or than French* mère *is
from Spanish* madre. *The words in each pair are cognates, not derivatives, i.e.,
they do not come one from the other but from a common source.* Liber *and*
eleutheros *are both descended from an Indo-European word posited by linguists
as* leudheros, free *and* frei *from proto-Germanic* frijaz, *which you mention (and
ultimately from I-E), and* mère *and* madre *from Latin* mater *(and ultimately
from I-E). English* liberty, *on the other hand, is indeed "taken from" Latin*
libertas *(by way of Old French).*

Louis Jay Herman
New York, New York

*"Freedom" and "liberty" have very long histories within the Western tradition.
Certainly in terms of the values they connote if not their actual etymological
origins, they both can be traced back to our heritage in the classical Greek
world; they come to us in the European world with over two thousand years of
history and accreted interpretation—we "know" what they mean, even if we
disagree (a curious if all too common paradox!).*

In distinct contrast, the term ziyou *has no tradition in China nor in any of
the Sinic family of languages. One will not find it in the major works of Chinese
thought, nor in the traditions of Chinese politics. The word, consisting of two
characters which may be translated as "self-reason" or "proceed from the self,"
was intially rendered by the Japanese, using Chinese characters, in the late
nineteenth century in order to translate the European term for which they had
no equivalent; the Chinese subsequently adopted it themselves, although not*

from Europe but Japan, thus distancing it even further from the original that we of the West all "understand." The same history is true of other such equally vital terms as "democracy" (minzhu zhuyi, *or "people's bossism"*) *or "republic"* (gonghe guo, *or "common harmony country"*).

The point is that such words have entered the Chinese (and Japanese) discourse without any of the bag and baggage they bear in the West; they are, in fact, virtually without meaning except as their users choose to invest them.

Ultimately, I would suggest, this becomes very important in resolving why the Chinese, when faced with the massive use of force in Tiananmen Square, retreated, while the Rumanians, for whom the words fit into a broader context, responded to equally if not more devastating force with mass outrage and further resistance. To the average Chinese—not the students who led the demonstrations, but the vast majority of the population—the words which were invoked as ideals carry no real meaning.

Hugh R. Clark
Associate Professor of Chinese
History
Ursinus College
Collegeville, Pennsylvania

Freedom *and* liberty *are not synonymous.*

Freedom is the absence of prescription, and liberty is the absence of proscription.

Prescription *is defined as a rule or course of action to be followed, or as a verb, the act of laying down a rule or course of action.*

Proscription *is defined as a prohibition, or as the act of prohibiting.*

With these definitions, I can easily imagine situations in which one has freedom without liberty, or liberty without freedom. The only situation in which I can envision freedom and liberty simultaneously is the absence of government.

Howard Hamer
Long Branch, New Jersey

The Words Not Used

"A naval blockade?" asked Sam Donaldson of ABC in his stentorian voice.

"Let's not use the word 'blockade,' " replied Secretary of State James A. Baker 3d, not yet replaced in the public eye by Defense Secretary Dick Cheney.

"Please supply a word for me," responded the no-nonsense, blockade-conscious journalist, "if you don't like the legal word, which is *blockade.*"

Mr. Baker had one on the tip of his tongue: "I'll give you, right now, *interdiction.*"

When asked the same question, President Bush also used "our policy of *interdiction,*" but Reuters characterized the policy with a more familiar word: "Bush has hinted the U.S. may *'quarantine'* the Jordanian port of Aqaba." United Press International reported that "White House press secretary Marlin Fitzwater said the *quarantine* should apply to all food."

This is an example of vintage diplolingo: the creative use of synonymy to put a peaceful spin on a warlike act.

The pioneer in avoiding the dread *B*-word was Franklin D. Roosevelt, who was working on a speech in 1937 critical of Hitler and Mussolini. Norman Davis of the State Department suggested the phrase "war is contagion," and Harold Ickes, the outspoken Interior Secretary, told F.D.R. that a neighborhood had a right to *quarantine* itself against threatened infection.

Roosevelt liked the metaphor; in a Chicago speech, he spoke approvingly of the way a community "joins in a quarantine of the patients in order to protect the health of the community" and made the foreign-policy connection: To stop the "epidemic of world lawlessness," he would adopt measures to "minimize our risk of involvement." The next day, reporters wondered how a quarantine fit a policy of neutrality; was he proposing *sanctions*?

"*Sanctions* is a terrible word," Roosevelt said; he liked his *quarantine,* especially since he did not apply it directly to diplomacy.

When John F. Kennedy was confronted by Soviet missiles in Cuba in 1962, he recollected the F.D.R. usage. "He again repeated his preference for a blockade," wrote Roger Hilsman, his State Department intelligence aide at the time, "and at this time supplied the word *quarantine* to describe it. This was a phrase with obvious political advantages both at home, where it was reminiscent of President Roosevelt's 'quarantining the aggressors' speech, and abroad, where it struck a less belligerent note than the word *blockade.*"

International law defines a blockade as an act of war, and leaders sometimes want to act more strongly than they speak. "The difference between *quarantine* and *blockade,*" says Goodwin Cooke, vice president for international affairs at Syracuse University, "is that a *quarantine* is not necessarily an act of war. A *blockade* is an act of war, as when the North blockaded the South in our Civil War." (That posed a semantic problem for Lincoln, who did not want to give the South the official status of a belligerent during what he termed an insurrection.)

"Similar to a blockade is an *interdiction,*" Mr. Cooke continues, "but that may block the shipping of a specific item. In discussions of Iraq, I suspect that the difference between *blockade* and *interdiction* is in the mind of the speaker.

Quarantine does not have to be an act of war; the word is related to 'forty'—it referred to keeping everything away from a given place or object for 40 days. Normally it's used for diseases."

Now we're down to hard etymology. *Quarantine* first appeared as a legal term in 1609, as the period of forty days in which a widow could remain in her dead husband's house before creditors could seize it.

A half-century later, the diarist Samuel Pepys noted the extension of the etymon: "Making of all ships coming from thence . . . to perform their 'quarantine for thirty days,' as Sir Richard Browne expressed it . . . contrary to the import of the word (though, in the general acceptation, it signifies now the thing, not the time spent in doing it)."

Interdiction originally meant "prohibition by saying or declaring," with the *diction* part the same as in *dictionary.* Church and Roman law picked it up in "interdiction of fire and water," which was a sentence forbidding the supply of the necessities of life to the criminal. Late in World War II, the word was used to mean "the interruption of enemy supply operations by bombing"; the BBC defined it as "rail-cutting by air attack."

The reader memorizing all this will recall F.D.R.'s comment that he considered *sanctions* "a terrible word." Mr. Roosevelt was right: It invites confusion. The root is *sanctus,* "holy," and as a verb, *to sanction* is to sprinkle approval on; however, the noun became associated with the penalty of proceeding without having been sanctioned, and *sanctions* are now "penalties" designed to coerce obedience.

A word that could be used before long is *siege,* with ancient connotations but no precise definition in law, which means "the use of a blockade to force a place to surrender." In a *siege,* incoming supplies are *seized;* one of those words has the *i* before the *e,* and the other is the other way around.

Year Reads Backward

Palindrome fans, your time has come: 1991 reads the same backward as forward. The last time this happened was in 1881, one of those years that Mark Schulte of New York thinks should be called a *palindromannum.*

Consider: In every century of this millennium, we have been treated to only one palindromannum—1001, 1111, 1221, et cetera—at intervals of 110 years.

But we fortunate humans have the prospect of two such years almost within a decade. The year 2002 is just around the corner. We live in interesting times.

Thank you for calling to our attention the palindromic aspect of 1991.

Perhaps you can suggest an appropriate term for 1961, which reads the same upside down as right side up? Don't worry if nothing comes to mind immediately; you have until 6009 to come up with an answer.

> Albert H. Teich
> Garrett Park, Maryland

Your observation that 1991 reads the same backward as forward called to mind my first day as a Harvard undergraduate (in September 1957) entering the class of 1961. In an apparent attempt to induce the assembled freshmen to work hard for the next four years, the auditorium speaker (I believe it was Dean McGeorge Bundy) informed us that our expected year of graduation, 1961, would read the same upside-down as right-side-up. To underscore the rarity of such an event, he pointed out that it had occurred only three previous times in this millennium (the years 1001, 1111 and 1691) and, more impressively, would not happen again until the year 6009.

> John C. Grosz
> New York, New York

I propose recognition of another class of even scarcer palindromanni. The recent MXM is an example.

> Carl G. Sontheimer
> Greenwich, Connecticut

You Know Who

The best rule for dealing with *who* vs. *whom* is this: Whenever *whom* is required, recast the sentence. This keeps a huge section of the hard disk of your mind available for baseball averages.

A dossier has been building up, however, on the use of *who* in a famous apothegm. "I was surprised and disgusted," wrote Janine M. Low to the New York University School of Continuing Education, "to see that a learning institution with the renown of N.Y.U. published a full-page ad using blatantly wrong grammar." She sent me a copy of her complaint, with the copy to me noted on the original, the same notation many people use who want to strike terror into the recipient's heart; it's like writing "cc: Better Business Bureau" on a letter to a corporate counsel, or "cc: Savings and Loan Institute" on a letter to a Congressman.

What infuriated Ms. Low was a line in the copy that read: "In business, it's not just who you know . . ." She believes it should be "it's not just *whom* you know."

In the same mail came this note from Clark M. Clifford, dean of Washington superlawyers: "There is an erroneous and moth-eaten cliché that I have always abhorred." (Clark minces no words about words.) "It is 'In Washington it is not *what* you know, but it is *who* you know.' A Britisher recently said, referring to this cliché, 'I do not know if the substance is correct, but I do know the grammar is ghastly.' "

Let us now deal with this cynical adage, derogating lobbyists and other innocent and useful intermediaries, in its pristine form: "It ain't *what* you know but *who* you know."

We all know that *who* is a pronoun that substitutes for the subject, and *whom* is a pronoun that substitutes for the object. (I hate this. I am doing it as penance for having written that those who counsel patience in the Persian Gulf were for "peace in our time"; that was an attempted allusion to Neville Chamberlain after the 1938 Munich sellout, when he said, "I believe it is peace *for* our time." The line with which this is often confused, "Give peace *in* our time, O Lord," is from Morning Prayer. That sort of error is unforgivable—I warned against it in my own political dictionary—requiring the writing of an item about *who/whom,* a stupefying MEGO.)

Take the sentence "It concerns the person you know"; *it* is the subject, *concerns* is the verb and *the person you know* is the object. Now insert a pronoun between "the person" and "you know"; since that person is the object of *concerns,* the pronoun should be *whom,* right?

Right answer, wrong reasoning. *Who* or *whom* must be used correctly within its own clause; if it is the subject of its clause, it is *who,* if the object, *whom.* (I'll never get this readership back. Next week, I'll try a sensational headline and see whom I can grab leafing through the paper.) In "the person whom you know," the object of the relative clause is *whom,* which stands for "the person"; you know *him.* Always substitute *whom* for *him;* you wouldn't say, "You know *he,*" would you? No; *he* and *who* are subjects; when you mean "he is the one you know," you can pop in the pronoun for a subject, as "who is the one you know." In the same way, when you are dealing with objects, receivers of the action, you go with *him/whom:* "you know him," "you know whom" or—here comes the thrilling denouement—"*whom* you know."

Thus, "it ain't what you know, it's whom you know." Now you're grammatically correct about *whom,* but linguistically in error. That's because "it's who you know" has been used so much for so long that it has become an idiom; the substitution of the "correct" pronoun, *whom,* becomes a pedanticism.

Now, just for fun (some fun), try killing the rest of the clause, leaving only the pronoun; if the context doesn't call for an object, *who* would be grammatically as well as linguistically correct: "The question isn't what; it is *who.*" That's because (this must be how Slick Willie Sutton felt, alone in a bank at night, pleased to be doing his thing with nobody looking) the *who* is a predicate nominative—that is, a noun, following a linking verb like *is,* making it equal to a subject, calling for the pronoun that is used to replace a subject.

If anybody challenges you on this, do not go into laborious detail about pronouns reflecting their positions inside clauses; do not justify your interest in the struggle between swinging idiom and sober syntax by quoting Slick Willie, who never said, "I rob banks because that's where the grammar is"; instead, tell whoever asks that you got it from a self-certified language maven, and in the usage dodge, as in business and in Washington, it isn't what you know . . .

CREDITS

Be careful with *thanks to*. This versatile idiom, used in English for more than two centuries, can be used to blame as well as bless ("Thanks to a plot by a pack of double-crossers, this prose was riddled with errors, the deadline for the manuscript was missed, etc."). Only in the idiom's positive sense (this manuscript was in on time) do I offer thanks to colleagues, sources and friends who help me watch your words and mine.

First, the leading lexies: Fred Mish of Merriam-Webster, Sol Steinmetz of Random House and Anne Soukhanov, formerly of American Heritage. When fellow philologists call these people, they get not only action but nuance. Also first (in a dead heat for my gratitude) is the "On Language" Board of Mentors—Olbom—Jacques Barzun, Fred Cassidy of the *Dictionary of American Regional English,* Alistair Cooke and Allen Walker Read. Good advice and sometimes astringent commentary were available from Allan Metcalf of the American Dialect Society, John Algeo, Cynthia Barnhart and James McCawley.

On quotations, James Simpson of *Simpson's Quotations* and Justin Kaplan of *Bartlett's* were always helpful, and Jeanne Smith at the Library of Congress has developed a skill at political phrase detection. My late brother, Len Safir, compiler of the "Good Advice" series of quotation anthologies, was a steady resource; I'll miss him for that, too.

At Random House, my editors are the legendary Kate Medina, as well as Jonathan Karp, Camille Capozzi, Beth Pearson, Margaret Wimberger, Patricia Abdale and Janet Wygal; Stacy Rockwood handled the production, and the index was done by Sydney Cohen & Associates. At *The New York Times Magazine,* where these columns first appeared, I am kept on the path of good taste, as one part of their jobs, by Jack Rosenthal, Harvey Shapiro and Michael Molyneux. (I wanted to use *Merkin* as a variant of *American* when writing about "Merkin English"; Molyneux pointed out to me that *merkin* is defined in *Webster's Third New International Unabridged* as an obsolete term for "the hair of the female genitalia," so I spelled my variant

Murkin.) At the *Times* Washington bureau, my linguistic support is led by Jeffrey McQuain, general editor of the fourth edition of *Safire's New Political Dictionary,* who is my chief research associate; Ann Elise Rubin, my assistant, who has an ear tuned to the latest neologisms and slang, and Rebecca Lawrence, who tries to keep up with the mail. (I get a lot of mail—three hundred letters a week, on average—mainly about language, the rest about politics. Replies go out on blue postcards; if you get two postcards of acknowledgment saying the same thing, send one on to a needy friend.) My political column's copy editors, Steve Pickering, Linda Cohn and Sue Kirby, often contribute suggestions for "On Language" based on mistakes they save me from making. In the bureau library, Barclay Walsh, chief librarian, Monica Borkowski and Marjorie Goldsborough are unfailingly helpful.

Finally, thanks to the Lexicographic Irregulars—the redundancy spotters of the Squad Squad, the etymologists of the Phrasedick Brigade, the Nitpickers' League and its shock troops called the Gotcha! Gang—for their useful emendations, instructive challenges and constant nagging.

INDEX

ABOUT THE AUTHOR

WILLIAM SAFIRE is a writer of many incarnations: reporter, publicist, White House speechwriter, historian, novelist, lexicographer and essayist.

His primary occupation since 1972 has been political columnist for *The New York Times,* usually taking the point of view of a libertarian conservative; in 1978, he was awarded the Pulitzer Prize for distinguished commentary. His column "On Language" in *The New York Times Magazine* is syndicated around the world and has made him the most widely read and argued-with writer on the subject of the English language.

Mr. Safire is married, has a son and daughter and lives in a suburb of Washington, D.C.

ABOUT THE TYPE

This book is set in Times Roman, designed by Stanley Morison (1889–1967) for *The Times* (London) as a universal type that could be used for everything from classified advertisements to the newspaper's headlines. It became popular for book text as well as newspapers because of its economy and elegance. The fine serifs were not well served by crude presswork and Times Roman might well have disappeared but for the arrival of photocomposition, which the fastidious Morison would probably have deplored. Morison was an acerbic historian of *The Times* as well as a typographer and adviser to the Monotype Corporation, though William Safire would like it to be known he thinks Morison's reputation owes a lot to a good press agent.